Proportion and Style in Ancient Egyptian Art

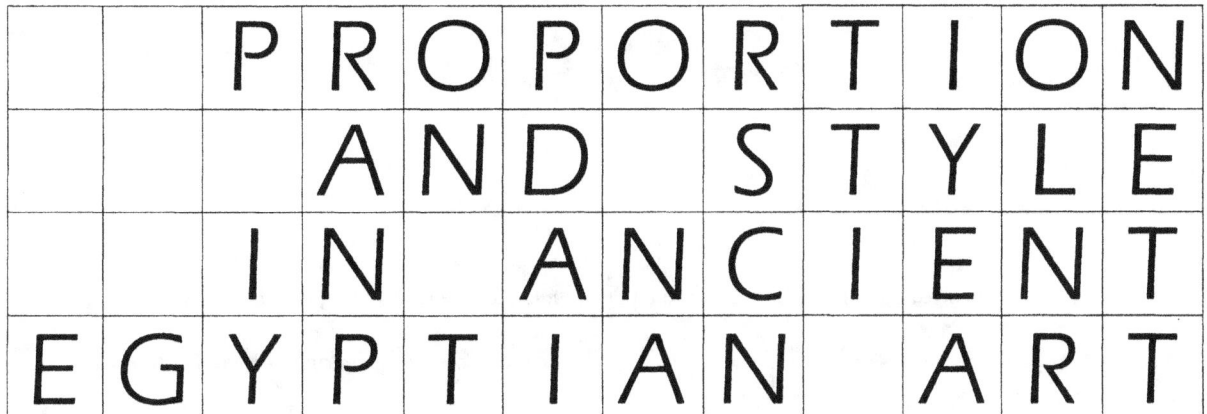

PROPORTION AND STYLE IN ANCIENT EGYPTIAN ART

BY GAY ROBINS

Drawings by Ann S. Fowler

University of Texas Press AUSTIN

This book has been supported by a grant from the National Endowment for the Humanities, an independent federal agency.

ISBN 978-0-292-75544-4 (library e-book)

ISBN 978-0-292-78774-2 (individual e-book)

Library of Congress Cataloging-in-Publication Data

Robins, Gay.
    Proportion and style in ancient Egyptian art / by
Gay Robins ; drawings by Ann S. Fowler. — 1st ed.
            p.   cm.
    Includes bibliographical references and index.

    ISBN: 978-0-292-77064-5

    1. Art, Egyptian.   2. Art, Ancient—Egypt.
3. Proportion (Art)   4. Composition (Art)   I. Fowler,
Ann S.   II. Title.
N5350.R65   1994
709'.32—dc20   93-65

Contents

Preface

It has long been known that much Egyptian art executed in two dimensions as painting or relief was conceived and carried out on a squared grid, which helped to determine the proportions of the human figure. Although there have been several previous studies of the Egyptian grid, these have been almost entirely limited to single standing or seated male figures, and in some cases have been bedeviled by preconceived theories that relate more strongly to the mind of the modern interpreter than to the intentions of the ancient draughtsmen.

In this book I have attempted to base my own ideas, and any theories that may be put forward, primarily on observations carried out on the actual monuments. I have considered female figures as well as male, other postures besides standing and sitting, and also the interrelationships of multiple figures, animal-headed as well as human, often in different postures and at different levels in a single scene. I show that the squared grid had an important influence on the composition of scenes as a whole and in helping to determine the characteristic style of a particular period. I consider the effects of the major change in the grid that occurred in the twenty-fifth dynasty and persisted thereafter, and elaborate my discovery of the grid system adopted during the Amarna period.

Although I have taken representative material from all stages in the development of Egyptian art, my treatment of the subject is not intended to be exhaustive. The plates and figures provide a corpus of material specifically designed to illustrate points relating to the use of the grid, and irrelevant details have been omitted from the drawings. Not every surviving grid, whether previously recorded or not, has been mentioned, and obviously there are thousands of scenes not illustrated here where further study involving the application of hypothetical grids might prove illuminating. I hope, therefore, that my work may stimulate other scholars to look at the art of different periods of Egyptian history from the points of view set out in this book.

Acknowledgments

This project began during my four-year tenure of the Lady Wallis Budge Research Fellowship in Egyptology at Christ's College, Cambridge, and I would like to thank the Master and Fellows for support and encouragement. I wish to thank the Egyptian Antiquities Organisation for permission to work and photograph in tombs at Thebes, Amarna, Meir, and Beni Hasan in 1984 and 1986. I am grateful for two grants that I received from the Wainwright Near Eastern Archaeological Fund toward the cost of my fieldwork in Egypt in 1984 and to help with expenses incurred in the preparation of this book. My fieldwork in Egypt during 1986 was funded by a Suzette Taylor Travelling Fellowship from Lady Margaret Hall, Oxford, and by grants from the University of Cambridge through the H.M. Chadwick Fund and the Thomas Mulvey Fund. I would like to thank Mr. Barry Kemp and the Egypt Exploration Society for allowing me to stay at the EES dig house at Amarna in 1984, and Dr. Lanny Bell and the Oriental Institute of Chicago for their hospitality at Chicago House, Luxor, while I was working at Thebes in 1984 and 1986.

I am also grateful to the Trustees of the British Museum and Mr. Vivian Davies, to the Committee of the Egypt Exploration Society and Dr. Patricia Spencer, to the Griffith Institute and Dr. Jaromír Málek, to the Musée du Louvre and M. de Cénival, to the Metropolitan Museum of Art and Dr. Catharine Roehrig, and to the Pelizaeus Museum Hildesheim and Dr. Bettina Schmitz for supplying me with photographs and permission to publish them. I would also like to thank Ms. Ann Fowler for her patience and skill in drawing the figures for the book.

A large number of other individuals have helped and encouraged me in this project, and to all of them I am grateful. I owe especial thanks to my teacher Prof. John Baines for all his encouragement over the years and also for sending me numerous references relating to this project. I would also like to thank Ms. Janine Bourriau for permission to measure figures on objects in the Fitzwilliam Museum, Cambridge; Mr. Vivian Davies for letting me have copies of photographs of the grids in the tomb of Ahmose son of Abana at el-Kab; Dr. Eiddon Edwards for his interest in my work on Tutankhamun; Mr. Harry James for finding me grids on objects in the British Museum; Mr. Ray Johnson for many fascinating discussions and for showing me his graphic reconstructions of scenes in the temple of Luxor; Dr. Candy Keller for sending me copies of her photographs taken in KV 22; Dr. Rolf Krauss for drawing my attention to the gridded "cube" in the Ägyptisches Museum, Berlin acc.no.3/70 and Dr. Settgast for permission to publish it; Mr. Christian Loeben for many discussions and for sharing with me his examples of Amarna grid traces; Dr. Jim Romano for tirelessly answering my questions about Brooklyn Museum 05.390 as well as for much other help; Prof. Harry Smith for his unceasing interest and encouragement; Dr. Donald Spanel for helping me in numerous ways; Dr. Patricia Spencer for help in looking through the EES photo archives of Meir and for providing me with copies of photos; Dr. Nigel Strudwick for lending me his mirror and diffuser, indispensable for my work at Thebes in 1986; Ms. Gabriele Wenzel for letting me see a copy of her master's thesis; and Dr. Helen Whitehouse for permission to measure the figures on the shrine of Taharqa in the Ashmolean Museum, Oxford, and for her help in doing so. In addition, I would like to thank everyone at the University of Texas Press who was involved in preparing *Proportion and Style in Ancient Egyptian Art* for publication. In particular, I am grateful to Frankie Westbrook, Theresa May, Carolyn Wylie, and Letitia Blalock for their indispensable help at different stages of the process.

Finally, I have to mention the part played by my husband, Prof. Charles Shute, whose inquiries about Egyptian metrology in the early years of our marriage led me to reread Iversen's *Canon and Proportion in Egyptian Art,* and so set this whole work in motion. I would like to dedicate this book to him.

Proportion and Style in
Ancient Egyptian Art

Introduction

This book is a study of a fundamental aspect of ancient Egyptian art, namely, the use of squared grids made by the artists in drawing preliminary sketches of scenes and figures. I have undertaken it because although some features of the grid are already known, particularly in relation to individual seated and standing figures, others have been subject to misunderstanding, the treatment of kneeling figures has been neglected, and there has been virtually no consideration of how the grid relates to the composition of whole scenes or to different styles adopted at different periods.

Before turning to the grid itself, however, it is necessary to have an understanding of the general principles by which Egyptian draftsmen worked to produce what is arguably the finest artistic achievement of the Prehellenic world, which still holds a place among the best today. Nurtured by the unique civilization of the River Nile, the art of ancient Egypt gave expression to the thoughts and aspirations of an extraordinary people, chronicling their views of the world, the gods, society, life, and afterlife for over three thousand years. It is well known that the Egyptians raised great monuments to their deities and their dead, and the decoration of temples and tombs is a major source for our knowledge of Egyptian art, but art was not confined to religious and funerary contexts. Kings decorated their palaces and ordinary people their homes, and many household objects in everyday use were also ornamented. In fact, art played a part in every aspect of Egyptian civilization, in the worlds of the gods and their rituals, and in the life and death of mortals.

Modern viewers find much of Egyptian art familiar and readily understandable, so that they can appreciate it without knowledge of the aims and principles underlying its composition. But it also surprises them that these superb artists never "discovered" perspective. A closer look produces the even more startling revelation that the Egyptians seemingly did not know their right from their left; right hands appear on left arms and vice versa. Further, couples are often grouped together with different parts of their bodies overlapping in ways that just cannot happen in reality. Clearly Egyptian artists were either incredibly incompetent or they were not working according to the rules that many modern viewers expect.

In two-dimensional art, artists have the choice of accepting the drawing surface as flat, in which case they cannot directly reproduce an image of the world in three dimensions, or of finding ways to create the illusion of depth in their pictures. In the modern world, we are familiar with schematic systems such as plans of electric circuits, ground plans and elevations of buildings, and maps, all of which are purely two-dimensional on the flat drawing surface. These we are unlikely to count as art. It is the second choice, the creation of depth or perspective in a picture, that we expect to find in Western pictures, at least until the advent of "modern" art.

In perspective representation, artists adopt techniques to show the decrease in size of objects at a distance, the foreshortening of objects lying at an angle to the picture plane, and the convergence of parallel lines as they move away from the viewer. Already by 500 BC, the Greeks were experimenting with foreshortening and, soon after, with empirically making parallel lines converge. It was not until the Renaissance that what we can call Western or geometric perspective was brought into use, in order to provide a way of accurately reproducing architecture in two dimen-

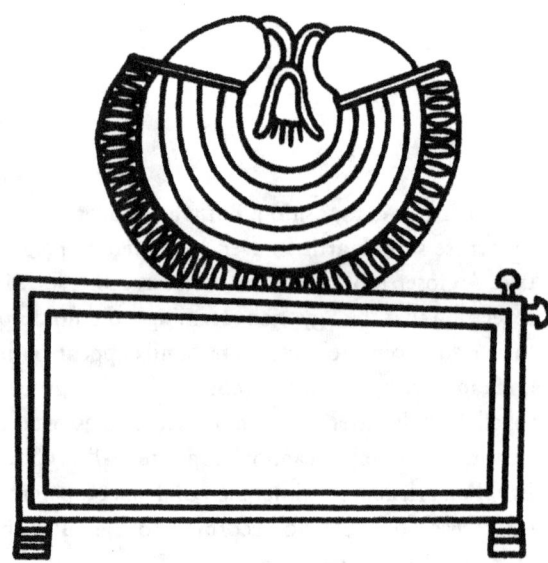

FIGURE 1.1

Representation of a box containing a necklace, TT 100, eighteenth dynasty, after Davies 1943, Plate 90.

sions. The system was rooted in the scientific study of optics, of which the oldest surviving work, written about 300 BC, is by the Greek mathematician Euclid. Later Greek and Arab mathematicians in Egypt took his work further and their treatises became available in Europe in Latin translations by the thirteenth century AD. Western scholars continued to be interested in the study of optics; it was much in vogue in fifteenth-century Italy, and as a result scientific principles were used to formulate the rules of geometric perspective. The method is based on the use of a single static viewpoint for a complete composition together with a system of central convergence in which parallel lines meet at a vanishing point. This enables artists to capture scenes and postures from specific angles at a

given moment of time. They can transfer what they see exactly onto the drawing surface, in much the same way that a camera transfers an image onto film.[1]

This method was adopted in Europe at the time of the Renaissance and was used during the next four centuries virtually without a break until the mid-nineteenth century when new developments occurred, which interestingly were stimulated by the discovery of sophisticated artistic traditions in non-European cultures. Yet for many Western people, the eye still feels most comfortable with the geometric perspective employed in the bulk of their European artistic heritage. In fact, this type of perspective was a uniquely Western phenomenon. For instance, although the representation of space was fundamental to Chinese landscape art, artists had no scientific interest in perspective and its rules. The spaces involved were conveyed by a combination of a shifting viewpoint and a bird's-eye view of the landscape, so that the eye is led over the painting and may, for example, be guided to follow a path up a mountain and then, on reaching the top, to look over at what is on the other side. Receding parallel lines in buildings are not generally shown as converging but as parallel, because this enables the eye to move more easily from one scene to the next.[2]

Similarly, Persian artists made no use of geometric perspective with its strict rules. Instead of one fixed viewpoint applying to all parts of the picture, they employed a system of multiple viewpoints, combining the resultant observations on one picture plane. Distance was usually indicated by placing items at different levels on the drawing surfaces, though without differentiation in scale.[3]

Western viewers must remember then that geometric perspective, which is so familiar, is not the only method of conveying the illusion of depth in a picture. But in ancient Egypt, artists did not even attempt to give depth as such to their compositions. They accepted the drawing surface as flat and represented the subjects of their composition through a series of symbols which they arranged over the surface. The aim of artists was to depict the enduring nature of the objects and scenes they portrayed; they were not interested in how these might appear at any one time from a particular viewpoint. They used established conventions to encode the information about the world that they wished to convey. Since viewers were familiar with these, they could easily grasp the meaning. A fundamental convention was that objects were shown in what was regarded as their most characteristic form, independent of time and space. They were usually represented by one of their surfaces, so a rectangular item like a box would be depicted by the side that gave the most immediately recognizable shape. If it was necessary to show the contents, these were drawn above the container (Fig. 1.1). If two or more surfaces of an object were considered important, they could be combined in one image; for instance, the legs of a stool could be shown in profile with the seat shown full view above them in the same plane (Fig. 1.2). These images were then arranged on the flat drawing surface to make up scenes.

The schematic nature of Egyptian art is well illustrated by the way in which gardens were depicted. A typical Egyptian garden was laid out around a pool which was shown from above as a rectangle (Fig. 1.3). Within the rectangle, the artist could draw water plants, birds, fish, or boats. In real terms, some of these merely float on the surface of the pool, while others are actually in the water. Rows of trees standing around

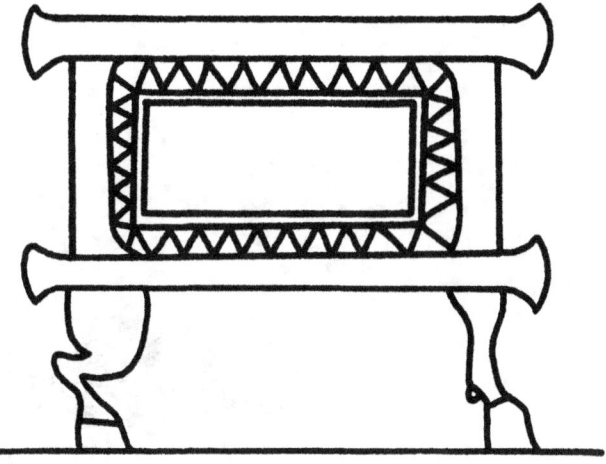

FIGURE 1.2

Representation of a stool, tomb chapel of Hesire, Saqqara, third dynasty, after Quibell 1913, Plate 18.

the pool to provide shade apparently lie flat on the ground. Nevertheless, the whole scheme provides a plan of a garden that can be readily understood and easily converted into real terms.

In the same way, architecture is sometimes represented by a plan of the building, within which individual elements like doors or pillars are shown in elevation (Fig. 1.4). Because these lie in the same drawing plane as the ground plan, they appear to be flat on the ground, just like the trees in relation to the pool.

These examples show that scenes in Egyptian art were built up from a variety of items, each represented on the drawing surface in its most characteristic form. It follows that artists were not reproducing directly

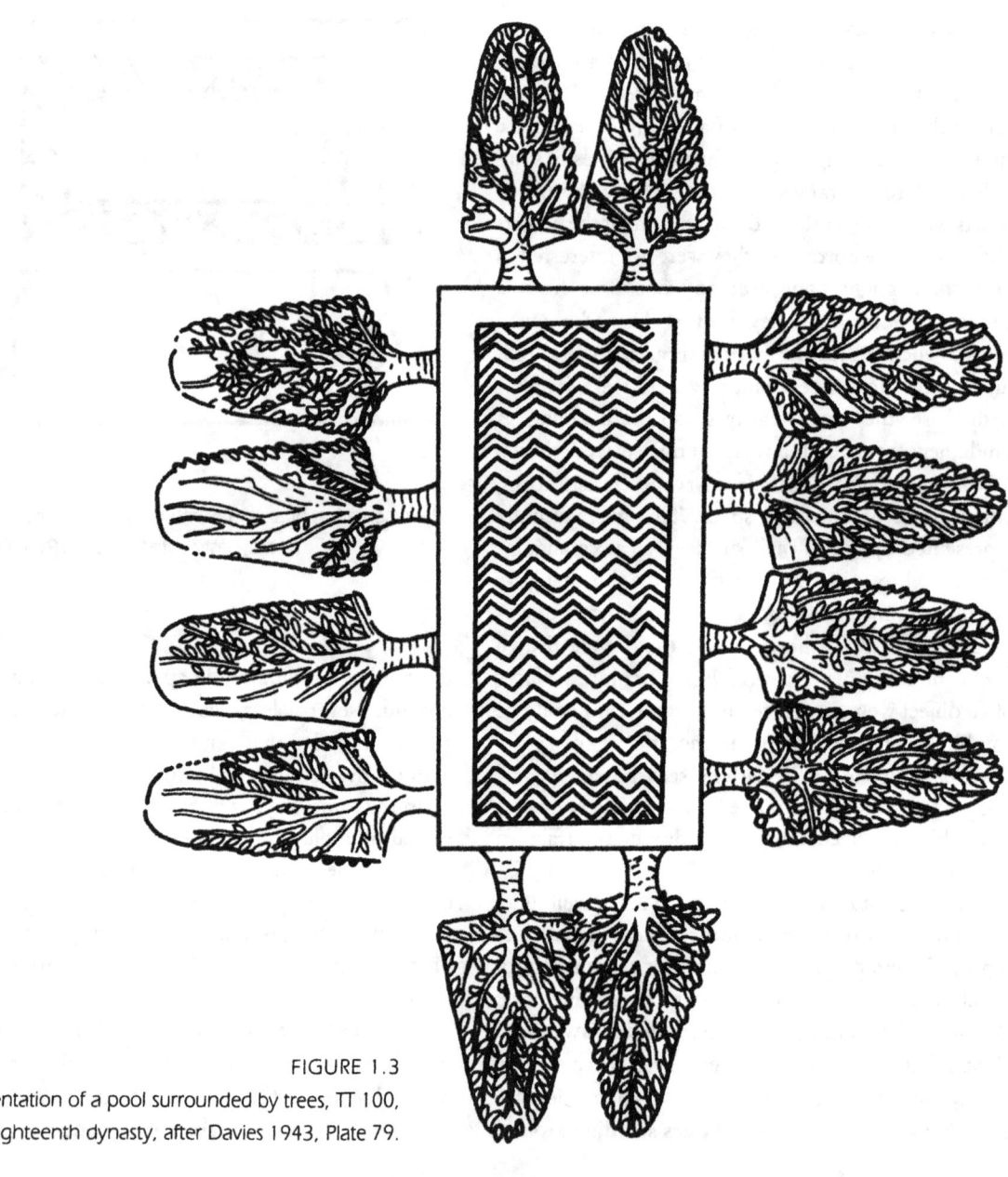

FIGURE 1.3
Representation of a pool surrounded by trees, TT 100,
eighteenth dynasty, after Davies 1943, Plate 79.

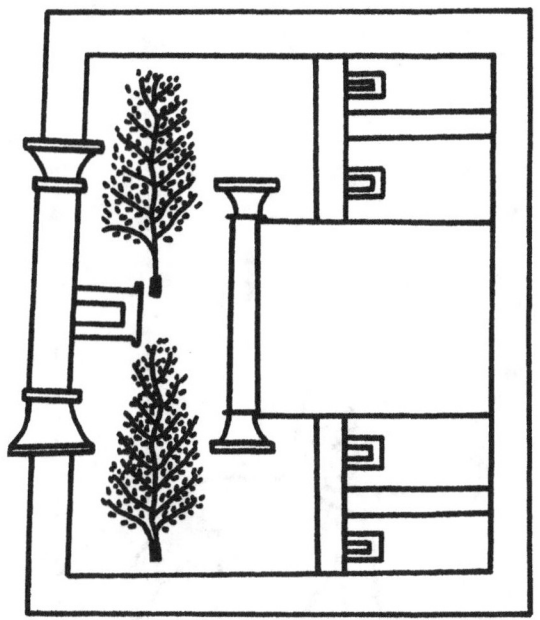

FIGURE 1.4
Representation of a building, TT 87, eighteenth dynasty,
after author's photograph.

FIGURE 1.5
Scene, tomb chapel of Ptahhotep, Saqqara, fifth dynasty,
after Davies 1900, Plate 21.

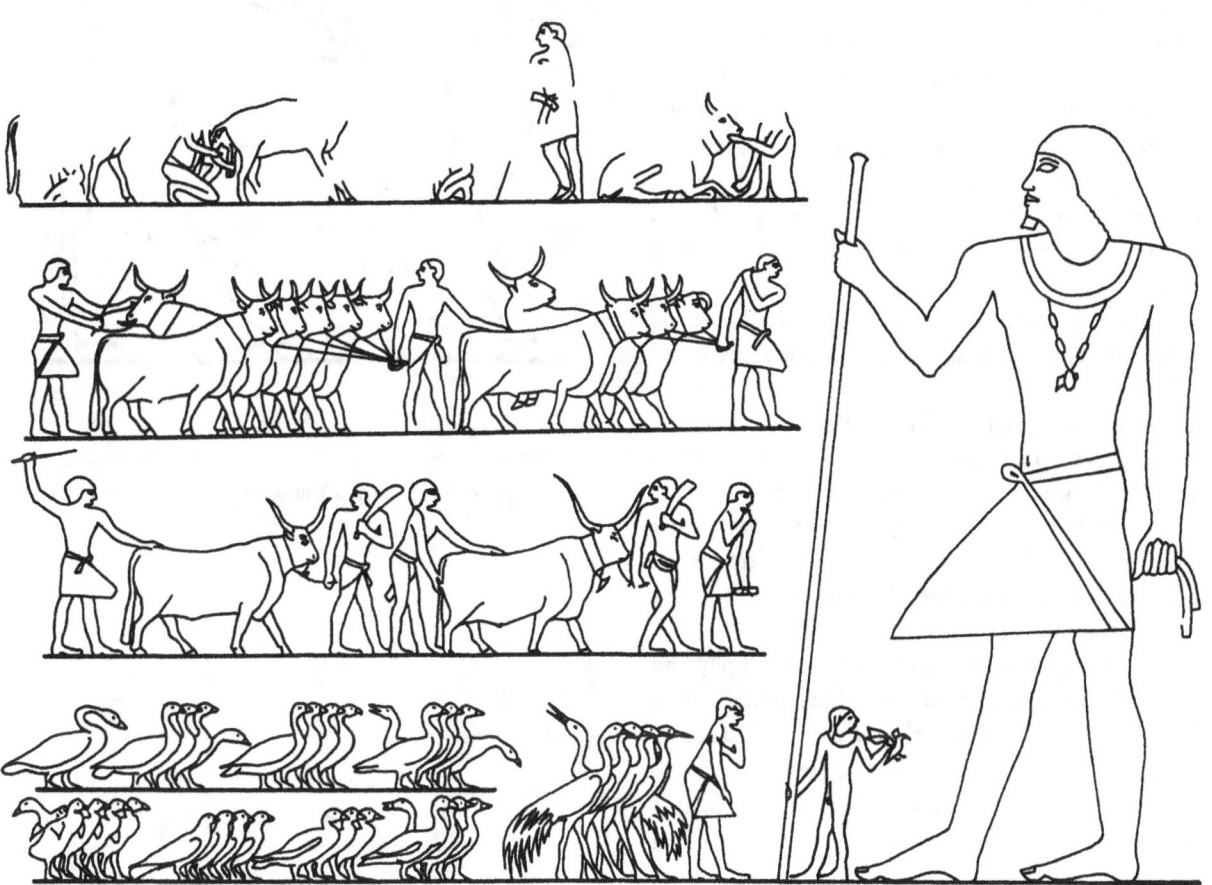

from what they saw. Instead, they encoded what they wished to show by drawing on a stock of learned forms which they then assembled to make a scene.

In order to organize this material on the drawing surface, artists divided the area into horizontal registers placed vertically above one another (Fig. 1.5). The surface itself was neutral in relation to time and space. Nor is there any indication of spatial or temporal relationship between the registers, although sets of registers were often given unity by setting a major figure at one end overlooking what was happening in them. The lower border of each register acted as the baseline for the figures within it. Sometimes part of a register was divided into subregisters which then provided baselines for smaller figures within the original register. Most commonly, the feet of all the figures in a register were placed on the baseline. This is true even of figures that overlap on the drawing surface, so that the true spacial relationship between figures as seen from above ground level was not represented (Fig. 1.6).

The register system was often relaxed in desert and battle scenes, partly because such scenes depict forces associated with chaos rather than the ordered world in which the Egyptians normally lived. So the register lines often undulate to represent desert terrain (Fig. 1.7), while in the confusion of battle scenes they may disappear altogether.

In some representations of desert topography and battlefields, artists adopted a technique similar to that used in their depiction of architecture. Instead of dividing the drawing surface into registers, they treated it as a flat area on which to draw a plan or "map." Within this, they then added the other elements of the

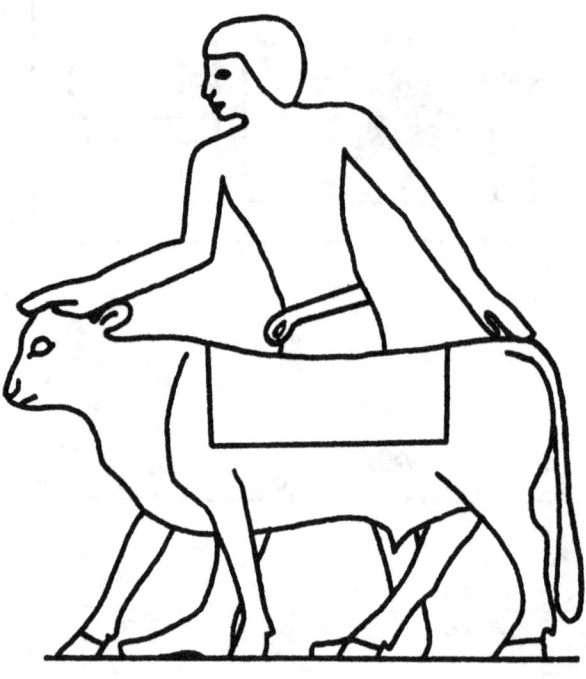

FIGURE 1.6
Representation of a man with a bull calf, tomb chapel of Nefer, Giza, fifth–sixth dynasty, after Junker 1943, 49 Figure 11.

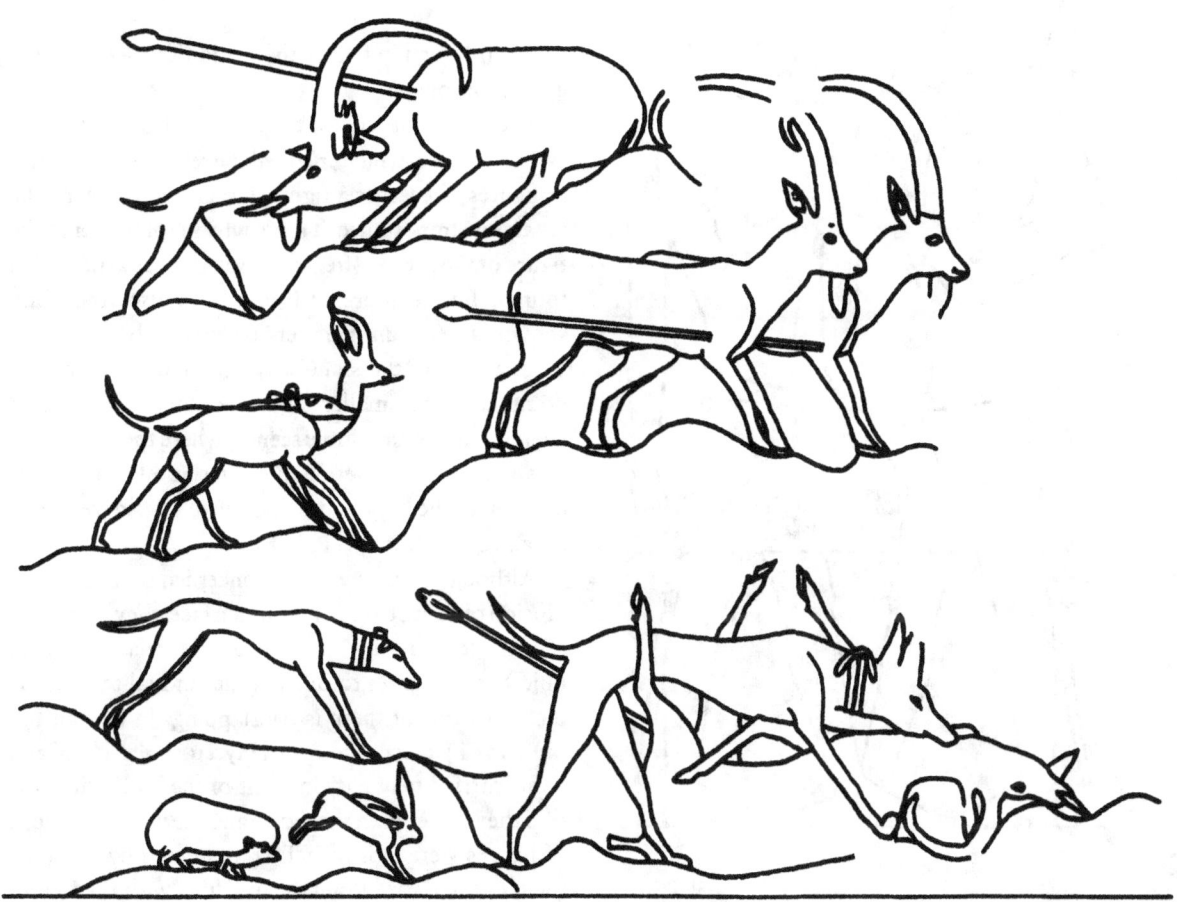

FIGURE 1.7
Detail of a desert scene, tomb chapel of Senbi, Meir B1,
twelfth dynasty, after Blackman 1914, Plate 6.

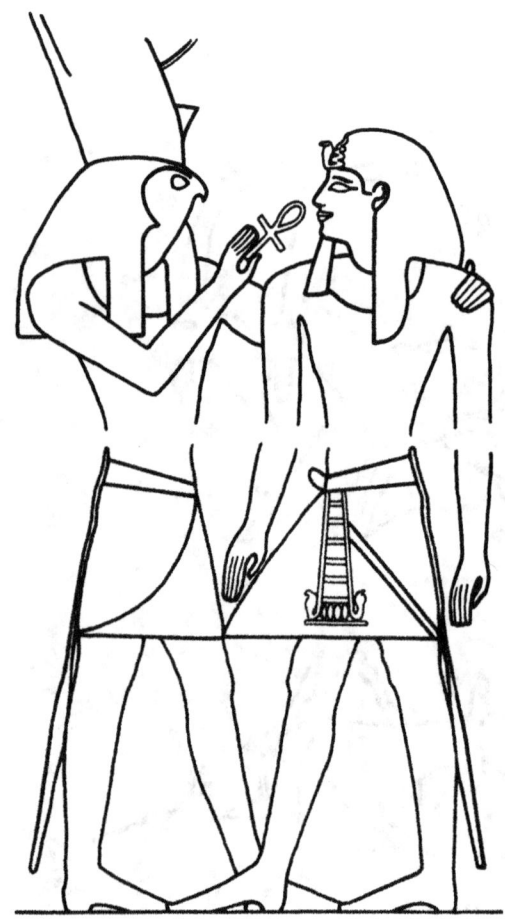

FIGURE 1.8

Scene showing a falcon-headed god offering life to
Thutmose III, temple of Buhen, eighteenth dynasty, after
Caminos 1974, Plate 58.

scene, although in reality these additions would lie in a different plane.

Artists also organized their material according to a system of scale, which encoded the relative importance of figures; the larger a figure in relation to others, the greater its importance. This is why in tomb scenes the figure of the owner often overlooks scenes arranged in four or five registers and why he is also frequently shown larger than members of his family (Figs. 1.5, 1.14, 1.15). In the same way, the figure of the king dominates the smaller figures of his subjects and enemies. In major temple scenes, where the king interacts with deities, there is little variation in scale because here the king and deities were considered to be on an equal footing (Fig. 1.8).

Although artists were not concerned with giving an illusion of depth to the drawing surface, they employed several "depth cues" to encode the relationship of objects and figures to one another in real terms. The most obvious of these is overlapping. In human figures, for instance, the arm may cross the chest and items carried may pass in front of the body, showing that they lie between the figure and the viewer. Groups of figures were most usually represented by stringing them out in a row along the baseline, with the figures in similar postures and overlapping horizontally to a greater or lesser extent. Their feet, as described above, all reach down to the baseline, but the overlapping of their legs and bodies is a cue to depth in their actual grouping (Fig. 1.9).

Other groups were built up from figures in different postures. Once again the baseline acts for all the figures, but the overlapping of the various figures clearly indicates the depth of the composition in reality (Fig. 1.10).

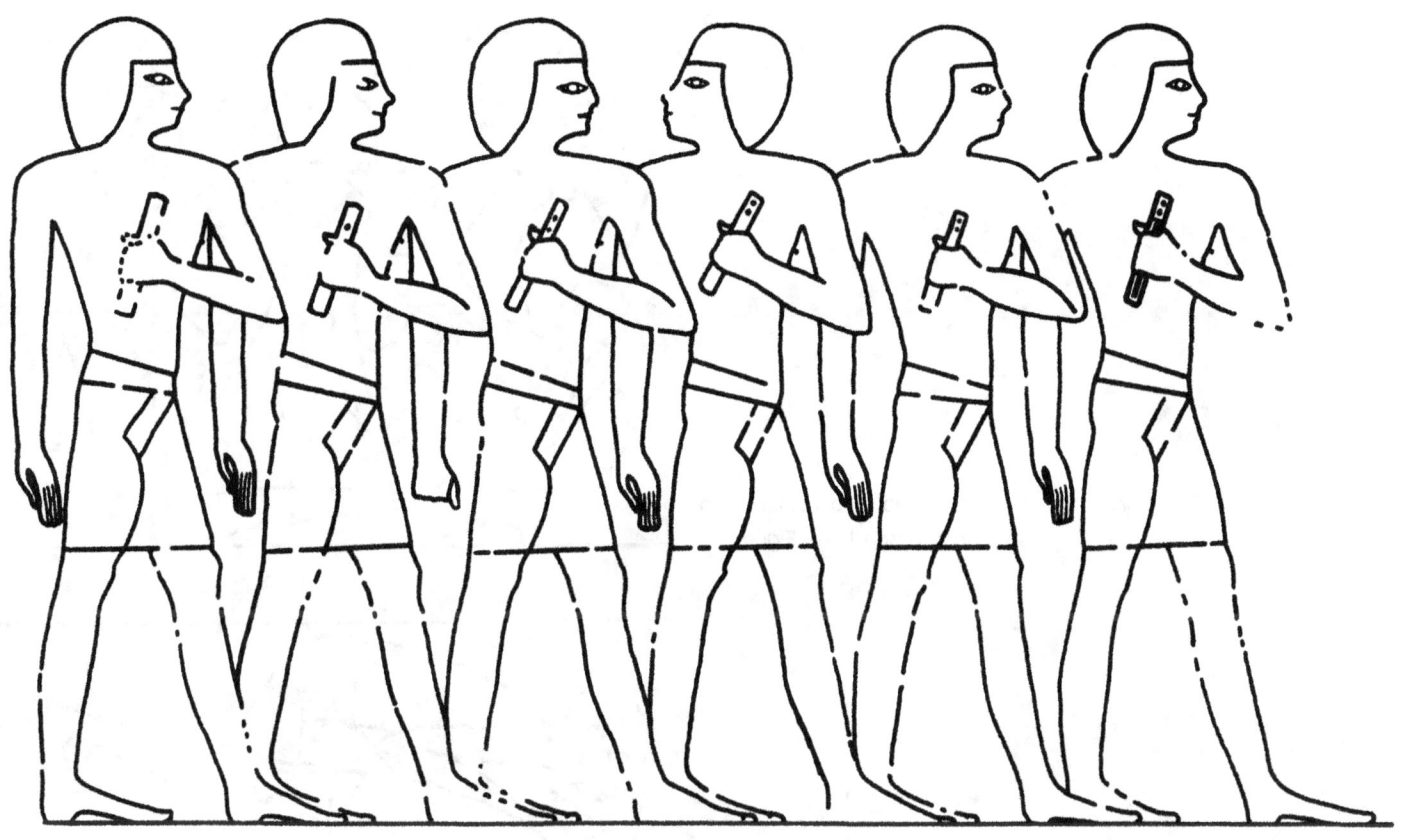

FIGURE 1.9
Group of scribes, TT 100, eighteenth dynasty, after Davies
1943, Plate 25.

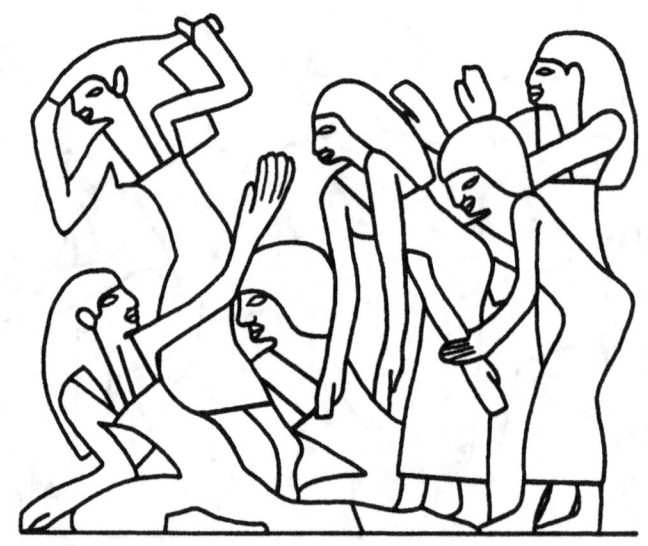

FIGURE 1.10
Group of mourning women, tomb chapel of Idu, sixth
dynasty, after Simpson 1976, Figure 35.

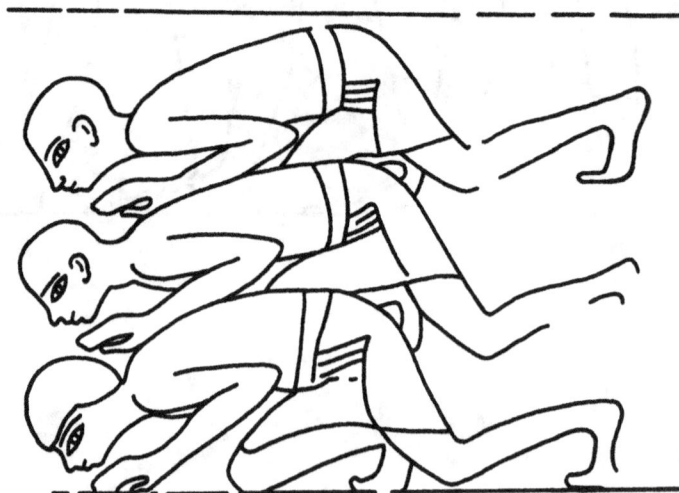

FIGURE 1.11
Group of prostrate figures, wall painting from the tomb of
Nebamun, British Museum EA 37978, eighteenth dynasty,
after author's photograph.

Artists also built up groups by overlapping figures in similar postures in vertical rows, so that only the lowest one was on the baseline and each subsequent row was placed higher (Fig. 1.11). It follows that depth could be indicated within a register by vertical positioning and that objects placed higher in the register can be interpreted as lying behind those below. So in elaborate piles of offerings composed of a number of groups heaped up one above another, the higher groups in reality lie behind the lower ones.

While overlapping obviously had a functional purpose in Egyptian art, artists also used it to create patterns on their drawing surface. Two fundamentals in good Egyptian art were the use of balance and space. These seem to have been particularly important because the acceptance of the two-dimensional nature of the drawing surface encouraged groups of objects and figures to be seen in terms of flat designs. So elements in a scene were balanced against one another, as, for instance, in the very common scene type in which two or more figures face each other in various ritual acts (Fig. 1.8). It was also common for two scenes of similar types to be placed back to back, forming a larger composition in which the two halves balanced each other.

Heaps of offerings form one of the commonest themes in Egyptian art. In a good composition, the whole pile was built up from individual items carefully balanced against each other to form small groups. These groups were then balanced against others until the final grouping was achieved. Overlapping helps to provide pattern and coherence to the whole, in addition to its function of encoding spatial distribution (Fig. 1.12).

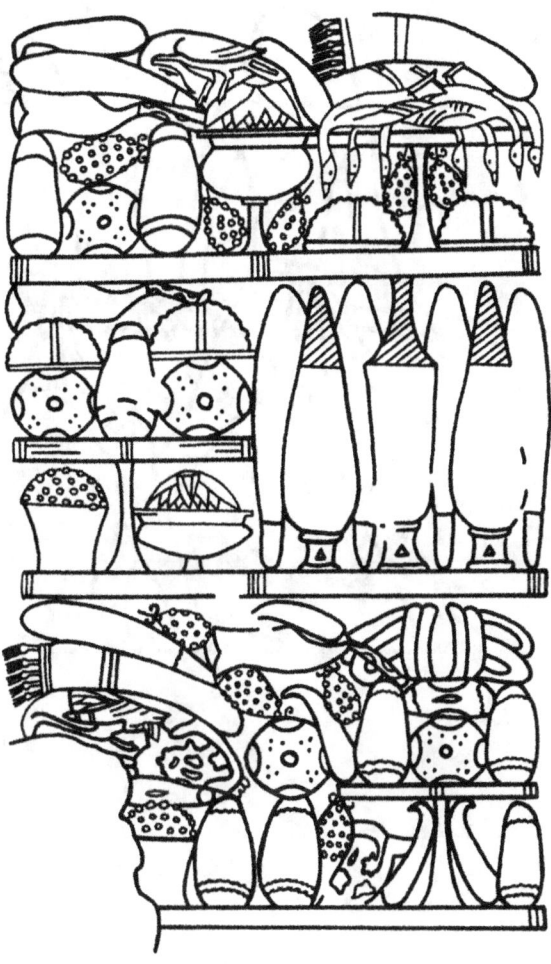

FIGURE 1.12
Representation of offerings, TT 251, eighteenth dynasty, after author's photograph.

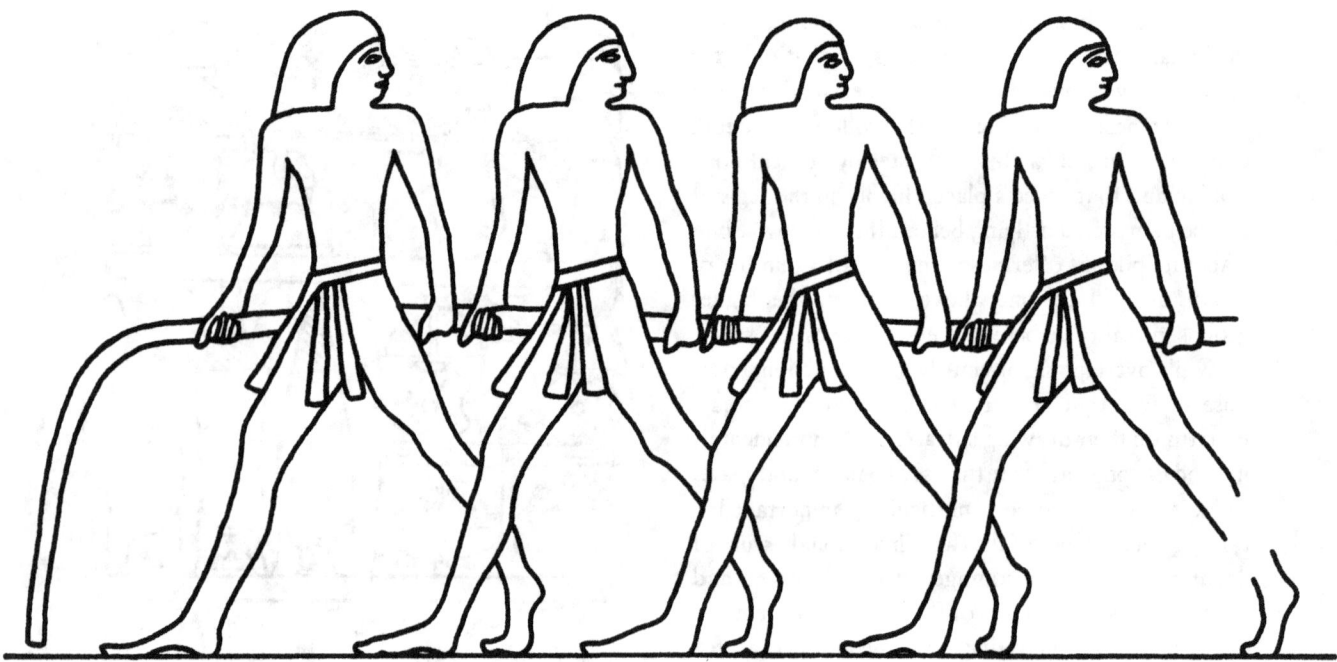

FIGURE 1.13
Representation showing men pulling a rope, tomb chapel
of Qar, sixth dynasty, after Simpson 1976, Figure 24.

Artists also frequently incorporated pattern into groups of human beings or animals. Where these groups were built up from a row of figures in the same posture, the limbs and bodies were overlapped to produce interlaced designs that are almost abstract (Figs. 1.5, 1.13). With groups composed of figures in different postures, artists were able to build up rhythmical patterns growing out of the interplay of limbs and bodies (Fig. 1.10).

Artists' use of space was governed by a sense of balance, which ensured that the elements on the drawing surface were not too crowded nor dispersed with wide intervening gaps that would break the rhythm of the whole composition. Inferior artists often lacked the ability to compose balanced scenes with a pleasing use of space.

1.1. The Human Figure

The principles of rendering the human figure were no different from those used to represent other items. Artists drew each part of the body in what was regarded as its typical aspect and put the parts together to form a composite diagram. The result is immediately recognizable as a human figure, although it plainly does not correspond directly with reality. The head was drawn in profile, to which was added at the appropriate levels a full-view eyebrow and eye and a half mouth. The shoulders and chest are full-view, but the nipple or breast, small of the back, elbows, buttocks, legs, knees, and feet are in profile. The navel was drawn full-view and placed near the front edge of the body behind the profile of the stomach. This treatment

made it clearly visible, whereas if it had been incorporated into the profile of the stomach, it would have been difficult to see (Fig. 1.14). Collars, necklaces, and straps of garments were drawn full-view lying on the expanse of the chest. In the usual image of a woman, one breast only, partly or wholly uncovered, appears in profile on the front line of the body, while the full-view dress strap runs across the chest (Fig. 1.15). On statues, the breast lay under the strap and was not visible.

In careful work, the drawing of the knee distinguishes the upper and lower borders of the kneecap or patella, together with a swelling below corresponding to the tibial tubercle where the patellar ligament attaches. Until the eighteenth dynasty, both feet were always shown from the inside with the big toe and the arch of the foot visible. This was because artists simply encoded the idea of a foot and attached their image of it without distinction to both legs of a figure, although it corresponded with reality only in the case of the far foot. Toward the end of the eighteenth dynasty, artists began to experiment with feet drawn from the outside showing all five toes, and from then on figures sometimes, but by no means always, employed the two images to distinguish the near and far feet.[4]

By contrast, artists had no one ideal image of the hand, since it could be shown not only empty but also holding or manipulating objects. It could be drawn either open or clenched, from the front or back, the two views being differentiated in careful work by the presence or absence of nails. Where the individual fingers manipulated objects, artists had a certain amount of freedom in creating the image. Although they were usually successful in conveying

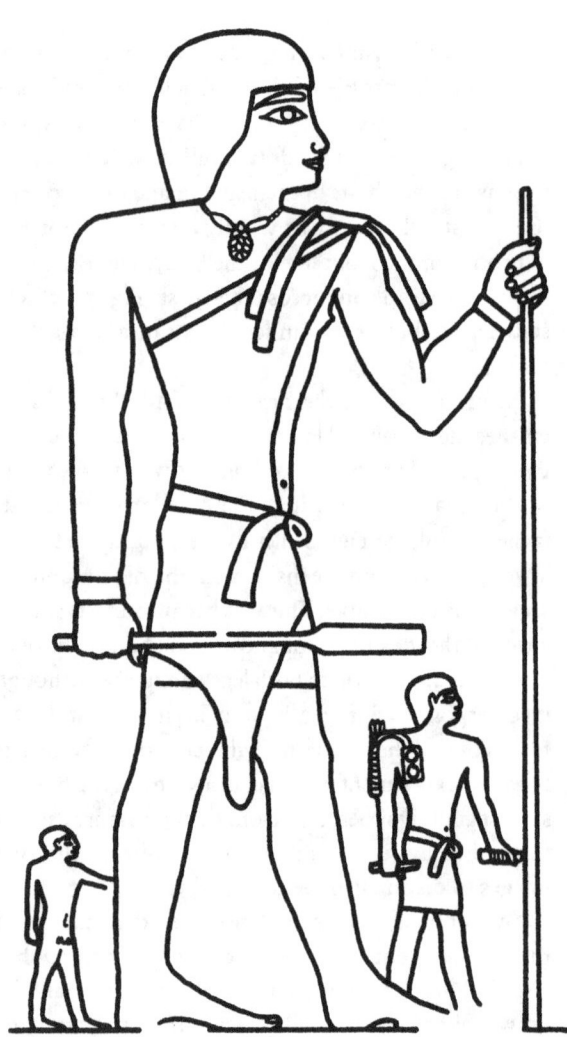

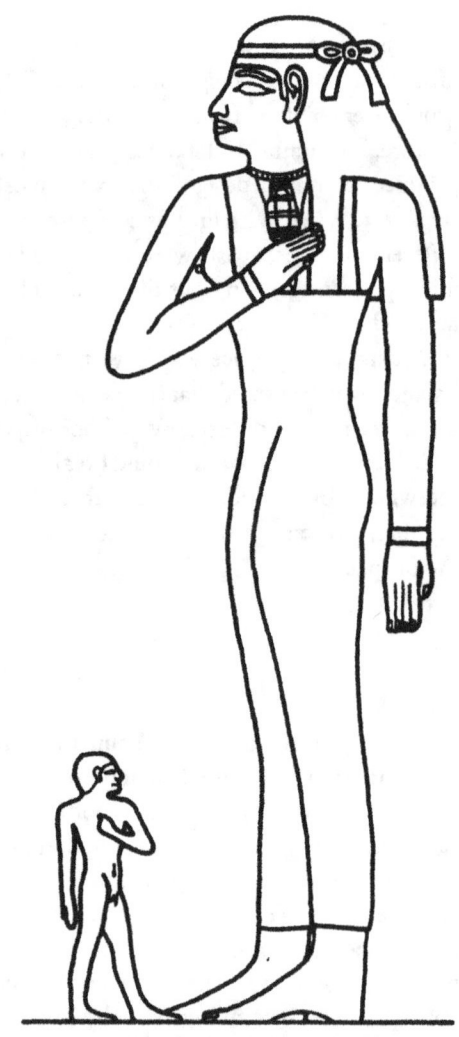

FIGURE 1.14
Standing figure of Iry on a block from his tomb, British
Museum EA 1168, fifth dynasty, after James 1961,
Plate 3 no. 3.

FIGURE 1.15
Standing figure of Inet on a block from the tomb of Iry,
British Museum EA 1170, fifth dynasty, after James 1961,
Plate 3 no. 4.

the desired gesture or action, their constructions do not, in many cases, reflect the postures that would occur in reality, and indeed are often anatomically impossible (Fig. 1.16).

One way of drawing the open hand was to show it full-view from the front or back with the fingers held straight, their lengths being differentiated, even if not always as much as in nature. This image of the hand occurs only with certain gestures, such as when the hand is held flat against the chest or the arm is outstretched to dedicate a pile of offerings (Fig. 1.20*a*, 1.20*b*).

More commonly, the open hand was shown from the back with the body and fingers slightly curved, as in the natural hand when relaxed. However, the nails were drawn in profile, not in full-view. The hand as a whole is therefore neither in profile or full-view but a combination of the two. Further, the fingers were usually all drawn the same length, in contrast to the more realistic depiction of the straight hand. This image of the hand is used when it hangs by the side of the body, is held up in adoration, reaches out to touch, is held above the knee of a sitting figure, is stretched out toward offerings, and holds items without manipulating them (Figs. 1.8, 1.15).

When the two hands hang open at the sides of the body, they are generally identical; the thumb of the forward one is next the body and that of the rear one away from it (Fig. 1.8). For the rear hand, this is contrary to what occurs in nature and means that in using this image artists did not distinguish between left and right. In contrast to this, the clenched fist may be shown full-view from the front or back and the two hands can be distinguished.

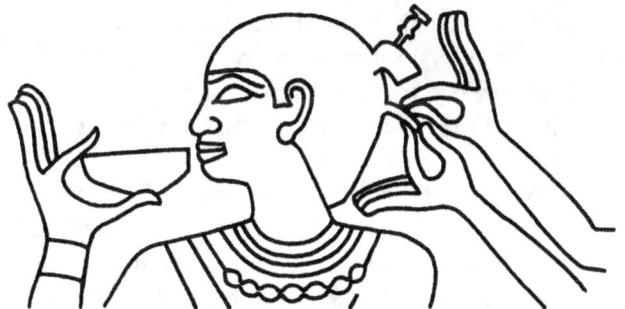

FIGURE 1.16
Detail of hands, coffin of Kawit, Cairo Museum JE 47397, Theban eleventh dynasty, after Lange and Hirmer 1961, Plate 83 top.

1.2. Problems of Right and Left

Right and left fists are often to our eyes reversed on figures, so that a left hand is attached to a right arm and a right hand to a left arm. This is not ineptitude on the part of the artist. The fist is clenched because it carries an object, such as a staff or scepter. From statuary we know that particular items were carried in a specific hand, and the reversal of hands is in fact a device that enabled artists to keep items in the correct hand without upsetting the composition of the figure. Take, for example, the image of an Old Kingdom tomb owner carrying a long staff in one hand and a scepter horizontally at his side in the other. Statues show that the staff was always carried in the left hand and the scepter in the right. In two-dimensional figures facing the viewer's right, the forward arm represents the left one and the rear arm the right one. The artist simply placed the long staff in the forward hand, which was equivalent to the left hand in life, and the staff was then held in front of the body. The scepter was placed in the rear hand, equivalent to the right hand, and held horizontally across the body at the level of the thighs. The result is closely related to the three-dimensional image (Fig. 1.14).

When artists needed to draw a similar figure facing the left, they encountered a problem. The forward arm was now equivalent to the right arm and the rear one to the left arm. If, however, they placed the staff in the left hand attached to the rear arm, it would no longer be held away from the body but would run unattractively close to it and threaten to obscure the face, while the scepter in the forward right hand would stick out in front of the body across the line of the staff. It seems

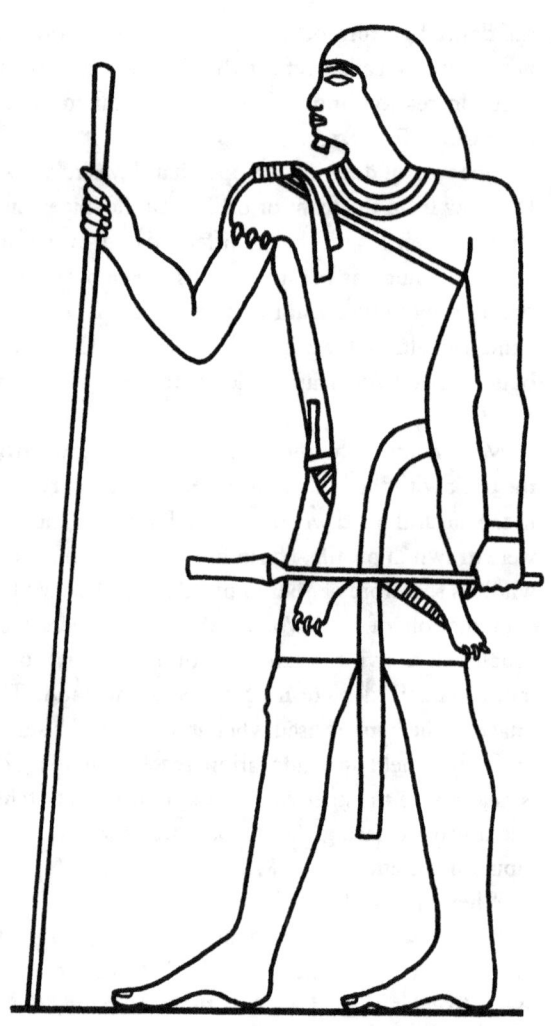

FIGURE 1.17
Standing figure of a man facing left, tomb chapel of Nefer and Kahay, Saqqara, fifth dynasty, Moussa and Altenmüller 1971, Plate 30.

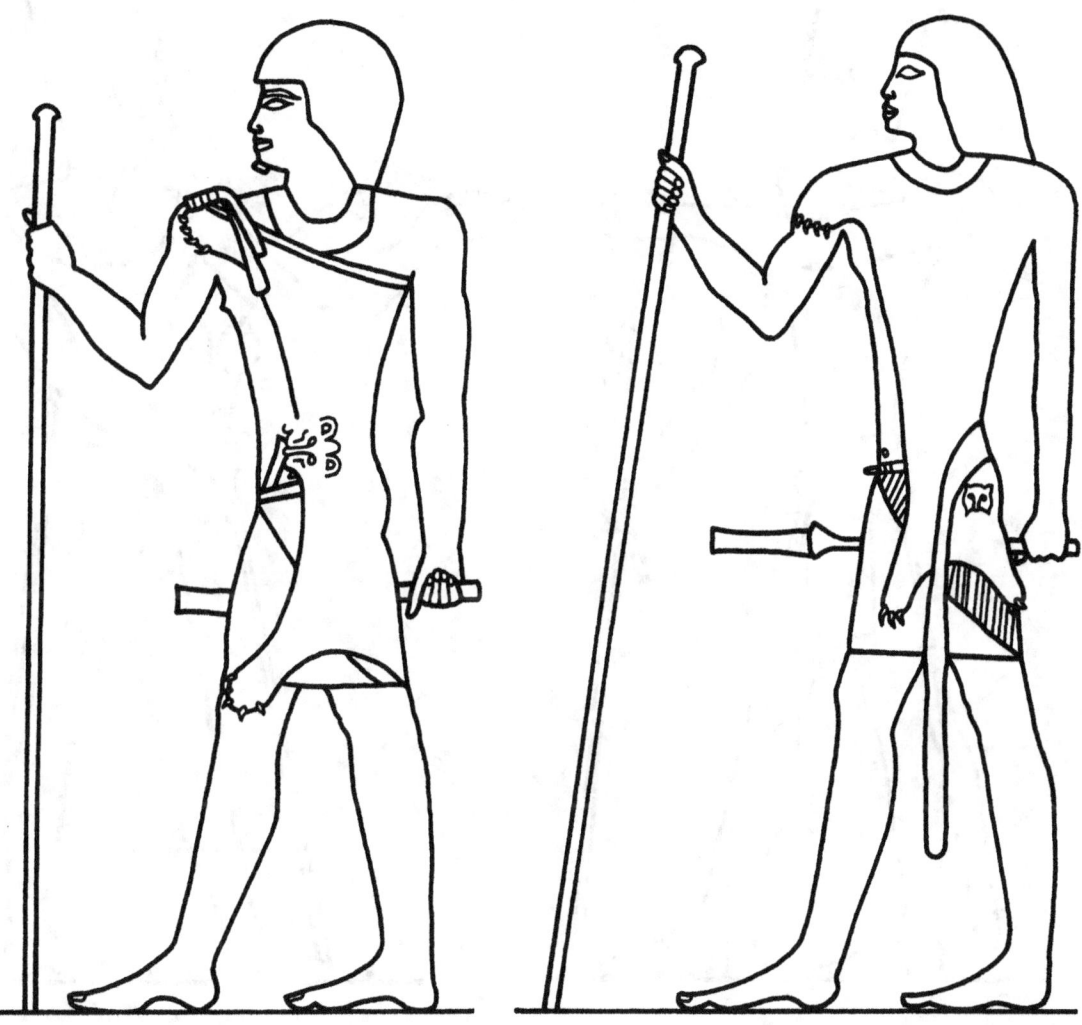

FIGURE 1.18

Standing figure of a man facing left, tomb chapel of
Niankhkhnum and Khnumhotep, Saqqara, fifth dynasty,
after Moussa and Altenmüller 1977, Figure 22.

FIGURE 1.19

Standing figure of a man facing left, tomb chapel of Nefer
and Kahay, Saqqara, fifth dynasty, after Moussa and
Altenmüller 1971, Plate 37.

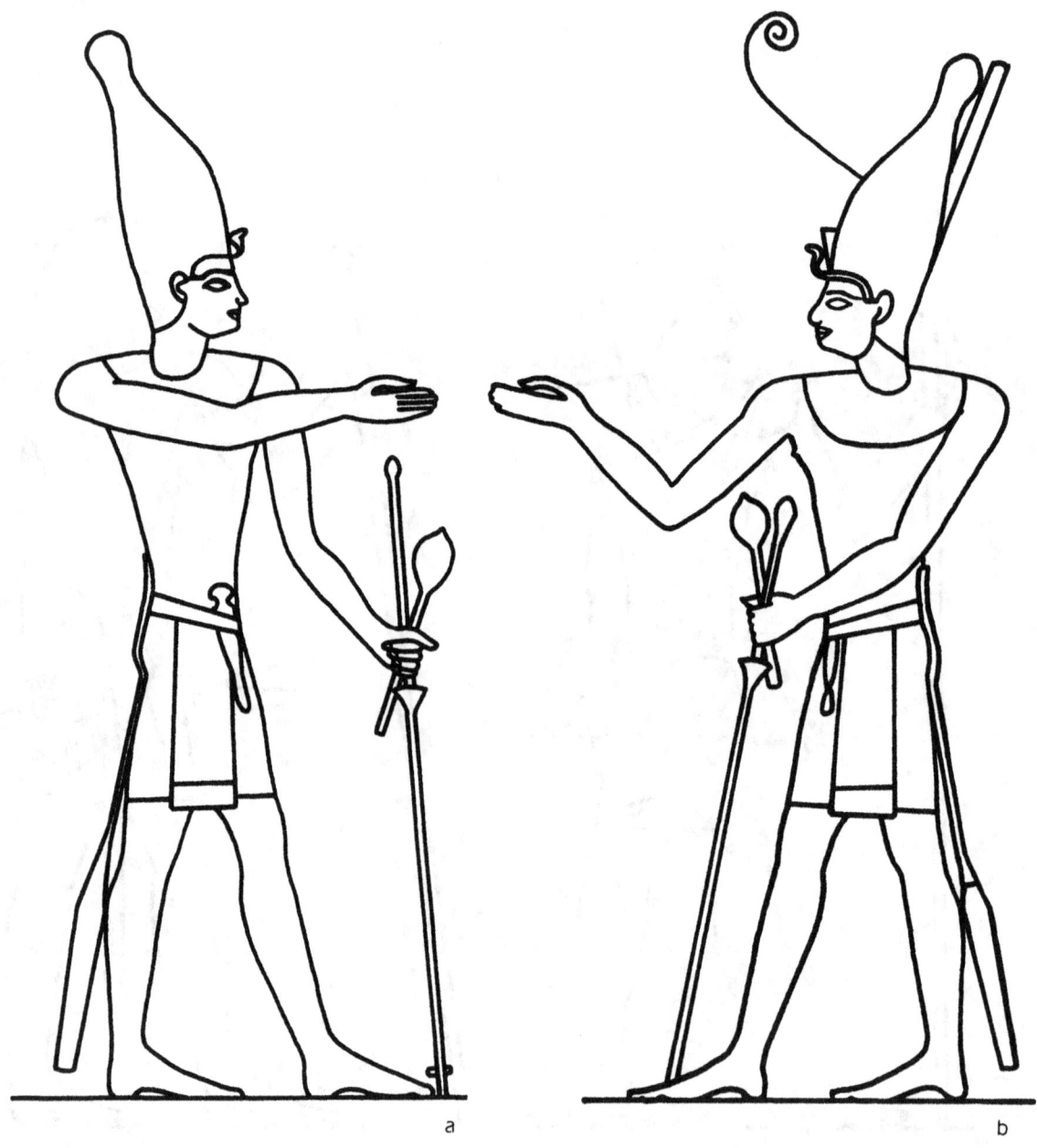

a   b

FIGURE 1.20
Figures of King Ahmose, stela dedicated to Tetisheri,
Abydos, Cairo Museum CG 34002, after Lacau 1909, Plate
2: a, figure facing right; b, figure facing left.

that artists decided that this would make an ugly and confusing image. So instead, when they drew left-facing figures, they continued to place the staff in the forward hand and the scepter in the rear one. However, the forward hand was now the right hand and the rear hand was the left one, so that in real terms the objects were in the wrong hands (Fig. 1.17).

To correct this, some (but by no means all) artists attached the image of a left hand to the forward arm and one of the right hand to the rear arm. This then tells the viewer that the staff is actually held in the left hand and the scepter in the right. In addition, the scepter often passes behind the body of the figure and not in front. This is because in reality when a figure faces left and holds a scepter in its right hand, the body of the figure must come between the scepter and the viewer (Fig. 1.18).

It is important to note that artists had a choice of solutions to the problems involved in drawing this type of figure. They could simply reverse a right-facing figure completely and not worry that the objects carried were no longer in the hands that would have held them in life. Alternatively, they could change over the left and right images of the hands to correspond with the hands which carried the objects in reality. Further, they could either pass the scepter in front of the body (Fig. 1.17), as in the right-facing image, or they could place it behind to indicate its true relationship with the body from the viewpoint of the observer (Fig. 1.19). There was no single rigid rule that dictated how these figures had to be drawn.

When figures held objects that could be retained in the correct hand without producing a clumsy image if they were reversed, there was no problem. So the king

in certain types of offering scenes carries a short staff and mace in his left hand, while he makes the gesture of offering with his right. When his figure faces right, the staff and scepter are held in his forward hand which is the left, and his rear right arm crosses his body to make the offering gesture. When turned to face left, his forward hand, now his right, is stretched out to make the gesture, while his rear left hand crosses his body holding the staff and scepter just to the front of his body. Because the staff is short, it does not obscure his figure. Both the right and left facing images are well balanced and easily understood (Fig. 1.20*a*, 1.20*b*).

Other problems concerning right and left arise for the modern viewer in the portrayal of male and female couples. In pair statues, the man almost always stands or sits beside the woman on her right, which is the more important position. In two-dimensional representations, couples were portrayed by placing one figure in front of the other. The man was set ahead of the woman because this is the more prestigious placement, equivalent to the right side in three-dimensions. In these groups the woman usually embraces the man by putting her forward arm round his shoulders. Now, obviously in reality with the man on the woman's right, she must embrace him with her right arm. In two-dimensions she can do this when the group faces left because then her forward arm is her right arm. But when the group faces right, her forward arm becomes her left one. Because of the disposition of the two figures, she cannot embrace him with her rear right arm, so her forward arm has to be used for the embrace and the image no longer corresponds with reality. However, in order to show that the man is really on the woman's right and not her left, artists sometimes made

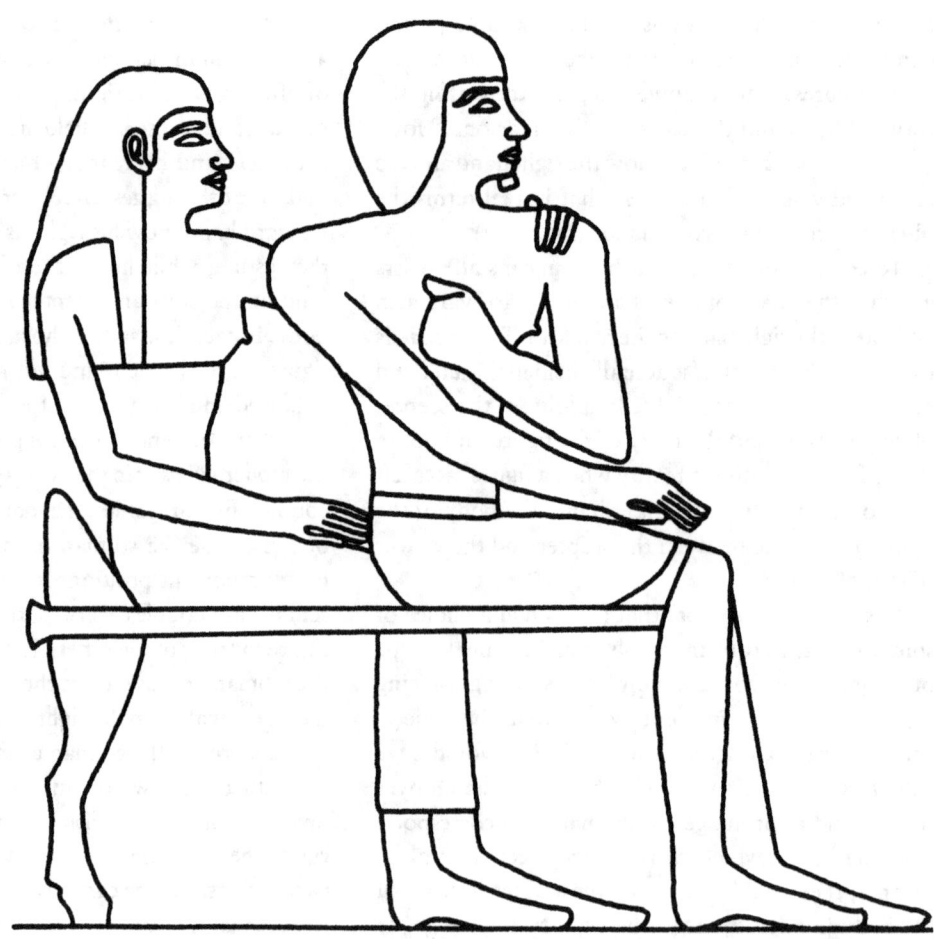

FIGURE 1.21
Representation of a seated couple facing right, tomb
chapel of Nefer, Giza, fifth-sixth dynasty, after Junker 1943,
49 Figure 11.

part of the man's body overlap the woman's; in seated figures the man's buttocks would overlap the woman's knees (Fig. 1.21) and in standing figures his heel would overlap her toes.

To complicate matters for the viewer today, we find as a secondary development similar overlapping occurring in left-facing figures where there seems to be no need for it. This is because orientation to the right is dominant in Egyptian art. Thus artists treated right-facing groups as the basic model which some then reversed unchanged in order to obtain left-facing groups.

This manipulation of left and right shows us a fundamental truth about Egyptian art. Artists were not reproducing the world as they saw it but were interpreting it as a series of concepts. This means that they produced images that had no direct relationship with reality but were constructed according to known conventions in order to convey desired information to the observer. If modern viewers do not understand this, they can never fully appreciate Egyptian art. If they regard art as slowly moving toward the discovery of geometric perspective and look for developments along these lines in Egyptian art, they will be searching for something totally alien to its spirit. Egyptian art was not evolving toward something better; it was a fully fledged representational system—subtle, mature, and conveying precisely the information that the Egyptians wanted conveyed. At the same time, artists had developed a harmonious system of composition so that the best works of art were not merely functional but also aesthetically pleasing.

It is often said that the Egyptians did not have "art for art's sake," but it is not clear how meaningful this phrase is. After all, it is possible to produce a highly functional object and also make it a work of art, and this is surely what the Egyptians did in their best works. Although artists did not transfer what they saw directly onto their drawing surface, their work leaves no doubt that they were good observers of the world about them. While they were trained in a repertory of learned forms, they did not simply reproduce these unchanged but would often add their own individual touches. Further, the Egyptians in general seem to have loved beautiful things. Although motifs used to decorate functional items were carefully chosen to enhance that function by their symbolism and associations, one cannot doubt that their owners also got great pleasure from possessing and using these beautiful objects.

1.3. Formal and Informal Art

According to the purpose for which a composition was designed, it is possible to distinguish between formal and informal art. The former consists of major scenes, which mostly depict ritual, in temples and tombs and on stelae. The scenes lie outside the time and space of this world and depict the changeless worlds of the gods and the dead. They tend to be static in character and energetic movement is mostly avoided. In potentially violent scenes like those depicting the king smiting his enemies, the artist concentrated on conveying a sense of perfectly balanced and controlled power rather than on the action itself (Fig. 1.22).

The protagonists in formal scenes are on the whole limited to deities, kings, and less often other members of the royal family, and to tomb owners and members of their families. These figures adopt a limited number of poses, standing, sitting, or kneeling. There is also a

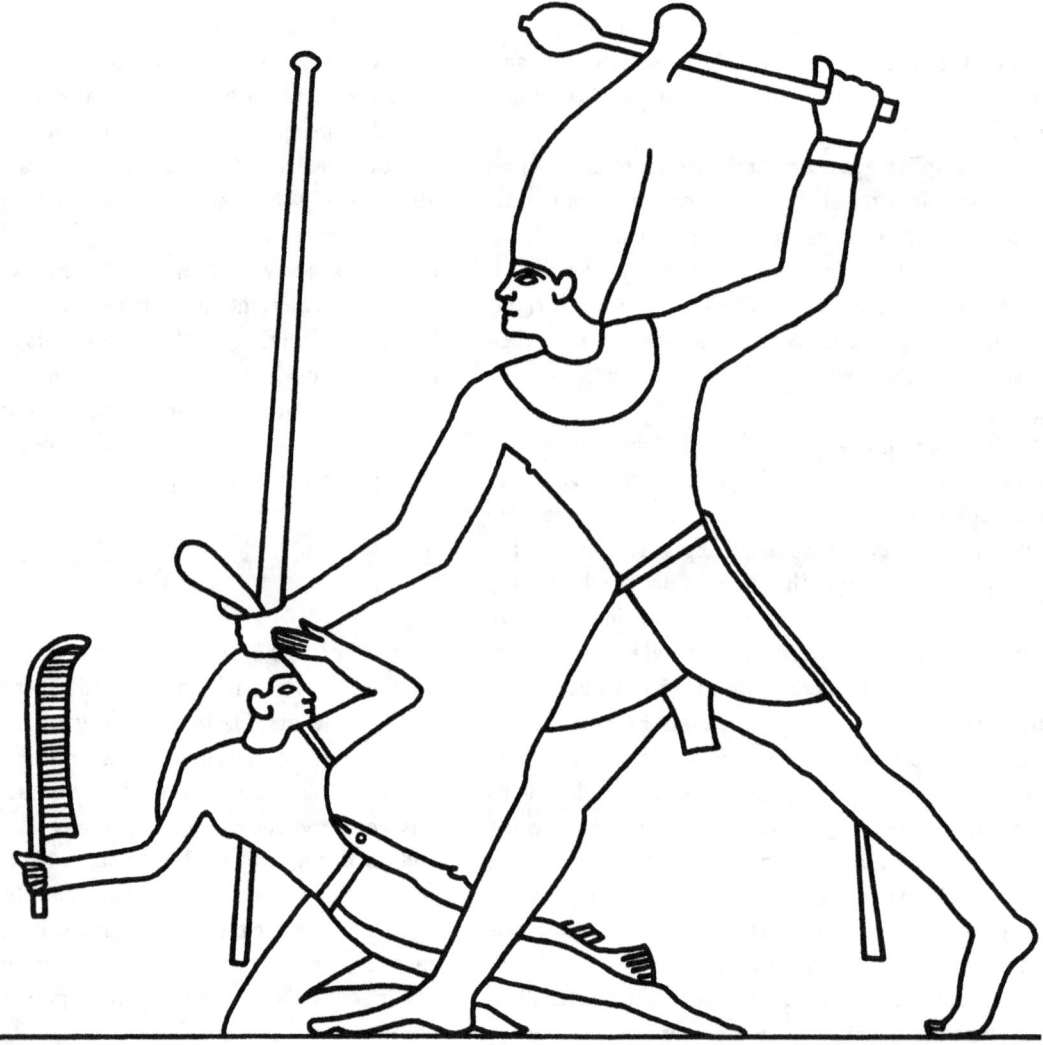

FIGURE 1.22
Representation of Nebhepetre Montuhotep smiting an
enemy, Gebelein, Cairo Museum, eleventh dynasty, after
Lange and Hirmer 1961, Plate 82.

narrow repertory of scene types. In temples, these center on the ritual performed by the king for deities and the reciprocal acts of deities toward the king. In tombs, the owner receives offerings from his family and his estates for his funerary cult, oversees activities connected with his estates or his office, and makes offerings to the gods. The figures involved in these scenes are always idealized. Men are shown either youthful and handsome or middle-aged and prosperous. Women are always young and beautiful, with little distinction made between different generations. Illness, deformity, and old age have no place here.

By contrast, subsidiary scenes contain a more informal art. They are set in the world of the living, often with a background to indicate their location, while time may be denoted by representations of the seasons. Movement is frequently present and may be energetic and violent, with figures caught in momentary attitudes (Fig. 1.10). In contrast to the formal art, there was an almost infinite variety of poses which the artist could create to capture the wide range of activities occurring in subsidiary scenes. These scenes mainly show aspects of everyday life on the estate or in the house of the tomb owner, or activities connected with his office. They include plowing, sowing, harvesting, netting fish, catching birds, animal husbandry, baking, brewing, cooking, entertainment with music and dancing, and the bringing of taxes or foreign tribute. An endless assortment of people appear, contrasting with the small number appropriate to major scenes. Moreover, far from being perfect, these figures may be shown as diseased or deformed.

The basic principles underlying both formal and informal art are the same. Formal art is more precise and has greater limitations, yet within these the varia-

tions are endless. No scene is ever exactly duplicated despite constant repetition of a small repertory of scene types. In informal art, the artist had greater scope and freedom which included room for some experimentation. This distinction between formal and informal art, and between major and subsidiary scenes, is important when it comes to considering the major topic of this book: the use of squared grids in composition to obtain proportions of figures. Such a technique was more readily adapted to the static figures and compositions of formal art than to the diversity of poses found in informal art, and gradually over time many subsidiary scenes came to be drawn freehand without the aid of grids.

1.4. Stages of Composition

The squared grid was a basic tool used by artists in laying out scenes and was part of the initial stages of composition. Egyptian artists worked on a number of materials, of which the foremost was stone, and much of our knowledge of Egyptian art comes from the decoration of tombs, temples, and stelae. Unfinished monuments show how the area to be decorated was prepared and how the various stages in the composition were executed. First, the stone was polished to a smooth surface and any flaws patched up with plaster. In rock-cut buildings where the stone was poor, the whole area was sometimes covered with a thick layer of plaster to provide a smooth surface for the cutting of relief. If the quality of the rock was particularly bad or perhaps if the tomb owner could not afford relief, the stone was only roughly cut and then covered with a thick layer of straw and mud. This was coated with

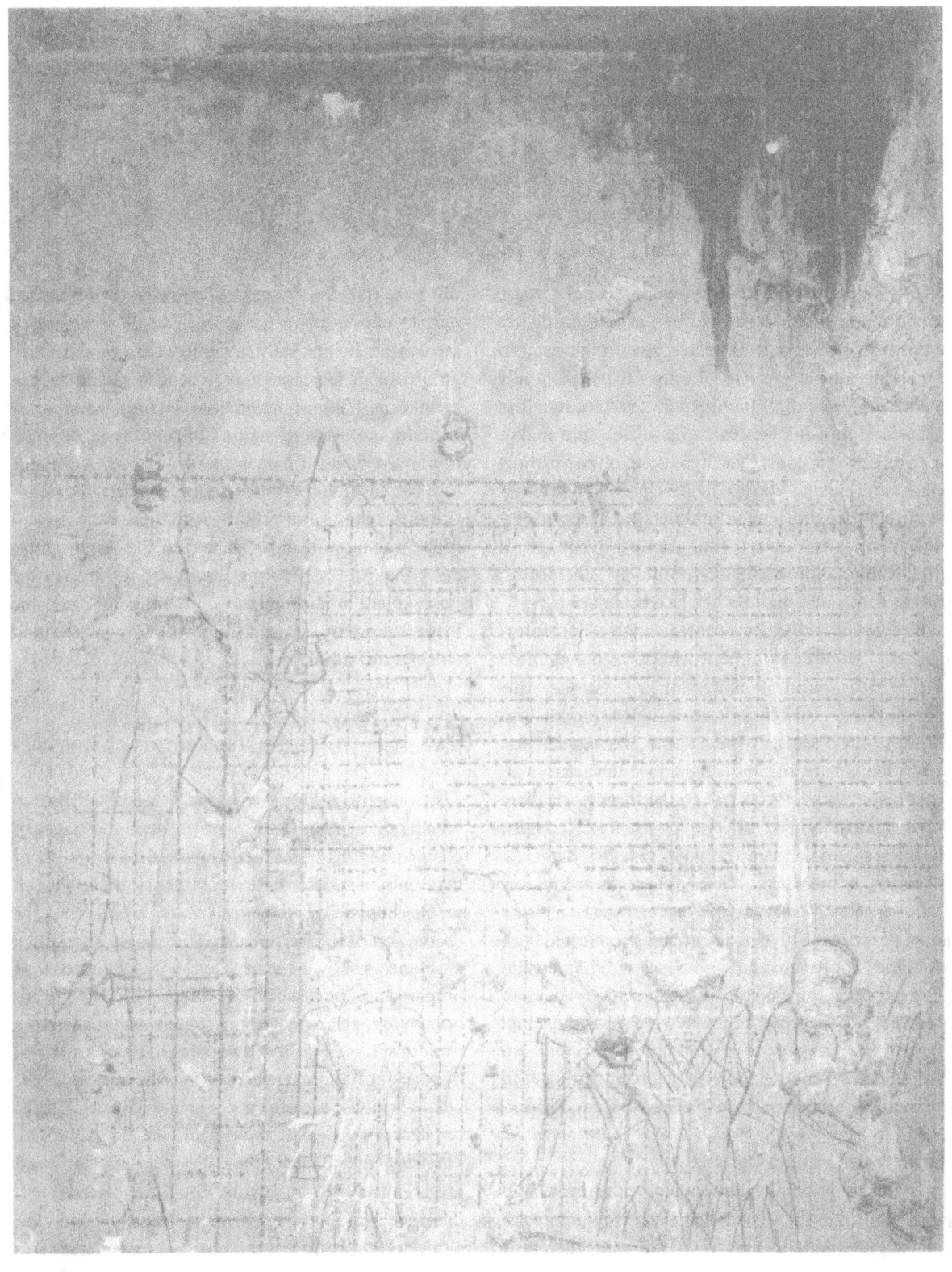

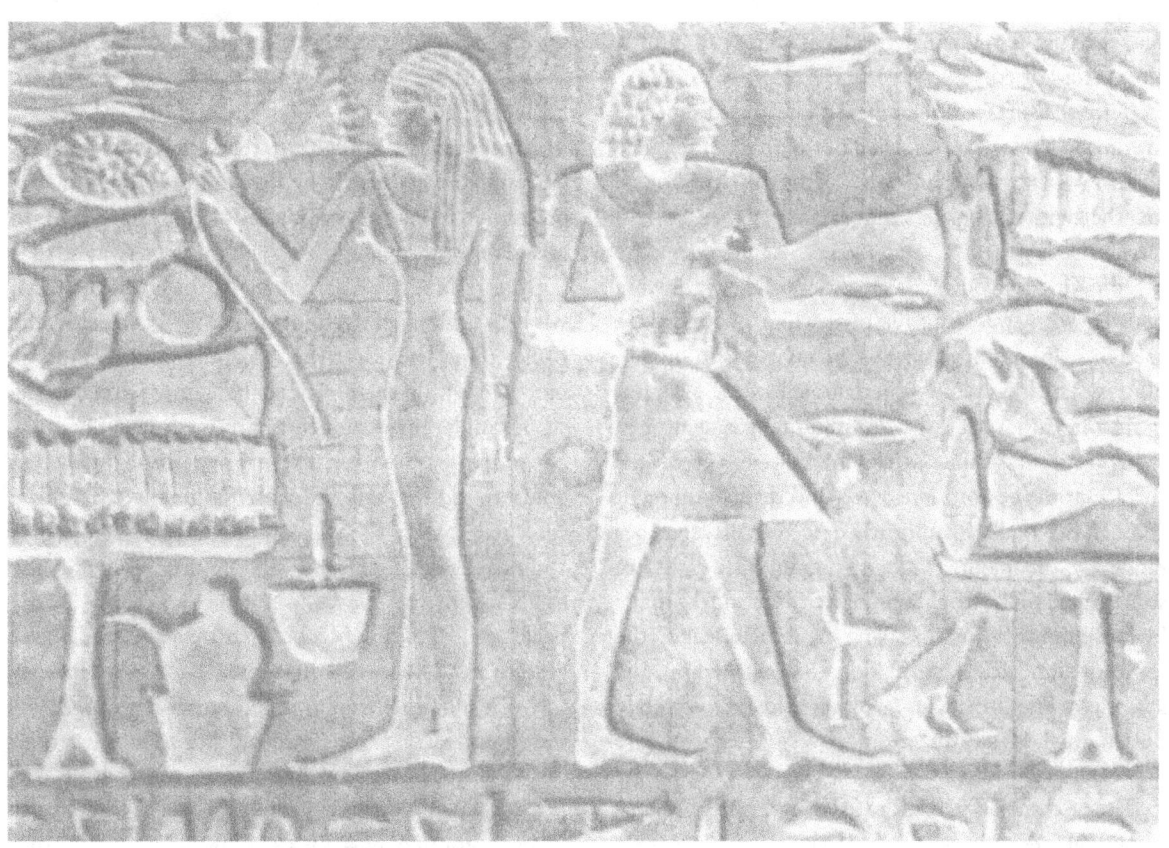

PLATE 1.1

Detail of unfinished scene in TT 92, eighteenth dynasty, Mond photo 2122, reproduced by permission of the Griffith Institute.

PLATE 1.2

Detail of stela of Userwer, twelfth dynasty, British Museum EA 579, reproduced by courtesy of the Trustees of the British Museum.

a layer of plaster on which the decoration was painted after it had dried.

Once the surface was prepared, the areas that were to contain scenes were marked out with red lines. The position of the frieze that ran along the top of the walls, together with the borders that ran around the scenes, might also be marked out in red at this time. From the Middle Kingdom onward, all or some of the walls were covered with squared grids of red lines, which were used to help obtain acceptable proportions in human figures. The lines were sometimes ruled (Pl. 5.4), but more often they were made by dipping a length of string into red paint, stretching it taut across the surface at the appropriate levels and then snapping it against the wall. In unfinished scenes the splashes made by the paint as the string hit the wall can sometimes still be seen, together with the marks made by loose filaments on the string. Also to be seen at the edges of some grids are the dots that marked out the spacing of the lines. The resulting grids are certainly not mathematically precise and very often they are visibly uneven (Pl. 1.1).

The next stage was to draw, also in red, the preliminary sketches for the scene (Pls. 1.1, 5.2). Artists worked in teams so that there would be different draftsmen employed on the different parts of a monument and even on the different parts of one composition. Nevertheless, the teams were overseen by a master draftsman who was probably responsible for the actual composition of the scenes. He would make corrections to his subordinates' work in black and approve the final version. Then, if the scene was not to be in relief, artists painted the composition color by color in flat washes, often starting with the back-

ground (Pl. 5.5). Lastly, the outlines of figures and details within them were redrawn with a fine brush (Pl. 1.4).

Most scenes were cut into relief. Two types, raised and sunk, were used. In both, the outlines in the preliminary sketch were incised with a sharp tool. In raised relief, the background was then cut away so that the figures stood out from the surface of the stone, while in sunk relief the figures were cut back below the background level. In either case, the figures could be modeled within their outline and details carved in the stone. Sunk relief produces sharp shadows so that it is particularly suited for use in bright sunlight, which tends to flatten raised relief. Originally, therefore, sunk relief was employed on the outside of buildings and raised relief inside. But since in sunk relief only the figures were cut away and not the larger area of the background, it came to be used on hard stones like granite, sandstone, and quartzite, which were less easy to work than the comparatively softer limestone. For the same reason it was also quicker to execute than raised relief, even in softer stones, so that it was favored during periods when there were large areas to be decorated in a hurry. However, artists using sunk relief found it difficult to obtain the subtlety of modeling and delicacy of line possible with raised relief.

When the relief had been cut, the stone was covered with a thin layer of plaster and the outlines of the figures were redrawn. The background and figures were then painted. Finally, details were picked out with a fine brush and the figures outlined for the last time. Today, the paint on many relief-cut monuments has disappeared.

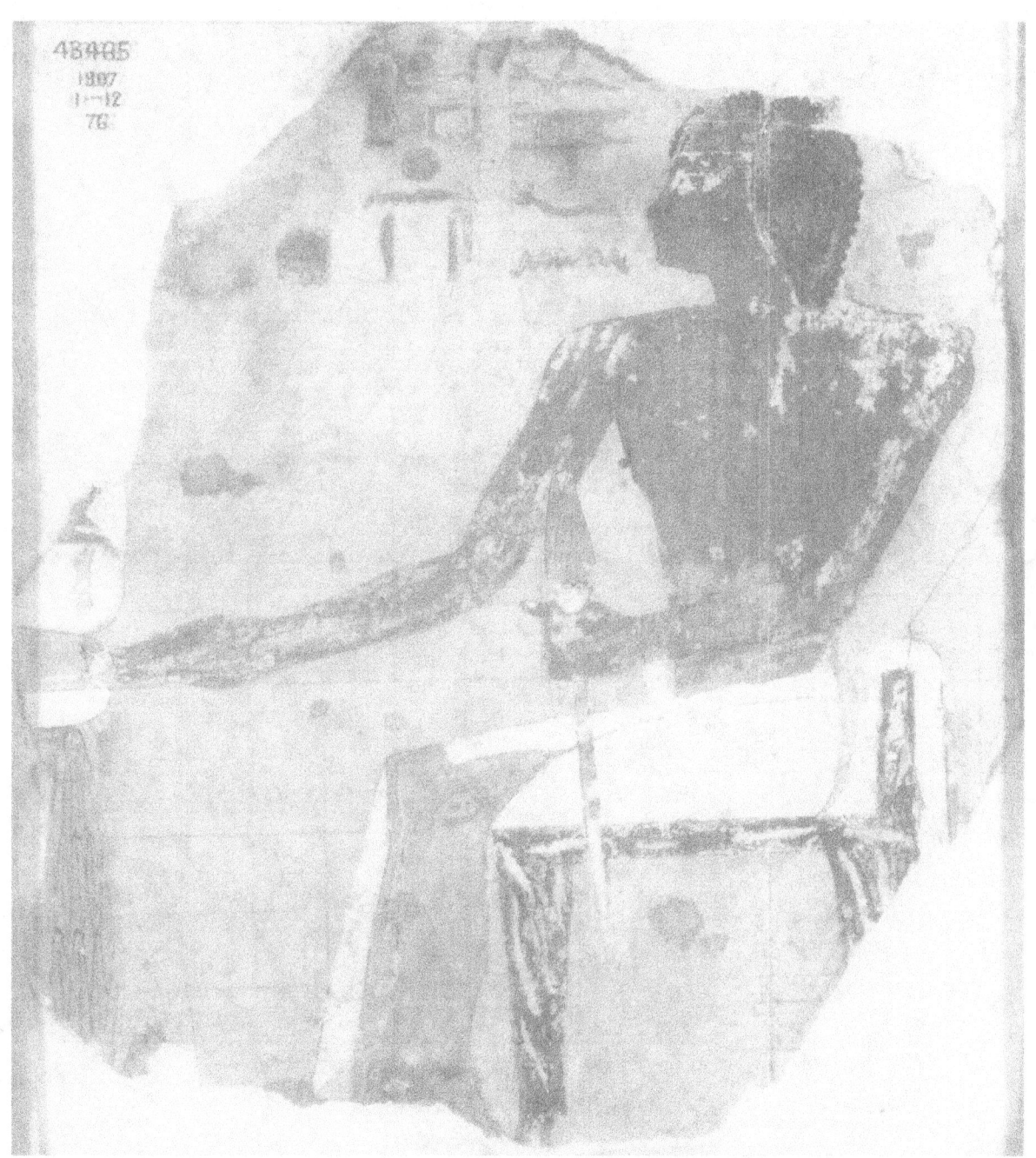

PLATE 1.3
Fragment of tomb painting, eighteenth dynasty, British
Museum EA 43465, reproduced by courtesy of the
Trustees of the British Museum.

28

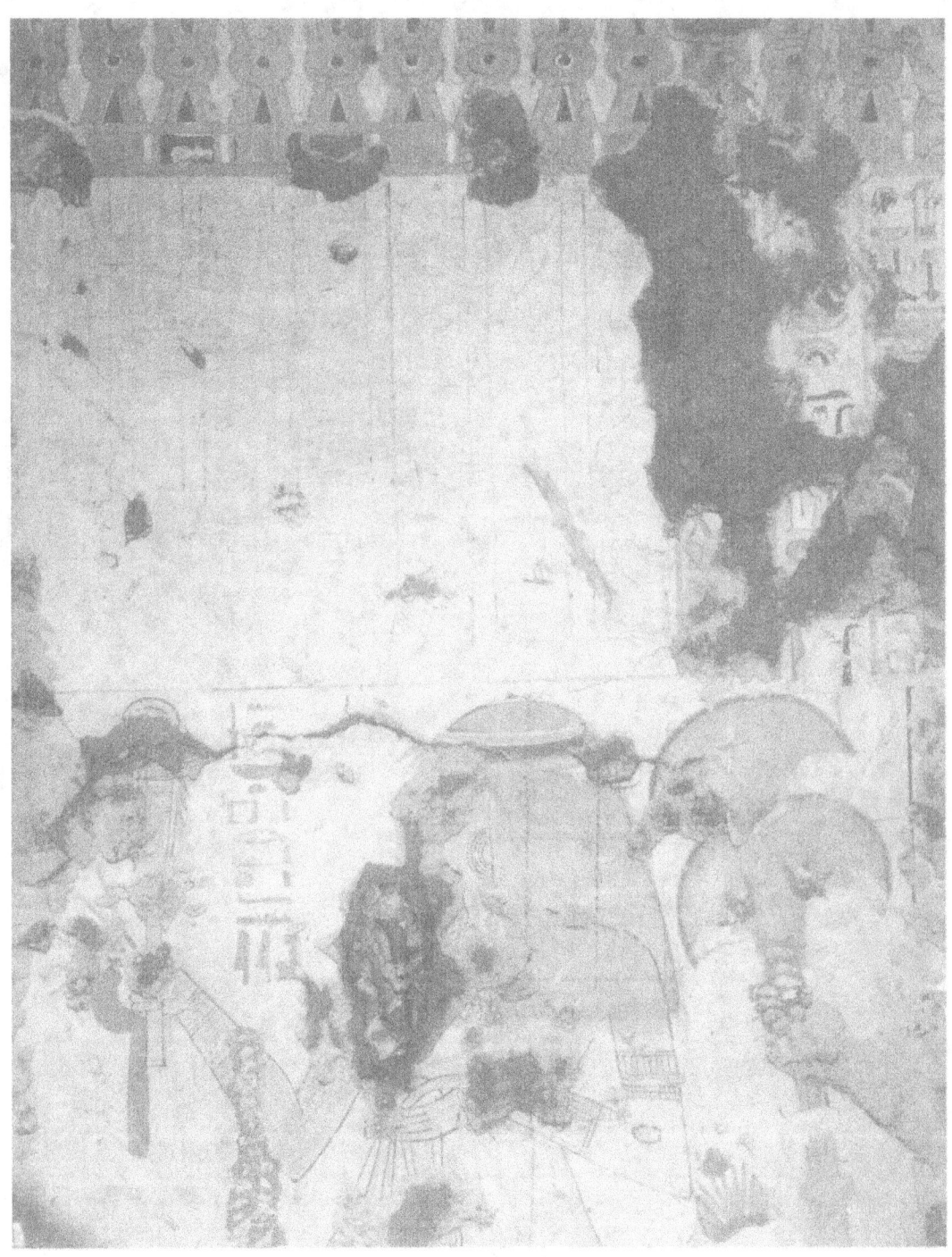

PLATE 1.4
Detail from a scene in TT 77, eighteenth dynasty,
Mond photo 6003, reproduced by permission of
the Griffith Institute.

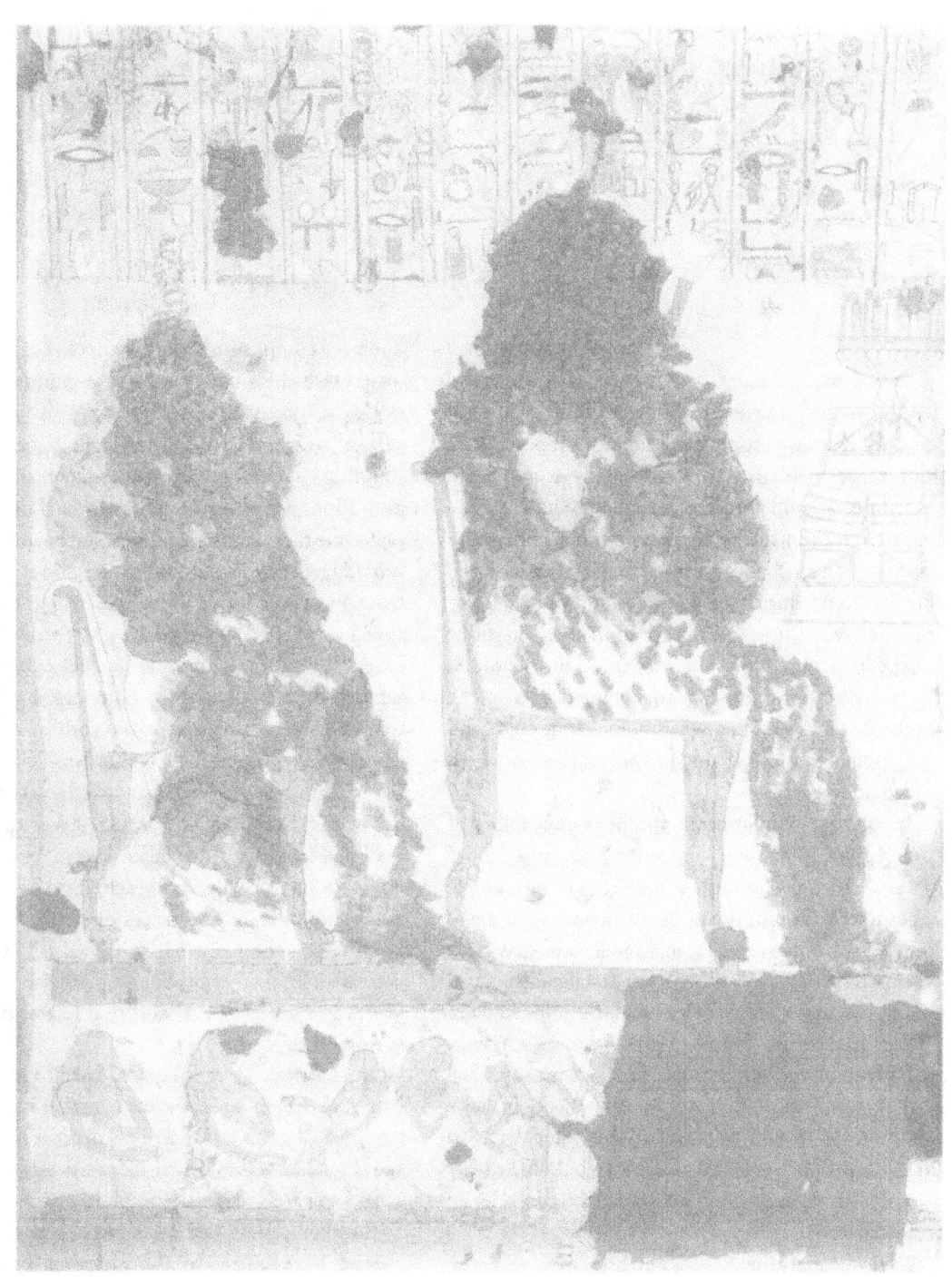

PLATE 1.5
Detail from a scene in TT 75, eighteenth dynasty, MMA
photo T 2093, photograph by the Egyptian Expedition,
courtesy of the Metropolitan Museum of Art, New York.

1.5. Survival of the Grid

Clearly, artists' grids were not meant to be seen once a piece of work was completed, so how is it possible to study them? The answer is that many scenes were never finished and so the grid is plainly visible. The majority of unfinished scenes are in tombs, and there is a very good reason for this. A man (rarely a woman) built his tomb during his lifetime, and once he was dead there was little incentive for his heirs to continue to expend resources on it. The decoration was therefore often left in varying stages of completion, from the outline sketches to scenes where some of the color had been applied to those where only the borders or frieze needed adding.

By contrast, temples were not the responsibility of a single man. What one king started the next would continue, so there was much less reason for temple scenes to remain unfinished. Nevertheless, grid traces do survive in some temples, making it clear that grids were used there as well as in tombs. In fact, it is logical to suppose that they were particularly important in temple decoration. Many of the large-scale scenes are high up on the temple walls, and artists must have worked from scaffolding to execute them. In such conditions, it would be impossible to step back to gauge the proportions, and grid lines would have been essential to ensure that acceptable figures were produced.

While the majority of grids and grid traces are to be seen in unfinished scenes, others appear in scenes that had been completed. Although in relief the grid was cut away with the stone (Pl. 1.2),[5] in painted scenes the grid lines were not physically removed but simply painted over. In every finished painted scene, the grids, initial sketches, and any subsequent corrections or alterations are all there underneath. If only we could penetrate the layers of paint without harming them, we would have a mine of information about artistic practices. However, there are places where damage over time has removed some of the paint from the walls to reveal for us traces of what lies below (Pl. 5.4). The whitish-blue color used to paint the background in many eighteenth-dynasty private tombs has often worn thin or flaked off (Pl. 1.3). But most commonly the black pigment used by artists failed to combine properly with the medium with which it was applied to the wall and has long since fallen away. As the standard color for hair or wigs was black, it is very common to be able to pick up grid traces on the heads of figures from which the paint has vanished (Pl. 1.4). Chairs were also frequently black and, with the loss of color, grid traces are often revealed that relate to the figures sitting on them (Pl. 1.5).

In addition, the red pigment used to mark the grid was very strong, and in some tombs it has penetrated the layer of paint above it. This process results in very faint, pinkish traces which are extremely easy to overlook and rarely show up on photographs.

Surviving grids had already been noticed and recorded by scholars in the nineteenth century. An outline of their observations is given in Chapter 2.

Previous Work on the Grid and Proportions

2.1. The Nineteenth and Early Twentieth Centuries

The nineteenth century, which was the great pioneering age of Egyptology, produced a remarkable number of outstanding figures in the field. One of the foremost was the Frenchman Achille Prisse d'Avennes (1807–1879), who went to Egypt as an engineer in the time of Mohammed Ali and while there single-handedly collected material for two large plate volumes recording the architecture and art of the monuments, published in the years 1847 and 1878. The text for the second book was completed from Prisse's notes by P. Marchandon de la Faye and published in 1879, the year of Prisse's death. In his second plate volume, Prisse included several figures drawn on squared grids, and a section in the text volume is devoted to his views on the canon of proportions.[1]

Prisse had no doubt that there was a system of proportions in use from the earliest times that acted as a guide for artists drawing human figures. He firmly denied the contention that the squared grids were used simply to copy figures onto walls from smaller sketches, as had been suggested by some. In fact, he believed that compositions were conceived in situ.

Prisse recognized that there were two basic grid systems, one in use until the twenty-sixth dynasty and the other from the twenty-sixth dynasty to Roman times. He described the standing figure in the first system as dividing into 19 parts from the soles of the feet to the top of the head. The head itself consisted of 3 parts, with the shoulders starting at 16 parts above the baseline. The pubis lay 9 1/2 parts up, so dividing the figure into halves. The knee was placed 6 parts up (Fig. 2.1).

Prisse was insistent that the height of the figure was to be reckoned as 19 squares to the top of the head. By contrast, some of his colleagues thought that the height

should be taken as 18 squares to the top of the forehead, excluding the part covered by hair. As we shall see later, Prisse was on the losing side in this argument. In most New Kingdom figures, the top of the head does indeed lie on grid horizontal 19, but in earlier figures it is rare for it to come up to this line; the top of the forehead or "hairline" is constant on horizontal 18.

Prisse also disagreed with some of his colleagues over the part of the body that might have acted as a unit module for the system. While he had no doubt that such a module existed, he rejected the foot, which some Egyptologists had proposed. Having noticed that the length of the middle finger or medius occupied one grid square, and thus was 1/19 of the height of a figure, he suggested this as the module.

In collecting material from the monuments, Prisse had observed that from the twenty-sixth dynasty until Roman times the total height of standing figures on the grid was divided into 23 squares (or into 21 1/4 squares to the top of the forehead [Fig. 2.2]); seated figures took up 19 squares. Although he did not think that this new grid system altered the proportions of figures in any great way, he felt it led to stockier limbs and a certain clumsiness. As we shall see, this impression was created by a return in art to Old Kingdom models, when figures were more sturdy than those of the later New Kingdom (Chap. 7).

Certainly Prisse did not regard the system of proportions as inflexible. Looking at the early grid system, he noted that there were different styles at different periods, remarking on the elegance achieved in the eighteenth and nineteenth dynasties compared with earlier times. He observed, however, that this did not alter the number of grid squares in a figure. He also

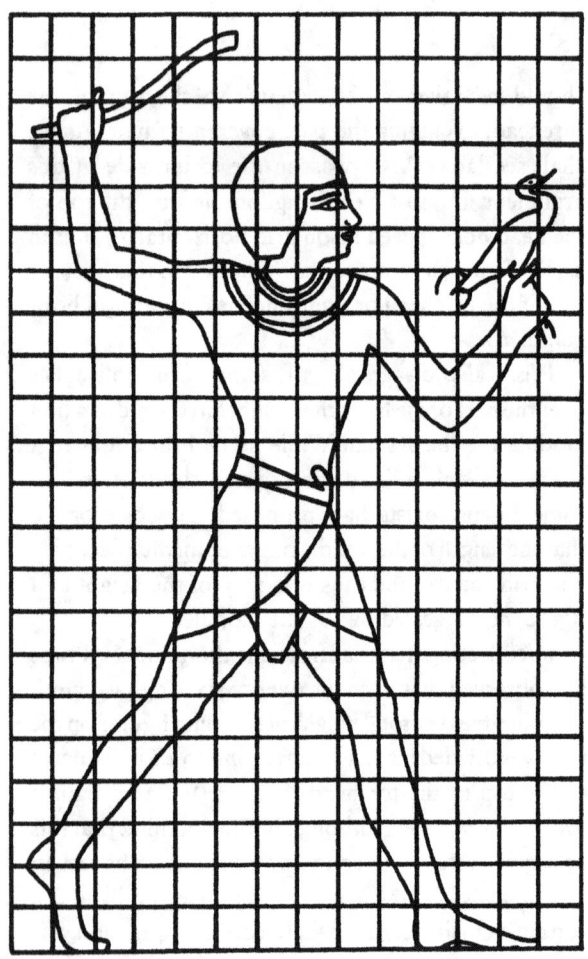

FIGURE 2.1

After Prisse 1879, 125, showing a figure on a grid in the early system (in TT 92).

stressed that neither of the two canons of proportion was so concerned with governing detail that drawing became mechanical. The grid was to prevent overall errors and to help the artist achieve harmony and regularity. Artists were not tied to the grid and, as he noted, did not always use it; this did not affect the quality of their work.

In 1869, a French art critic, Charles Blanc (1813–1882), went on a visit to Egypt. He described his adventures in *Voyage dans la Haute Egypte,* published in 1876. He had already given a description of the early grid system in his *Grammaire des arts du dessin* of 1867. Like Prisse, he described the total height of the body as being divided into nineteenths. He then listed the parts of the body through which grid horizontals run. Although he did not give numbers to these lines, an accompanying diagram enables the reader to do so simply by counting upward from the baseline, which is horizontal 0 (Fig. 2.3). Horizontal 1 runs through the ankles, 4 through the curve of the calf, 5 through the bottom of the kneecap and 6 at the top, 7 through the tip of the middle finger when the arm hangs at the side of the body, 8 through the base of the middle finger, 9 through the wrist, 11 through the navel, 12 through the elbow of the hanging arm, 14 through the lower border of the pectoral muscle, 16 through the Adam's apple (shown by his drawing to be at the same level as the junction of the neck and shoulders), 17 through the point of the nose, 18 through the forehead, and 19 through the top of the head. Like Prisse, he considered that the medius at 1/19th of the body height served as the unit module for the system.

During his trip to Egypt, Blanc had been excited to notice on the walls of the sanctuary at Karnak a figure

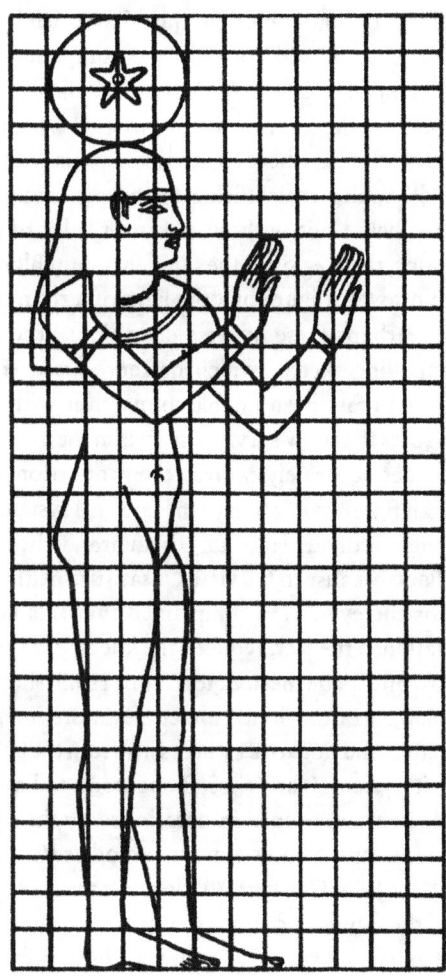

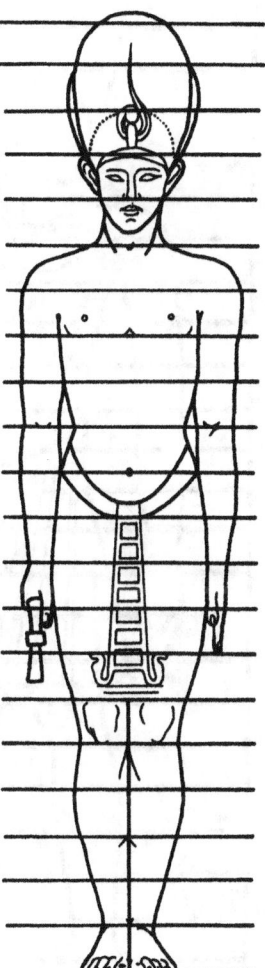

FIGURE 2.2
After Prisse 1879, 128, showing a figure on a grid in the
later system (in the temple of Kom Ombo).

FIGURE 2.3
After Blanc 1876, 233, showing a constructed figure
divided by horizontal lines according to the early
grid system.

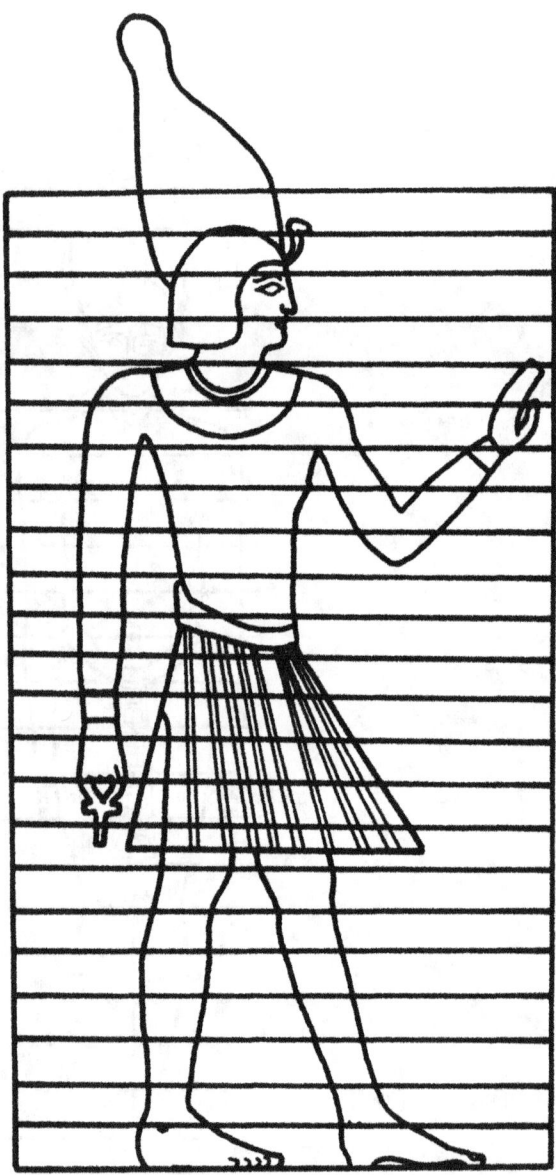

FIGURE 2.4

After Blanc 1876, 230, showing a figure divided by horizontal lines according to the later grid system, copied by Blanc in the temple of Karnak.

drawn on a grid. He determined to revisit it in order to copy it, and did so with two companions late one evening. He described how they made their return there by the light of torches carried by their donkey boys, the ram-headed sphinxes taking on a strange look under their flickering beams. Finally, having clambered not without risk over piles of fallen columns, they regained the sanctuary, and Blanc was able to draw his figure by "the light of a resin torch."[2]

Perhaps these adverse conditions account for his appalling sketch, which he reproduced (Fig. 2.4). I have in fact been unable to match it with any of the figures that now survive on grids in the area. However, it does accurately portray the proportions of the human figure in relation to the late grid system. The total height is divided into 22 1/4 squares, which displeased Blanc because in his view "it satisfies neither the spirit nor the eyes." He complained that this later system flattened the feet, reduced the knees, put the navel too low and made the neck too short. I shall show later that changes of this kind, sometimes more imagined than actual, did not arise by necessity from the change in the grid system. Like Prisse, Blanc seems to have observed changes in proportion occasioned by the return in art to Old and Middle Kingdom models (Chap. 7).

Sir John Gardner Wilkinson (1797–1875) was one of the founders of English Egyptology and spent more than twelve years in Egypt traveling, excavating, surveying, and copying the monuments. During his work in the Theban tombs, he came across examples of unfinished scenes showing figures on their original grids, and in some of his published works he made brief references to the early grid system.[3] He too described the body as being divided into 19 parts, and noted that the knee lay on horizontal 6. He pointed out, however, that in the eighteenth and nineteenth dynasties the knee lay higher than in earlier periods. This acute observation rests on the fact that originally it was most commonly the top of the knee that lay on horizontal 6, but later the lower leg was lengthened so that horizontal 6 ran through the bottom edge of the kneecap, pushing the top of the knee above the line (Chap. 5).

Among the giants of Egyptology for all time must be counted the great German scholar Karl Richard Lepsius (1810–1884). Of all his many achievements, one of the most outstanding in a remarkable and incredibly productive career was the publication in 1859 of the twelve plate volumes of the *Denkmäler aus Aegypten und Aethiopien,* which is still an indispensable tool of the modern Egyptologist. This vast work contains the results of the Prussian expedition to Egypt and Nubia that Lepsius led between 1842 and 1845. The expedition traveled throughout Egypt and into Nubia surveying the monuments and recording their texts and decoration. In the course of his journey Lepsius came across a number of scenes that still showed traces of the original artists' squared grids. Others preserved human figures drawn not on a grid but on a series of horizontal lines.

In 1884, the year of his death, Lepsius published a book on the units of length used in the ancient world, to which he added an appendix on the proportions of human figures in art based on his observations. He began by noting that standing figures were originally conceived as dividing into 6 equal parts between the soles and the top of the exposed forehead beneath the wig or headdress. This point, the hairline, was used rather than the top of the head because crowns and other headgear obscured the actual position of the top. Here he differed from those colleagues who thought

the body was divided between the soles and the top of the head.

Lepsius made it clear that he felt it was unimportant whether this sixth part of the body corresponded to a particular unit of measurement or not, because the proportions of a figure were relative, not absolute. However, in one Old Kingdom example, he had noticed that the length of the foot had been clearly marked off, and that this distance was similar to a sixth part of the hairline height. He thought, therefore, that it might be possible for the foot to have been used as the module for the construction of the whole system.

As a result, he examined the question of whether the "natural" foot on the figure could be related to the cubit system and the foot as a unit of measurement. In many parts of the ancient world, the metrological foot was normally equal to two-thirds of the small cubit. The latter in modern terms is roughly 45 cm, making the foot 30 cm long. But Lepsius calculated that if the human figure up to the top of the exposed forehead or hairline consisted of 6 feet of 30 cm each, this would come to 1.80 m, and that a further 6 cm would have to be allowed to reach to the top of the head. He found this to be unacceptably tall for the ancient Egyptians, adding that 1.82 m is the required height for "the first company of our Guards." In fact, by 1884 Lepsius clearly felt that the whole debate was rather pointless, because in the Egyptian system of measurement, two-thirds of a cubit was never called a "foot"; indeed, the foot did not play a part as a definite length in the cubit system.

When Lepsius came to describing the original system of proportions in the Old Kingdom, he admitted that his division into 6 parts was to some extent theoretical and that not all these divisions were marked off by lines. He called the length equal to a figure's foot a "square," and described how in practice a line 2 squares above the baseline runs through the middle of the knee; another, 1 square higher, beneath the buttocks; yet another, again 1 square higher, through the joint of the elbow; and finally another, 2 squares higher, through the hairline. In addition, between the elbow and hairline, there are another two lines, of which one runs through the armpits and the other through the junction of the neck and shoulders (Fig. 2.5). Neither of these last two lines fits exactly into the square module.

He then moved on to discuss the squared grid, which he demonstrated was merely a modification of the earlier system he had described. From the twelfth dynasty onward, the 6 equal parts of the figure were each further divided into 3, so that there were 18 parts between the soles and the hairline. If, as has become the custom, we take the baseline as 0 and count upward, horizontal 5 runs beneath the kneecap, 6 above the kneecap, 7 beneath the tips of the fingers of the hand hanging by the body, 8 under the thumb, 9 beneath the buttocks, 11 through the navel, 12 through the elbow, 14 through the nipple, 16 through the junction of the neck and shoulders, 17 beneath the nose, and 18 through the hairline. Thus, the horizontal lines of the early system found in the Old Kingdom that ran through the knee, beneath the buttocks, through the elbow, through the junction of the neck and shoulders, and through the hairline in fact correspond with the grid horizontals 6, 9, 12, 16, and 18. The old armpit line, however, had no corresponding grid horizontal; on the grid the armpits fell roughly halfway between horizontals 14 and 15.

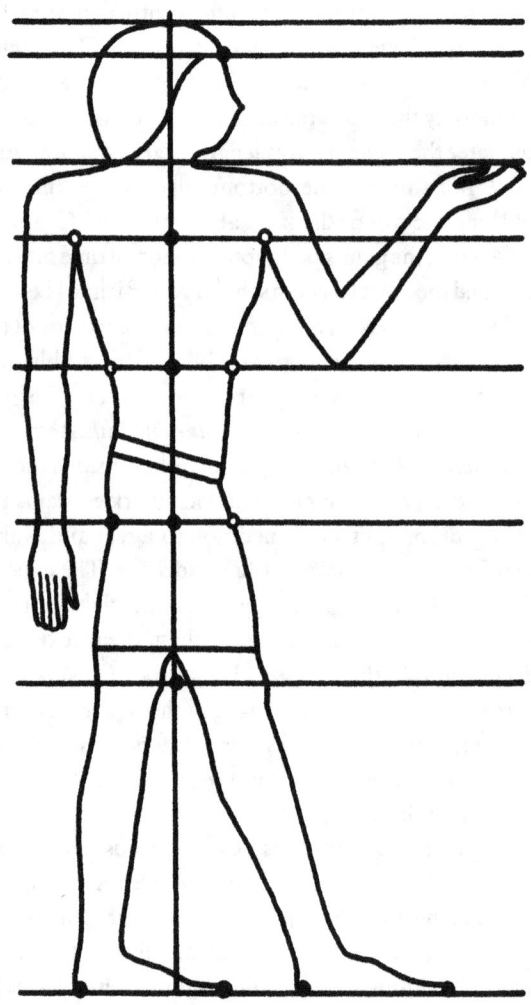

FIGURE 2.5
After Lepsius 1897, 242, showing a constructed figure based on LD 2, 65 divided by the guidelines in use in the Old Kingdom.

For Lepsius, his observations left no doubt that human figures were drawn according to an established set of proportions obtained originally by a set of horizontal guidelines and then secondarily by the use of a squared grid. While the foot as drawn was one-sixth of the hairline height, he specifically rejected any connection between this and the system of measurement based on the small cubit.

These were the conclusions that Lepsius chose to publish at the end of his life. However, they were not his first thoughts on the subject, which are preserved in the text to his great work, *Denkmäler aus Aegypten und Aethiopien.* He died without actually having produced the text, and it was left to the Swiss Egyptologist Henri Edouard Naville to compile it from Lepsius' papers. In the first of the five volumes, appearing in 1897, there is a discussion of human proportions in art[4] based on the same unfinished figures from an Old Kingdom tomb published in LD 1, Pl. 65, which formed the basis of the description in the 1884 book. In these earlier notes, Lepsius described the divisions of these figures and their relationship to the 18-square grid system much as in the later book, but there are two major differences.

In this earlier work, Lepsius assumed that the foot in art, equal to one-sixth of the hairline height, was the equivalent of two-thirds of a small cubit, that is, 30 cm in modern terms. Second, he took the length of the small cubit to be equivalent to the distance from the elbow bone to the middle knuckle of the middle finger. But as we have seen, by 1884 he no longer believed that the length of the foot in art should be linked with a metrological unit equal to two-thirds of a small cubit and was at pains to point out that any such equation

produced figures that were unbelievably tall in absolute terms; also there was no separate unit of measurement in the Egyptian metrological system that was based on the foot. The second change to be found in the 1884 book concerns the relationship between the length of the small cubit and the human forearm. By this time, Lepsius had come to regard the small cubit as the length of the forearm from the elbow to the tip of the outstretched middle finger,[5] rather than to the middle knuckle of the middle finger.

Clearly Lepsius' later work superseded his earlier thoughts on the subject, and the latter would hardly be worth mentioning if they had not been made generally available as part of the text to the *Denkmäler.* As such, they were to be a major influence on one Egyptologist, Erik Iversen, who would, as we shall see, make the subject of canon and proportion very much his own.

Let us, however, for the moment remain in the nineteenth century. While Lepsius was formulating his description of the grid system and canon of proportions, two Frenchmen, Georges Perrot (1832–1914) and Charles Chipiez (1835–1901), were engaged in writing a book entitled *L'Histoire de l'art dans l'antiquité,* of which the first volume, appearing in 1882, was devoted to Egypt. In this, the authors disputed both the very existence of a formalized canon of proportions and that figures were drawn on a consistent number of grid squares. The authors cited examples of standing figures consisting of 16, 19, 22 1/4, and 23 squares. In their view, the only function of the grid was to enable artists to transfer figures from sketches to the working surface.

Yet another Frenchman writing on Egyptian art expressed much the same opinion. This was the eminent Egyptologist Gaston Maspero (1846–1916), who in his day was one of the dominant figures in the field. He wrote strongly against the existence of a theoretical canon based on a module representing, for example, the length of a finger or of the foot.[6] Of course, the parts of the body would naturally stand in a fixed ratio to one another, as in life, but it was not necessary, in his view, to tabulate them into a system. The squared grid was merely for transferring figures from a sketch to the wall. After all, the grid was not even in universal use, as is shown by unfinished figures, for example, in the tomb of Sety I in the Valley of the Kings.

This challenge to the canon of proportions was taken up and refuted by the Scottish Egyptologist and Greek scholar C.C. Edgar (1870–1938). Edgar had a long connection with the Cairo Museum and produced a number of volumes of the *Catalogue générale des antiquités égyptiennes du Musée du Caire*. These included one published in 1906 entitled *Sculptors' Studies and Unfinished Works*. The objects described are late, dating in the main to the Ptolemaic period. They included models of royal heads in various stages of execution; where the surface of the stone had not been cut away or modeled, traces remained of horizontal and vertical lines forming squares, together with secondary lines which Edgar showed marked the levels of various facial features.

As a spin-off from his work for the catalog, Edgar published an article in 1905 in which he examined the markings on these heads and put them into the context of the grid system and canon of proportions in general.[7] He met the challenge of Perrot, Chipiez, and Maspero that the markings were purely arbitrary and did not represent a canon of proportions by showing that although some of the secondary lines were indeed

variable, the size of the square was always "in a fixed ratio to the proportions of the head." Therefore, far from being arbitrary, the square formed the unit on which the proportions of the head were based. But did this unit relate to any natural feature of these heads, such as the height of the ear or breadth of the forehead?

In response to this question, Edgar looked at the proportions of two-dimensional figures surviving on their original guidelines or grids. Here, too, he countered Perrot's assertions that there was no canon of proportions and that the grid was only a method of transferring a small-scale composition to a larger surface. Edgar took the examples used by Perrot to demonstrate the inconsistent nature of the grid and showed that the figures either fitted into the early or later grid system already described by a number of scholars or were smaller subsidiary ones drawn, presumably freehand, on a grid belonging to a larger canonical figure.

Having come down firmly in favor of the existence of a canon of proportions, Edgar was less bothered about whether one part of the body acted as a unit module for the system. He saw no reason why the canon should not simply be a set of rules governing fixed ratios between all the parts of the body. That these might have been tabulated by reference to one particular part was to him of secondary importance.

When it came to the problem of the later grid system, he said that he could "discover no marked difference . . . in the proportions of the figure." He doubted, in fact, that the introduction of the later system was ever intended to alter them.

Although Edgar had no doubt that the canon was concerned with the main proportions of the human figure in art, he nevertheless saw it only as a guide, not a "strict law." He thought that artists worked with a good deal of freedom "especially on informal figures" and that in reality the artist "no doubt drew his figures with practised ease and was content to come within reasonable closeness to the conventional standard."

Another scholar who contributed a study on grids in the early decades of this century was an English archaeologist, Ernest Mackay (1880–1943), who began his career in Egypt under the great Sir Flinders Petrie. From 1913–1916, he took part in a photographic survey of the Theban tombs, and during this time he studied and copied a number of scenes with surviving grid traces. In an article published in 1917,[8] he gave what amounted to a practical description of the artist's squared grid as found in the tombs and the way in which standing and seated figures related to it, drawing on his own observations in the field. Like Lepsius and Edgar, he had no doubt that the purpose of the grid was to ensure the correct proportions of the human figure, and he firmly refuted the idea that it was merely a method for transferring compositions from a draft to the wall. He pointed out, however, that many minor figures in scenes were drawn either without any grid or with the aid of a few guidelines only. Mackay called the grid square a unit and was content to leave it at that. He did not try to tie it to a particular part of the body or to the system of metrology.

Most of his examples of grids were taken from eighteenth dynasty tombs, but he reproduced one showing a twenty-sixth dynasty standing figure drawn, according to the later grid system, on 21 squares from the soles to the upper eyelid. His description shows that, unlike Edgar, he thought this new grid had altered the proportions of the figures. Like others before and after him, he was misled by the fact that

artists had abandoned the style of the New Kingdom and returned to earlier models (Chap. 7).

Mackay's work was important not only for the examples of grids that it provided but also because his description of the grid system was based on close observation in the field. This left him in no doubt that there was a canon of proportions but that it was not unyieldingly rigid, and that in many cases less important figures were drawn freehand, showing that artists were not tied to the grid.

Nearly two decades later, a French scholar, Marcelle Baud, set out for the Theban necropolis in order to study unfinished scenes there. She published her results in 1935 in a book called *Les Dessins ébauchés de la nécropole thébaine*. This brought together a large body of material which she had copied showing scenes in various stages of completion. While some figures were drawn on grids, others were sketched with the aid of only a few guidelines and yet others were drawn freehand. In her view, the grid had been used to enable artists to reproduce their figures at different scales, as had been suggested by Perrot and Maspero. However, she acknowledged that there was a fixed relationship between the squared grid and figures in certain postures, such as standing figures adoring, harpooning fish, or hunting birds and seated figures receiving offerings. These consisted respectively of 19 and 15 squares to the top of the head, so that in these cases there was a canon of proportions.[9] It is interesting that the major figures in any tomb are usually limited to such poses; less important figures in tomb scenes, including those in other postures, were very often drawn without a grid, as Mackay pointed out in his article.

Since Baud considered that the rules governing

proportions had long since been described by others, she did not bother to repeat them. For her, the size of the grid square was the basic unit of measurement that fixed the proportions of the figures. As far as she was concerned, there was no one rigid, immutable system encompassing the drawing of all human figures. The approach by artists was varied, ranging from the formal treatment of major figures drawn on grids with a set number of squares appropriate to their posture, down to subsidiary figures sketched out completely freehand.

To sum up, it is quite clear that despite the views of Perrot, Chipiez, and Maspero, most scholars who worked on the problem of grids agreed both on the description of the two grid systems and on relating these to a canon of proportions. Whether a particular part of the body acted as a unit module for the whole system of proportions was discussed by early writers, but later ones seem to have regarded this as a matter of secondary importance. Lepsius raised the idea that there might be a connection between such a unit—in his view the foot—and the Egyptian metrological system, only to reject it. The relationship between the early and later grid systems was not examined in any depth, and there were differing opinions as to whether or not the change from one system to the other caused changes in proportions.

And there it was left: Lepsius was dead; Edgar moved on to other work after publishing the *Sculptors' Studies* for the Cairo Catalogue; Mackay left Egypt to excavate in Palestine, Iraq, and finally India; Baud shifted her studies to other aspects of Egyptian art, the grid having been only a minor part of her interest in unfinished tomb scenes. Then, in 1955, a book appeared by a Danish Egyptologist, Erik Iversen, entitled

Canon and Proportions in Egyptian Art, which was devoted entirely to the grid system and the proportions of the human body. Its basic concerns were to demonstrate that Egyptian metrology and the proportions of the human figure in art and life were indissolubly linked, and to undertake a theoretical approach to the subject rather than a practical one based on field studies.

2.2. The Work of Erik Iversen

2.2.1. *Canon and Proportions in Egyptian Art (1st Edition, 1955)*

Erik Iversen begins his study by criticizing the work of his predecessors. His basic charge is that they were "untheoretical," the fault as he sees it lying in the fact that their views were "based simply on direct practical observations on figures inscribed in their original grid."[10] The reader is told that "Lepsius never appreciated the natural consequences of his discovery nor did he realise its full scope."[11] As for Edgar, he failed to discuss "the theoretical problems of the canon and its relation to the grids,"[12] while "Mackay avoids theoretical discussion about the origin and basis of the grids."[13] Similarly, Marcelle Baud "does not contribute to a solution of the theoretical problems."[14]

What are these theoretical problems? Iversen believes that the human figure is drawn according to natural proportions and that these are directly linked to Egyptian metrology; in art, the proportions are expressed in terms of grid squares, so that the square itself is the basic module of the whole system. He consequently regards it as fundamental to identify both the metrological unit and the part of the body to which the grid square corresponds.

2.2.2. Iversen's Metrology

The basis of our knowledge of Egyptian units of linear measurement was laid down by Lepsius,[15] although a number of points remain obscure. The most important of these units in everyday life was the small cubit, which surviving measuring rods show to have been about 45 cm in length. The small cubit was divided into 6 palms. Each palm was further divided into 4 fingers, and on some rods these might be divided into halves, thirds, quarters, fifths of a finger, and so on, up to sixteenths.

In addition to the small cubit, there was a larger unit of measurement called the royal cubit which consisted of 7 palms. In other words, an extra palm was added to the small cubit, making a unit of approximately 52.5 cm in modern terms. This larger unit was used in architecture and land measurements, and cubit rods were the length of a royal cubit or 7 palms, which of course incorporated the small cubit. The word for cubit was written with a hieroglyph depicting the forearm from the elbow to the fingertips.

Of the smaller divisions of the cubit, two have special significance for Iversen. The first is written with a hieroglyph that is most commonly used to write the word *djeser* "sacred, holy." Its significance in metrology is unclear, but according to Lepsius the same unit is also written with the sign for two-thirds.[16] This together with its position on cubit rods seems to indicate a value of two-thirds of the small cubit, equal to 4 palms or 30 cm. Iversen accordingly speaks of this unit as "the two-thirds measure."

The second unit to which Iversen gives great importance is written with a clenched fist. On measuring rods where the palms are divided into fingers, the first division often contains a hieroglyph showing 1 finger, the second 2 fingers, the third 3 fingers, the fourth a hand with 4 fingers, the fifth a hand with 4 fingers and a thumb, and the sixth a clenched fist. Divisions seven and eight each contain a hand with 4 fingers, which taken together signify a double palm or 8 fingers in all (Fig. 2.6). Because of its position in the sixth division of the rod, Lepsius took the fist to signify a length of 6 metrological fingers.[17]

Iversen complains that this interpretation does not fit the "simple pictorial meaning of the sign."[18] He prefers to understand it as representing the measurement of an actual fist consisting of the distance across the 4 fingers at the knuckles, making a palm, plus the thumb. The thumb, as he admits, is not a unit of measurement in the Egyptian system, so he has to find a way of estimating what its value might be. He considers it wider than 1 finger, but not as wide as 2 fingers. From looking at his own thumb, he plumps for it being wider than a finger by one-third. So he reckons the fist had a value of $4 + 1 1/3 = 5 1/3$ fingers.

He can offer no proof except to look ahead to his reconstruction of the canon of proportions and its relation to the squared grid system. He claims that in art the width of the fist "always equals exactly the length of the side of one square of the grid."[19] Now, according to him, the side of a square is a third of the length of the foot, and the foot, in art, is always equal to the forearm length from elbow to wrist. He regards the elbow-to-wrist length as being in life two-thirds of a small cubit—the "two-thirds" measure mentioned above—which is 4 palms equal to 16 fingers. The side

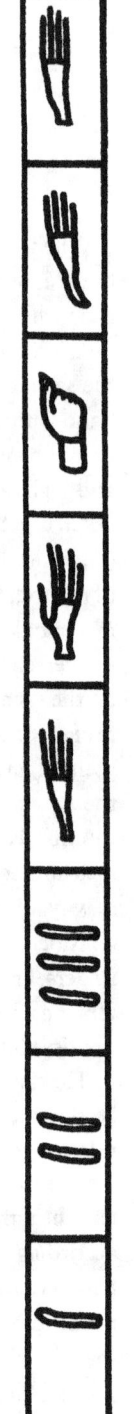

FIGURE 2.6
The divisions into fingers of the first 2 palms
on a cubit rod, after Lepsius 1865, Plate 1b.

of a square, therefore, is equivalent to a third of 16 fingers, or 5 1/3 fingers. This must also be the width of the fist, the result happily already reached by a consideration of the natural proportions of thumb and finger.

In spite of the apparent neatness of the fit, there are some serious objections to be raised against Iversen's analysis. First, in arbitrarily assessing the width of the thumb as 1 1/3 fingers, he seemingly has failed to observe that while the fingers are shown full-view in drawings of the fist, the thumb is seen from the side. In side view, the thumb has much the same width as a finger, and is not thicker by a third. One cannot, therefore, on anatomical grounds claim that the fist has a width of 5 1/3 fingers.

Second, there is no textual evidence that a fist is the metrological equivalent of 5 1/3 fingers. The only corroboration offered by Iversen relates to the supposed length of the male forearm from elbow to thumb tip, which he takes to be 4 1/2 squares in art and a small cubit of 24 fingers in life. If the fist in art is always equal in size to a grid square and if art obeys natural proportions, it follows that the width of the fist is 24 fingers ÷ 4 1/2, that is, 5 1/3 fingers. Unfortunately this result leads to an absurdity, as I shall now show.

Iversen's assumption that the length of the forearm from elbow to thumb tip is a small cubit is apparently based, although he does not fully acknowledge this, on Lepsius' earlier notion, recorded in the text to the *Denkmäler,* that the small cubit was measured from the elbow to the first joint of the middle finger,[20] which in practice is approximately level with the tip of the thumb. Lepsius' revised opinion, published in 1884 and so written after the *Denkmäler* text, that the small cubit was equal to the length of the forearm up to the tip of the outstretched middle finger,[21] is not mentioned by Iversen. Now, if the elbow-to-thumb-tip distance is in life a small cubit of 45 cm and in art 4 1/2 grid squares, as Iversen supposes, 1 square must represent a length of 10 cm. The standing height to the hairline, which consists of 18 squares, would then be 180 cm or nearly 5 feet 11 inches, and the total stature to the crown of the head over 6 feet. As Lepsius realized, ancient Egyptians were just not that tall.

The same untenable conclusion stems from a consideration of the length of the forearm from elbow to wrist, and from the length of the foot, both of which are 3 grid squares and, according to Iversen, represent two-thirds of a small cubit. Since a small cubit measures 45 cm, two-thirds of it is 30 cm. If, then, in art the elbow-to-wrist length and the foot length are each one-sixth of the hairline height, it follows that the living height is 6 x 30, or 180 cm as before. It was the impossibility of this result that led Lepsius to abandon the very ideas about the metrological relationships of the forearm that Iversen was so eager to espouse. In so doing, he constructed a theoretical system that is internally consistent but that fails to conform with actuality.

2.2.3. *The First Explanation of the Later Grid*

In the second part of his book, Iversen goes on to consider the later grid system of 21 squares from the soles to the upper eyelid. Here he tackles the old problem of whether or not it altered proportions. Like Mackay, he argues that it did, because "the proportional length of the figure has been increased in the new canon by 3 squares."[22] His explanation is that the royal cubit of 7 palms had replaced the small cubit of 6 palms as the universal unit of measurement.

Now in the first system of proportions, Iversen claims that the figure to its hairline height was 1 fathom equal to 4 small cubits or 24 palms (18 squares of 1 1/3 palms = 24 palms). In the new system he thinks this distance had become the equivalent of 4 royal cubits or 28 palms. However, according to him, there was no change in the relationship between the fist and grid square side, which were still equal to one another. Because the grid square was still the equivalent of 1 1/3 palms, "more squares would be needed for the height of the standing male figure."[23] In the old system, a height of 24 palms divided by a fist or grid square of 1 1/3 palms had given 18 squares. In the new one, a height of 28 palms divided by 1 1/3 palms gave 21 squares. The height therefore was increased by 3 squares, of which 1 was added in the legs, 1 in the waist above the navel, and 1 at the breast. As a result, the torso between the front of the belt and forehead was increased by 2 squares, accounting for "the 'unnatural' elongation of the upper part of the body."[24] Clearly this explanation must lead to the conclusion that human figures were no longer being drawn in accordance with natural proportions.

When the first edition of *Canon and Proportions* was published, it provoked a critical reply from the German Egyptologist Rainer Hanke.[25] Interestingly enough, he accepted Iversen's metrology and its connection with the proportions of the human figure and grid system without question. But he showed that Iversen had made a major miscalculation in his section on the later grid system when he assumed that it had necessitated a change in the proportions of the human figure. He demonstrated what should have been obvious, that provided the ratios between the various elements of the body in each of the two systems remained the same, there would be no overall change in proportions between one system and the other. He also demonstrated that Iversen was wrong in thinking that the fist and grid square size also corresponded in the later grid system by the simple expedient of referring to Iversen's own illustrations. In fact, Iversen's drawings showed that the fist was larger, as one would expect, since a grid square in the later system was smaller in relation to the figure than in the earlier system.

Hanke clinched his demolition of Iversen's hypothesis with illustrations of two figures, one from the Old Kingdom and one from the Late Period. He divided each of them into both 18 and 21 parts. In the Old Kingdom figure, the distance divided in both cases was between the soles and the hairline, while in the Late Period figure it was between the soles and upper eyelid. Therefore, the demonstration did not quite correspond with reality, for on both figures the division into 18 should have been from the hairline, while that into 21 should have been from the upper eyelid. Nevertheless, Hanke made clear that the change in grid system did not involve any major change in proportions and that Iversen had misunderstood the nature of the grid system that he was studying.

It is surprising that after the discovery of such a fundamental error, Iversen's other hypotheses concerning metrology and the grid were not critically examined. However, he was still considered to be the authority on the subject and contributed a chapter on it to *The Legacy of Egypt*, published in 1971.[26] Here he reiterated his ideas on metrology, giving a revised account of the later grid system with due acknowledgment to Hanke.

2.2.4. *Canon and Proportions in Egyptian Art (2nd Edition, 1975)*

In 1975, a second, completely rewritten edition of *Canon and Proportions* finally appeared. The revised edition incorporates of course a new explanation of the later grid system, but also generally expands the whole account of both systems. Nevertheless, as far as the first grid system is concerned, the basic metrological schema and its relationship to the human figure and grid remain unchanged. It still rests on the two assumptions that the small cubit was equal to the distance from elbow to thumb tip in real life and comprised 4 1/2 squares on the grid, and that the fist was a unit of measurement equal to 5 1/3 fingers and the equivalent of one grid square side.

It must be said at this point that Iversen has set up a theoretical system connecting metrology, human proportions, and the early grid system but that he fails to provide firm proof on which to base it. His arguments turn out on examination to be circular and only prove that his hypothesis is internally consistent. For it to have external validity the following would have to be true: the clenched fist would always have to be equal to the length of a grid square side; the fist would have to be a metrical unit equal to 5 1/3 fingers; the length of the small cubit would have to equal the distance from elbow to thumb tip.

While in art the clenched fist is often approximately the size of a grid square, there are many cases in which it is either larger or smaller. Therefore one can say that the size of the fist was not rigidly equated with grid square size. As for the fist as a metrical unit, there is no independent evidence for its existence. The value of

5 1/3 fingers was arbitrarily assigned to it by Iversen simply because he decided to give a width of 1 1/3 fingers to the thumb after looking at his own. The equivalence of the small cubit to the distance from elbow to thumb tip was rejected by Lepsius in favor of a distance from elbow to fingertips.

Iversen, however, now holds this last distance to be the equivalent of a royal cubit of 7 palms or 52.5 cm and a distance on the grid of 5 1/4 squares. This is open to the objection that measurements made on a large corpus of artistic material show that the length of the forearm is by no means invariable, and it may be suggested that the basic length was 5 squares (Sec. 5.7).

In fact, if we work from the hypothesis that the forearm was 5 squares from elbow to fingertips and that this distance represented a small cubit of 45 cm, as Lepsius said, the grid square size becomes equal to 45 ÷ 5, or 9 cm, not the 10 cm postulated by Iversen. Figures consisting of 18 1/2 to 19 squares from the soles of the feet to the tops of their heads would then represent a height of 166.5 to 171 cm. Not only is this more believable than the 185 to 190 cm produced by Iversen's system, but it ties in with actual estimates of living stature made from ancient Egyptian skeletal material.[27] In a sample from the predynastic cemeteries from Naqada, the average male living stature can be estimated at 170 cm.

Although Iversen tests his hypothesis on figures drawn either on their original grids or on hypothetical grids obtained by dividing the distance between the upper measuring points and the baseline by the appropriate number of squares, his results are open to criticism.

First of all, the material illustrated in his plates, which he uses to demonstrate his hypothesis, is drawn in the main from other scholars' publications. There is no evidence from the book that Iversen, unlike his predecessors writing on the subject, ever went to look at and collect grids in the field. Yet much of this material is in the form of drawings and there is always a chance that these have been incorrectly copied. For instance, a number are taken from Lepsius' magnificent *Denkmäler*. While this work was an incredible achievement for its time, modern copyists checking the drawings against the originals have to admit that they are not always strictly accurate. But for the precise measurements that Iversen is attempting, anything that fails to represent the original exactly should not be used.[28]

One scene in the tomb of Amenhotep III preserves the figures of the king and the goddess Hathor on their original grid. It was copied and reproduced as LD 3, Pl. 78*f*, and Iversen uses it to illustrate the "archetypal standing figure."[29] The figures are less well preserved today than when Lepsius recorded them, but a comparison between modern photographs[30] and the drawing shows clear discrepancies (Figs. 2.7, 2.8). In the drawing, the shape of the back of Hathor's wig is wrong; the position of her uraeus and the line of her face are incorrectly placed in relation to the vertical grid line; a horizontal runs through her mouth but on the original passes higher (just beneath the nose); the line of the breast and the lower edge of the forward arm touch the dress strap but on the original meet without coming near the strap; Hathor's buttocks touch her rear arm but on the original there is a clear gap between them; and the elbow bones are carefully marked but in fact are not clearly distinguished on the original.

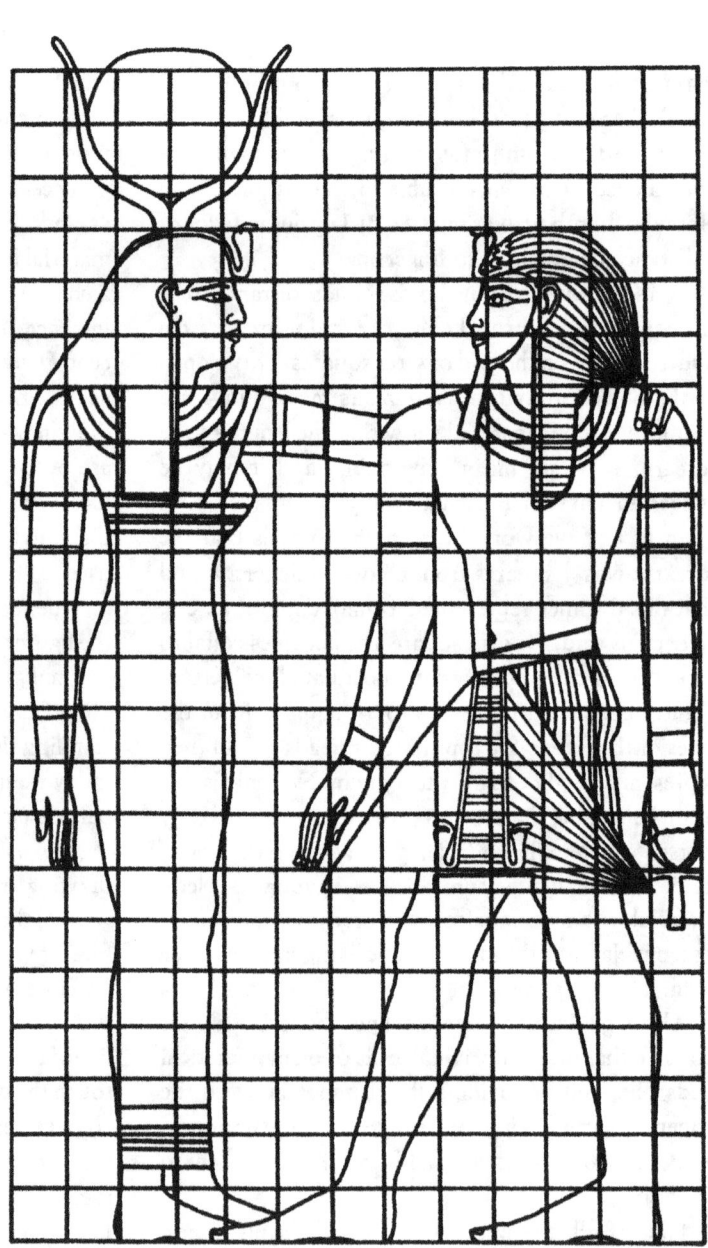

FIGURE 2.7
After LD 3, 78f, showing Hathor and
Amenhotep III on an original grid in KV 22.

FIGURE 2.8

Figure of Hathor on an original grid, KV 22, drawn from a photograph taken by C. Keller.

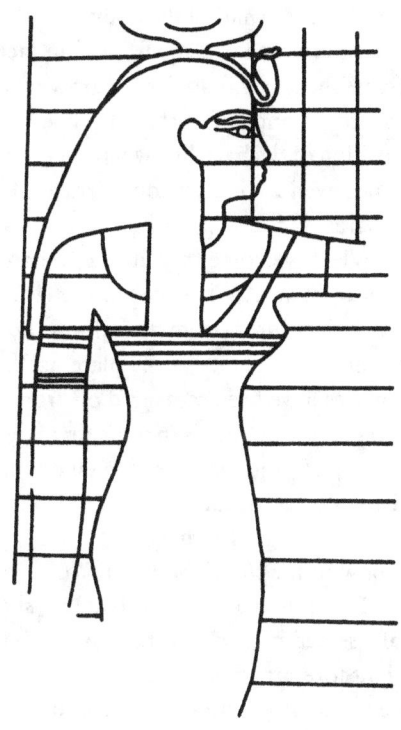

A second criticism of Iversen's results rests on the fact that what he states in his text often does not correspond to what he shows in his plates. Third, he is inconsistent in how he takes his measurements of the parts of the human body, working from arbitrary points to produce the result he thinks he ought to get. Finally, when even this fails, it is allegedly because of foreshortening, an incompetent artist, or an inaccuracy in the original (but now vanished) grid.

Iversen's most recent summary of his hypotheses concerning the grid and metrology appeared in an article published in 1990. In it, he reiterates what he said in the second edition of *Canon and Proportions in Egyptian Art*. He makes no attempt to meet the various objections that have been raised with regard to his theories.

2.2.5. *Discrepancy between Text and Plate*

In the chapters of the second edition of *Canon and Proportions* where he analyzes his material, Iversen describes most of the figures illustrated in his plates individually, so it is easy to see where there is a discrepancy between his text and a plate. In his description of Plate 6.2, the reader is informed that the "front half [of the figure] has, as always, the correct measure of 3 squares, when measured at line 15."[31] It is Iversen's practice to measure the widths of the two halves of the body from the vertical line marked *M* in his plates along horizontal 15. Now a look at the illustration in question here shows that the front line of the upper arm between the shoulder and the elbow is obscured by the rear hand coming across it, but it is easy to see where it should run (Fig. 2.9). By no stretch

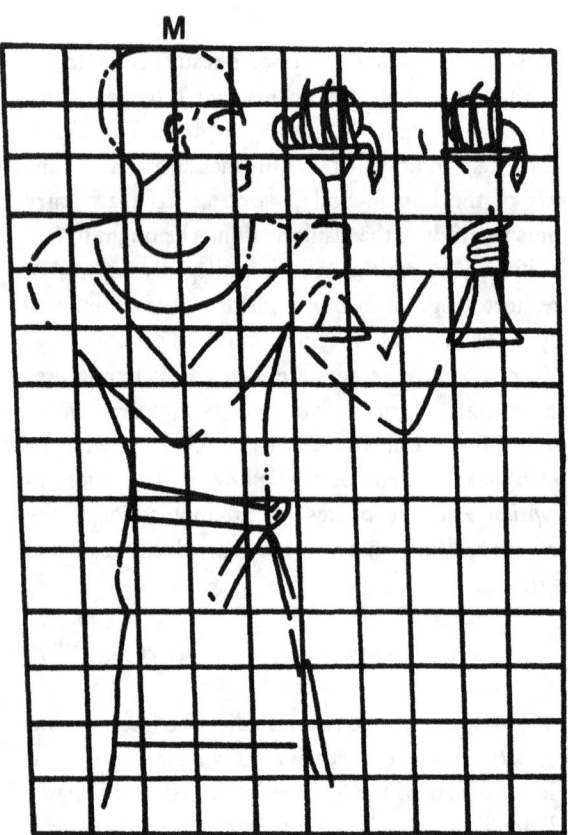

FIGURE 2.9

After Iversen 1975, Plate 6.2, showing a figure on an original grid.

of the imagination can this line be made to touch the grid vertical 3 squares from Iversen's line *M*.

In Plate 7, there is a subsidiary figure of a man marked *A* by Iversen. In the description we are told that "the rear half of the body is . . . foreshortened by 1/2 square to 2 1/2 squares."[32] In fact, in this minor figure the rear shoulder is not drawn full-view at all but in profile and set within the line of the back. The position of the back line where it crosses horizontal 15 is not even 2 squares from vertical *M*, let alone 2 1/2 squares (Fig. 2.10).

When we come to Plate 11, we are informed that "the right arm . . . has the same length of 4 1/2 squares when measured from the elbow bone . . . to the thumb."[33] A glance at the plate itself, in which 4 1/2 squares have been measured off from the elbow bone along the arm, shows that the tip of the thumb is more than 4 1/2 squares from the elbow bone (Fig. 2.11). This also contradicts the earlier statement that the extended arm is in general "4 1/2 squares from the elbow to the *tip* of the thumb" (my italics).[34]

The text accompanying Plate 20, showing the figure of a seated man, claims that the "cubital length of the right fore-arm from elbow to thumb is 4 1/2 squares, because the thumb is seen in its full extent and therefore not foreshortened."[35] However, in the plate itself, not only can it be seen by eye that the distance is less than 4 1/2 squares but it is actually labeled 4 1/4 squares (Fig. 2.12).

2.2.6. *Inconsistency in Taking Measurements*

Iversen explains that he measures the forearm from the elbow line—that is, horizontal 12 of the grid—to the tip of the thumb, and that "each typological change in

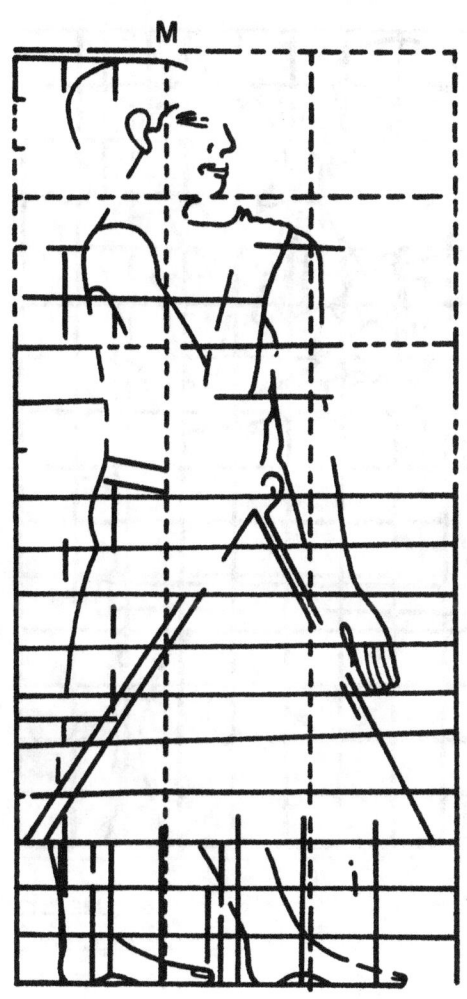

FIGURE 2.10
After Iversen 1975, Plate 7A, showing a figure on
an original grid.

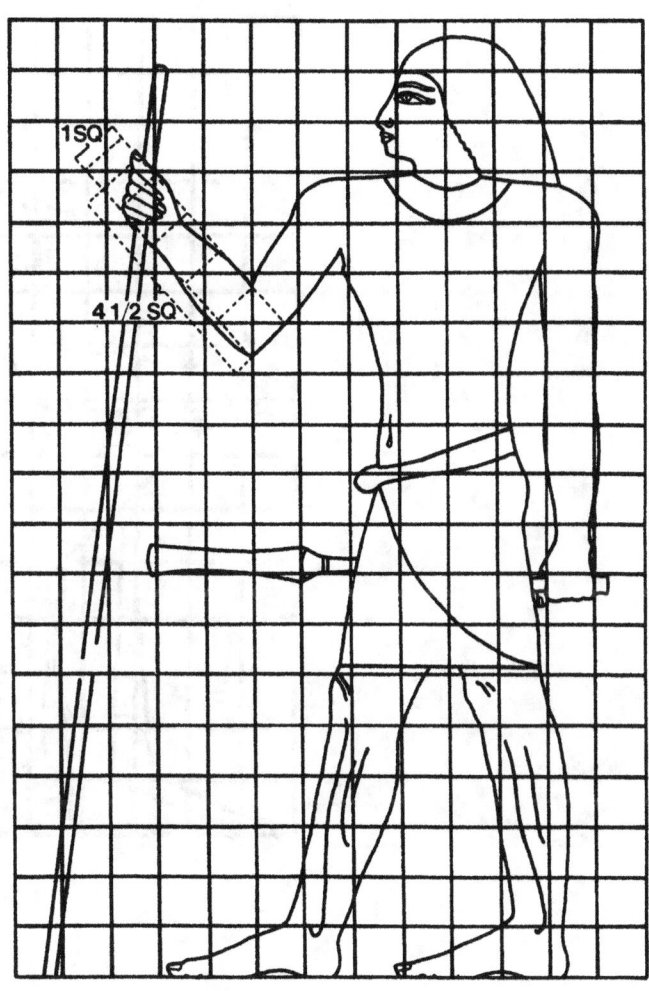

FIGURE 2.11
After Iversen 1975, Plate 11, showing a figure on a
hypothetical grid.

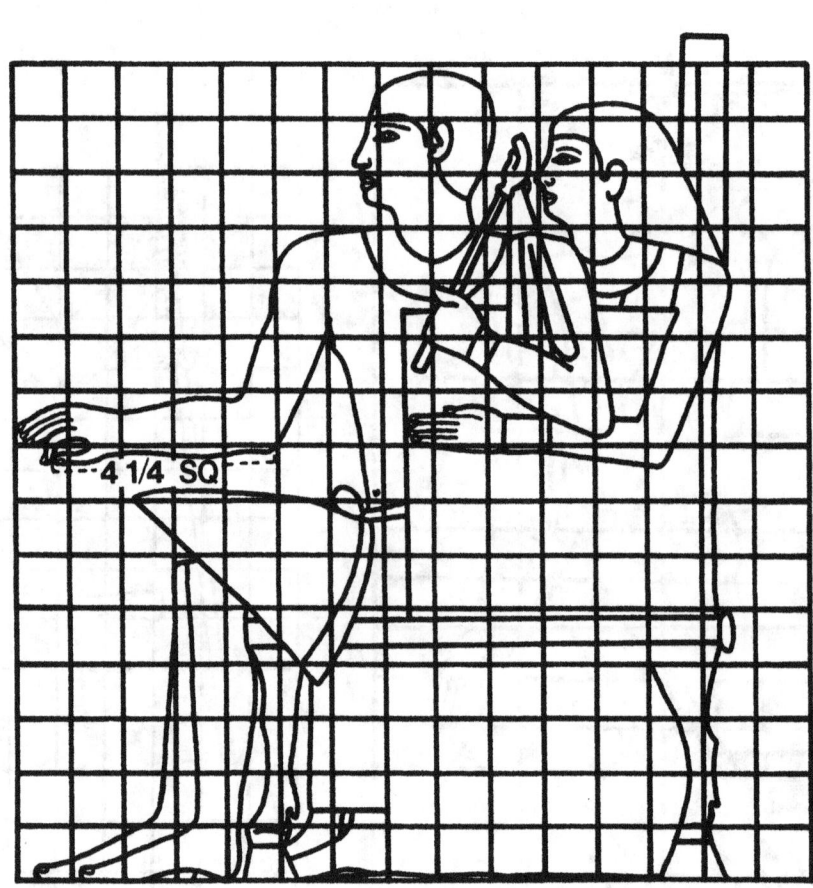

FIGURE 2.12
After Iversen 1975, Plate 20, showing a figure on a
hypothetical grid.

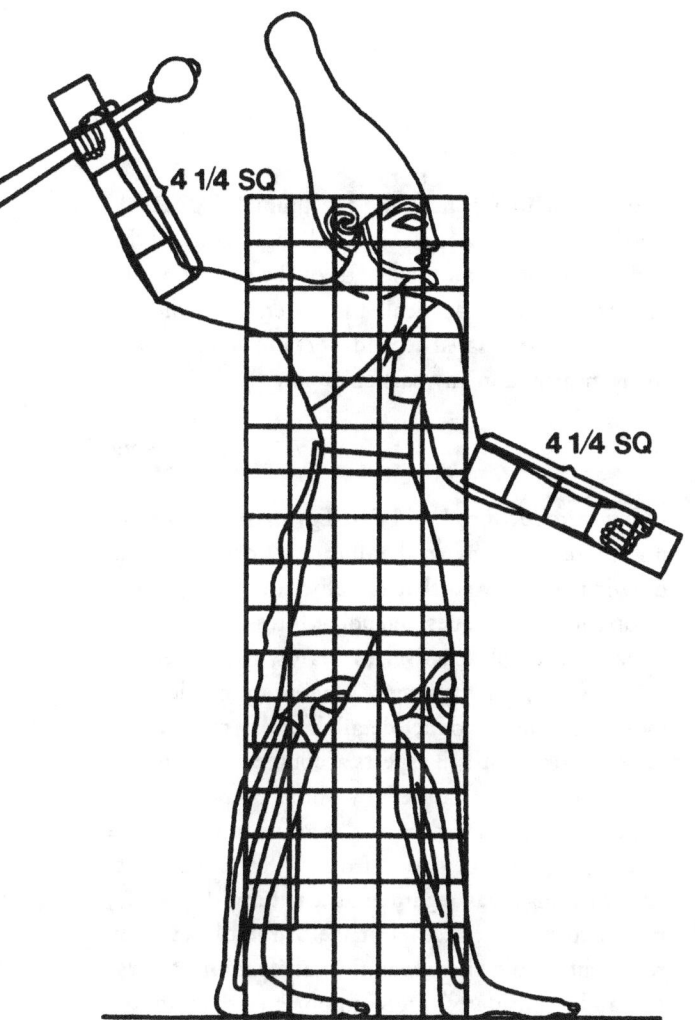

4 1/4 SQ

4 1/4 SQ

FIGURE 2.13

After Iversen 1975, Plate 15, showing a figure on a
hypothetical grid.

the position or the gesture of the hand had its own
canonical registration . . . but in some positions the
methods used for the establishment of these measures
remain obscure."[36] Indeed, if we look at his plates we
find that measurements may be made from the elbow
crease or the elbow bone or even some other point,
along the axis of the arm or at an angle to the axis. In
Plate 15, on one and the same figure, the rear arm is
measured from the elbow bone while the front one is
measured from the elbow crease, despite the fact that
the elbow bone lies almost exactly on horizontal 12,
which is the elbow line mentioned by Iversen as a point
of measurement (Fig. 2.13). Similarly, if we examine
Plate 13, we find that on the rear arm the distance from
the elbow to the wrist is measured to the edge of the
bracelet nearest the hand. On the forward arm it is
measured to some unmarked point in the middle of the
bracelet (Fig. 2.14). One cannot help feeling that the
desired result controls the way in which the measurement is made.

Iversen's attempts to show that the fist is always
equal to a grid square size are also suspect. On page 53,
referring to his Plate 11, he points out that when a
figure is shown with two fists, one seen from the front
and one from the back, the view from the front shows
the "knuckles" (heads of the first phalangeal bones)
and that from the back the "first finger joints" (heads
of the metacarpal bones of the hand); since the hand is
wider at the first finger joints, some artists excluded
the thumb from the grid square measurement in the
back view. Unfortunately, according to Iversen's measurements shown on Plate 8, where the major male
figure has two fists, one shown from the front and one
from the back, it is the one seen from the back that fits

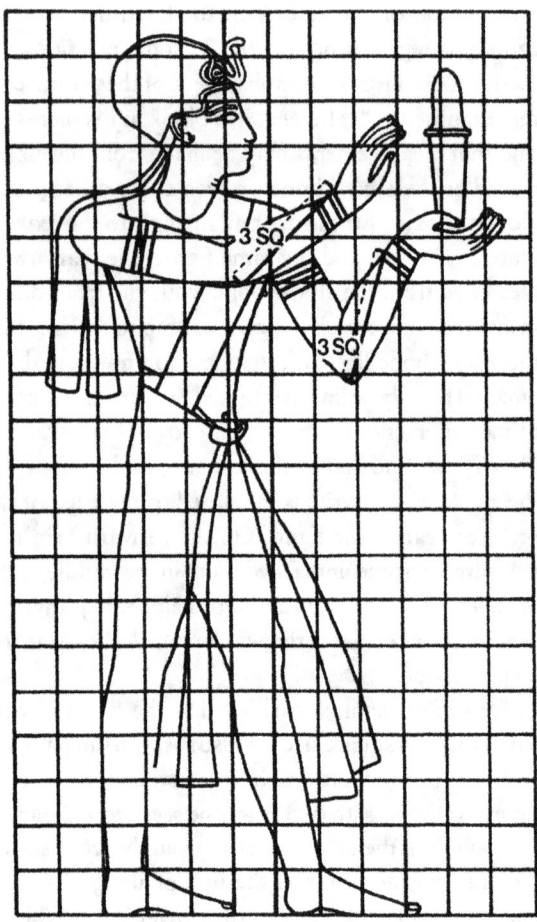

FIGURE 2.14

After Iversen 1975, Plate 13, showing a figure on a
hypothetical grid.

into a grid square including the thumb (Fig. 2.15). Despite the constant repetition of the assertion that the width of the fist and the length of the side of a grid square are always identical, it is evident that whether the two can be equated depends very much on how the fist is measured in any particular case.

2.2.7. Foreshortening

In my introduction, I said that Egyptian artists were not interested in giving the illusion of depth to their drawing surface and that therefore they did not develop those techniques, including foreshortening, associated with perspective. In his own introduction Iversen says much the same: "Wherever possible, each individual object and each detail should be represented in its entirety, with all aspects accounted for, with no parts hidden or distorted by shifts of perspective, because parts omitted or not seen, were considered missing, and any deviation from the factual appearance of things was regarded as a natural deficiency, bound to mar the eternal image of the objects they represented. Nowhere was the satisfaction of these demands considered more important than in the representation of the human body."[37]

Iversen does not seem to find this statement at odds with his later contention that the thumb and fingers of the hand are sometimes foreshortened: "When the hand is bent around an object the tip of the thumb is frequently raised 1/4 square in the grid by geometrical foreshortening, and in such cases the cubital length of the arm is shortened by 1/4 square . . . , a possibility always to be taken into consideration at the reconstruction of the proportional schema of any figure. The bending of the other fingers or the palm of the hand called for similar adjustments, demanding that the fingers were raised 1/4 square in the grid."[38]

In other words, he finds that the distance from elbow to thumb tip is sometimes nearer 4 1/4 squares than the desired 4 1/2 squares, while the length from elbow to fingertips may be only 5 squares, not 5 1/4 squares. To explain this he has to fall back on a claim that the thumb or fingers were foreshortened, although artists did not usually draw objects "distorted by shifts of perspective." In fact, in many figures where the forearm from elbow to fingertips is only 5 squares, the fingers are scarcely bent at all and it is hard to see that further straightening of them would give an extra quarter square in length.[39] Further, there are examples where the fingers are undoubtedly straight, yet the length from elbow bone to fingertips is clearly no more than 5 squares (Fig. 9.12).[40]

2.2.8. Bad Artists and Inaccurate Original Grids

Once Iversen has established his hypothetical system, he attributes discrepancies between it and the material to errors arising from incompetence on the part of the artist. So in one figure where the hands are "too wide by a fraction" in relation to the grid square, this is to be blamed on "the lack of consistency characteristic of the artist responsible for the decorations of the tomb."[41] In fact, Iversen sums up his position with the statement: "The frequent errors and mistakes found in the proportioning of all categories of figures are therefore in most cases due to carelessness, bad workmanship, or ignorance."[42] In other words, the artists are chided for not conforming to Iversen's system.

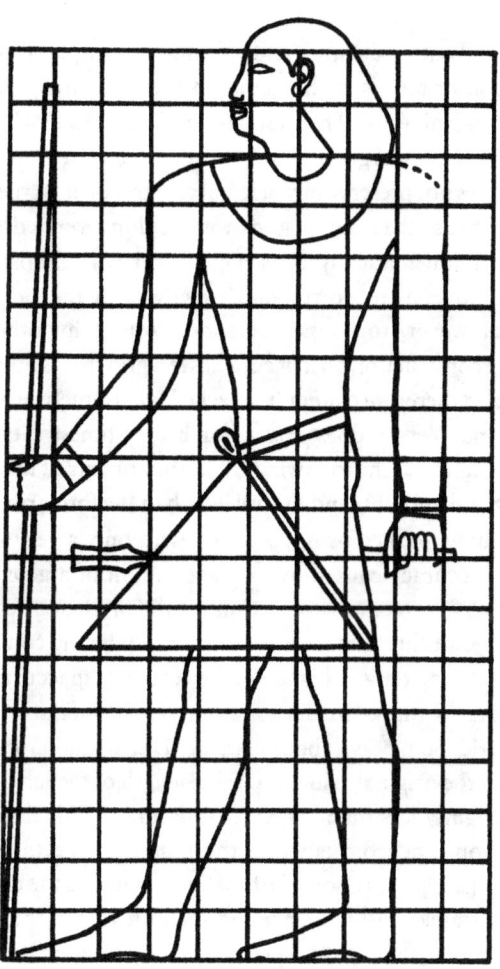

FIGURE 2.15

After Iversen 1975, Plate 8, showing a figure on a hypothetical grid.

Another excuse that Iversen uses to explain lack of conformity is to blame it on the inaccuracy of the original grid. This applies in those cases where a hypothetical grid has been constructed for a figure that does not preserve any original grid traces. It is true that because the original grids were seldom evenly drawn, a mathematically constructed grid will almost certainly fail to correspond exactly with the original. However, to blame deviations from a hypothetical reconstruction on inaccuracies in a grid that is now lost and therefore cannot be checked is extremely unscientific. Yet he does this a number of times; a typical example is the following: "The four fingers of the right hand are bent, and the full length of the fore-arm from elbow to medius is 5 squares, with only a very slight inaccuracy caused by the substitution of a geometrically correct reconstruction for the original grid."[43]

In other instances we find that when it comes to entering data in his tables, he corrects "inaccuracies" that he thinks are due to the unevenness of the original grid. So he says about Plate 8: "Due to an inaccuracy in the original grid, the cubital length of the left arm is slightly less than 4 1/2 . . . squares."[44] This does not stop him from entering the thumb in the tables as 7 1/2 squares above the baseline,[45] which is the desired distance. In fact, since the forearm to the thumb is shorter than 4 1/2 squares, the thumb must be more than 7 1/2 squares from the baseline.

There are a number of other occasions when Iversen enters into the tables of analysis figures that fit his system although examination of the relevant plates tells a different story. For instance, the table relating to Plate 14 enters the level of the armpits as 14 1/2 squares and the wrist as 9 squares above the baseline.[46] In the plate they lie lower than the claimed positions. Further, the level of the knee is entered as the expected horizontal 6, but no mention is made of the fact that horizontal 6 does not run through the top or point of the knee, as in the majority of figures illustrated, but through the lower border of the kneecap. Consequently the top of the knee is pushed up to about 6 1/2 squares above the baseline.

As a result of these constant adjustments to figures entered in Iversen's tables, a reader working through them obtains the impression of almost universal conformity with his theory. If the figures had not been adjusted, an alternative picture of possible variation within the system would have been given.

In fact, Iversen, having proposed his system, instead of testing it with an open mind on the material at his disposal, forces the material to fit his model. For example, in his description of Pl. 7, he informs the reader that: "the distance from elbow to wrist is 3 squares, the cubital arm length 4 1/2 squares."[47] However, in a note he admits "the tip of the thumb is not seen, but its theoretical position is clear."[48] In other words, he has assumed the length of 4 1/2 squares because his hypothesis demands it.

2.2.9. *The Rigidity of Iversen's System*

It is undoubtedly worrying that Iversen appears to be forcing the material to fit his hypothesis rather than checking his system against the material. Further cause for misgiving lies in the absolute rigidity of the system in which "the relations of the grids to all types of representations are fixed and immutable in all cases."[49] Such a strict relationship between the proportions of the human figure and the grid would have acted like a straitjacket on artists, confining them within an inflexible set of rules so that they would have been virtually painting by numbers. But familiarity with Egyptian art reveals how subtle and varied artists were in their work and how in producing the same scene type over and over again they rarely, if ever, made exact copies. It seems contrary to the spirit of Egyptian art that artists should have produced their human figures by a mechanical system based on an unvarying set of rules. If this had been so, how would different styles have appeared: the chunky, robust figures of the Old and Middle Kingdoms and the slender, long-legged figures of the New Kingdom?

Iversen seems to be oblivious to these changes in style. Thus he claims that "the canon of the New Kingdom in no ways differed from that of earlier times."[50] He tries to demonstrate this by comparing a figure from the sixth dynasty with a figure in the tomb of Amenhotep III dating to the second half of the eighteenth dynasty. He states: "Although separated from one another by nearly 8 centuries, the reconstructed grid of plate 12 and the original seen on plate 4 will be seen to intersect the two figures at identical places, to effect the same division, and to reflect the same proportions, thereby demonstrating the absolute identity of the canons used in the Old and the New Kingdoms."[51] This is just not true, as a comparison of the two figures shows (Figs. 2.7, 2.16). In the Old Kingdom figure, the lower border of the buttocks lies on horizontal 9, the small of the back and navel on 11, and the knuckles of the rear fist just below horizontal 8. In the figure of Amenhotep III, the lower border of the buttocks is 9 1/2 squares above the baseline, the

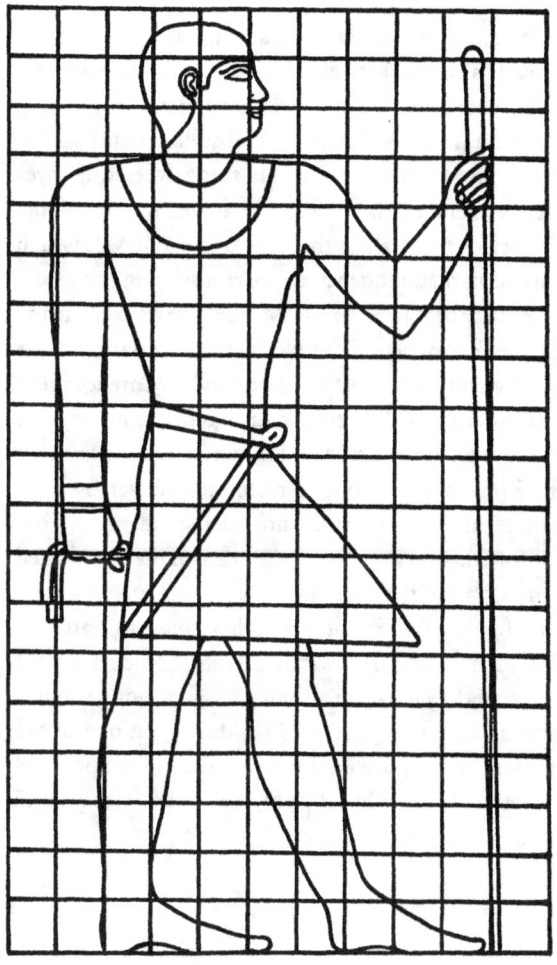

FIGURE 2.16
After Iversen 1975, Plate 12, showing a figure on a hypothetical grid.

small of the back and navel approximately 11 1/2 squares above the baseline, and the knuckles of the rear fist about a quarter of a square below horizontal 8. Although the two figures indeed have much in common, there is clearly not "absolute identity" between them. Of course, in his study Iversen ignores inconvenient levels such as the lower border of the buttocks, the small of the back and the navel, which have a marked tendency to move about on the grid.

Even more surprising is Iversen's claim concerning the figures on the famous Narmer palette dating to the very beginning of the dynastic period. We are told that "irrespective of . . . minor divergencies, mostly the result of technical errors or inaccuracies, the figures of the King as shown on the recto and the verso of the palette are consequently not merely identical, but conform in every respect to the norm of the established canon."[52] Yet the knees lie on horizontal 7, not 6 as in later figures; the armpits are on horizontals 14 and 15, not 14 1/2; and the width of the shoulders across horizontal 15 is no more than 5 squares, not 6 squares as found later (Fig. 2.13). In addition, on one of the figures (for they are not identical) the lower border of the buttocks lies almost as high as horizontal 11 and

the small of the back around 12 1/2. Although these are not levels considered by Iversen, they are in fact higher than in other figures analyzed by him, where the lower border of the buttocks usually lies anywhere from horizontal 9 to 10 and the small of the back from 11 to 12.

However hard Iversen tries to force the material to fit his preconceived theories, it must become obvious to a careful reader that it keeps escaping from the constraints he has imposed. Plainly Egyptian artists were not working within a rigid, unchangeable system from which only bad practitioners deviated. Edgar surely came much nearer the mark when he commented: "The squares did not of course ensure exact conformity to the ideal type unless the draughtsman measured all the minor distances with slavish care; in reality he no doubt drew his figures with practised ease and was content to come within reasonable closeness to the conventional standard . . . . When squares were used the artist often worked with a good deal of freedom, treating them as a guide to the eye rather than as a strict law to the hand."[53] In other words, as others have also stressed, the Egyptians were accomplished artists, not mechanical copyists.

Methods

3.1. Surviving Grids

The work of Erik Iversen that I examined in the last chapter came to be regarded as the standard study of grids and the canon of proportion, but as I have shown it does not stand up to close scrutiny. It seemed necessary to me, therefore, to undertake my own research, and that meant beginning with a study of grids in situ. Only in this way would it be possible to understand the rules by which artists were working and the amount of latitude allowed to them within these rules. Thus I began to make plans for a season of fieldwork in Egypt.

The first priority was to find a source of material that was both accessible and plentiful. Since tombs were more often left unfinished than temples, and painted scenes preserve the grid which may then be revealed over time as the paint flakes off, I decided that my main fieldwork should center on a study of eighteenth-dynasty painted Theban tombs, following in the footsteps of Mackay and Baud. In the end, I was able to arrange two major working trips, one in spring 1984 and one two years later in spring 1986. During the course of the earlier trip, I was also able to work briefly in some of the private tombs at Beni Hasan, Meir, and Amarna in Middle Egypt.

Although all the Theban tombs that I had permission to work in had been carefully chosen through references in the literature to the presence of grids, many of the tombs were unpublished so that I did not really know what to expect in them, nor was there any way of knowing what condition the monuments would be in. Some tombs turned out to have been beautifully cleaned and conserved by the Egyptian Antiquities Organisation. Even so, in many the ravages of time and human depredations had left only fragments offering tantalizing glimpses of what had once been fascinating scenes. Other tombs were filthy, with thick dust and grime on the walls obscuring the color of the paint and making it difficult to see the scenes.

On entering a tomb, the first step was to locate and record the position of all grid traces from virtually complete grids down to the smallest traces. I also recorded a number of measurements: the sizes of the grid squares; the distances of the various grid horizontals above the baseline passing through the soles of the feet; the height of the hairline. With a calculator, it was easy to find out how close these lines ran to a mathematically calculated grid. It was also important to note where grid lines ran in relation to the key points of the body to see whether they always coincided with exactly the same points or whether variation was allowed.

In examining the scenes, I was interested to find traces of previous workers in the tombs. A number of figures had had their outlines enhanced in black, presumably to aid copying in modern times—and no wonder, when one sees the thickness of the tracing paper used by the early copyists. It is surprising that they could see anything through it, and the temptation to darken the outlines to render them more visible must have been too great. Who the culprits were we shall probably never know. Norman de Garis Davies noted the phenomenon in the tombs at Amarna and commented that "it is sufficient for us to condemn the practice without attempting to fix the blame."[1] It is a relief to know that Davies himself, one of the greatest of copyists, was not responsible.

It was vital for me to make full notes in the tombs because it was not always possible to get satisfactory photographs. Nevertheless, most of the material could be photographed to obtain a visual record as well. In

1984, I found the results from flash photography to be disappointing, because of the bright reflection off the whitish-blue background paint used in many of the scenes. In 1986, the use of flash photography in tombs was banned. Since I was unable to transport lighting equipment to Egypt, or indeed around the Theban necropolis, as it is a very steep climb to many of the tombs, a way had to be found to use natural light. I therefore decided to use a mirror and diffuser.[2] Sunlight could be beamed into the tombs with the mirror and spread evenly over the walls by the diffuser, which consisted of a board covered with aluminum foil. To make the most of the available light, I used fast color film and also black and white. On the whole, the system worked well so long as the weather was sunny and dust storms did not obscure the light.

Although my main aim in these tombs was to find grids, there was incidentally plenty of evidence to be gathered concerning the different stages used in constructing the scenes themselves, and also in producing the borders around the scenes, the friezes at the tops of walls, and the ceilings. The last are usually decorated with geometric patterns, and unfinished examples show that they too were laid out on grids.[3] I was interested to find on a later trip when I visited the ruins of the Coptic monastery of St. Simeon at Aswan that the same technique of drawing on squared grids had been employed for the ceilings there.[4]

The tombs at Beni Hasan date to the eleventh and twelfth dynasties. They were published in four volumes by Percy Newberry,[5] and one of his plates shows a female offering bringer in tomb 2 with some grid traces.[6] Lepsius had earlier recorded a gazelle and a bull on grids from the same tomb,[7] but there was no indication of these traces in Newberry's publication.[8]

I wanted to see if I could identify these figures and find out if there were any more grid traces in this tomb or any of the others. Many of the tombs have suffered badly over time, especially from Coptic occupation. In some cases walls and ceilings are blackened by the use of lamps inside, and scenes are covered by later graffiti and drawings. Four tombs, however, have recently been cleaned, of which two, numbered 15 and 17, date to the eleventh dynasty and two, numbered 2 and 3, to the twelfth dynasty. On first sight, none of these tombs shows evidence of grids. But knowing there were supposed to be at least traces in tomb 2, I looked again more carefully. Part of the difficulty in seeing lines lies in the great height of the tombs and the fact that the lowest register of decoration is halfway up the wall, already at about eye level. To search the walls properly for grid traces one would need scaffolding to reach the higher registers, which was impossible to arrange in the time available.

By careful examination I managed to identify on the south wall in the second register up the female offering bringer and the gazelle and bull that I knew were associated with grid traces, although I failed to find these on the wall. However, in the bottom register at eye level, close scrutiny revealed a number of tiny grid traces the whole way along the register. Each trace was so minute as to be easily overlooked, and in no case was there enough left to reconstruct the grid. Although I was unable to pick up any traces on the other walls, the importance of those on the south wall was to confirm that grids were used in this tomb. I had no luck at all in finding signs of grids in any of the other tombs. A more prolonged examination of the walls of the better preserved tombs using scaffolding to get close up, together with good lighting equipment, might produce some results. The presence or absence of grids is of some interest because as yet there is no evidence for use of the grid before the early twelfth dynasty. Since these tombs span the eleventh and twelfth dynasties, it would be valuable to determine whether or not grids were present in the tombs dating to the earlier period.[9] As things stand, however, the lack of discernible traces in the earlier tombs is clearly not significant.

The rock-cut tomb chapels at Meir were published by Aylward Blackman in the first half of this century,[10] and one, numbered B2, has subsequently become well known for its surviving grids, as much of the decoration was still only drawn in and the squared grids remained in evidence. My aim, then, was to study these scenes, to examine others with less spectacular grid traces preserved in tomb chapel C1, and to see if any other of the tomb chapels also had grid traces. In the time at my disposal I was unable to get to all the tombs, but I was able to visit the group numbered B1–B4 and a tomb chapel dating to the Old Kingdom numbered A2.

I was unable to detect any grid traces in B1 and B3, but they were present in B4, although they only showed in places where the finished painted background had flaked off. It was in B2, however, that I spent the most time, seeing for myself the grids that I had become familiar with in Blackman's publication. When I at last finished, our guide moved us on to the nearby tomb, A2. It was so large and dark that our torches proved to be inadequate lighting. But we found our way to the serdab which has an interesting history. As is so often the case in a serdab, which was specially designed to hold statues of the tomb owner, the walls were originally covered with representations of rows of statues depicting the owner. But the upper parts of the walls were then cut back all the way around, leaving a narrow shelf halfway up, and the newly revealed rock surface was decorated with scenes showing funerary rites.[11] These had never been completed, and on the west and east walls were simply drawn in black outline; in some places the original Old Kingdom guidelines are still visible. On one group of figures a squared grid had been added, though whether contemporary or later is impossible to tell. The height of the drawings above ground level and the bad lighting unfortunately made photography impracticable with my equipment. Sadly, although Blackman had published these drawings, neither guidelines nor grid lines were included.[12] Some guidelines can be seen in the two photographs he published.[13] Other photographs of the scenes are in the Egypt Exploration Society archives. It is clear from these that Blackman was not totally able to overcome the bad working conditions in the tomb, but his photographs show some of the relevant lines, although they are often difficult to pick out.

The original decoration of the serdab surviving on the lower part of the wall was also of great interest. Many of the representations of statues still showed their original guidelines, as Blackman had indicated,[14] and these I was able to see.

The private tombs at Amarna were published by N. de G. Davies with line drawings and some photographs early in the century.[15] Davies rarely included grid traces in his drawings, but in one of his photographs of a scene in the tomb of Ay it is possible to make out traces of squares just behind the king's figure.[16] The tombs are decorated in sunk relief, so that the figures themselves are cut away but not the background as in raised relief. There was a slight chance, therefore, that grid traces might survive on the uncut background if it was merely painted over and not polished, and that loss of paint would reveal them. My aim was to see if I could find any more scenes with grid traces and to study the one shown in Davies' photograph in situ.

The tombs at Amarna divide into two distinct groups: the north tombs in the cliffs to the north of the wadi containing the royal tomb and the south tombs in the cliffs to the south of the royal wadi.[17] Some of the tombs are small, undecorated, and mostly uninscribed, and were of no interest for my work. It was the larger decorated tombs that I was eager to visit: northern tombs 1–6, and southern tombs 7–11, 14, 23, and 25. Tomb 14 turned out to be used as a magazine, however, and therefore impossible to enter. Most of these tombs are considerable in size with more than one chamber, but often the cutting was never completed, while large areas of their walls were left undecorated. The finished scenes were cut into sunk relief and painted, but in a number of instances they were merely sketched out and never subsequently carved. Both deliberate damage and the passage of time have taken their toll of the decoration.[18] After the death of Akhenaton and the rejection of the Aton cult, the sun disk, the figures and especially the faces of the king and queen, and their cartouches together with those of the god were willfully mutilated in many places. Later, the northern tombs were lived in by Copts and the tomb of Panehesy was turned into their place of worship. This new use for the tombs often involved altering their structure, removing walls, and cutting niches for lamps and holes to take various fittings like pegs or ropes for tethering animals. In modern times, much damage was done by tomb robbers attempting to cut out pieces for sale. Over time most of the color has been lost from

finished scenes. While this might have revealed any underlying grid lines, I suspect that in many cases these too have worn off.

Although I was unable to find many grid traces in the unfinished scenes that were merely sketched on the walls, the figures involved were mainly subsidiary or sometimes those of the tomb owner, but rarely those of the king and queen. They were clearly sketched freehand with no trace of a grid.

In the tomb of Ay (no. 25), I found the scene showing the king and queen that Davies had published in a photograph and there, indubitably, were the traces of the grid lines behind the king's figure. I was able to take my own photographs of them and, in addition, measure the grid square size. I found one other standing figure of the king with related grid traces in the tomb of Mahu; the traces were not recorded by Davies.[19]

A sketched scene in the tomb of Parannefer shows the king in a kiosk. Drawn in red paint that is now very faint, it is hard to make out and much of the upper part of the body, including the face, is lost where there is damage to the rock. In his publication, Davies marked in some lines that might be interpreted as grid traces, but he does not comment on them in his text.[20] These lines and a few others can just be made out in situ, but their positioning makes it difficult to see how they can be incorporated into a single reasonably regular grid.

3.2. The Construction and Use of Hypothetical Grids

Since grids survive on a very small proportion of extant representational material, it would be a pity to have to limit this study to figures that by chance preserve grid traces. This would mean that the art of some periods and also some types of material would be virtually excluded from my work. In fact, it is possible to take an accurate reproduction of any figure and analyze it on a hypothetical grid obtained by dividing the distance between the hairline and baseline by the appropriate number of squares. Since original grids were frequently irregular in their construction, one can see that even the most precisely calculated and carefully drawn hypothetical grid will not correspond exactly with the original one. However, the result will certainly be close enough for such grids to be used as a tool for analyzing samples of material, provided that one does not try to work to too fine a degree of precision.

In the early grid system, standing and seated figures occupied 18 and 14 squares respectively on the grid from the soles of their feet to their hairlines (Chaps. 4–5). After the change to the later grid system, they consisted of 21 and 17 squares respectively from the soles of the feet to the upper eyelid (Chap. 7). So in order to construct a hypothetical grid for a figure, the distance between the soles and hairline, or later the upper eyelid, must be divided by the appropriate number of squares to obtain the individual square size, from which the grid can be calculated.

I find it convenient to use a calculator for this operation and to place the square size in the memory. By repeatedly adding this as often as necessary, the spacing of the grid lines can be worked out. I reckon that it is possible to draw to an accuracy of a quarter of a millimeter, so that I correct the calculation for each line to the nearest 0.25 mm. Then I rule out the grid on transparent acetate using a Rotring drawing board. The acetate can then be placed over the figure and its position adjusted until satisfactory.

Obviously, unless the metric value for the height to

the hairline according to the early grid system is exactly divisible by 18 for standing figures and by 14 for seated ones, and the value for the height to the upper eyelid in the later system is exactly divisible by 21 for standing figures and 17 for seated ones, some approximation is inevitable in the placement of the lines. Usually, if the lines are carefully drawn with the slant of the pen kept constant, there is no detectable irregularity, but since the eye is extremely sensitive to small differences in spatial separation, some unevenness may occasionally be apparent, especially if the approximations displace adjacent lines in opposite directions. Fortunately, the methodology is such that slight malpositioning of any particular line will not invalidate the grid as a whole. Since each line is drawn as close as possible to its theoretical position, an approximation determining the site of a particular line does not affect that of any other, so that errors are not cumulative.

The position of the horizontals in relation to a given figure is governed by the baseline and the level of the hairline or upper eyelid. When these coincide with the constructed grid, the horizontals can be taken as matching as nearly as possible the position of the originals, so long as it is remembered that there are likely to have been irregularities in the grid as it was originally drawn by the Egyptian draftsman. It is more difficult to place the verticals, because there are no points to which they are exactly fixed. Where figures survive on original grids, one vertical, more or less central with respect to the upper part of the body, virtually always runs through some part of the ear, but this may be the front, middle, or back, allowing some latitude in the placing of the vertical on a hypothetical grid. In surviving grids this "axial" vertical commonly passes between the thighs. It may run down the front line of the tress of long wigs[21] and down the front edge of the lappet of the *nemes* headdress of striped cloth often worn by the King.[22] When pairs of horns or symmetrical double feathers are worn, the axial line may bisect these.[23] Draftsmen also like to place male standing figures on the early grid so that a vertical passed through each armpit and others ran down the outside of each upper arm.[24] The position of the arms and other compositional considerations can nevertheless override this preference. So while there is some guide as to how the verticals might have been placed, there is far less assurance than with the horizontals that one is matching the original grid.

A word of caution is needed here. Often in putting a grid on a figure, a number of verticals or grid intersections will coincide with lines or parts of the scenes in such a way as to convince one that this must be how the artist drew it. But move the grid a quarter- or half-centimeter in either direction and different elements of the scene will lie convincingly on grid verticals and intersections. The lesson has to be that if one imposes a grid on a scene, however one places it, some grid lines will correspond with salient points of the composition. Coincidence, therefore, between verticals or intersections of the grid and elements in the scene cannot be taken as proof that the hypothetical grid duplicates the position of the original grid.

In the interest of clarity, grid lines have not been given numbers in my illustrations. To determine vertical proportions, the reader is asked to count upward from a putative horizontal 0 through the soles of the feet, horizontal 1 through the ankle region, and so on to the upper limit defining the figure, that is, the hairline or upper eyelid. Vertical lines are not so easily numbered because there is no obvious point of departure similar to the baseline. Horizontal proportions are, therefore, normally obtained by counting the number of grid squares between two points of the body lying on the same level—for instance, the distance between the outer edges of the forward and rear upper arms at the point where they cross the horizontal one square below the line marking the junction of the neck and shoulder.

While in theory there is a large amount of representational material surviving from ancient Egypt that could be used for the study of proportions in figures, in order to apply a hypothetical grid to any scene, that scene must be accurately reproduced in a photograph or drawing.[25] Yet many monuments are simply unpublished. I have already mentioned the difficulties with drawings, particularly those made by early copyists, because they are often inaccurate. Even photographs may be useless for my work, because if there is any distortion in them they will give misleading results when a hypothetical grid is added. Such distortion can arise from tilting the camera up or down, which causes vertical lines to converge in one direction and diverge in the other, or from obliquity of the camera, which similarly affects horizontals. Taking pictures obliquely is frequently done to obtain a more "artistic" result, to prevent relief being flattened as it often is when photographed straight on, and sometimes from sheer necessity in order to get a whole scene into one frame. Tilting the camera, especially up, is often adopted to get pictures of scenes not at eye level.

A further problem with distortion arises if one attempts to apply grid analysis to statues. There can be no doubt that Egyptian sculptors obtained acceptable proportions for their figures by drawing squared grids on the original block before carving it, but these proportions cannot be recaptured for all depths of a statue by superimposing a single hypothetical grid onto a photograph of the statue. Because of perspective distortion, nearer parts of a three-dimensional object will be enlarged relative to those parts further away, so that the true proportions are falsified. Such distortion, however, may not be significant if the object is diminutive enough for its thickness to be small compared with its distance away from the camera. It may be possible to determine the degree of distortion in, say, a frontal view by checking against photographs taken from other angles. If the analysis of a figure is restricted to points on the body profile that lie on a plane parallel to the camera film, perspective distortion is avoided. In Chapter 6 of this book, I describe some photographic results that I have been able to obtain on statuettes from the Amarna period. These are small standing figures with little depth to them. Seated three-dimensional figures cannot be satisfactorily analyzed from photographs.

All these factors limit the amount of published material suitable for my project. Certainly I have made use of publications, but they cover a tiny proportion of the material available in Egypt today that could be used if only one were able to obtain an accurate record of it. The obvious solution was to collect as much as I could myself during yearly trips to Egypt. To overcome the problem of tilted photographs I acquired a shift lens. Such a lens, which moves up or down, enables the surface of the film to be kept parallel to the surface being photographed, so that objects not at eye level can be photographed without tilting. Since it also moves sideways, it can help to overcome the need for obliquity.

In this way I have been able to collect material for analysis from a number of monuments that would otherwise have been unavailable to me. This has played a large part in my understanding of style and composition in Egyptian art, but my application of hypothetical grids has always been governed by what surviving originals have taught me about how Egyptian artists themselves used the grids.

Proportions in the Old and Middle Kingdoms

4.1. Old Kingdom Guidelines[1]

The system of drawing figures on squared grids is not attested on surviving material before the Middle Kingdom. However, from the fifth dynasty onward, through the First Intermediate period into the eleventh dynasty, there are examples of figures drawn out on a system of guidelines (Figs. 4.1–4.3).[2] In most cases, there is an axial vertical that runs over the position of the ear and divides the body into two parts, together with up to 8 horizontal lines that pass through key points of the body: the crown of the head, the hairline, the junction of the neck and shoulders, the armpits, the elbow and bottom of the ribcage, the lower border of the buttocks, the knee, the middle of the lower leg. It is not common for all of the lines to be present on any one figure, but they are found on a stela from Naga ed-Der[3] and on some of the figures in the eleventh dynasty tomb of Inyotef at Thebes (Fig. 4.3).[4] In most surviving Old Kingdom examples, the crown of the head is not marked, but the hairline is present in almost all cases.[5] This vindicates Lepsius' contention that measurement was made to the hairline and not to the crown of the head. Lines through the junction of the neck and shoulders, the armpits, the elbow level, the lower border of the buttocks and the knee occur in the majority of examples. The line marking the middle of the lower leg first appears in the sixth dynasty. A female standing figure in the sixth dynasty tomb of Djau at Deir el-Gebrawi was given an extra line marking the bottom of her dress.[6]

A figure on a private stela from Abydos (CG 20131) dating to year 3 of Senwosret II of the twelfth dynasty is drawn on guidelines,[7] although the grid system had by this time been introduced. In addition to the lines for the top of the head, hairline, junction of neck and shoulders, lower border of the buttocks, and knee,

there are two extra lines, one running through the bottom of the nose and one roughly through the maximum convexity of the buttocks. It is interesting that both these points are also marked by horizontals in the grid system.

If the distances between the horizontals of the guideline system and the baseline are measured, we find that the knee line is roughly half the height of the elbow line and one-third of the height of the hairline horizontal; the line marking the lower border of the buttocks is roughly half the height of the hairline horizontal; the line at the junction of the neck and shoulders is approximately eight-ninths of the hairline height or, measuring up from the elbow level, two-thirds of the distance between the elbow line and hairline horizontal; the level of the armpit line is roughly four-fifths of the hairline height.

It is necessary to realize that in many examples the guidelines are only approximately placed and have clearly not been measured with great accuracy. For instance, Clarence Fisher pointed out how, in the mastaba of Snofruhotep at Giza, the line marking the junction of the neck and shoulders has been placed too low in one of the registers of offering bearers where guidelines have survived (Fig. 4.4).[8] Further, the figures in the mastaba of Manufer from Saqqara, used by Lepsius for his study of guidelines and proportions,[9] are very inaccurate as they appear in LD 2, Pls. 65 and 68 (Fig. 4.5). The dots that supposedly mark the knee level are less than half the height of the elbow level and clearly less than a third of the hairline height, and the dots assumed to mark the lower border of the buttocks lie lower than half the hairline height. Prisse, who knew and illustrated the figures as evidence that draftsmen were already using guides for drawing figures,

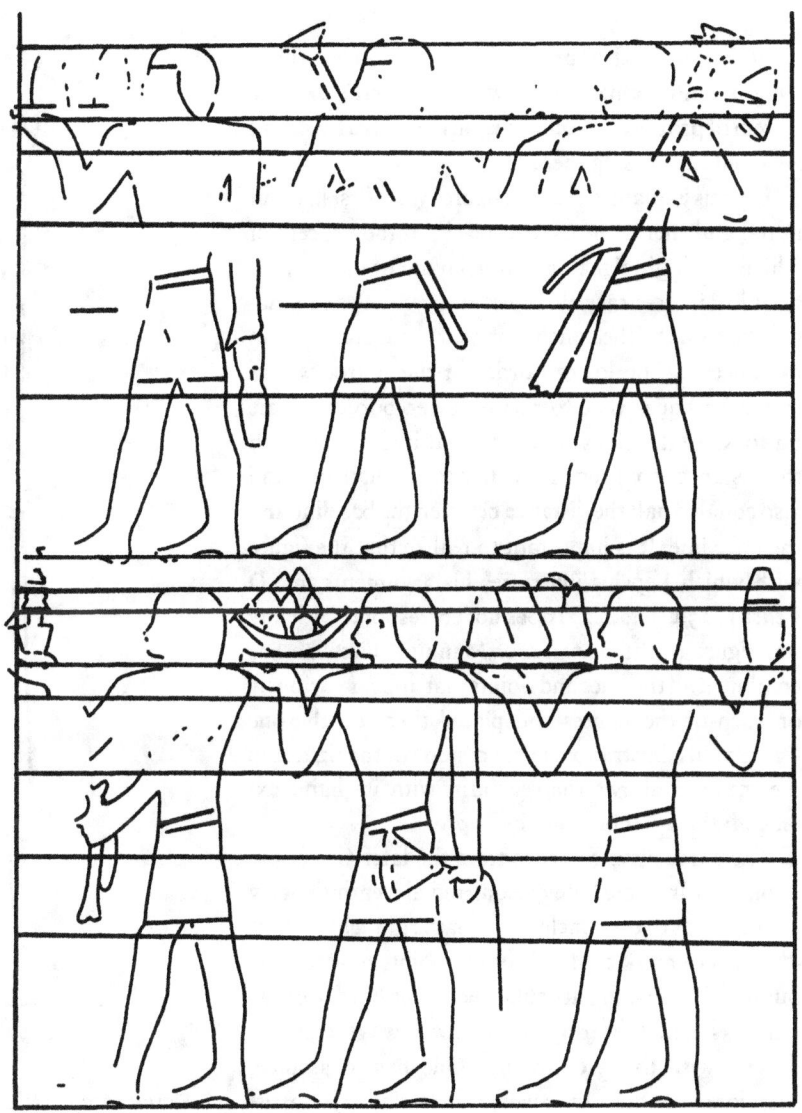

FIGURE 4.1

Rows of offering bearers with guidelines, tomb chapel of Akhtihotep,
Saqqara, fifth dynasty, after Davies 1901, Plate 17 bottom.

obviously found their proportions puzzling; he said he could see no connection between the marks and the system of proportions otherwise in use at this time, and he avoids discussing them.[10]

Lepsius explained that the figures were first laid out in red and then gone over in black, in the process of which the original mathematical layout of the proportions lost its accuracy.[11] However, after long examination he came to the conclusion that the distance from the knees to the lower border of the buttocks was meant to equal that from the lower border of the buttocks to the elbow line, and that it should be half the distance from the elbow line to the hairline, and also equal to half the distance between the baseline and the knee line. It is important to realize that the figure with which Lepsius illustrates his arguments in LD *Tekst* 1, 234 (Fig. 2.27) does not correspond with any one figure in the mastaba of Manufer. First, he has combined all the lines and points that appear variously on each of the figures and placed them on the one figure of his illustration. Second, none of the figures in the mastaba shows the rear arm with its hand extended; this is a construct by Lepsius.

The cumulative evidence from the later Old Kingdom, First Intermediate period, and eleventh dynasty plainly leads to the conclusion that the guidelines were designed to mark the levels of key points of the body, but these points, in particular the lower border of the buttocks and the armpits, do not always coincide exactly with the relevant line. One has to assume, therefore, that these lines were merely aids to the artist and that he was not tied to them. There also survive unfinished scenes where it seems no guidelines were used at all, showing that artists could draw freehand with perfect competence.

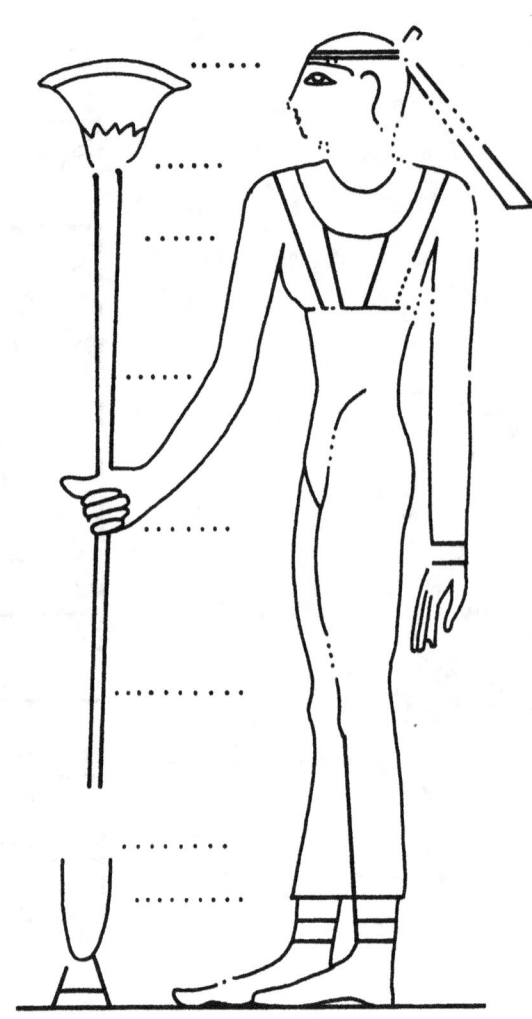

FIGURE 4.2
Figure of the wife of Djau with guidelines, tomb chapel of Djau, Deir el-Gebrawi, sixth dynasty, after Davies 1902, Plate 6.

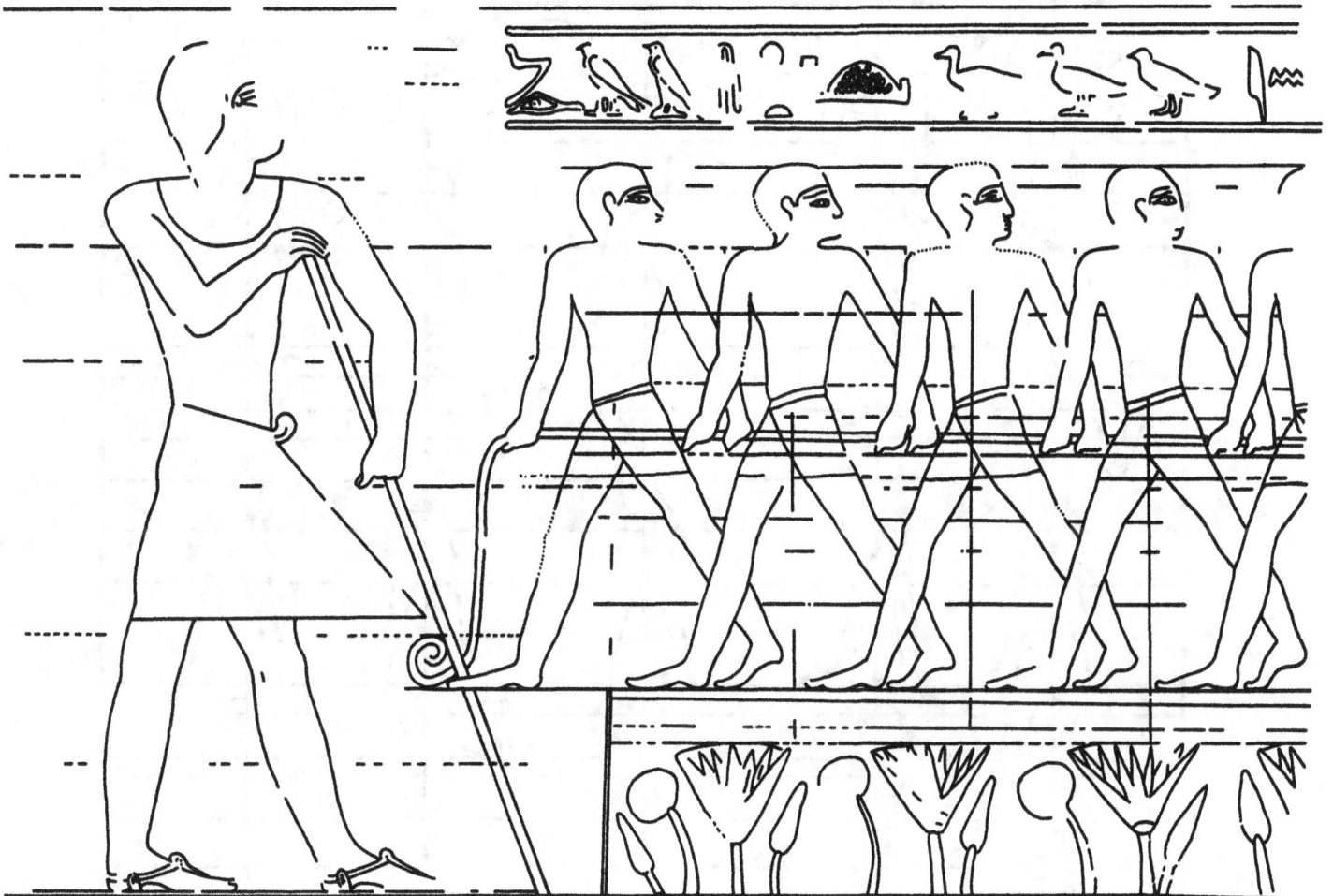

FIGURE 4.3
Figures in the tomb chapel of Inyotef with guidelines,
TT 386, eleventh dynasty, after Jaroš-Deckert, 1984,
foldout 4.

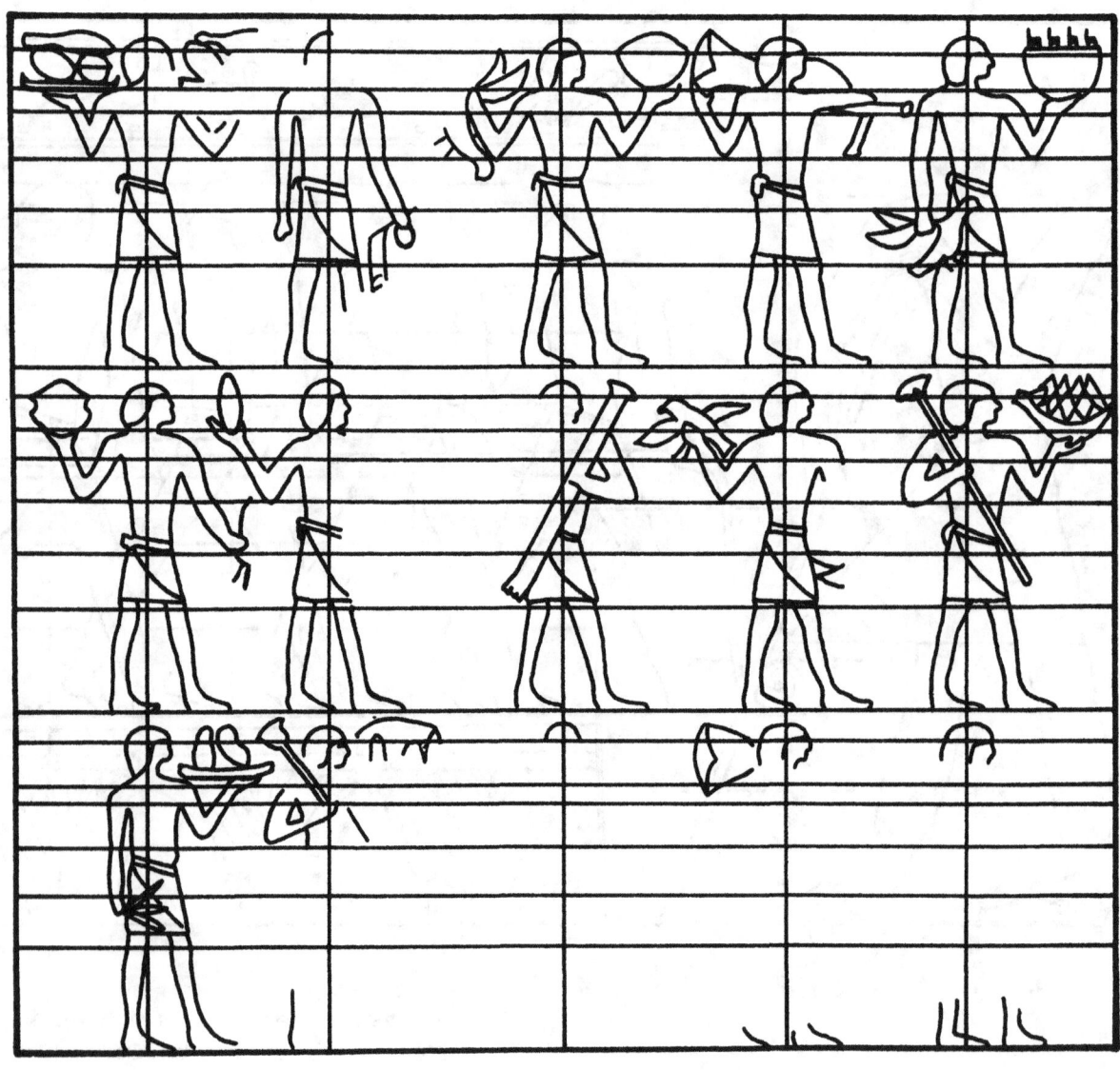

FIGURE 4.4
Offering bearers with guidelines, tomb chapel of Snofruhotep,
Giza, sixth dynasty, after Fisher 1924, Plate 55.

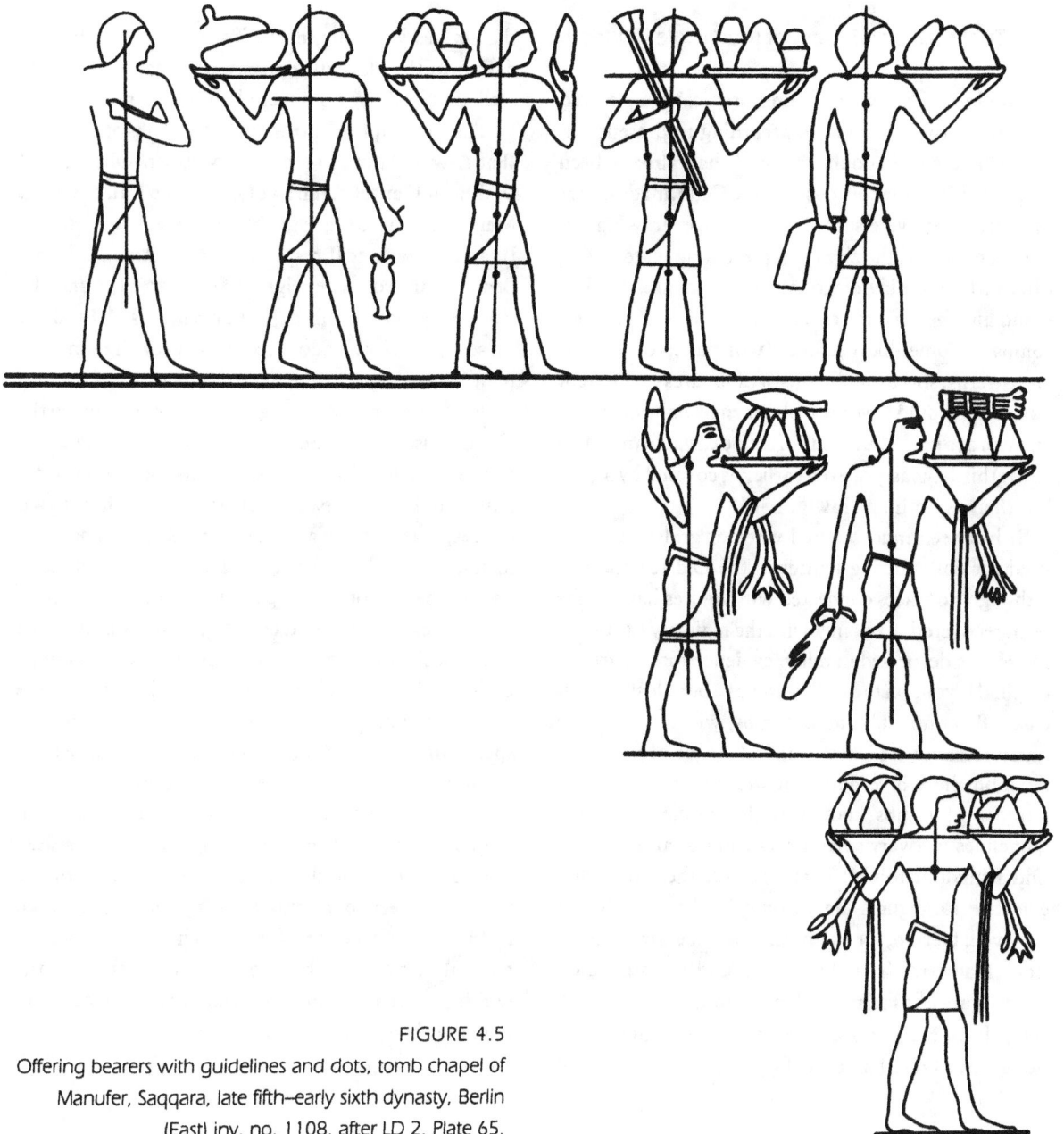

FIGURE 4.5
Offering bearers with guidelines and dots, tomb chapel of
Manufer, Saqqara, late fifth–early sixth dynasty, Berlin
(East) inv. no. 1108, after LD 2, Plate 65.

4.2. The Basic Grid System of the Middle Kingdom

Squared grids on which figures are drawn appeared first in the twelfth dynasty, according to present evidence. There is no doubt that grids had already been employed for other purposes in the Old Kingdom; for instance, they were sometimes used for drawing expanses of water, the zigzags representing water being obtained by joining diagonals of the squares.[12] They could also be used to set out offering lists.[13] Further, tombs are sometimes decorated with panels of geometric patterns; some simply consist of squares of different colors that could have been obtained by painting in the squares of a grid.[14] One side of a block, which may date to the third dynasty or even earlier, is covered by a grid, but there is nothing drawn on it.[15]

It has been much argued whether grids were also used for constructing figures in the Old Kingdom,[16] although no traces connected with figures have so far been recovered. Certainly with the majority of surviving tombs decorated in relief, evidence for the artist's original layout on the wall must have been lost in most cases. By contrast, painted tombs, which were more likely to show evidence of initial stages of working, have on the whole not been well preserved. So the number of tombs known at the moment to have guidelines is a very small proportion of all surviving Old Kingdom tombs. It is possible, therefore, that evidence for figures drawn on grids has simply not survived: Iversen, for example, thinks it entirely fortuitous that grids have not been found in association with figures.[17] From the First Intermediate period, stelae from Naga ed-Der preserve traces of guidelines, not grids, in relation to the figures of the owners and

their wives.[18] Finally, in the Theban tomb of Inyotef dating to the eleventh dynasty, the major figures as well as subsidiary ones were laid out on guidelines.[19]

These examples contrast with the tombs of Sarenput II at Aswan dating to the reign of Amenemhat II;[20] of Wahka at Qaw el-Kebir;[21] of Ukhhotep I, II, and III at Meir belonging to the reigns of Senwosret I, Amenemhat II, and Senwosret II respectively;[22] of Amenemhat at Beni Hasan from the reign of Senwosret I;[23] and the twelfth-dynasty tomb of Ihy at Saqqara.[24] In all of these, grids were undoubtedly used for drawing human figures.

An interesting stela bought in Luxor and now in the Cairo Museum (CG 20003) has been variously dated to the First Intermediate period, to the eleventh dynasty, and to the twelfth dynasty.[25] It shows two figures, a seated man and a smaller seated woman, cut in sunk relief (Figs. 4.6–4.7). The background stone has not been worked or painted, and red horizontal and vertical lines behind each figure still survive. The lines consist of 13 fairly regularly spaced horizontals between the soles of the feet and the junction of the neck and shoulders, with 13 much more narrowly spaced lines above. Of these latter, the fifth above the shoulders passes beneath the nose and the tenth through the hairline. These lines can be shown to correspond to horizontals 0–14 of the squared grid on which seated figures came to be drawn (Secs. 4.4–4.5), with the spaces between horizontals 12–13 and 13–14 each further subdivided into fifths. Each figure, however, has only 6 vertical lines; counting from the left, the width between the first and second is slightly greater than that between the horizontals; the width between the second and third is just over 4 times the width

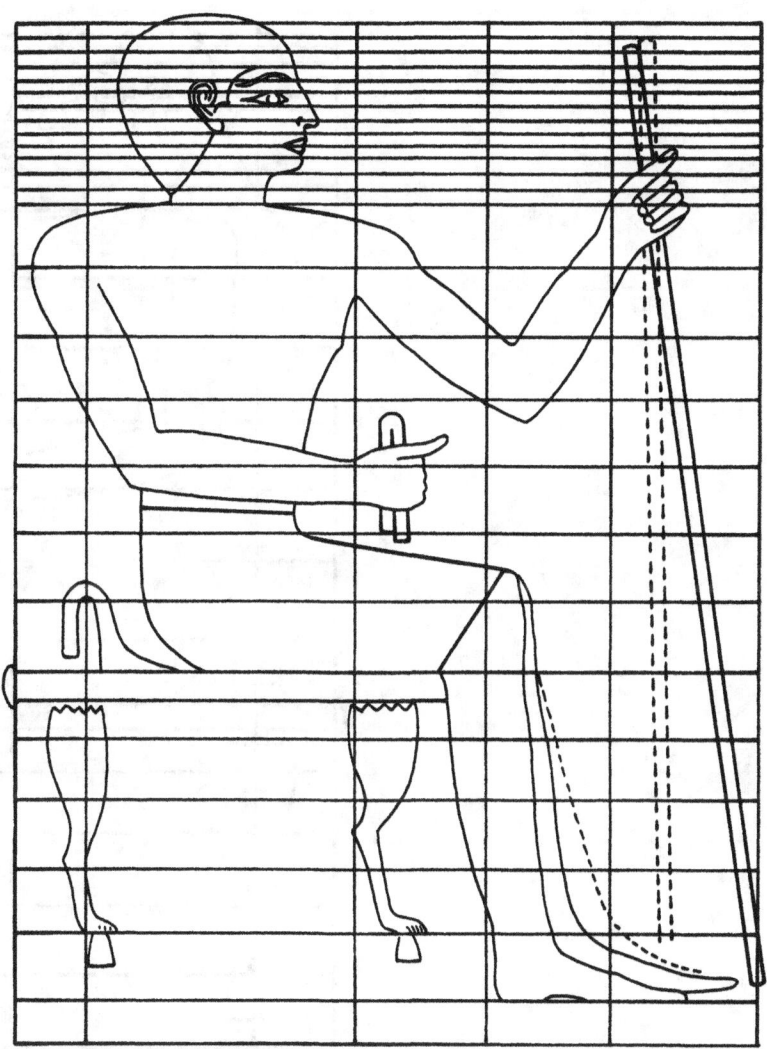

FIGURE 4.6

Detail from stela of Inyotef son of Khuu, Qurna, eleventh dynasty,
CG 20003, after Lange and Schäfer 1902b, Plate 118.

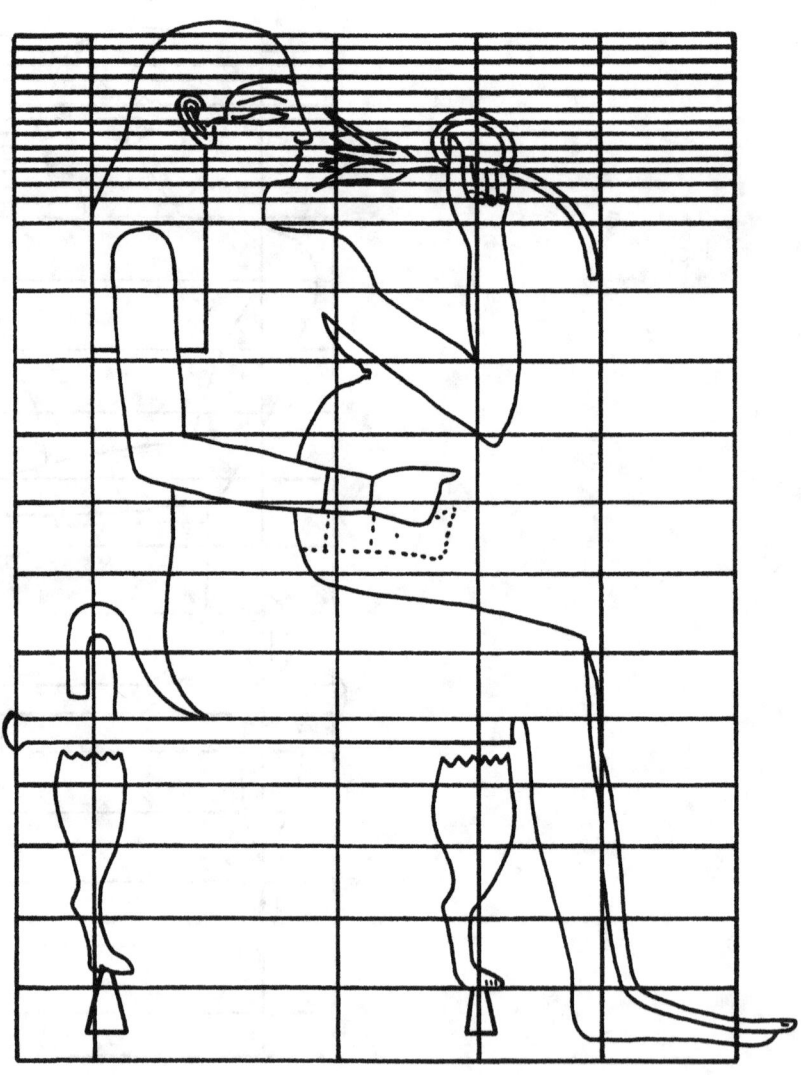

FIGURE 4.7
Detail from stela of Inyotef son of Khuu, Qurna, eleventh
dynasty, CG 20003, after Lange and Schäfer 1902b, Plate 119.

between horizontals in the case of the man and 3 1/2
times for the woman; the width between the remaining
lines approximates in each case to roughly 2 times the
width between horizontals. While the figures are not
drawn on a squared grid, the system of lines employed
is more developed than the standard guideline system
and is perhaps an intermediate development between
the old guidelines and the squared grid.

On the whole, the evidence as it stands at the
moment would suggest that the squared grid was not
used in the Old Kingdom for obtaining the proportions
of human figures. The earliest surviving figures drawn
on such grids that can be certainly dated come from the
reign of Senwosret I of the twelfth dynasty.

4.3. Male Standing Figures on the Grid

A close examination of any sample of figures still on
their original grids shows that artists did not have to
conform exactly to the system.[26] Nevertheless, it is
possible to abstract from such a sample an ideal
relationship between the figure and the grid. It is this
"typical" figure that I shall describe in the following
sections.

Standing figures consisted of 18 squares from their
soles on the baseline to their hairlines (Figs. 4.8–4.10,
8.3). As Lepsius pointed out,[27] the hairline was used
rather than the top of the head presumably because the
latter might be obscured in the case of the king's figure
by his various crowns. Typically, horizontal 18 of the
grid ran through the hairline; horizontal 17 through or
near the bottom of the nose; 16 through or near the
junction of the neck and shoulders; 14 through or near

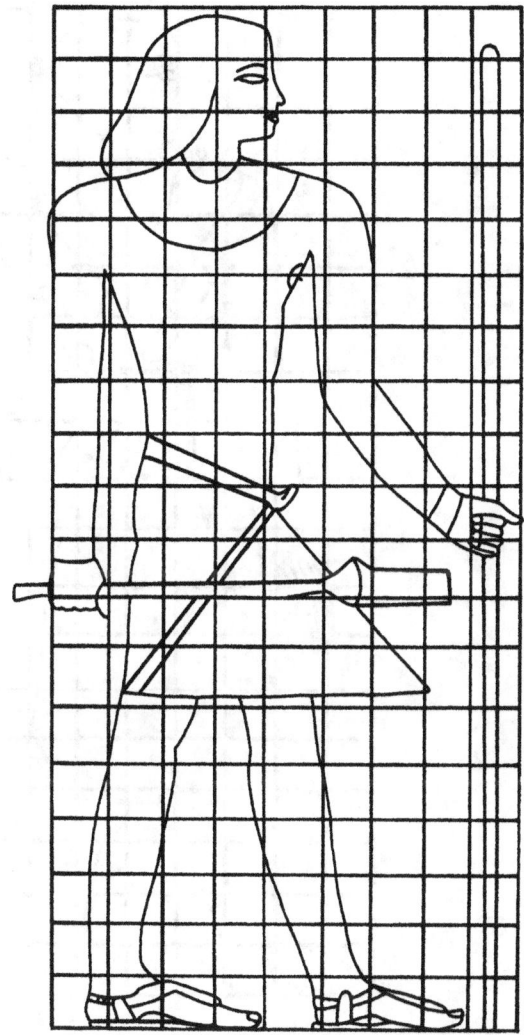

FIGURE 4.8

Standing figure of Sarenput II with grid completed from
surviving traces, Qubbet el-Hawa, twelfth dynasty, after
author's photograph.

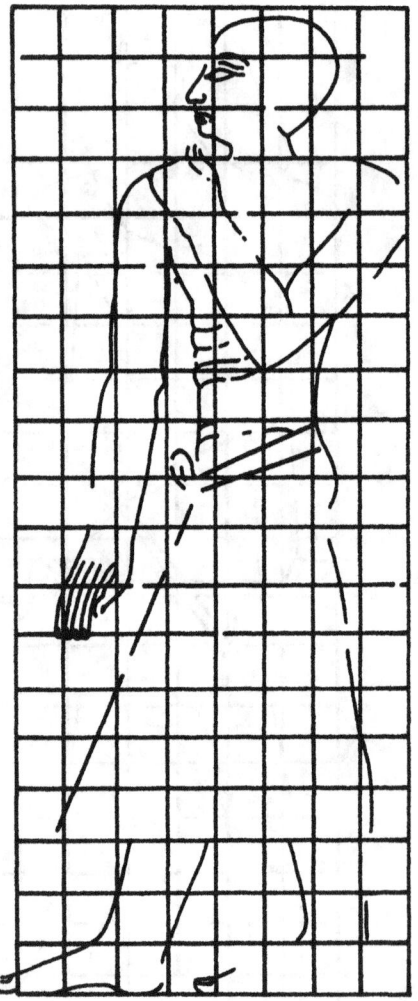

FIGURE 4.9

*Standing figure on original grid, tomb chapel
Meir B2, twelfth dynasty, after Blackman 1915a,
Plate 10 bottom right.*

the nipple; 12 through the bottom of the ribcage and through or near the elbow of the hanging arm; 11 often through or near the navel when shown, the small of the back, and sometimes the top of the belt at the back; 9 through or near the lower border of the buttocks; 6 through the knees; and 0 below the soles.

The other horizontals do not mark such obvious parts of the body; however, 10 often passes through the front of the belt and through the maximum convexity of the buttocks, 5 sometimes runs at the bottom of the bulge of the tibial tubercle where the patellar ligament attaches, 4 through the maximum swelling of the calf, and 1 through the ankle. There is no fixed point for the top of the head, which lies somewhere between horizontals 18 and 19; at this period it rarely touches 19.

A vertical grid line, which can be termed the axial line, usually passes through some part of the ear and divides the neck and upper torso roughly in half; the vertical line immediately in front runs through the eye.[28] Often when a major figure stands with the arms hanging vertically by the side, the armpits lie on verticals 2 squares to the left and right of the axial line, so that they are 4 squares apart. The width of the upper arm is usually 1 square, so that the body from the outer edge of one arm to that of the other, most conveniently measured along horizontal 15, is approximately 6 squares wide (Fig. 4.8; Pl. 1.1; see also Fig. 4.9).[29] The distance across the body at the level of the small of the back is usually 2 1/4 to 2 1/2 squares. The feet are most often 3 squares in length. Sometimes they are longer; less frequently they are shorter. The width of the fist often, but by no means always, fits into a grid square and may, for instance, be larger.[30]

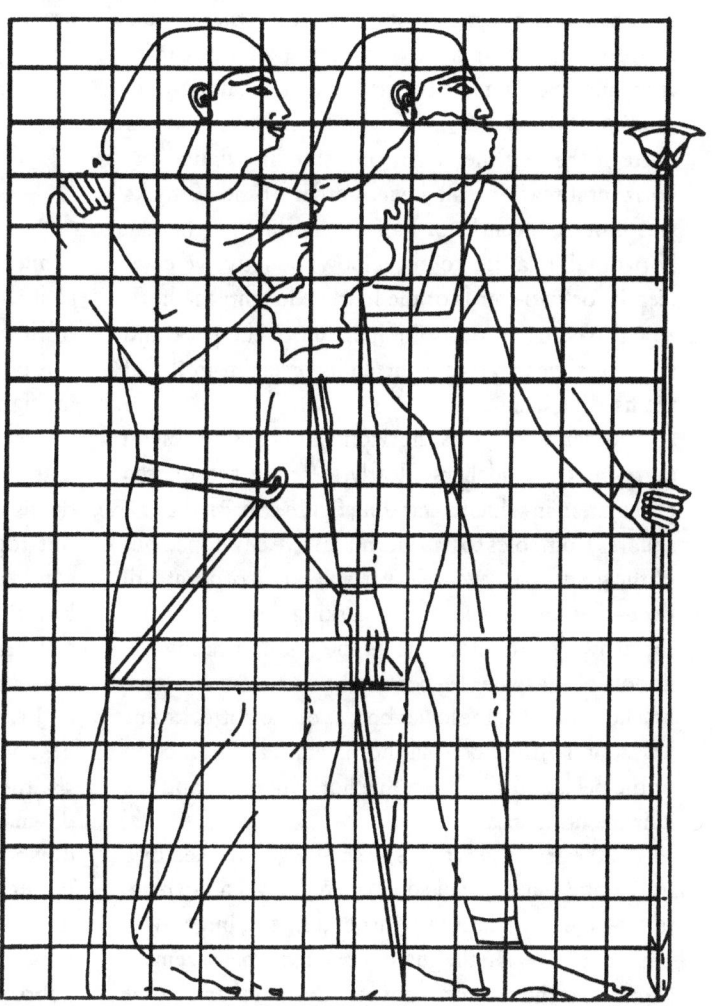

FIGURE 4.10
Standing couple with original grid traces completed, tomb
chapel Meir B2, twelfth dynasty, after Blackman 1915a,
Plate 2.

Lepsius demonstrated long ago that the Middle Kingdom grid system developed out of the earlier guidelines (Sec. 2.1). In the grid system, the horizontal running through the knee was six-eighteenths or a third of the hairline height of a standing figure; the horizontal marking the lower border of the buttocks was nine-eighteenths or half the hairline height; the horizontal relating to the elbow was twelve-eighteenths or two-thirds of the hairline height; the horizontal passing through the junction of the neck and shoulders was sixteen-eighteenths or eight-ninths of the hairline height.

In other words, these horizontals in the grid system correspond to guidelines. Clearly, therefore, the squared grid system in which a standing figure consisted of 18 squares from soles to hairline must have developed out of the guideline system. It was able to incorporate all the earlier lines except those marking the armpits and the crown of the head. Thus the line indicating the middle of the lower leg became horizontal 3, the knee line horizontal 6, the lower border of the buttocks line horizontal 9, the elbow line horizontal 12, the junction of the neck and shoulders line horizontal 16, and the hairline horizontal 18.

On the grid, the armpits are no longer marked by a horizontal line but fall somewhere between horizontals 14 and 15. This is often around 14 1/2, but may be higher or lower. In the guideline system, measurement shows that the distance between the lines marking the crown of the head and the hairline was less than one-eighteenth of the hairline height; in fact it varies between approximately one-half and three-quarters of one-eighteenth of the hairline height. This is reflected in the Middle Kingdom grid system where the crown of the head lies lower than horizontal 19, somewhere

between 18 1/2 and 18 3/4 squares above the baseline. The old vertical axial guideline became incorporated as a vertical grid line.

4.4. Male Seated Figures on the Grid

While standing figures were drawn on a grid of 18 squares, seated figures usually consisted of 14 squares from their soles to their hairline (Figs. 4.11–4.12).[31] The bodily proportions remained the same as in standing figures, but now the thigh no longer contributed to the overall height. The number of squares from the hairline to the lower border of the buttocks, on which the figure now sits, is still 9, as in standing figures, and this together with the height of the seat, which is 5 squares, makes 14 squares in all. The height of the lower leg from soles to the top of the knee remains 6 squares, but the top of the knee lies 1 square above the lower border of the buttocks on which the figure sits.

Just as in standing figures, the bottom of the nose lies roughly 1 square below the hairline, on horizontal 13, the junction of the neck and shoulders 2 squares down on 12, and the nipple approximately 4 squares down on or near 10. The belt of the kilt tends to be flatter than on standing figures; the front of the belt, usually 8 squares below the hairline on standing figures, is frequently raised in the sitting position to approximately 7 squares below. Although the back of the belt may be slightly higher than the front, the vertical separation between back and front is usually less than the whole square common on standing figures. Horizontal 5, which runs along the top of the seat, often passes through the bottom of the bulge of the tibial tubercle.

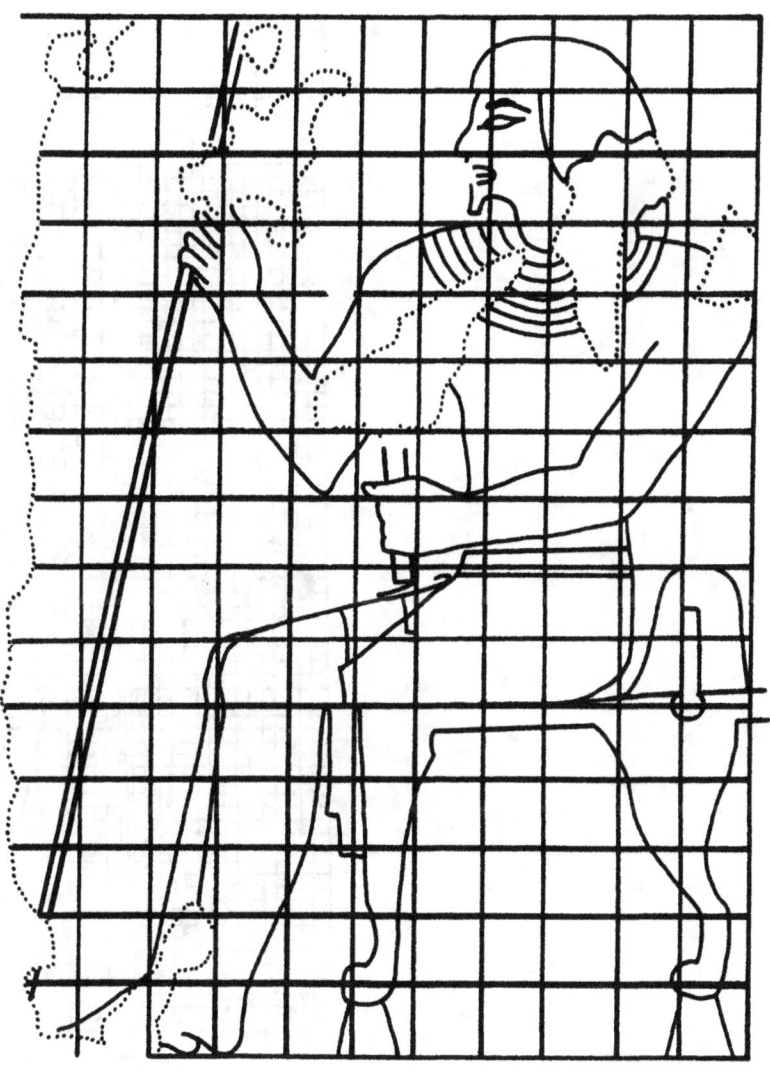

FIGURE 4.11
Seated figure of Sarenput II with grid completed from
surviving traces, Qubbet el-Hawa, twelfth dynasty, after
Müller 1940, 86 Figure a.

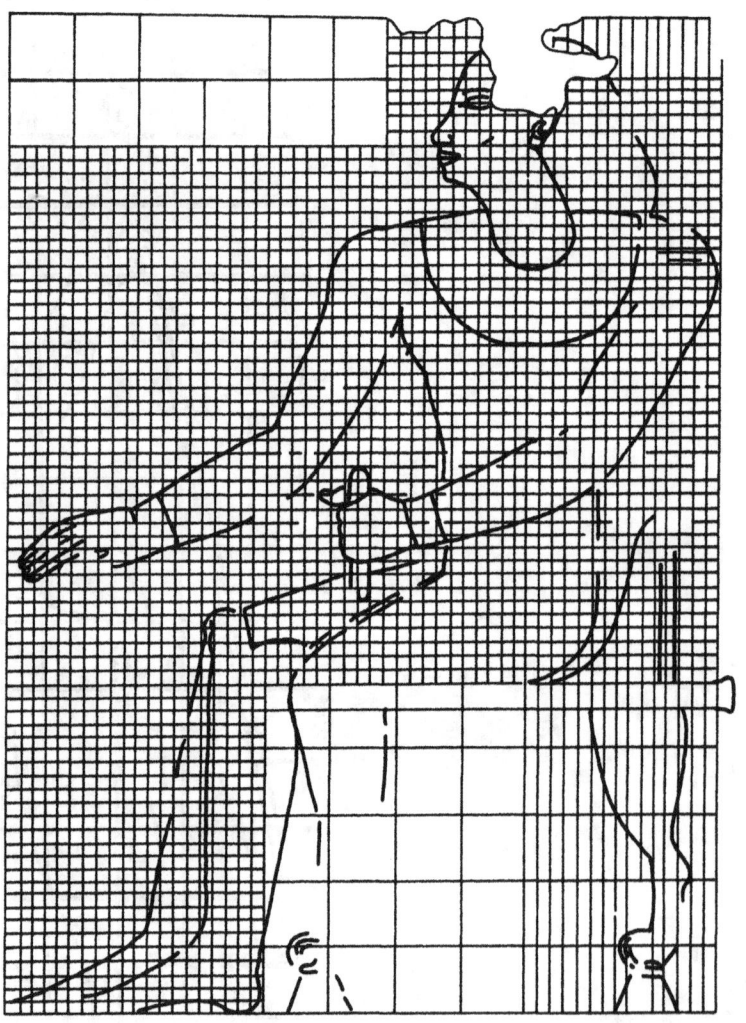

FIGURE 4.12

Seated figure of Ukhhotep on original grid from his tomb chapel, Meir B2, twelfth dynasty, after Blackman 1915a, Plate 10. The spaces between the horizontals and verticals of the 14-square grid have been subdivided into fifths.

4.5. Female Standing and Seated Figures

Female figures on surviving grids show that from the hairline to the soles standing figures consist of 18 squares and seated figures of 14, just as for male figures (Figs. 4.10, 4.13–4.14).[32] However, there are differences in the proportions of male and female figures that, on the whole, reflect differences found in real life (Pl. 1.2, Fig. 4.15). In standing figures, the bottom of the nose, the junction of the neck and shoulders, the nipple, and the knee lie on or near horizontals 17, 16, 14, and 6, but the buttocks are usually more pronounced than in male figures, extending upward so that the small of the back is pushed up, often to horizontal 12 and sometimes to 13.

In both seated and standing figures, the width of the body is narrower than in male figures: from armpit to armpit is usually approximately 3 rather than 4 squares; the full width across horizontal 15 is 5 squares or less; across the level of the small of the back is often 2 squares or less, instead of the 2 1/4 to 2 1/2 squares of the male figure. Like their male counterparts, female figures usually have an axial vertical that runs through the ear when it is visible. Since the widths between the armpits and between the outer edges of the upper arms are an odd number of grid squares, both the armpits and the edges of the upper arms lie between grid verticals and not on them as in their male equivalents (Figs. 4.13, 4.15).

4.6. Kneeling Figures

Few kneeling figures with grid traces have survived. Two examples of male figures occur in tomb chapel B2 at Meir (Fig. 4.16)[33] and four of women in tomb chapel

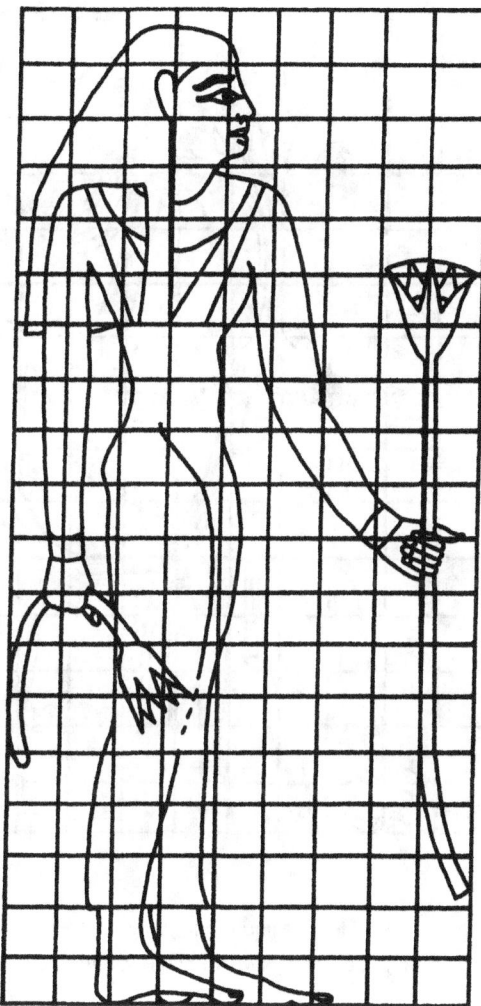

FIGURE 4.13

Standing female figure on original grid from tomb chapel of Sarenput II, Qubbet el-Hawa, twelfth dynasty, after Müller 1940, 84 Figure c.

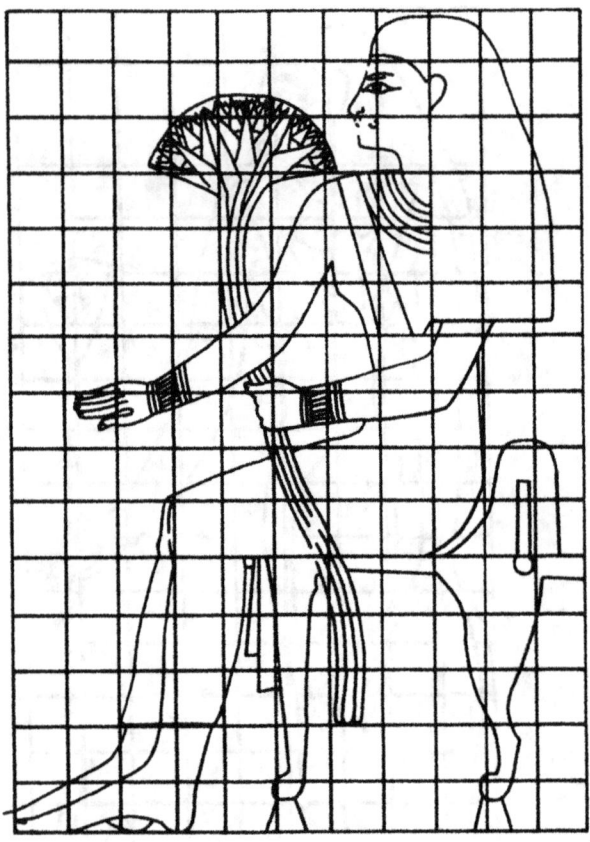

FIGURE 4.14

Seated female figure from tomb chapel of Sarenput II,
Qubbet el-Hawa, twelfth dynasty, after Müller 1940, 86
Figure b.

C1 (Pl. 4.1).[34] The figures kneel so that the buttocks rest on the heel of the vertically raised foot; they consist of 11 squares from the hairline to the baseline. In many ways, their proportions are similar to those of standing and seated figures. The bottom of the nose lies 1 square below the hairline, the junction of the neck and shoulders 2 squares below, and the nipple or breast region 4 squares below.

In the male standing figures at Meir, the top of the back of the belt most commonly lies on or near horizontal 11, that is, 7 squares below the hairline; the bottom part of the front of the belt is usually on horizontal 10, or 8 squares below the hairline. In the figures of the kneeling men, the top of the belt at the front is pushed up to 7 squares below the hairline, and at the back the belt is raised by half a square. The small of the back is also raised, lying only 6 squares below the hairline, not 7 as in standing figures.

In all the examples of kneeling figures, the lower border of the buttocks rests on the heel of the raised foot, which is roughly 8 3/4 squares below the hairline. The height of the foot with the toes turned under is about 2 1/4 squares, bringing the total height of the figure to 11 squares. The shortfall of a quarter square in the distance between the lower border of the buttocks and the hairline as compared with the ideal of 9 squares should not be made too much of, since in many standing figures the lower border of the buttocks is not placed exactly on horizontal 9.

Other figures kneel with one or both of their lower legs lying along the baseline, with the foot placed horizontally, sole upward, and the toes pointing backward; in the former case, the other leg is bent with the knee raised in front of the body. Two groups of

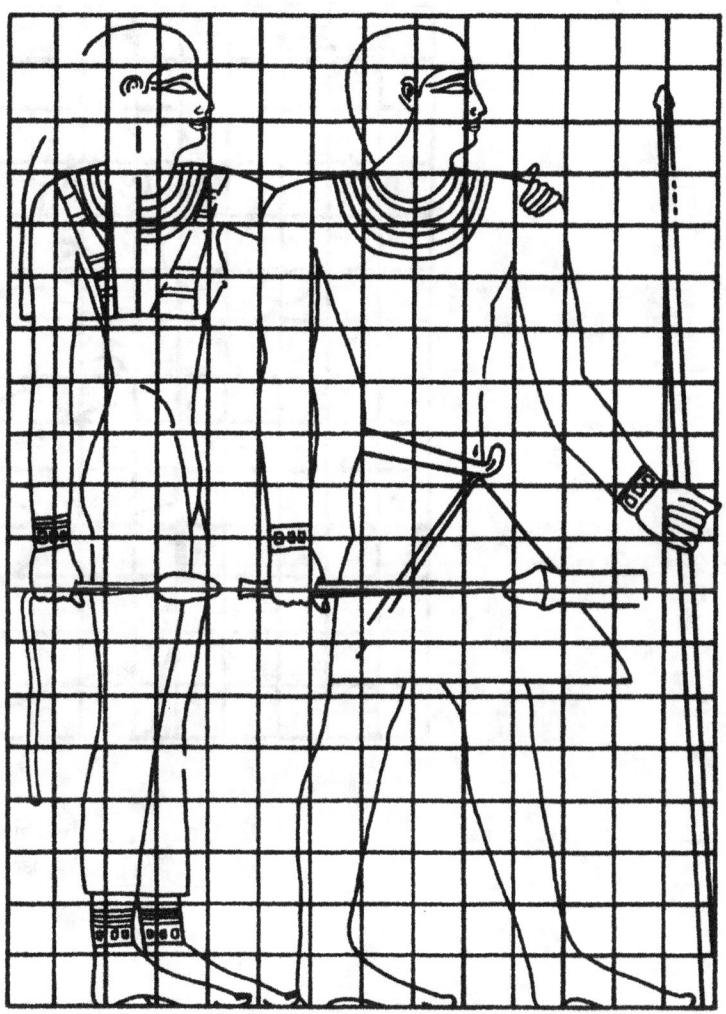

FIGURE 4.15
Standing male and female figures on hypothetical
18-square grid, Naga ed-Der, twelfth dynasty, Boston
MFA 25.659, after Freed 1981, Figure 2.

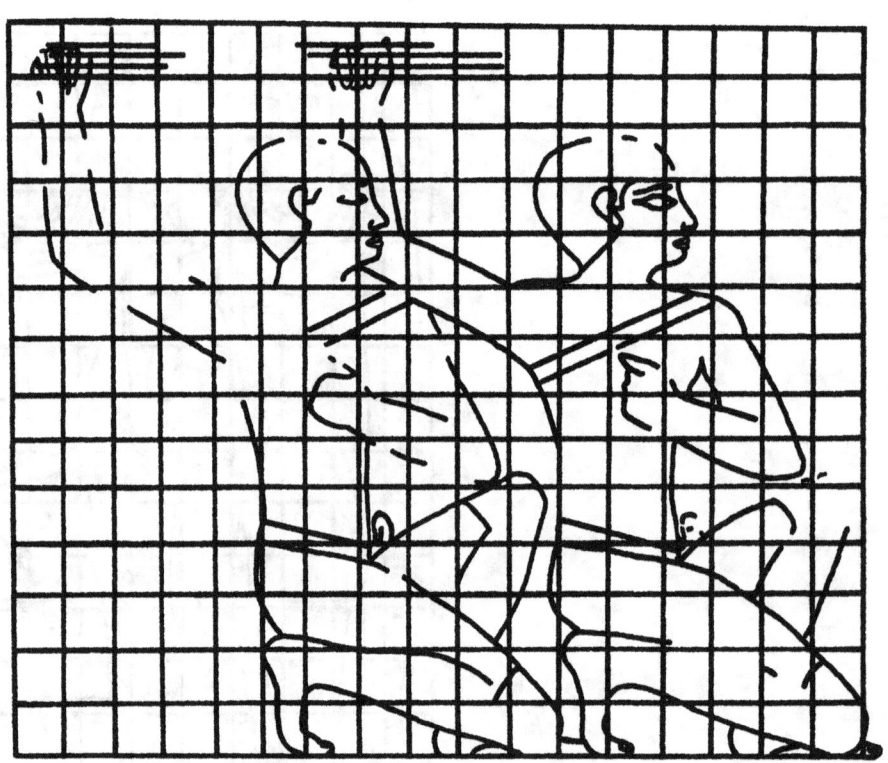

FIGURE 4.16
Two male kneeling figures on original grid from tomb chapel of Ukhhotep, Meir B2, twelfth dynasty, after Blackman 1915a, Plate 10.

musicians, one male and one female in tomb chapels B2 and C1 respectively at Meir,[35] kneel in this way, and are associated with grid traces that can be extended to run over their figures (Fig. 4.17). The results show that each figure comprises 10 squares from hairline to baseline. The line formed by the lower border of the buttocks and the back of the thigh resting on the calf and heel of the lower leg runs roughly along horizontal 1, so that the lower border of the buttocks is 9 squares below the hairline; the thickness of the lower leg is 1 square, making a total hairline height of 10 squares. The length from the top of the knee to the heel is approximately 6 squares as in standing figures. The raised knees of the women, in which the lower leg is vertical, are roughly 5 3/4 to 6 squares above the baseline. In the group of male musicians, the raised knee of the left-hand figure reaches to horizontal 5 and of the others to horizontal 4; in all the figures the lower leg is held obliquely compared to the women in C1, but on those where the knee only reaches to horizontal 4, the leg is even more oblique.

4.7. Subdivisions of the Grid

In a very few cases, the grid squares have been subdivided into smaller squares.[36] In tomb chapel B2 at Meir, a seated figure of the tomb owner is sketched on the usual 14-square grid from soles to hairline but the sides of the squares have been subdivided into fifths, so that the large squares now contain 25 smaller squares (Fig. 4.12).[37] Undivided squares at the top left-hand corner of the grid and under the seat suggest that the scene was first laid out with a conventional grid. This is confirmed by the dots marking the spacing of the intermediate lines. The lines of the main grid run on without interruption; between them dots clearly show where the subdivisions were measured out after the fundamental grid had been drawn. These subdivided squares cover the whole of the figure except for the rear portion of the lower leg, yet although the whole scene is clearly preserved, it is difficult to understand what the purpose of the subdivision was.

This seated figure is the only one in B2 that is drawn on a subdivided grid. However, in tomb chapel C1 at Meir, there is similar evidence of subdivision in some of the grids. The tomb is in a poor state of preservation, and Blackman does not mark these grids in his publication, but they can be seen in his photographs of the scenes, now in the E.E.S. archives.[38] One scene shows the owner in a boat hunting birds. Grid horizontals are preserved between the back of his head and the streamers falling from his fillet,[39] and also above the baseline around the figure of a kneeling woman.[40] In the companion fishing scene, grid lines occur between the owner's legs beneath his kilt.[41] Finally, a standing figure of the tomb owner shows grid horizontals relating to the foot, and horizontals and verticals behind the figure below the clenched hand, roughly at knee level.[42] In all these cases the lines are too close together to represent standard grid squares. However, both the grids and the figures are too damaged to show whether we are again dealing with subdivisions into fifths.

I have already mentioned the stela in the Cairo Museum, CG 20003, dating to the First Intermediate period or the eleventh dynasty, that shows two seated figures, the larger male and the smaller female, drawn on a "proto-grid" (Figs. 4.6–4.7). On each there are 12 horizontals above the baseline up to the junction of the

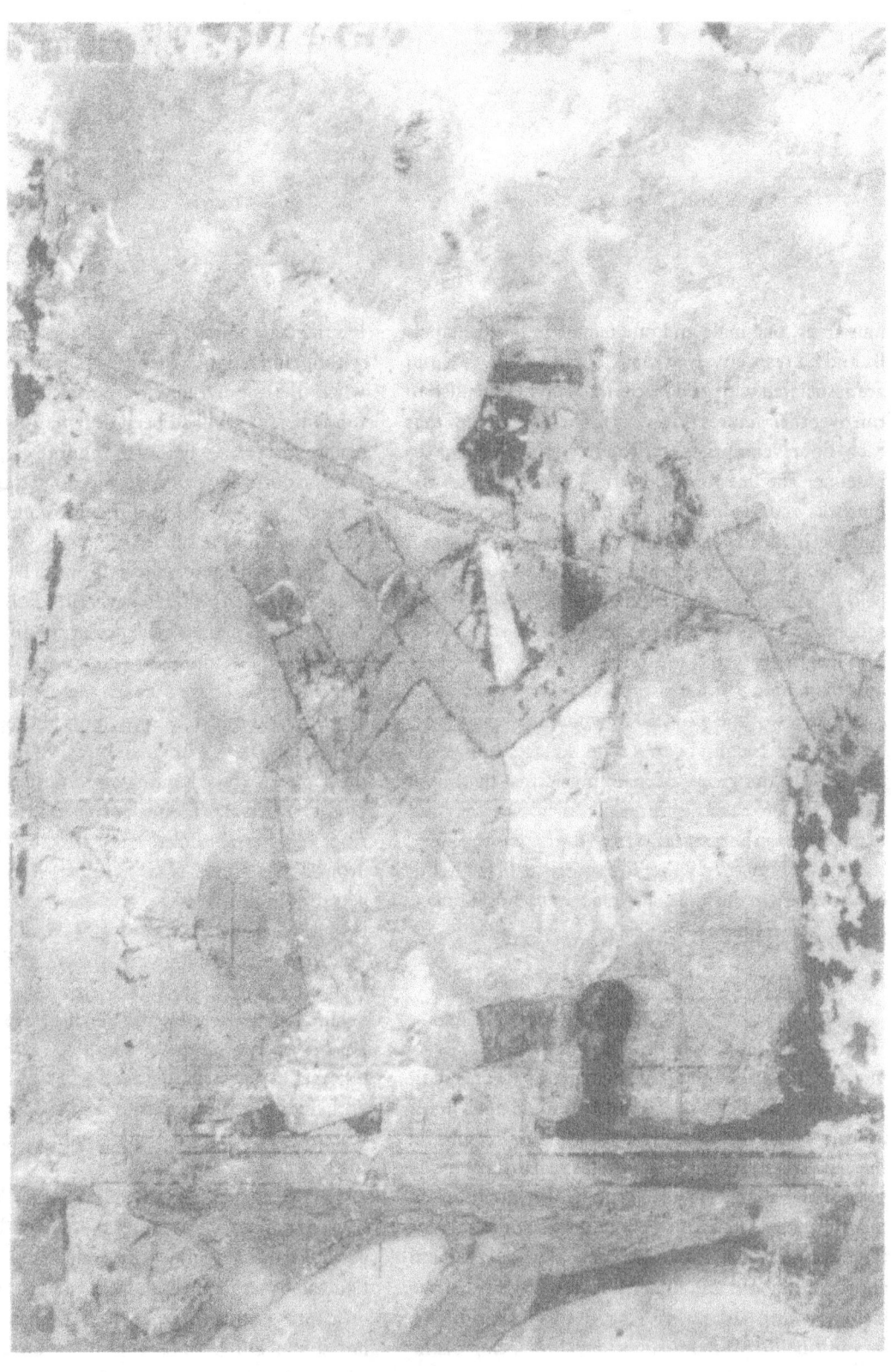

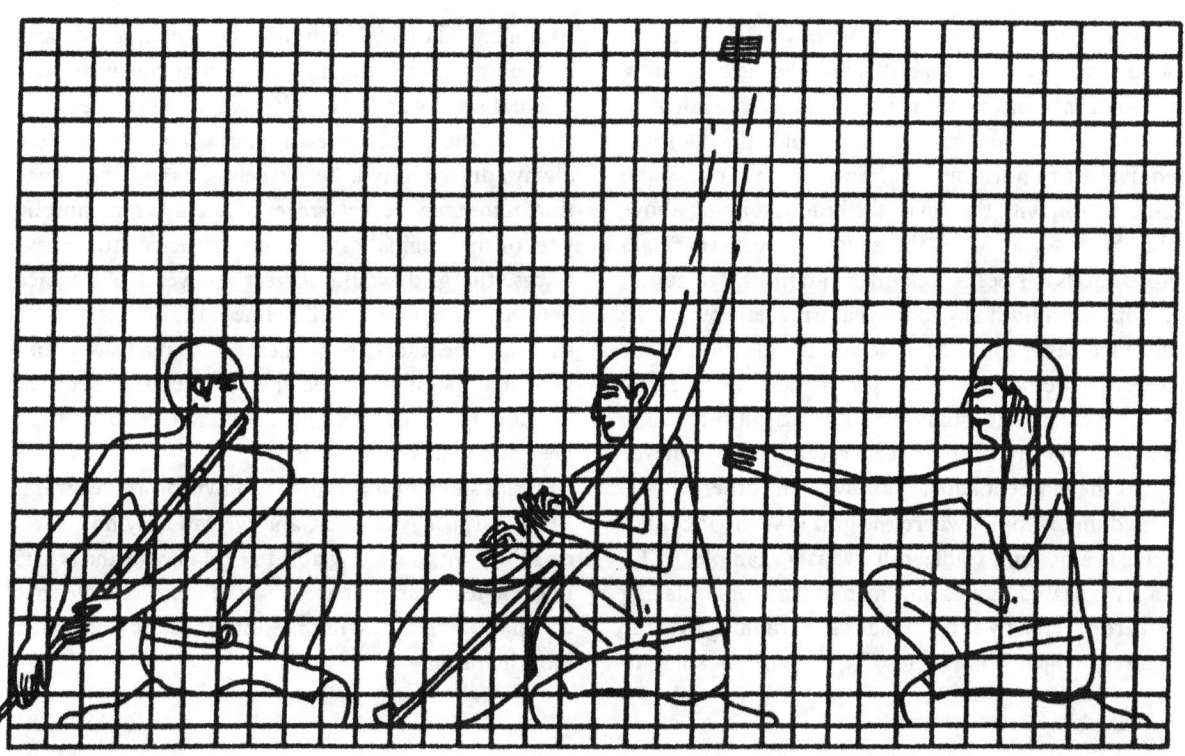

PLATE 4.1

Detail from a scene in Meir tomb C1, twelfth dynasty, detail of EES photo B97, reproduced by permission of the Committee of the Egypt Exploration Society.

FIGURE 4.17

Group of kneeling musicians with original grid traces extended to cover them from tomb chapel of Ukhhotep, Meir B2, twelfth dynasty, after Blackman 1915a, Plate 3.

neck and shoulders. Above horizontal 12 there is a series of 13 closely spaced lines, the fifth running through the bottom of the nose, and so equivalent to horizontal 13, and the tenth through the hairline, equivalent to horizontal 14. There are 3 more of the lines above, with the top of the head just rising above the third. As at Meir, the space between the main horizontals has been subdivided into fifths. The subdivisions are admittedly somewhat irregular, but as the distance between the hairline and the junction of the neck and shoulders is only 3.4 cm in the case of the man and 2.8 cm in that of the woman, this is not surprising; accuracy on such a small scale is difficult to achieve.

At the moment I do not know of any other Middle Kingdom examples where the grid is subdivided, but there is a possible eighteenth-dynasty example. In TT 81, two seated figures of a man and a woman facing left are covered by a grid of black lines running over the figures, which consist of 9 squares from soles to baseline.[43] The fact that the lines cross completed parts of the figures is enough to show that this is not the original artist's grid, as is also suggested by the black color of the lines, since original grids were almost always drawn in red. Nevertheless, careful examination of the scene reveals traces of red lines that must be part of the original grid. If reconstructed from these traces, the grid would correctly cover the distance between the hairline and baseline of the figures with 14 squares. The traces are plainest on the man's wig, and here it is possible to see that the squares between horizontals 12 and 13 and between 13 and 14 have been subdivided into fifths.[44]

Grids showing any sign of subdivision are very rare. Their purpose is unclear, and we can only note their existence without being able to explain why the artists in these few instances went to the extra trouble that calculating and drawing the intermediate lines must have involved.

In the New Kingdom, except during the brief Amarna period (Chap. 6), the number of grid squares in standing and seated figures did not alter, but the relationship of some parts of the body to the various grid lines did change, producing a change in style. In addition, there is evidence that at some point in the later eighteenth dynasty an extra square was introduced into the height of royal kneeling figures.

5.1. Male Standing and Seated Figures

At the beginning of the eighteenth dynasty, the proportions of male standing figures were very much the same as their Middle Kingdom counterparts (Fig. 5.1).[1] However, evidence shows that sometime in the reign of Thutmose III, and certainly by the reign of Amenhotep II, changes in proportion were taking place (Figs. 5.2–5.4). The small of the back came to be more often situated on or near horizontal 12 rather than 11, and the lower border of the buttocks was most often placed above horizontal 9, sometimes as high as 10.[2] It also became common for the top of the head to be extended up to horizontal 19.[3]

Although surviving grids from the nineteenth and twentieth dynasties are rare, analysis of material on hypothetical grids (Sec. 3.2) shows that these trends continued throughout the New Kingdom. In addition, by the nineteenth dynasty it was usually the lower border of the kneecap that lay on horizontal 6, instead of the top or point of the knee (Figs. 5.5, 9.8, 9.10).[4] This pushed the top of the knee above horizontal 6, so lengthening the lower leg. By the twentieth dynasty, the knee frequently lay as high as 6 3/4 squares above

the baseline, with horizontal 6 passing through the tibial tubercle below the kneecap (Fig. 5.6). Lengthened leg proportions were transferred to seated figures from the nineteenth dynasty on.

Throughout the eighteenth dynasty, the relationship of seated figures to the grid remained traditional, as figures surviving on grids testify (Pls. 5.1, 8.1; Fig. 8.1).[5] By contrast, when figures from the nineteenth and twentieth dynasties are analyzed on hypothetical grids, we can see that the lower leg has become longer in proportion to the rest of the body (Figs. 5.13, 9.13).[6] In the earlier figures, the top of the seat had lain on horizontal 5 with the top of the knee a square higher on 6. From the nineteenth dynasty, the top of the seat generally lay about 5 1/2 squares above the baseline with the top of the knee a square higher, 6 1/2 squares up. Horizontal 6 ran through the lower border of the kneecap as in standing figures. On occasion, the top of the knee might be placed as high as horizontal 7 with the top of the seat on 6, so that the lower leg consisted of a total height of approximately 7 squares (Figs. 5.7, 9.16).[7]

It is interesting to note that even in Old and Middle Kingdom figures, in relation to natural proportions the lower leg had been somewhat elongated.[8] In life the femur in the thigh is longer than the tibia in the lower leg. In natural standing figures, the head of the femur, articulating with the hip joint, lies between the upper and lower margins of the buttocks, roughly on a level with their maximum convexity; the lower end of the bone meets the upper end of the tibia on a level with the lower border of the kneecap. The extreme lower end of the tibia at the ankle is marked on the surface of the leg by the inner malleolus, which is often shown in the art

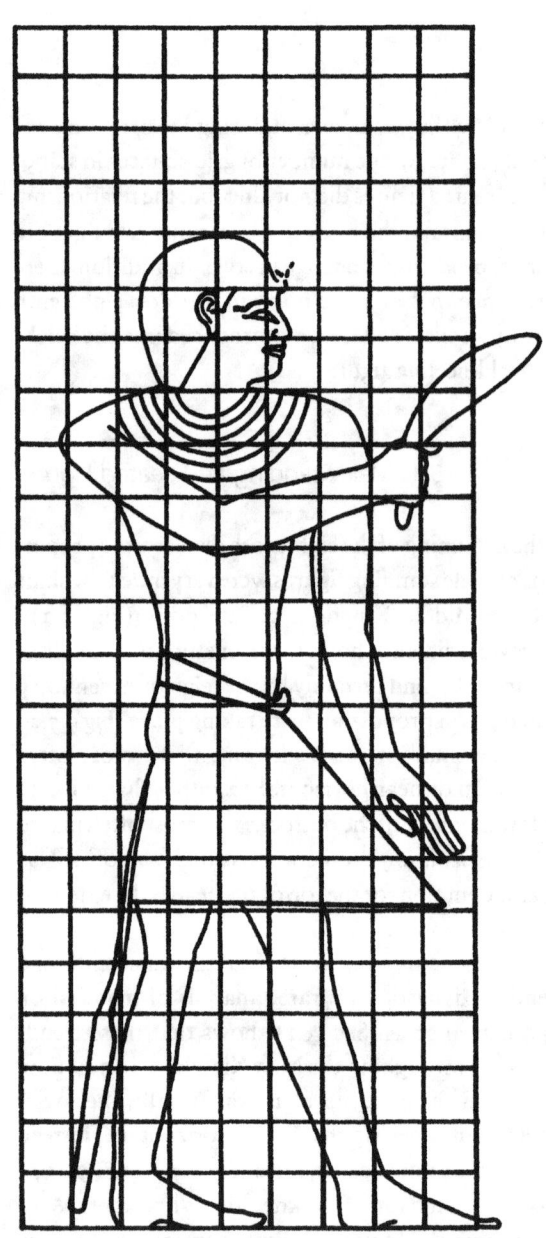

FIGURE 5.1
Figure of Amenhotep I on hypothetical 18-square grid,
Karnak, eighteenth dynasty, drawing from author's
photograph.

FIGURE 5.2
Figure on grid completed from surviving traces,
astronomical ceiling, TT 353, eighteenth dynasty, after
MMA photo. M8C 191.

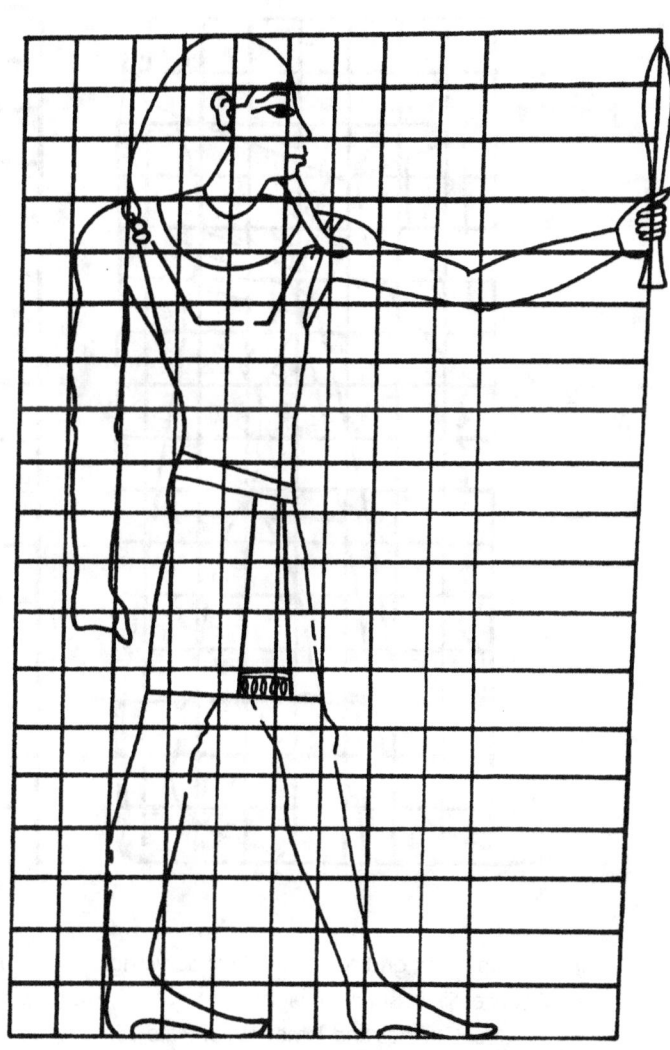

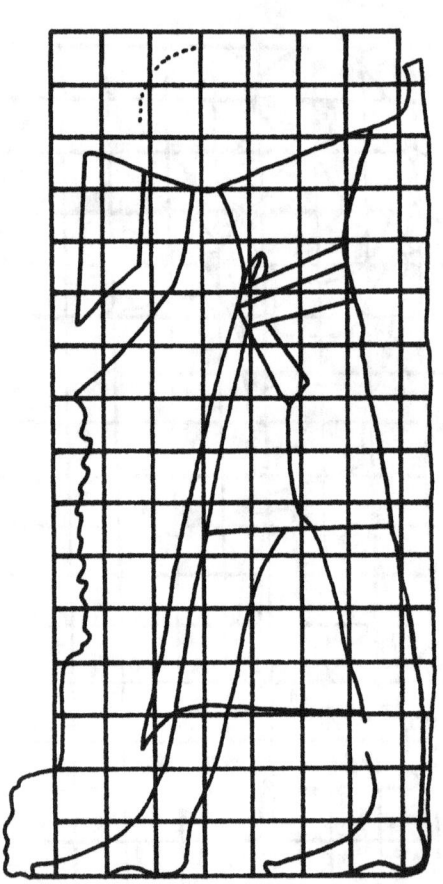

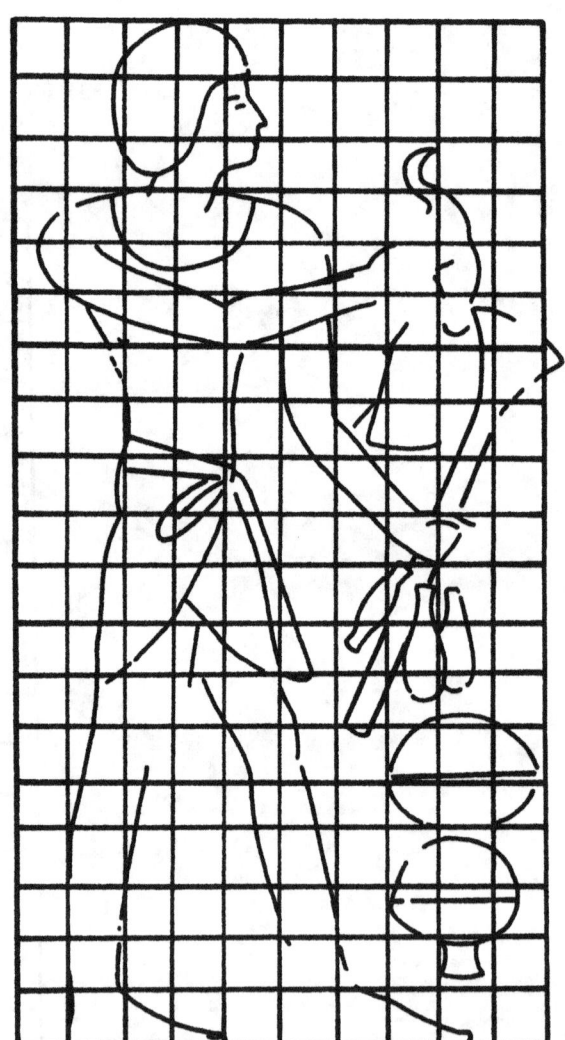

FIGURE 5.3
Unfinished figure on grid completed from surviving
traces, Gebel es-Silsila, shrine 5, eighteenth dynasty,
after Caminos and James 1963, Plate 15.

FIGURE 5.4
Unfinished figure on grid completed from surviving
traces, TT 92, eighteenth dynasty, after Mackay 1917,
Plate 16 no. 2.

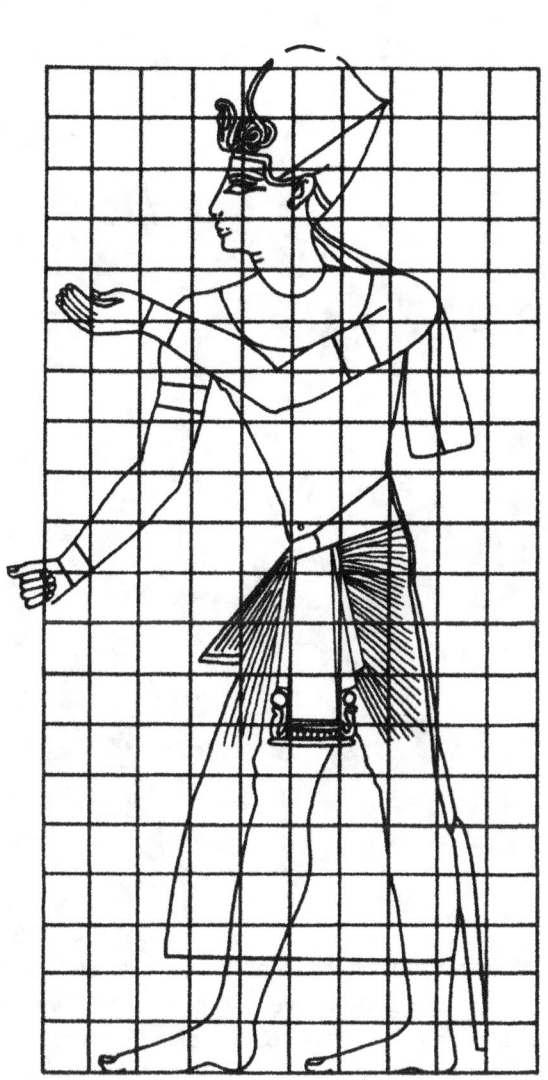

FIGURE 5.5

Figure of Sety I on hypothetical 18-square grid, temple of Sety I at Abydos, nineteenth dynasty, after Calverley 1938, Plate 45.

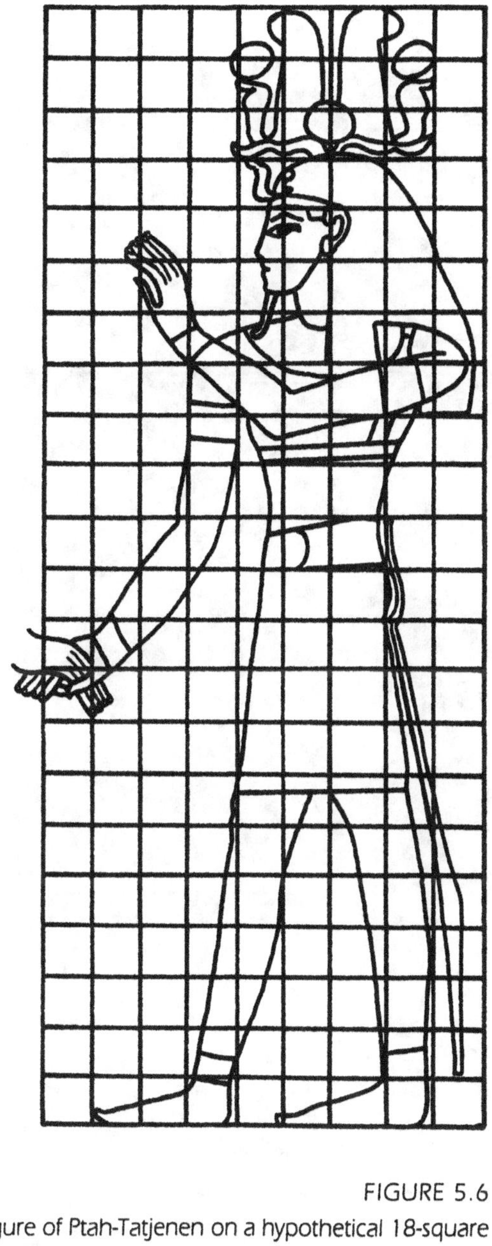

FIGURE 5.6

Figure of Ptah-Tatjenen on a hypothetical 18-square grid, tomb chapel of prince Amonhirkhopshef, Valley of the Queens, Thebes, twentieth dynasty, after Kamal el-Mallakh 1980, 84.

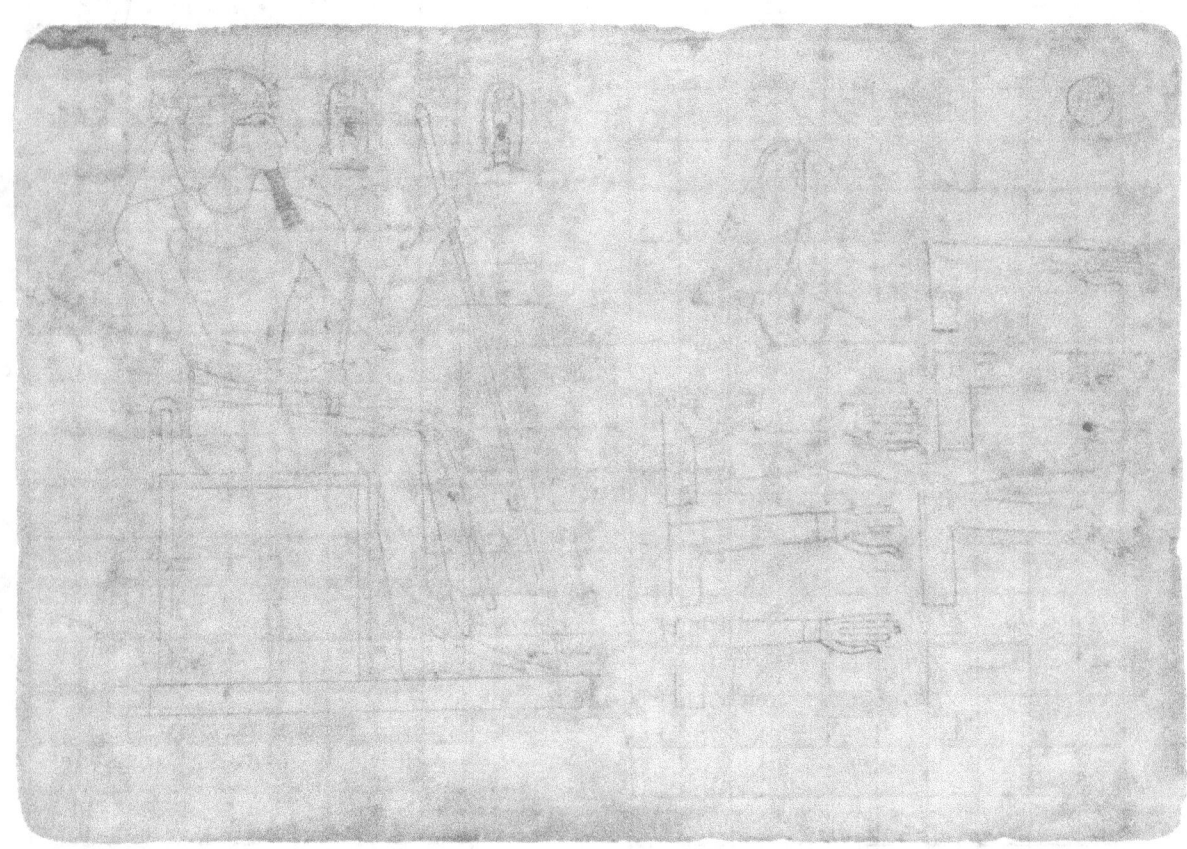

PLATE 5.1
Drawing board with figure of Thutmose III sketched out
on an original grid, eighteenth dynasty, British Museum
EA 5601, reproduced by courtesy of the Trustees of the
British Museum.

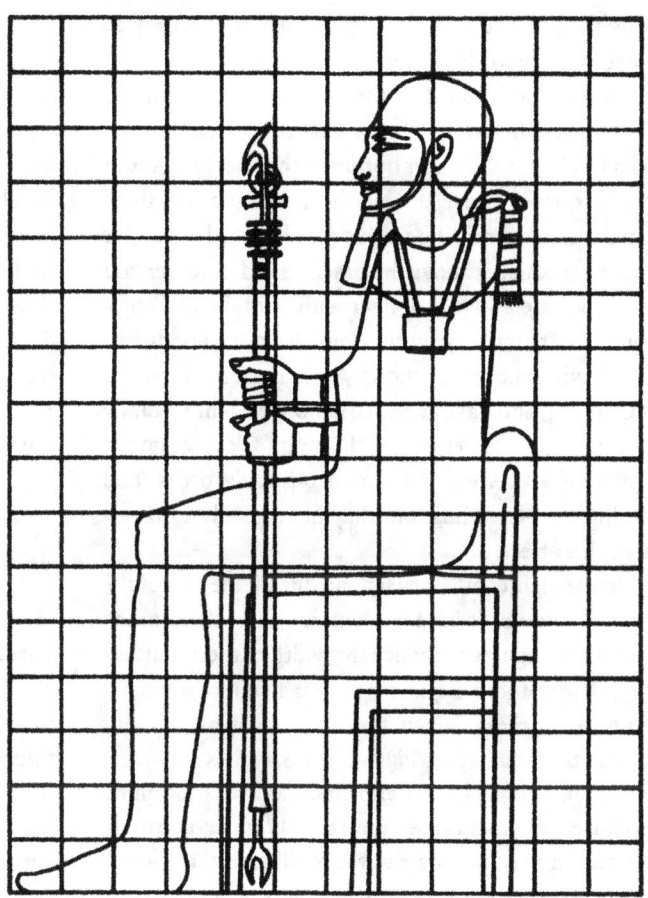

FIGURE 5.7
Seated figure of Ptah on hypothetical 14-square grid,
temple of Sety I at Abydos, nineteenth dynasty, after
Calverley 1935, Plate 27 lower register.

roughly half a square above the baseline. It is easy to work out for Middle Kingdom figures on a grid that the top of the femur near the maximum convexity of the buttocks lies around horizontal 10 and the bottom, on a level with the lower border of the kneecap, about 5 1/2 squares above the baseline, giving a length of 4 1/2 squares for the bone. But the tibia, with its upper end 5 1/2 squares above the baseline and its lower end half a square above, is longer with a total length of 5 squares. Artists in many cultures have often felt dissatisfied with the proportions given by nature to the human leg, and have achieved a more elegant result by elongating the lower part of the limb.[9] Clearly ancient Egyptian artists did the same from early times, and during the New Kingdom they increasingly exaggerated this effect.

In the eighteenth dynasty and during the rest of the New Kingdom, it became common in both standing and seated figures to reduce the width of the shoulders slightly, by about a quarter to half a square or sometimes even more, when the rear arm was brought across the body (e.g., Figs. 5.3–5.6, 5.8, 5.11–5.12; Pl. 5.1). This has been explained as foreshortening because the pose causes the rear shoulder to rotate forward and so lie closer to the midline of the body.[10] However, since foreshortening was not generally practiced by Egyptian draftsmen, the narrowing of the shoulders is more likely to have been a method for increasing the effective reach of the whole arm across the body without lengthening it disproportionately. The practice was not common in the Old or Middle Kingdoms; in major figures the width across the shoulders was usually 6 squares whatever the position of the arm (e.g., Figs. 4.11–4.12, 10.13, 10.20–10.22).

5.2. Standing and Seated Female Figures

As in the Middle Kingdom, female standing figures were drawn on grids of 18 squares (Fig. 5.8) and seated ones on grids of 14 squares (Pls. 5.2–5.3) between the baseline and hairline. The small of the back, however, tends to lie higher than in male figures,[11] and the width of the body is narrower across the shoulders and waist (Figs. 8.2–8.3, 8.5, 9.7, 9.9).[12] In other words, the distinctions between male and female figures found in the Middle Kingdom (Sec. 4.5) persist into the New Kingdom, even when the small of the back of male figures rises from horizontal 11 to 12 (Fig. 5.8).

5.3. Minor Seated Figures of the Eighteenth Dynasty

Besides the normal 14-square seated figure, which sits on a chair 5 squares high, there are others that are placed on lower chairs. These are not usually major figures in scenes; they may, for instance, be guests at a banquet, drawn on a smaller scale than the tomb owner and less important.[13] In fact, unfinished scenes show that such minor figures are most often drawn not on a grid but with the aid of a few guidelines[14] or freehand.[15] There are, however, examples with surviving grids that make it clear that the proportions of these figures are similar to those found in major standing and seated figures.

In TT 85, dating to the reigns of Thutmose III and Amenhotep II, a group of male figures sit on low stools.[16] Grid traces on their wigs can be used to reconstruct a complete grid (Fig. 5.9). This shows that

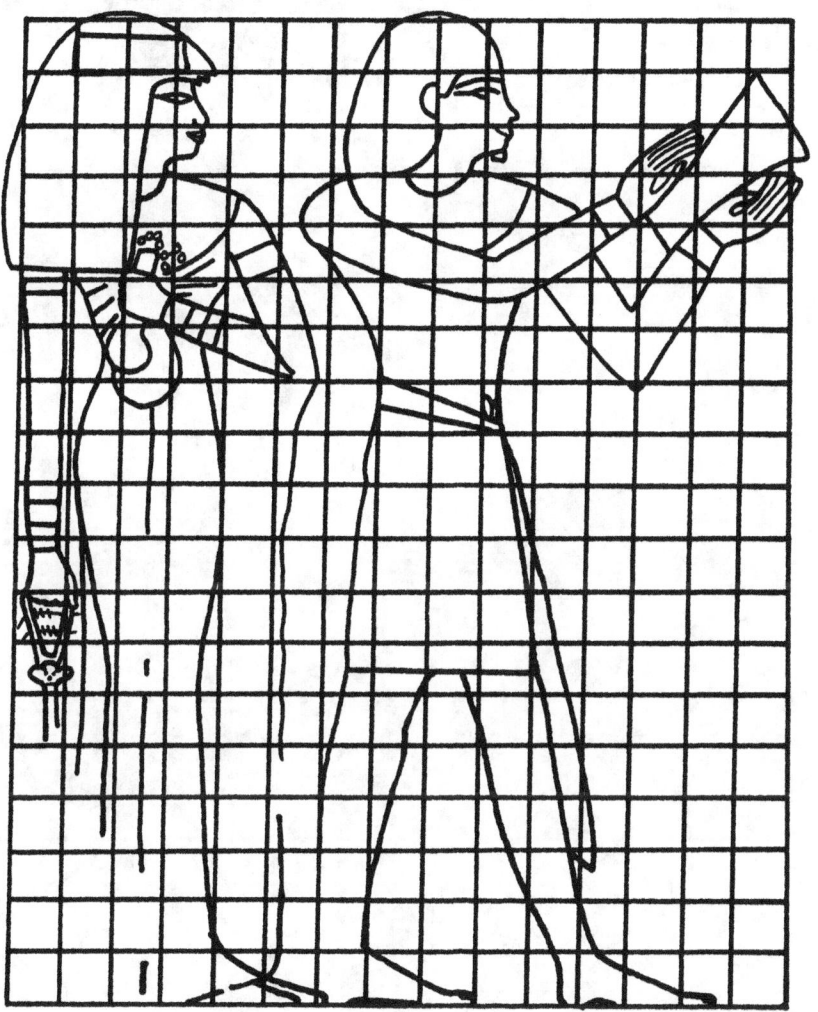

FIGURE 5.8
Standing figures of Nakht and his wife on grid
completed from surviving traces, TT 52, eighteenth
dynasty, after Mackay 1917, Plate 15 no. 6.

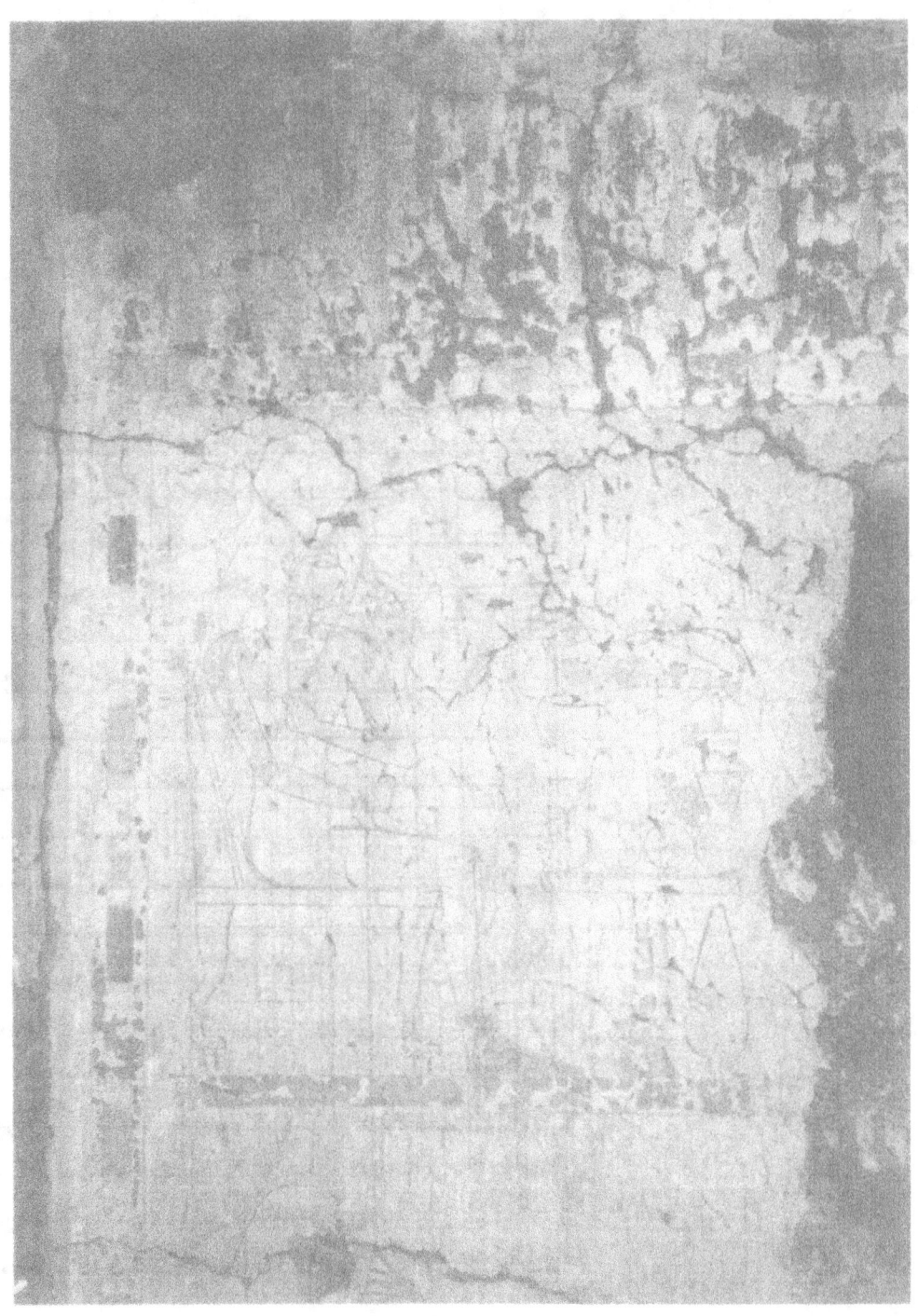

PLATE 5.2
Seated female figure on original grid, TT 89, eighteenth
dynasty, Mond photo11006, reproduced by permission
of the Griffith Institute.

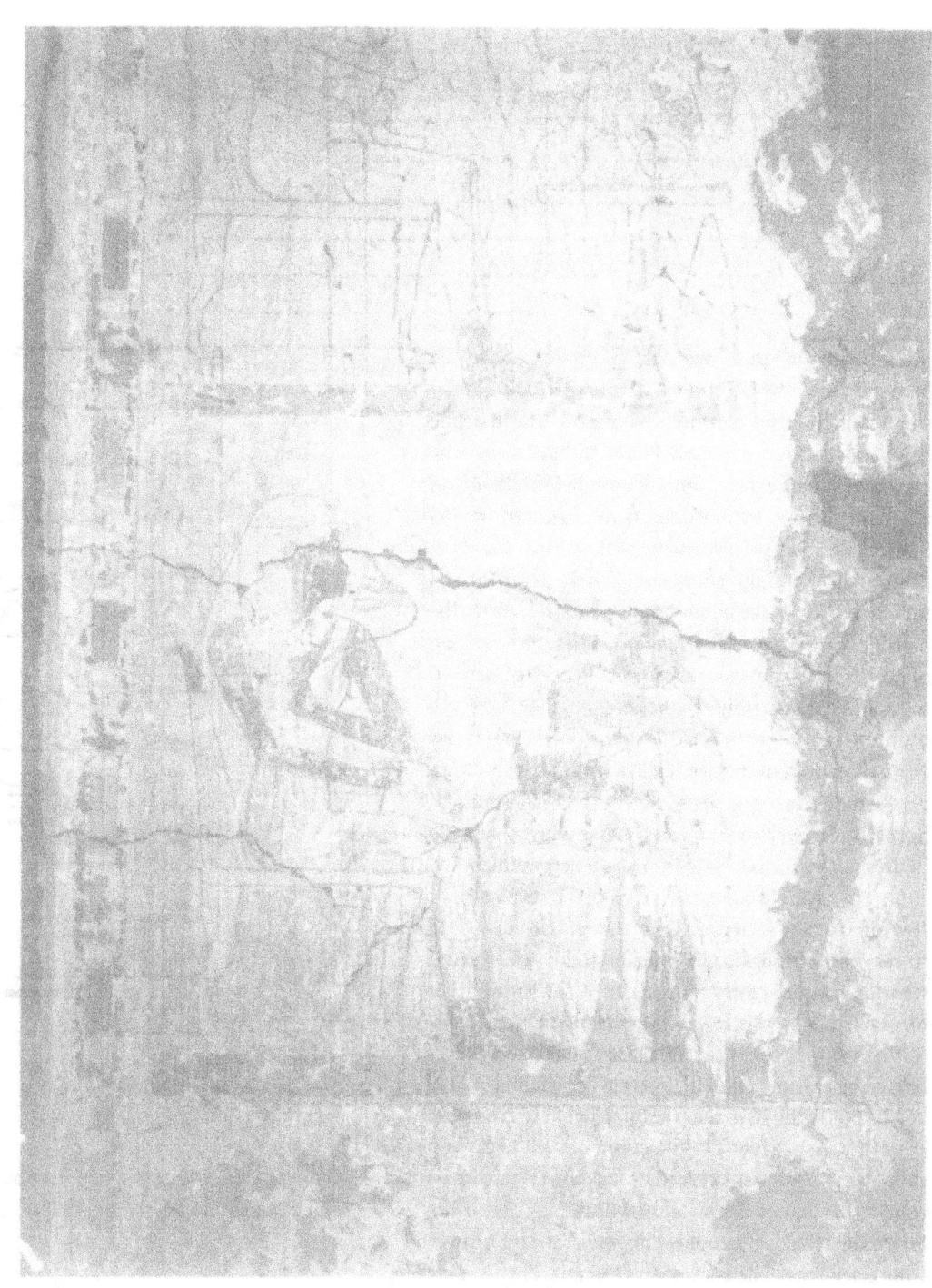

PLATE 5.3
Seated female figure on original grid, TT 89,
eighteenth dynasty, Mond photo 11013, reproduced
by permission of the Griffith Institute.

the tops of the stools are only 3 squares above the baseline; the lower borders of the buttocks are 9 squares below the hairline, making a total hairline height of 12 squares for each figure. The junction of the neck and shoulders is 2 squares and the nipple region 4 squares below the hairline. As in 14-square seated figures, the belt is pushed up at the front above its position in standing figures, so that here the front and the back are on the same level 7 squares below the hairline. The knee in these examples lies in the region of horizontal 6, but since the lower leg above horizontal 3 does not contribute to the height of the figure, the position of the knee in relation to the horizontal is less exact than in standing figures. The width of the shoulders across horizontal 9, equivalent to 15 in a standing figure, is just over 5 1/2 squares, in line with other male figures where the rear arm is brought across the body.

In TT 200, dating to the reign of Thutmose III, a row of women seated on low chairs also have grid traces on their wigs from which a grid can be reconstructed for the figures (Fig. 5.10).[17] This shows that for each figure the lower borders of the buttocks, resting on the top of the seat, are roughly 9 squares below the hairline as usual, but that the chair is only 4, not 5, squares high, so that the total height of the figure is only 13 squares. The junction of the neck and shoulder is 2 squares below the hairline and the breast roughly 4 squares below, although in one case it lies approximately 4 1/2 squares down, a variant known from elsewhere. The knee is about 6 squares above the baseline. An axial line runs through the front of the ear and down the front edge of the wig. The width across the shoulders along horizontal 10 is less than 5 squares, since women were normally drawn as more slender than men.

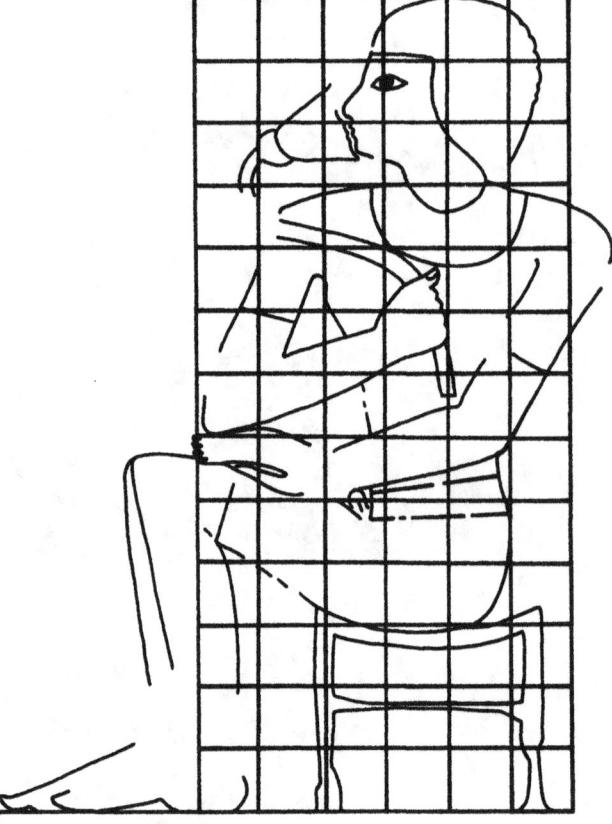

FIGURE 5.9
Seated figure on grid completed from surviving traces, TT 85, eighteenth dynasty, after Mond photo. 18030.

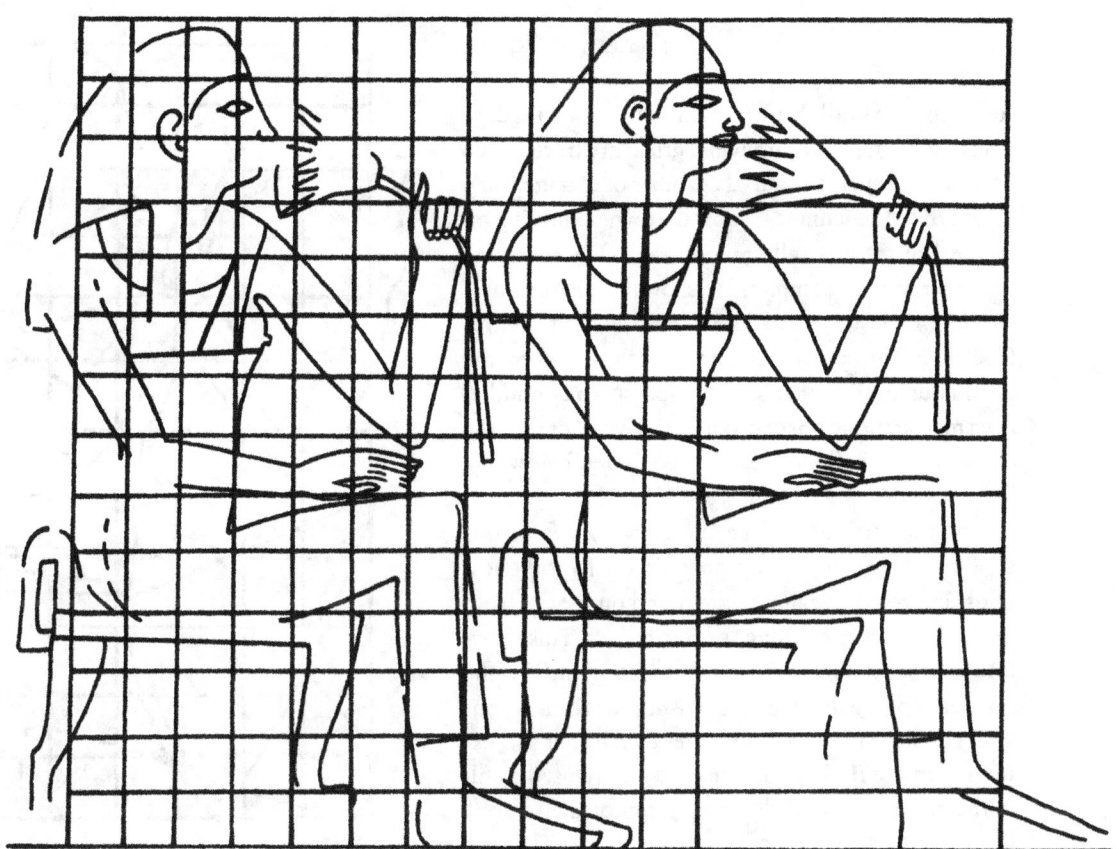

FIGURE 5.10
Seated figures on grid completed from surviving traces,
TT 200, eighteenth dynasty, after MMA photo. T 3545.

5.4. Kneeling Figures

Just as in the Middle Kingdom, so in the New Kingdom kneeling figures on surviving grids are rare. Two figures in TT 353, the burial chamber of Hatshepsut's great official Senenmut,[18] show the owner kneeling on the heel of his vertically raised foot.[19] The surviving grid traces can be completed to show that these figures consist of 11 squares as in Middle Kingdom figures (Sec. 4.6; Fig. 5.11). Senenmut is shown with the pendulous breasts that signify a prosperous middle-aged man at the height of his career. Because of this, the nipple on each figure lies 4 3/4 squares below the hairline rather than 4 squares.

The proportions of other kneeling figures of this type can be examined by analysis on hypothetical grids. Interesting examples are found on blocks from the so-called *chapelle rouge* of Hatshepsut. This structure had probably been intended to stand in the sanctuary of the main temple of Amun at Karnak, but after Hatshepsut's death it was rejected by her successor Thutmose III. Instead, the blocks were used as fill in the construction of the third pylon of the temple, from where they were recovered this century. They are now on display in the open-air museum at Karnak.[20] Some of the scenes on these blocks show figures of the king kneeling before a seated god, all on the same baseline.[21] If a 14-square hypothetical grid is placed on the seated figures, the proportions are as one would expect for the period: horizontal 12 passes through the junction of the neck and shoulders; 10 through the nipple region; 6 through or near the top of the knee; 5 near or along the top of the seat (Figs. 5.12, 8.3). When the grid is extended over the associated kneeling figure, horizontal 11 runs through the hairline, the junction of

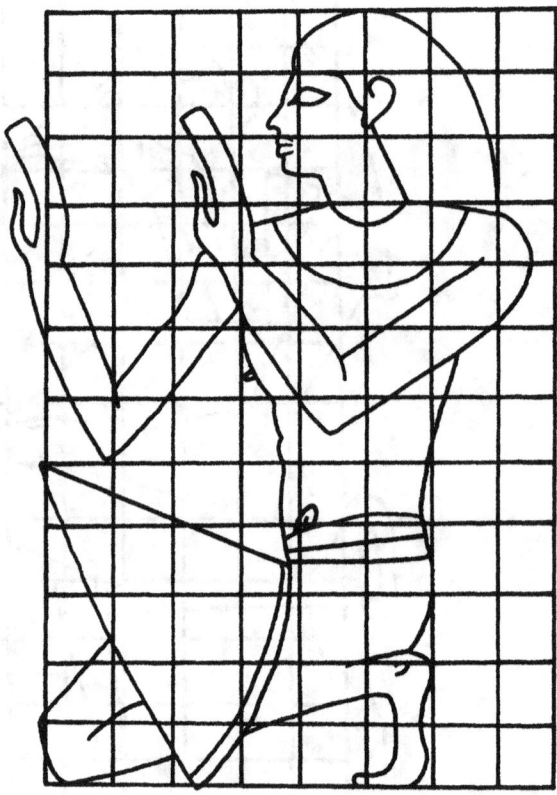

FIGURE 5.11
Kneeling figure of Senenmut on grid completed from surviving traces, TT 353, eighteenth dynasty, after MMA photo. M8C 183.

FIGURE 5.12
Scene from a block of Hatshepsut's *chapelle rouge* with a hypothetical 14-square grid calculated for the seated figure, Karnak, eighteenth dynasty, after author's photograph.

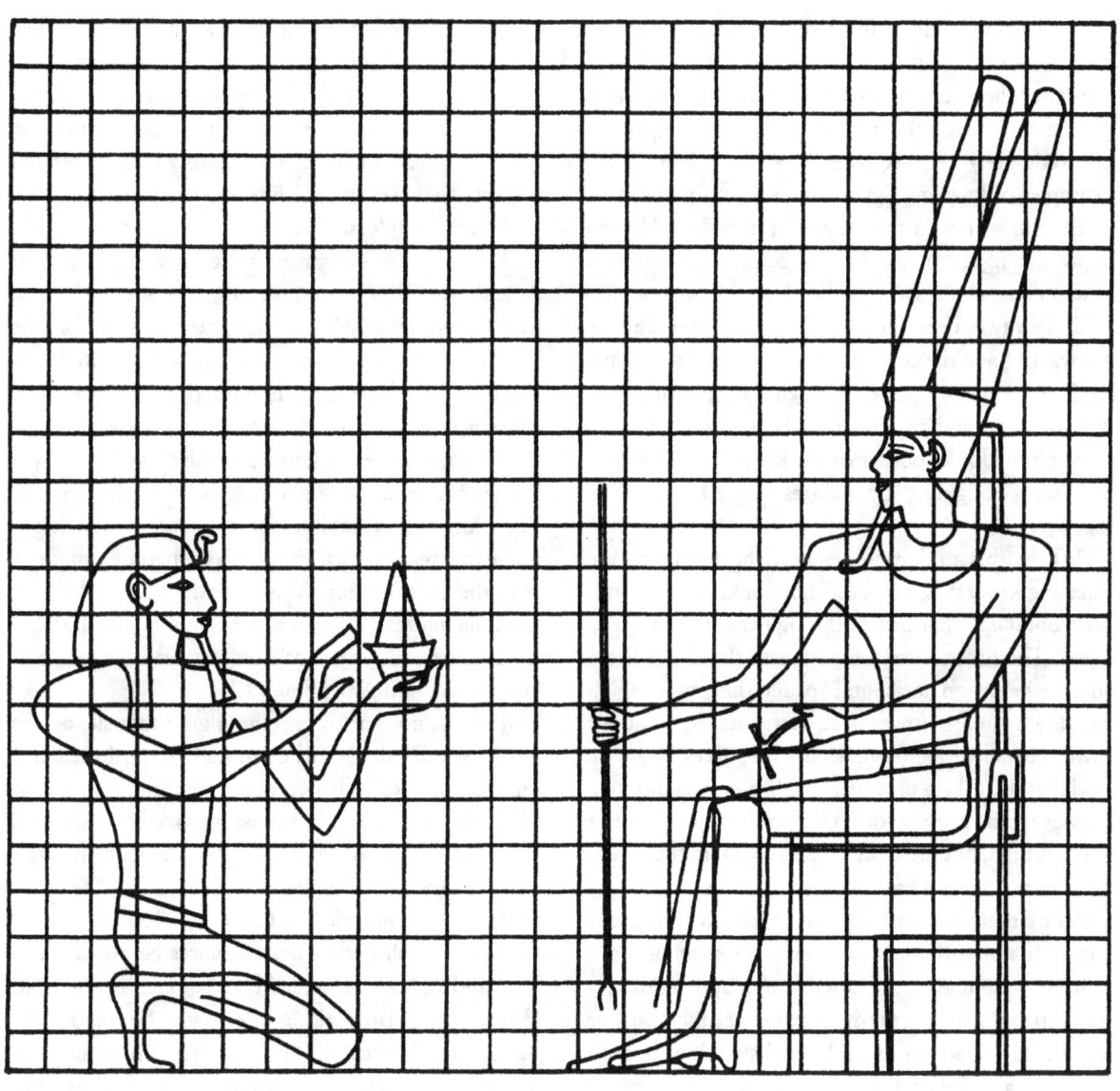

the neck and shoulders lies 2 squares below, and the nipple region is another 2 squares down. The lower border of the buttocks is roughly 8 3/4 squares below the hairline with the height of the foot equal to approximately 2 1/4 squares, as we have seen in the examples of kneeling figures that survive on grids.

Several scenes in the temple of Sety I at Abydos show the figure of the king kneeling between two seated gods, all on the same baseline.[22] If a 14-square grid is drawn over the seated figures, they can be shown to have the proportions expected for this period: horizontal 12 passes through the junction of the neck and shoulders; 10 near the nipple region; 6 through the lower border of the kneecap. The top of the seat is roughly 5 1/2 squares above the baseline (Sec. 5.1).

Where this grid passes across the figure of the kneeling king, it is, however, horizontal 12, and not horizontal 11, that passes through the hairline (Fig. 5.13). The junction of the neck and shoulders lies 2 squares below on horizontal 10, and the nipple region roughly 2 squares lower near horizontal 8, while the lower border of the buttocks lies 9 squares down on horizontal 3. These proportions, then, are traditional. However, the raised foot on which the figure sits is 3 squares high, not the 2 1/4 squares found in the earlier 11 square kneeling figures.

So by the nineteenth dynasty, artists had added 1 square to the traditional 11 squares for kneeling royal figures by elongating the raised foot to approximately 3 squares and making the distance between the hairline and the lower border of the buttocks a full 9 squares. Whether a kneeling figure was drawn on 11 or 12 squares is reasonably easy to distinguish by eye. In an

11-square figure, the distance between the hairline and the junction of the neck and shoulders, which is 2 squares, should be only slightly less than the height of the foot at 2 1/4 squares; in the 12-square figure, the foot of 3 squares will be considerably longer than the distance between the hairline and the junction of the neck and shoulders.

A spot check on some of the kneeling figures of Amenhotep III in the temple of Luxor shows that the foot is considerably longer than the distance from the hairline to the junction of the neck and shoulders. Analysis on a 12-square hypothetical grid produces canonical proportions: horizontal 10 passes through the junction of the neck and shoulders, and the lower border of the buttocks is 9 squares below the hairline. The width across the shoulders is 6 squares. The height of the foot is 3 squares. This analysis therefore suggests that the extra square was already being added to kneeling figures by the time of Amenhotep III, and that the change must have occurred between the reigns of Hatshepsut and Amenhotep III.

The second type of kneeling figure that sits on the lower leg and foot placed horizontally along the baseline only occurs for private, not royal, figures. A few examples of figures in this posture survive on squared grids from the eighteenth dynasty. The majority consist of 10 squares from hairline to baseline,[23] as in the Middle Kingdom (Pl. 5.4; Fig. 5.14). The junction of the neck and shoulders lies 2 squares below the hairline, and the breast a further 2 squares below that. Horizontal 1 runs along the lower border of the buttocks and the calf of the lower leg. Where the axial line survives, it runs through the front of the ear and along the front edge of the forward tress of the wig.

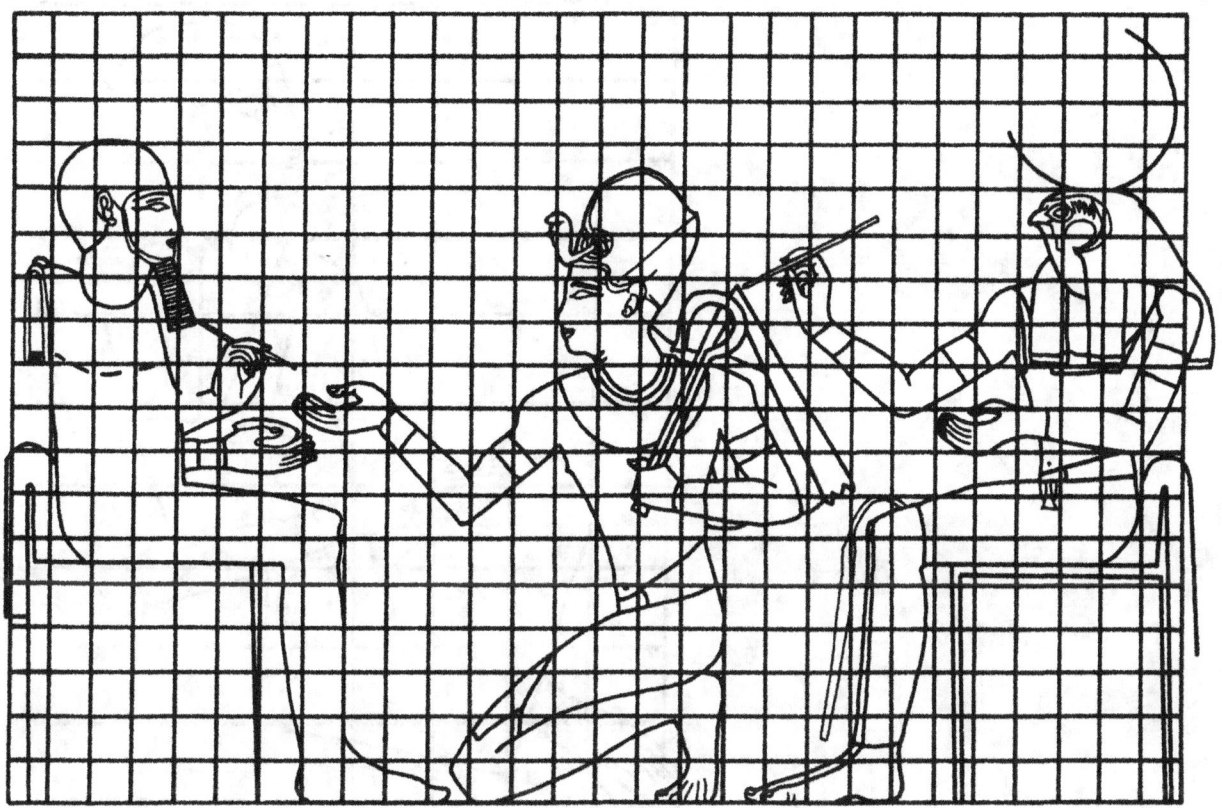

FIGURE 5.13
Scene with a hypothetical 14-square grid calculated
for the seated figure, temple of Sety I at Abydos,
nineteenth dynasty, after Calverley 1958, Plate 25.

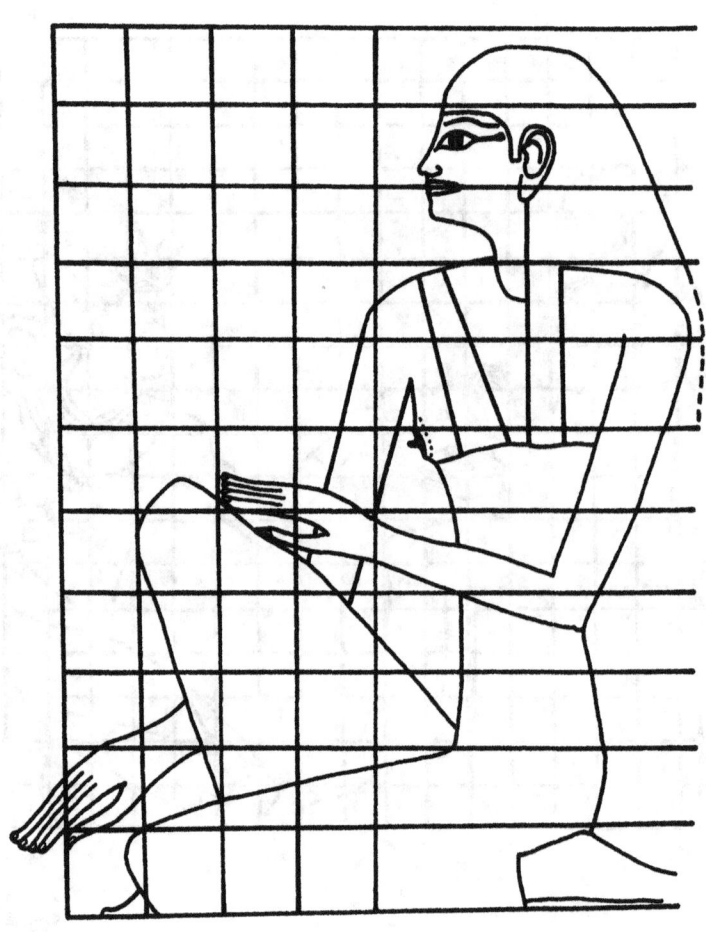

FIGURE 5.14

Kneeling figure from a fragment of wall painting with
surviving grid traces, Walters Art Gallery, Baltimore
32.2, eighteenth dynasty, after museum photograph.

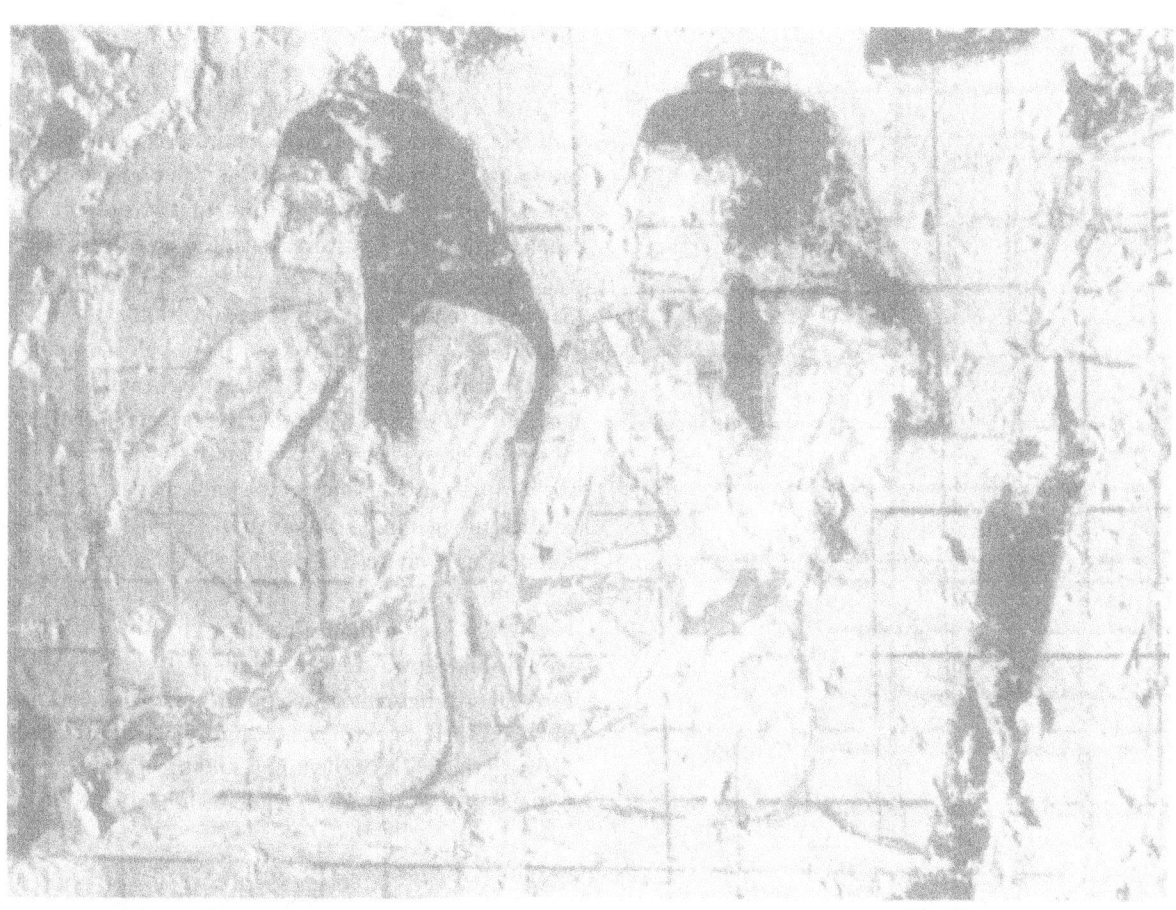

PLATE 5.4
Two kneeling female figures on original grid, TT 154,
eighteenth dynasty, author's photograph.

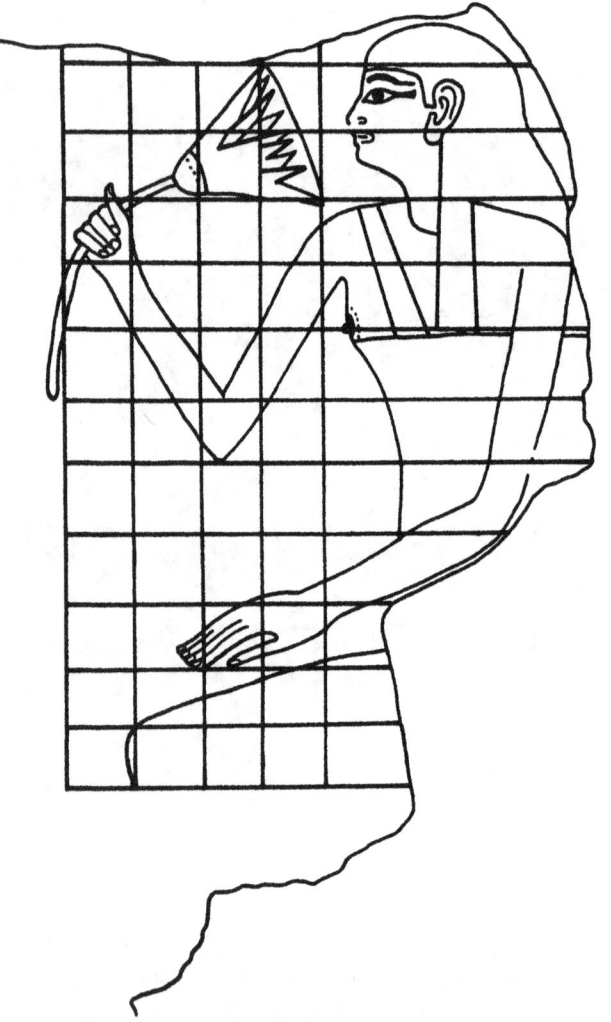

FIGURE 5.15

Kneeling figure from a fragment of wall painting with surviving grid traces, Brooklyn Museum acc. no. 05.390, eighteenth dynasty, after museum photograph.

The horizontal lower leg is roughly 6 squares from knee to heel. The knee of the obliquely raised leg lies 5 to 5 1/2 squares above the baseline.

One fragment, Brooklyn Museum no. 05.390, which probably belongs to a group of wall paintings dating to the early eighteenth dynasty,[24] portrays a woman in an apparently similar posture, but the grid traces show that there are 11, not 10, squares between the hairline and the baseline (Fig. 5.15).[25] The junction of the neck and shoulders is 2 squares and the nipple 4 squares below the hairline as usual. The buttocks and foot are lost, but comparison with other figures seated on their horizontal lower legs suggests that the lower border of the buttocks and the back of the thigh met the calf and the heel along a line 1 square above the baseline. The figure is unlikely to be kneeling with the foot raised vertically as the number of squares might suggest, because in such a figure the upper line of the thigh would slope upward more obliquely. It seems, therefore, that the figure is sitting on the foot held horizontally, and that an extra square must have been added between the levels of the nipple and the lower border of the buttocks, the effect being to elongate the back.

5.5. Animal-headed Figures

In Egyptian art a number of deities are represented with human bodies and animal heads. In human-headed figures the proportions are based on the distance between the soles of the feet and the hairline. When it comes to determining the proportions of animal-headed figures, there is no obvious hairline to act as the upper point of measurement. No examples are preserved on grids from the Middle Kingdom, but

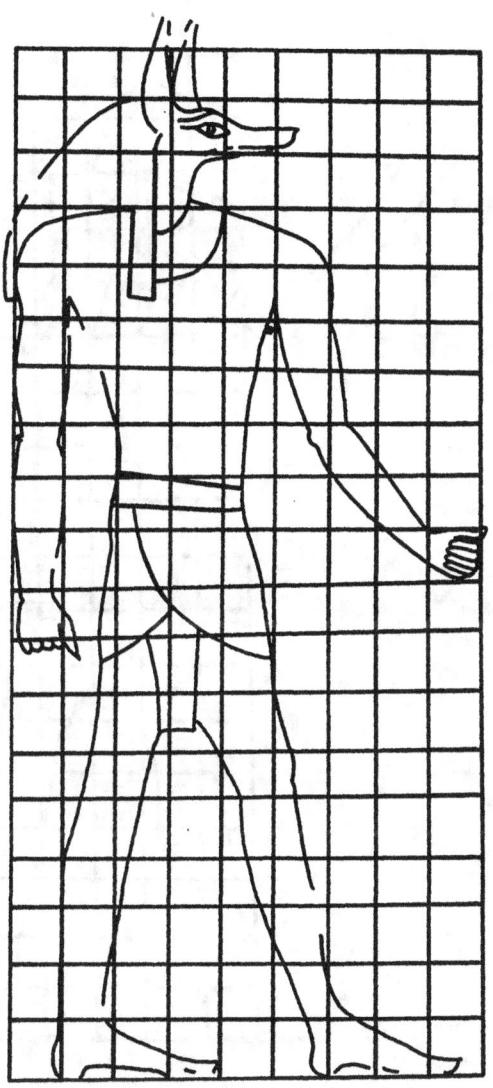

FIGURE 5.16

Jackal-headed figure on grid completed from surviving traces, astronomical ceiling, TT 353, eighteenth dynasty, after MMA photo. M8C 191.

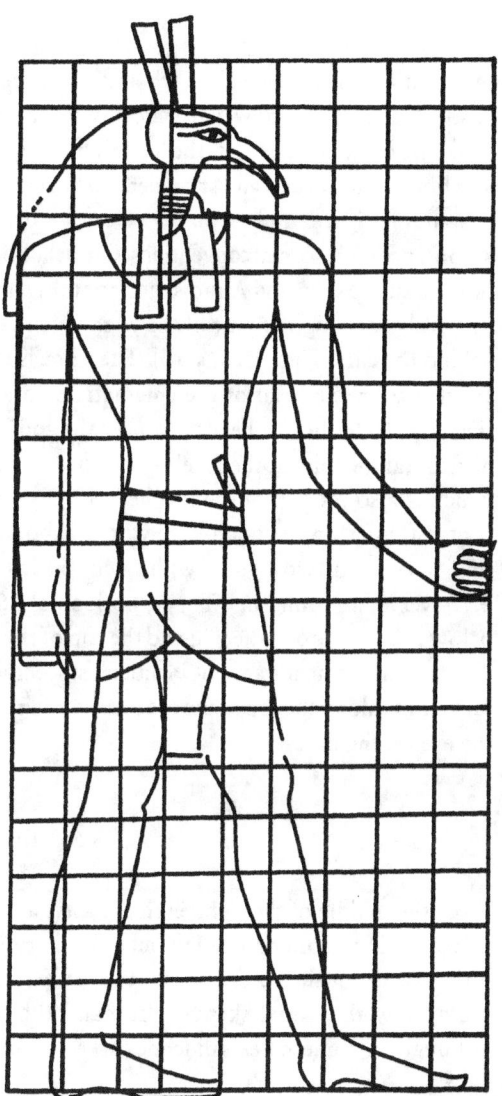

FIGURE 5.17

Seth-animal-headed figure on grid completed from surviving traces, astronomical ceiling, TT 353, eighteenth dynasty, after MMA photo. M8C 191.

some survive from the eighteenth and nineteenth dynasties, which show how artists dealt with this problem.[26] As one would expect, the human body up to the junction of the "neck" and shoulders on horizontal 16 in standing figures and 12 on seated ones is drawn in accordance with normal conventions. On jackal-headed figures, such as the god Anubis, horizontal 18 runs at the level of the highest part of the wig, which lies just behind the ears (Figs. 5.16, 5.19). The same is true of a figure with the head of the enigmatic Seth animal (Fig. 5.17). On the ibis-headed form of the god Thoth, horizontal 18 runs at the level of the top of the wig, which is also the top of the ibis head (Fig. 5.18). By contrast, in examples of a figure with a baboon head (Fig. 5.19) and two figures with falcon heads (Figs. 5.20–5.21), all found in TT 353, horizontal 18 runs below both the top of the wig and the top of the head. The two falcon heads are not identical, since horizontal 18 runs along the top of the eye on one and through the eye on the other.

5.6. Guidelines

From the middle of the eighteenth dynasty, it became increasingly uncommon to lay out subsidiary scenes on grids. Unfinished work shows that instead artists often drew the initial sketches freehand (Pl. 1.5),[27] although in some cases guidelines were used as an aid.[28]

In TT 42, a scene showing rites being carried out before the mummy is laid out in five registers.[29] Each row of figures is drawn on five horizontal lines marking the top of the head, the junction of the neck and

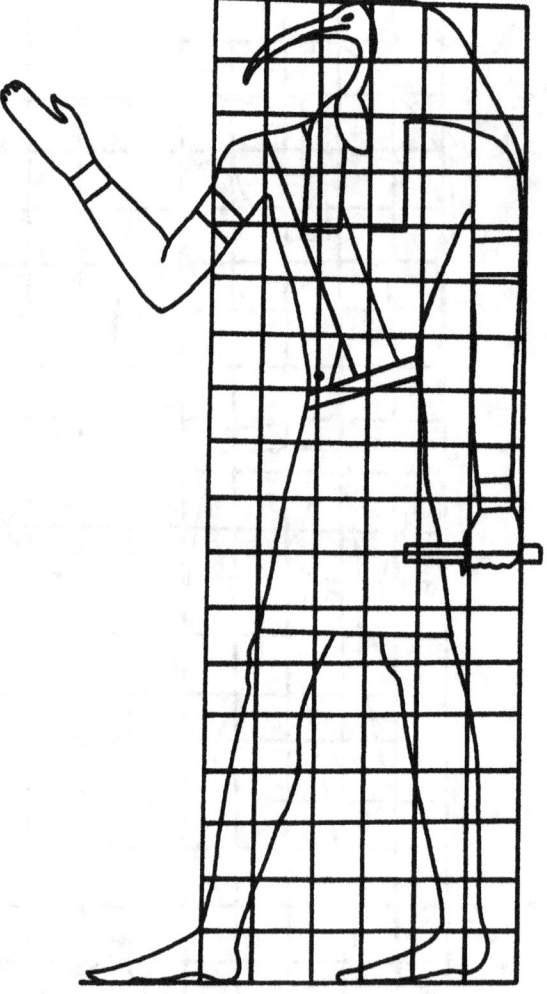

FIGURE 5.18

Ibis-headed figure on grid completed from surviving traces, temple of Ramesses II, Abydos, nineteenth dynasty, after author's photograph.

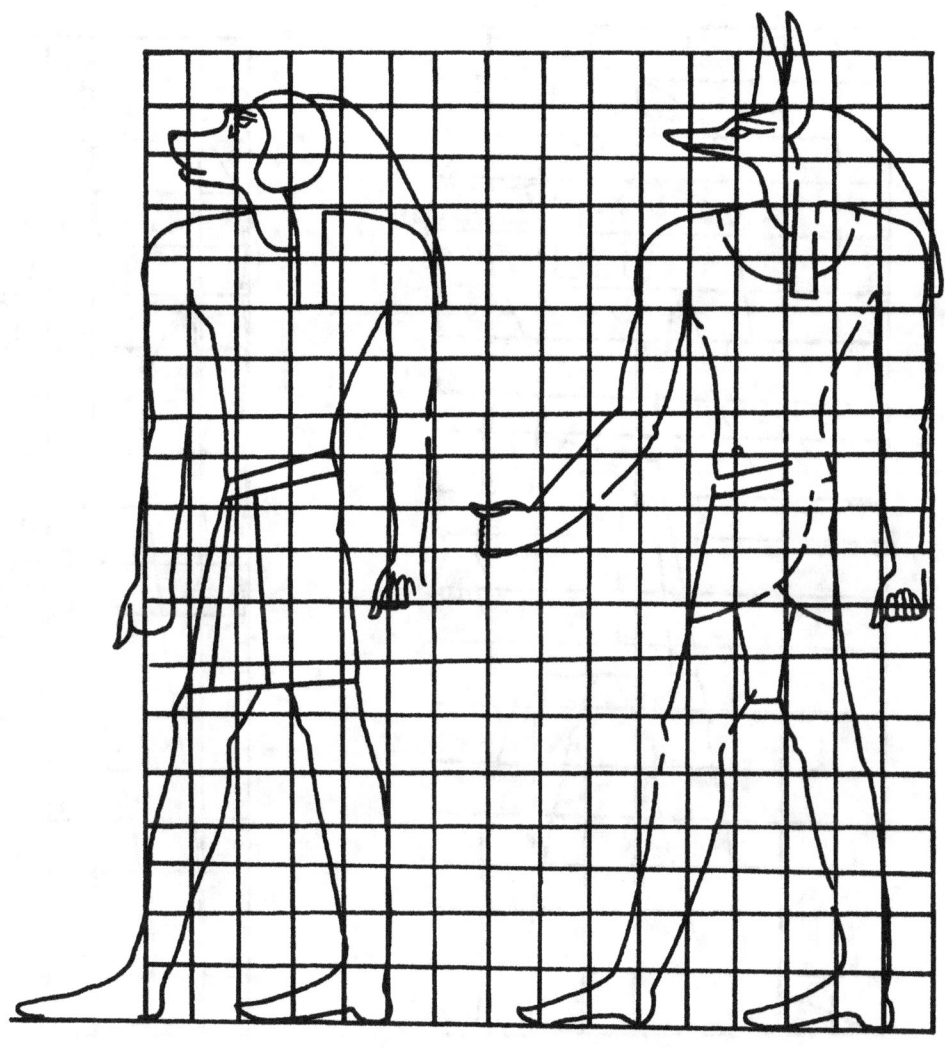

FIGURE 5.19
Baboon-headed and jackal-headed figures on grid
completed from surviving traces, astronomical ceiling, TT
353, eighteenth dynasty, after MMA photo. M8C 189.

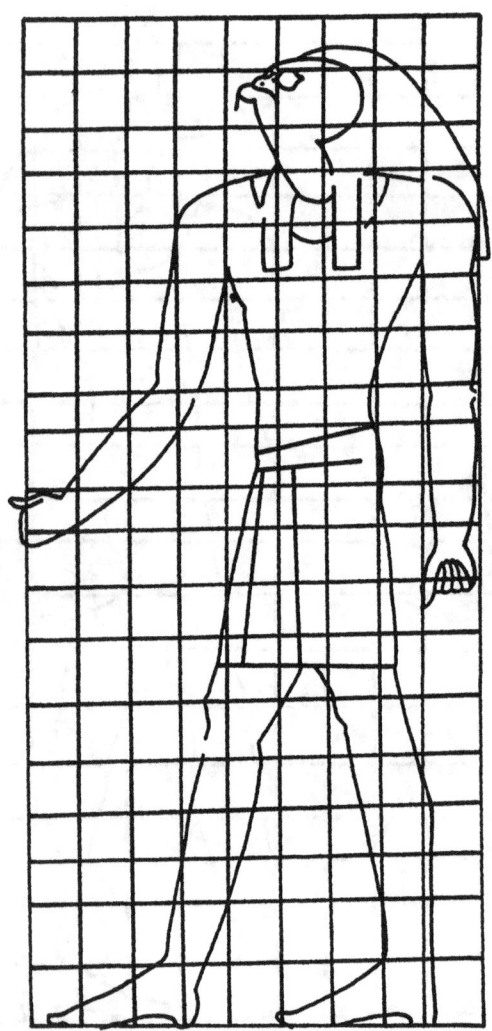

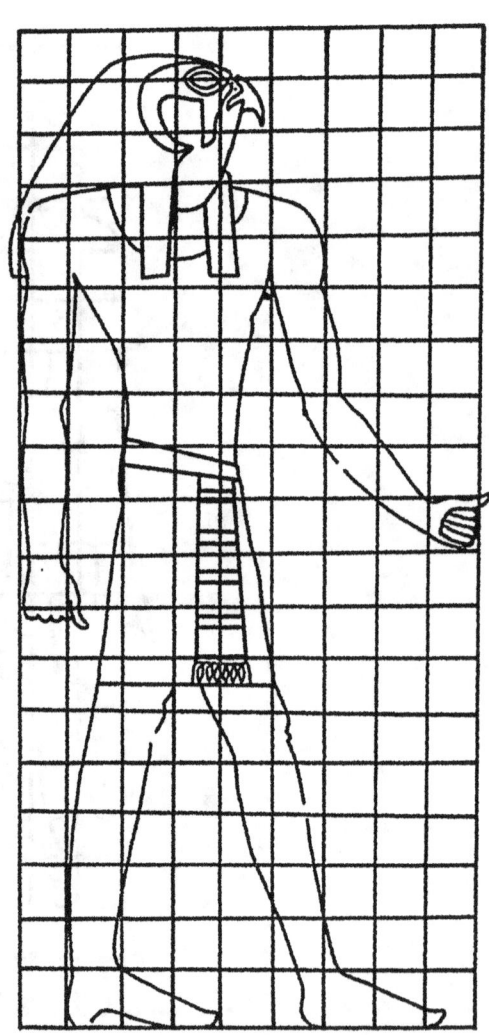

FIGURE 5.20
Falcon-headed figure on grid completed from surviving traces, astronomical ceiling, TT 353, eighteenth dynasty, after MMA photo. M8C 189.

FIGURE 5.21
Falcon-headed figure on grid completed from surviving traces, astronomical ceiling, TT 353, eighteenth dynasty, after MMA photo. M8C 191.

shoulders, the lower border of the buttocks, the bottom of the kilt, and the baseline. If the uppermost line is taken as the equivalent of horizontal 19 on a grid, the lines marking the shoulders and lower border of the buttocks run approximately at the levels of 15 1/2 to 16 1/4 squares and 10 squares respectively above the baseline, close to the position of the junction of the neck and shoulders and the lower border of the buttocks on an eighteenth-dynasty grid. The kilt lines run along levels equivalent to 6 3/4 to 7 squares. It is difficult to see how the spacing of these lines was determined. The buttock line lies just above half the height of the figure, and the kilt line is somewhat more than a third of the same height. An approximation to the shoulder line can be obtained as five-sixths of the total height. However, there are slight differences in the spacing of the lines in each register, suggesting that they were not measured with great precision.

In TT 92 there is a wall laid out in four registers,[30] each with two guidelines marking the levels of the top of the head, and the junction of the neck and shoulders. In two of the registers, a third guideline marks the bottom of the kilt, while in the two others the top of the knee is marked by an additional guideline (Pl. 5.5). The registers were meant to contain rows of figures, but the draftsman never got beyond sketching in the first figure in each register. Measurement shows that the lines are slightly differently spaced in each of the four registers. Their heights above the baseline can be converted into numbers of grid squares by taking the top line as horizontal 19. Then the shoulder lines in the four registers vary from approximately 15 to 15 3/4 squares, instead of 16 as expected on a grid, and the kilt or knee lines from just above horizontal 6 to just

above 7. In registers 1 and 2, counting down from the top, these lowest lines lie at approximately 6 2/3 and 7 squares on a grid, running along the bottom of the kilts. In registers 3 and 4, the lines are lower, at just above 6 to 6 1/2 squares, and pass through the knee below the kilt. In the top three registers, the actual tops of the heads of the figures have been drawn lower than the guidelines, while in the fourth the junction of the neck and shoulders lies above the shoulder line. In other words, the guidelines have been drawn with little precision; there is too much space between the two upper lines in each register, while the third line in the series runs at levels more appropriate to the bottom of the kilt in the two top registers and to the top of the knee in the two bottom ones. The artist has adjusted his figures accordingly.

In TT 108, one unfinished scene shows a sketch of figures performing rites before statues of the tomb owner (Pl. 5.6).[31] There is only one register drawn with figures. It contains five guidelines above the baseline: one running above the heads of the figures; one at approximately shoulder height; one roughly marking the lower border of the buttocks; one running through the knees; and one marking the top of the statue bases. The spacing of the lines varies slightly from left to right, but at the left-hand end of the scene the shoulder line is roughly five-sixths of the height of the upper line, the buttock line half, and the knee line a third. However, as the upper line runs above the heads of the figures, the knee line in fact places the knee a good deal higher than a third of the hairline height, giving long lower legs to those figures with their feet on the baseline. The legs of the figures that are raised on statue bases are, of course, shorter.

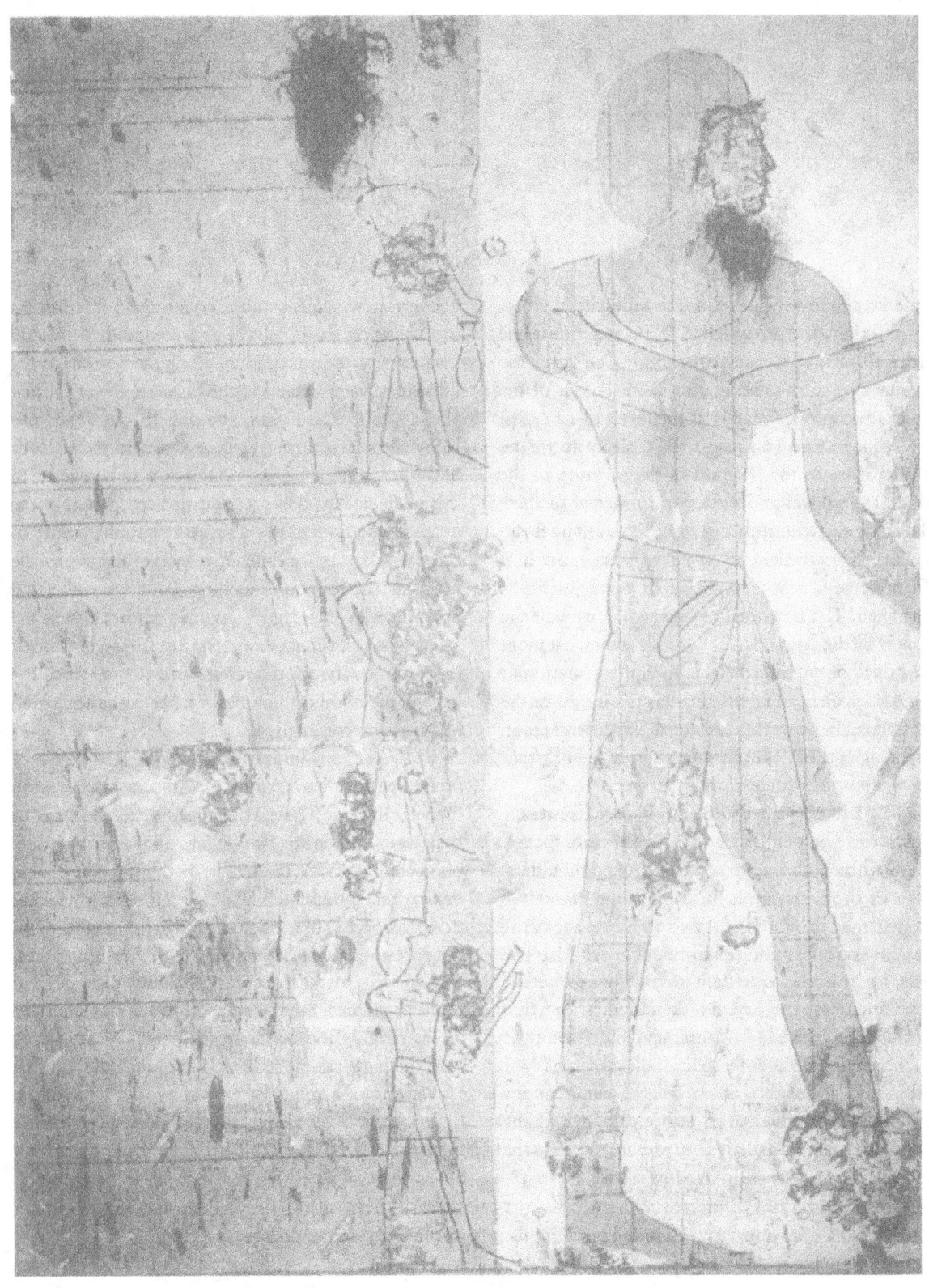

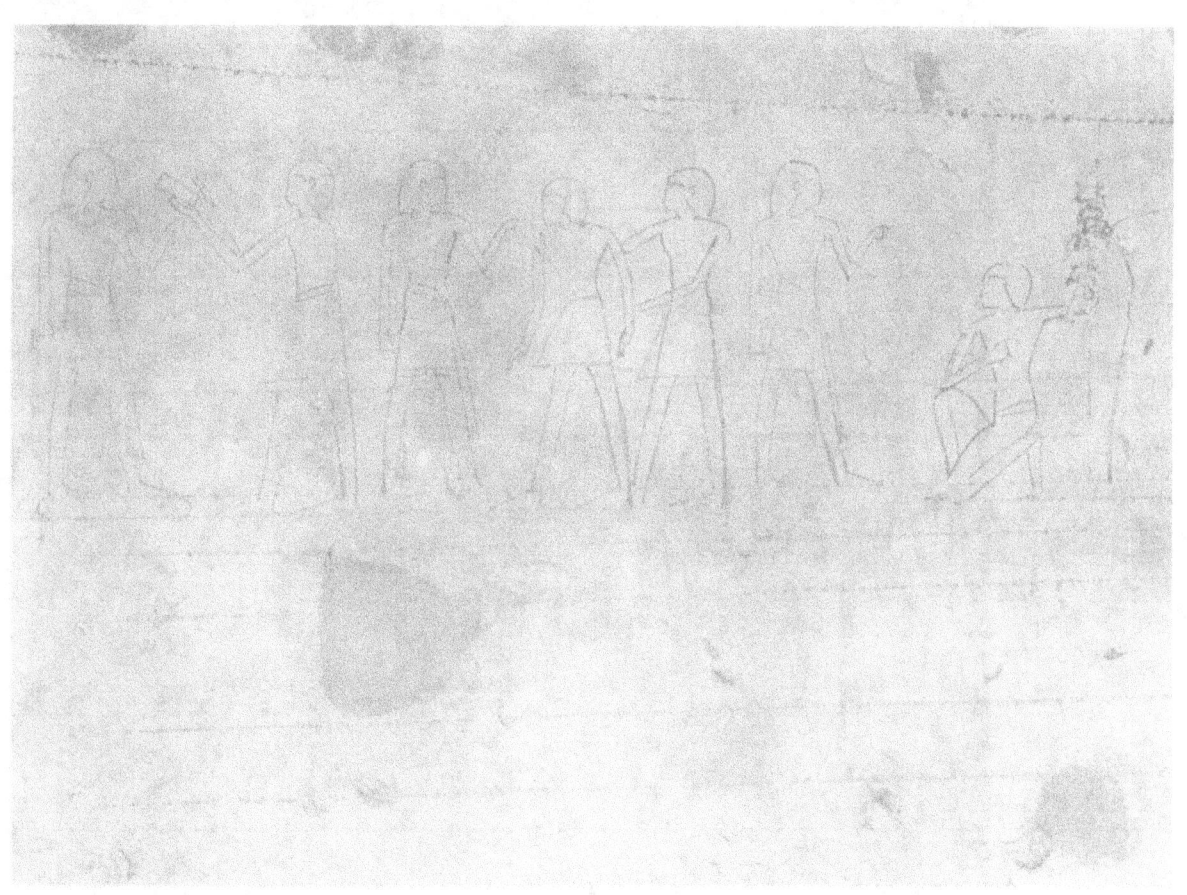

PLATE 5.5
Three registers laid out with guidelines, TT 92,
eighteenth dynasty, Mond photo 2067, reproduced
by permission of the Griffith Institute.

PLATE 5.6
Scene with guidelines, TT 108, eighteenth dynasty,
MMA photo T 3403, photograph by the Egyptian
Expedition, courtesy of the Metropolitan Museum of
Art, New York.

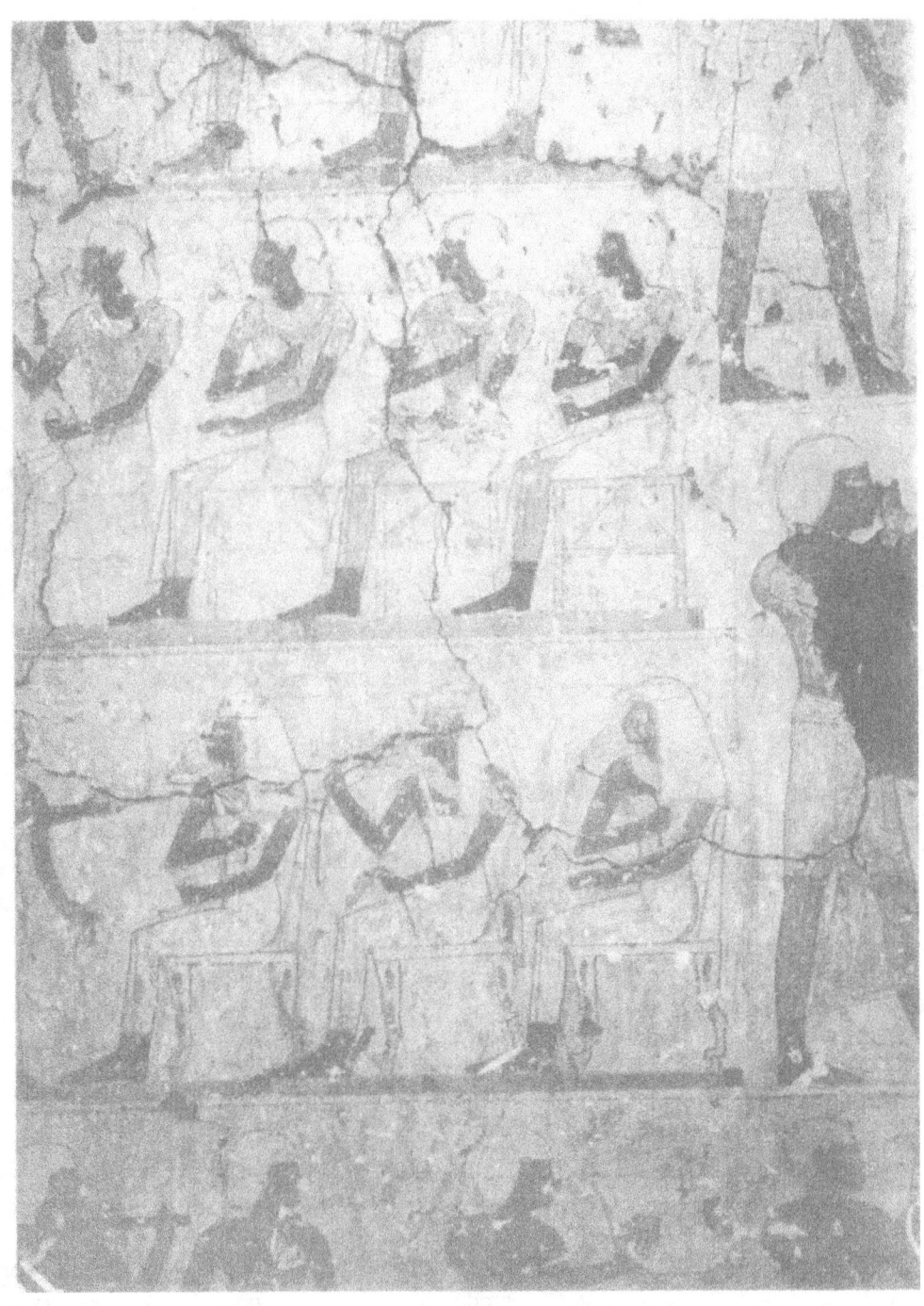

PLATE 5.7
*Scene with guidelines, TT 89, eighteenth dynasty,
Mond photo 11011, reproduced by permission of the
Griffith Institute.*

In a banquet scene in TT 89, three registers of seated guests are drawn with the aid of a few guidelines (Pl. 5.7).[32] One horizontal runs through the tops of the heads, one through the junctions of the neck and shoulders and one along the tops of the seats. At this period, seated figures on a grid usually occupied 15 squares to the top of the head with the junction of the neck and shoulders on 12, at four-fifths of the total height, and the top of the seat on horizontal 5, at a third of the total height. The guidelines on these figures are simply drawn at levels approximately four-fifths and one-third of the height to the tops of their heads.

These examples show that guidelines in subsidiary scenes were not measured and drawn with any great care, and that if they were too inaccurate, the draftsman might choose to draw his figures according to the proportions he knew to be correct, virtually ignoring the lines. On the whole, guidelines were used to lay out rows of figures, and one purpose was probably to line up different figures in these rows to get the key parts of the body roughly level. The top of the head rather than the hairline may have been marked, because by the mid-eighteenth dynasty this point normally lay on a grid horizontal, which had not been the case earlier. Further, the types of figures found in the various subsidiary scenes laid out on guidelines were unlikely to wear elaborate headgear that might obscure the top of the head.

5.7. The Length of the Forearm

One of Iversen's main contentions is that good artists always measured the length of the forearm precisely,

so that whatever the position of the forearm was in relation to the body, it comprised 5 1/4 squares from the elbow to the middle fingertip, or 5 squares when the distance was reduced because of foreshortening of the relaxed hand.[33] I was interested to find out if there was in fact a fixed length for the forearm and whether it really was invariable. In order to investigate the matter, it was first necessary to decide how to measure the forearm. Iversen used no one way to measure its length, but took his measurements from either the elbow bone or the elbow crease, along the axis of the arm or diagonally across the arm (Sec. 2.2.6). This must have given rise to the temptation to adopt the method in any given instance that produces the desired result.

I decided always to measure from the elbow-bone[34] to the fingertips along the long axis of the forearm, rather than to measure directly to the fingertips in whatever direction they might lie as a result of the flexion of the wrist and hand. When the arm is straight, the elbow crease and elbow bone lie opposite each other on the same level, but when it is bent, the crease lies nearer than the bone to the fingers. It therefore makes a difference which is taken as the point of measurement. To be consistent, it should always be the same point, and I have chosen to use the elbow bone. This seems to be in keeping with how the Egyptians themselves might have thought of the extent of their own forearms as an equivalent of the small cubit; it would have been convenient to make rough estimations of length by laying the forearm flat with the palm down, along whatever was to be measured, and reckoning from the elbow bone to the tip of the middle finger.

I began by measuring the forearms in four samples of New Kingdom published material from the temple of Amenhotep III at Luxor,[35] the temple of Sety I at Abydos,[36] the temples of Ramesses III at Medinet Habu[37] and in the main Amun enclosure at Karnak,[38] and the temple of Khonsu at Karnak decorated by Ramesses XI, Herihor, and Pinudjem I.[39] In each publication, I measured the elbow-to-fingertip distances on all the undamaged forearms with open hands on all male and female standing, seated, and kneeling figures, excluding those where the wrist was excessively bent back. I then calculated the grid size for each figure by dividing the hairline height by the number of squares appropriate for the pose of the figure. The length of the forearm from elbow bone to fingertips could then be divided by the grid square size to obtain the number of squares in the forearm. Since Iversen claimed that straight hands were longer than relaxed ones by a quarter of a square, I have kept the two types of hand separate in my samples.

In the sample from the temple of Luxor, the lengths of the forearm with a straight hand ranged from 4.8 to 5.2 squares with a mean of 5.0 squares, while those with a relaxed hand ranged from 4.6 to 5.5 squares with a mean of 5.1 squares. In the temple of Sety I at Abydos, the range for the forearm with a straight hand was 4.9 to 5.8 squares with a mean of 5.4 squares, and with the relaxed hand 4.5 to 5.8 squares with a mean of 5.0 squares. The sample from the reign of Ramesses III produced a range for the forearm with a straight hand of 4.6 to 6.3 squares with a mean of 5.4 squares, and with a relaxed hand, 4.4 to 6.8 with a mean of 5.3 squares. The final sample from the very end of the New Kingdom gives a range for the straight-handed fore-

arm of 4.6 to 5.9 squares with a mean of 5.0 squares, and for the forearm with a relaxed hand of 4.3 to 5.4 squares with a mean of 4.8 squares.

What this analysis shows is that the length of the forearm varies and is not exactly drawn to conform to an unchanging number of squares. This is hardly surprising, as many artists no doubt simply drew the forearm by eye so that it looked right. Often female figures have shorter forearms than male ones, which actually reflects natural proportions. But there are frequently compositional reasons for changes in the length of the forearm. Sometimes artists wished to emphasize the function of the arms—for instance, the gesture of adoration, when the arms are raised in front of the face—and so they lengthened them. In other cases, because the hand may have needed to touch a specific object, the arm may have been either lengthened or shortened to bring it to the correct position. Further, some scenes may simply have been cramped for space, necessitating the shortening of the forearm in order to fit it in.

Was there then a basic length for the forearm on Egyptian figures? The four New Kingdom samples of forearms that I analyzed in fact suggest that the length may have varied according to sex, pose, and period. In the earliest sample from the temple of Amenhotep III at Luxor, male forearms with straight hands and with relaxed hands average 5.0 (most 5.1) and 5.1 (most 5.3) squares respectively, while in the temple of Sety I at Abydos, the average length of the forearm with a relaxed hand is 5.0 (most 5.0) squares. However, if this latter sample is divided into male and female figures, the average length for males is 5.1 (most 5.0) squares and for females only 4.8 (most 4.8) squares. In the same temple, male forearms with straight hands are longer with an average length of 5.4 (most 5.4) squares. The figures concerned consist mainly of the ithyphallic form of the god Amon-Re with one arm raised vertically behind the head, and figures of the Inmutef priest or Thoth with one arm stretched out to dedicate offerings; the longer arm may be a deliberate device on the part of the artist to emphasize this part of the body. By contrast, the small number of figures of the king with a straight-handed forearm have a shorter mean length of 5.1 squares. Similar figures of the king in the nearly contemporary temple of Ramesses II at Abydos have a mean length of 5.0 (most 5.0) squares.

Differences according to sex and pose are also present in the sample from the reign of Ramesses III. The average length of the straight-handed forearm on ithyphallic figures is 5.6 (most 5.5) squares, but on figures of the king it is less at 5.3 (most 5.3) squares. With the relaxed hand, the mean length of the forearm on male figures is 5.4 (most 5.4) squares and on females 5.2 (most 5.0) squares. It is noticeable that overall the mean lengths from the reign of Ramesses III are longer than in the samples from the earlier reigns. By contrast, the length has shortened again in the sample from the temple of Khonsu. The forearms of ithyphallic figures have a mean length of only 4.9 (most 4.8) squares. The forearms of male figures with relaxed hands have a similar mean length (most 5.1 squares), but those of female figures have a shorter average length of 4.8 squares.

Perhaps we can get nearer to finding a basic length for the forearm by looking at figures where the arm hangs vertically by the side with a relaxed hand. In an ideal figure, the elbow should lie on horizontal 12, and

we could then see how many squares below the artist had placed the fingertips. Unfortunately, few examples of this type survive, since the hand usually holds an object and the fingers are not extended. Nevertheless, one such figure is to be found in the twelfth-dynasty tomb chapel B2 at Meir, where the elbow lies on horizontal 12 and the fingertips 5 squares below on horizontal 7.[40] A second example in the same chapel is unusual in placing the elbow bone virtually on horizontal 11, not 12, but the fingertips still lie 5 squares below on horizontal 6.[41] On an unfinished stela, the sketched rear arms of the last two women and the two men who follow them in the bottom register have their fingertips on horizontal 7.[42] The rear arms of the three leading figures that have been cut into relief are, however, longer. The fingertips of the first female figure extend half a square below horizontal 6, making a length for the forearm of 6 1/2 squares; the fingertips of the third figure touch horizontal 6; those of the middle figure lie about a quarter of a square below horizontal 7. In the upper register, however, a standing figure of a woman, which has also already been cut into relief, also has the fingertips just touching horizontal 7 like the sketched figures (Pl. 1.2). There is no way of telling whether the great disparity of forearm lengths is due to the draftsman or to the relief cutter, but one may suspect the latter, since the quality of drawing is better than that of the relief cutting. In any case, the majority of figures on this monument with hanging rear arms have their fingertips resting on horizontal 7.

It is possible therefore that the forearm was originally taken to be approximately 5 squares in length, whether the hand was relaxed or straight. A 5-square forearm would be in accordance with natural proportions in males with the probable stature of ancient Egyptians, granted that the forearm was approximately a small cubit in length (Sec. 2.2.4). Clearly, however, draftsmen did not hesitate to vary the length according to circumstances. Further, in the reign of Ramesses III, the forearm was generally longer than it had been in the reign of Sety I and earlier, perhaps to balance the extreme lengthening of the lower leg at this time. However, although the long lower leg is still found in the temple of Khonsu at the end of the New Kingdom, the forearm is shortened once again, resulting in figures in which the upper part of the body now appears relatively small by contrast with the lower.

6

Changes in the Amarna Period

Towards the end of the eighteenth dynasty, in about 1350 B.C., a new king, Amenhotep IV, ascended the throne. He is better known today as Akhenaton, the king who promoted the cult of the sun disk Aton, finally declaring the Aton to be the sole god.[1] At the same time, a new and distinctive style of art was developed, probably at the instigation of the king himself to express his religious ideas.[2]

Many Egyptologists have regarded Amarna art as throwing off the restraints of traditional art and adopting a new naturalism or realism. Thus John Wilson could talk of the "extremely naturalistic art"[3] of Akhenaton's reign, while John Cooney could say of the Amarna style that "realism . . . is the most conspicuous feature."[4] Robert Hari talked of Akhenaton's "quest for naturalism and realism"[5] and described Amarna art as "this liberated art, taken from life. . . ."[6] Seton Lloyd went so far as to refer to "Akhenaton's . . . passion for 'actuality'—for the visual representation of things as they are, as opposed to the conceptual portrayal of how they should be."[7]

If these descriptions of Amarna art are correct, then clearly there was a revolution in the basic principles of Egyptian art, since traditional art is conceptual, that is, the very opposite of naturalistic.[8] So we must ask whether Amarna art was really liberated from traditional artistic conventions or whether the very marked changes in style have led some Egyptologists to a false conclusion. In fact, William Stevenson Smith hit the mark when he observed that "the innovators of the Amarna period had left intact the foundations of Egyptian art."[9] A look at any Amarna scene shows that objects were still depicted in their most characteristic aspect, as in traditional art, and that the basic rendering of the human figure as a composite built up from its individual parts did not change (Fig. 6.1). The head is still in profile with a full-view eye, the shoulders are still seen from the front, while the nipple or breast, waist, legs, and feet are, as before, in profile (Chap. 1).

Furthermore, draftsmen continued to accept the drawing surface as two-dimensional rather than incorporating any illusion of depth. While scenes might now run from one wall to an adjacent one, instead of each wall being self-contained, this did not change the draftsmen's perception of the nature of the drawing surface. Material was still ordered through the use of registers, with figures placed on the baseline. Movement could be expressed by raising the feet of figures off the baseline, but this was in no way an innovation and certainly did not negate the baseline's fundamental importance. Occasionally registers might be linked by making objects from one register cross into another, but this device did not become common.

In traditional art, the registers gave a unity to a number of loosely associated activities that might or might not be contemporaneous or linked by location, and that were ultimately held together by the major figure dominating the registers. In Amarna art, it became common to devote one or more walls to one scene set in a specific location, often representing activities belonging to a particular occasion. The background was usually a definite area within the city with detailed representations of temples and palaces. These buildings, however, were depicted according to the principles developed for the representation of architecture in earlier times, that is, through a combination of plan and elevation. The traditional use of scale to indicate importance remained unchanged, so that scenes are dominated by the large figures of the king and queen, while other figures are much smaller.[10]

It would seem then that the differences between traditional and Amarna art do not stem from fundamental changes in the principles of representation employed by artists. Many changes result rather from the elevation of the Aton to the position of sole god. This meant the rejection of traditional deities together with their cults, mythology, and promise of afterlife, all of which had provided iconographic themes in temples and tombs. It follows that many scene types were either banned altogether or reinterpreted to fit the new cult. For instance, the series of ritual scenes in temples based on cult actions carried out before the anthropomorphic statue of the god, in which the king adores or offers to the god, or is himself embraced by the god or offered the breath of life, was now replaced by an unvarying scene type in which the king adores or offers beneath the sun disk, the nonanthropomorphic symbol of the Aton who was never represented by a cult statue, while at the same time the Aton rays embrace the king and offer the sign of life.

In the decoration of private tombs and stelae, the common scene types showing the owner before a table of offerings or offering to a deity almost totally disappear,[11] as do the so-called scenes of daily life. Instead the main decoration is concerned with the king and members of his family, often in an apparently domestic situation.

Other changes also contributed to the unique Amarna style without affecting the basic artistic principles employed. Subsidiary scenes were depicted on a much smaller scale than before, so that temple and tomb walls seem to be teeming with a whole range of different activities.[12] Amarna artists showed a distinct preference for curves as opposed to straight lines, apart from the Aton rays; this is seen, for instance, in the

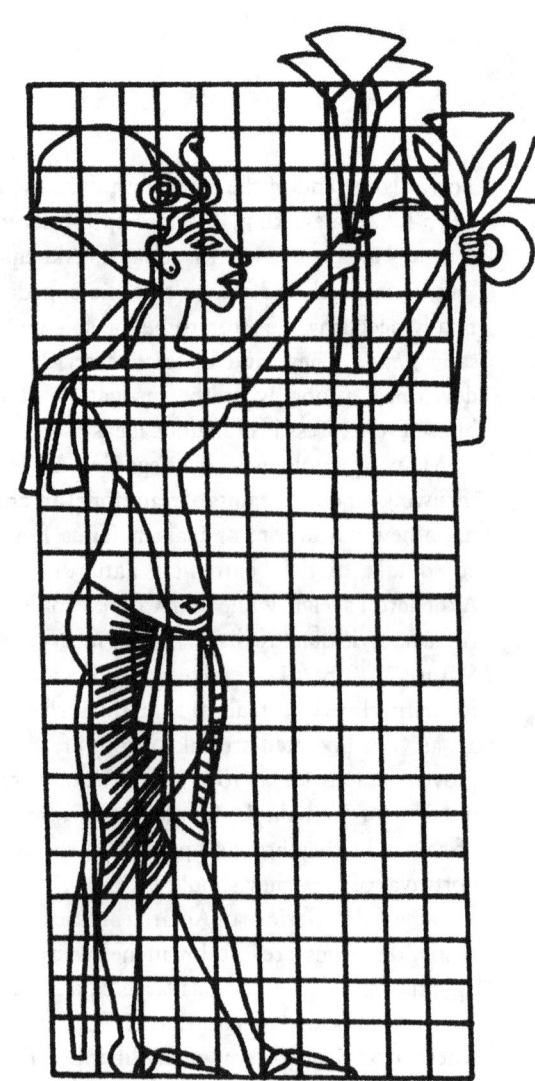

FIGURE 6.1

Standing figure of Akhenaton with grid completed from surviving traces, limestone slab from royal tomb, Amarna, eighteenth dynasty, Cairo Museum 10/11/26/ 4, after Martin 1974, Plate 54 no. 395.

curve of the thighs of a seated figure or the curve of the hand.[13] In minor figures, the body is frequently bent in obeisance to the king.[14] Loose pleated garments began to be depicted in the reigns of Amenhotep II and Thutmose IV, and the Amarna artists clearly reveled in these draperies with their floating streamers and sashes, which owe much to art and little to reality.[15] In the reigns of Thutmose IV and Amenhotep III, artists for the first time experimented on minor figures with the depiction of the near foot from the outside with all its toes.[16] In the Amarna period, this becomes the hallmark of the royal family, while private individuals are still given undifferentiated feet.[17]

One of the most obvious changes in Amarna art is in the style and proportions of the figures, especially those of the king and his family. Akhenaton is shown with drooping features, a long neck, pot belly with pronounced belly fold, heavy buttocks and thighs, short legs, narrow shoulders, and spindly arms.[18] Such an image could only have been sanctioned, and possibly devised, by the king himself. Wilson talked of "the broodingly introspective figures of this king, rendered in an extremely naturalistic art,"[19] and some authorities have thought that they portray the actual physical characteristics of the king and that he suffered deformity as a result of some disease.[20] The problem is that the sort of medical condition that would have produced this type of appearance, such as Fröhlich's syndrome, would have prevented the king from fathering the six "king's daughters" who figure so prominently on the monuments.[21] If we posit that the figure of the king, like the rest of Egyptian art, is conceptual rather than naturalistic, we may instead speculate that Akhenaton's image arises in some way as an expression of his religious ideas. As he never systematically

expounded these in writing, we shall probably never truly understand the meaning of the royal image.

6.1. Grids at Amarna

Because of the feeling that Amarna art somehow threw off conventional restraints and became naturalistic, it has been thought that the artists' grid system was also abandoned. This is to some extent understandable since very few figures with grid traces survive, mainly because most work was carried out in relief. While in painted scenes the grid is never removed but simply painted over, in relief the stone is cut away, taking with it the artist's original grid and outline sketch of the scene. Sometimes with sunk relief, however, the background is left unworked at least in places and the red grid traces would just have been painted over. These may then be revealed if the paint comes off, although over time the red ochre of the grid, like other colors, may also be lost.

Thus although surviving grid traces are rare, there is in fact enough evidence to show that squared grids remained in use, at least in the drawing of royal figures. A limestone slab found in the royal tomb at Amarna preserves grid traces, which relate to a complete figure of the king.[22] In the tomb of Ay at Amarna, grid traces survive behind a figure of the king, but unfortunately the head is missing.[23] Grid traces that relate to another figure of the king survive in the Amarna tomb of Mahu, but only the lower horizontals are in any way preserved.[24] Grid traces can be seen on a block from Karnak that preserves the legs of the queen,[25] but none survive in relation to a complete figure of Nefertiti. Finally, a block from the great temple at Amarna, now

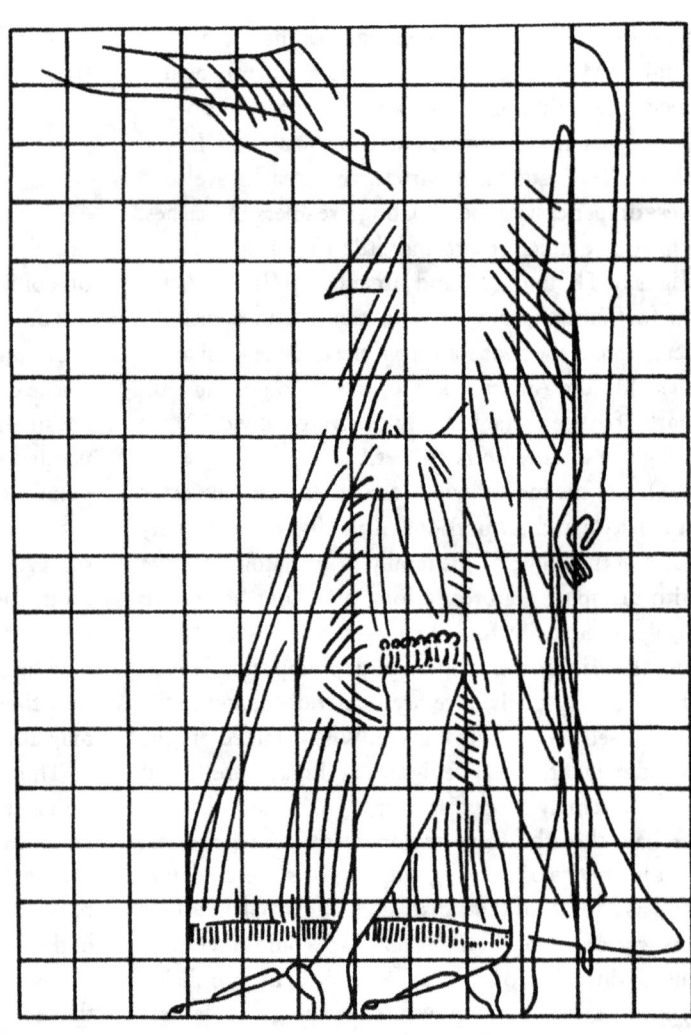

FIGURE 6.2
Standing figure of Akhenaton, head lost, with grid completed from surviving traces, tomb chapel of Ay, Amarna, eighteenth dynasty, after Davies 1908b, Pls. 26, 40.

in the Ashmolean Museum, Oxford, which shows part of the wheel of a royal chariot, has very clear traces of grid lines, but no human figures are preserved.[26] At Thebes, a few grid traces survive in the tomb of Ramose in the Amarna-style scene showing the King and Queen giving audience from the window of appearance, but there are not enough to reconstruct the grid for the scene.[27]

The grid on the slab from the royal tomb can be completed to run across the king's figure (Fig. 6.1). It was clearly not put on very carefully, but between the baseline and the horizontal nearest the hairline, there are 20 squares instead of the traditional 18 squares. The top of the knee is not very distinct, but seems to lie on horizontal 6, the lower border of the buttocks lies a little above 9, the bottom of the belly fold is about 10 1/2 squares up, and the navel is on 11. The breast region lies near horizontal 15, the junction of the neck and front shoulder near 17, and the throat on 18. Horizontal 19 runs through the nose and ear. An axial vertical also runs through the ear with the vertical in front passing through the eye.[28]

If the grid traces are completed to run over the figure of the king in the tomb of Ay, we find that the top of the knee lies on horizontal 6, the lower border of the buttocks a little above 9, and the belly fold on 10 (Fig. 6.2). It is likely that 17 lay near the now vanished junction of neck and shoulders and that the hairline lay on 20 as on the slab from the royal tomb.[29] The height of 20 squares is confirmed by measurements on the figure in the tomb of Mahu that preserves some grid traces. The hairline height is 90 cm and the height from the baseline to horizontal 1 is 4.5 cm. Since 90 + 4.5 = 20, the hairline height is 20 squares above the baseline.[30]

6.2. Standing Figures of the King

The evidence therefore suggests that during the Amarna period, the number of squares for a standing figure on the grid was increased from 18 to 20 squares. In order to test this hypothesis, 20-square grids can be applied to other figures of the king, calculated by dividing the hairline to soles distance by 20, to see how consistent the results are. The number of reasonably complete figures of the king that survive are unfortunately few, but I was able to collect a sample of fourteen that were suitable.

It has long been recognized that Amarna figures can be divided into at least two different styles.[31] The early style, in use at the beginning of the reign, which is found on the blocks from the dismantled temples of the Aton at Karnak and during the early years at Amarna, is more extreme, while the later style, occurring throughout most of the Amarna private tombs shows less exaggeration of the human figure. In analyzing figures of the king on hypothetical grids, it can be shown that a broadly similar scheme of vertical proportions applies to all the figures. The knee lies on horizontal 6 in both early and late styles, but in most of the early-style figures analyzed, the lower border of the buttocks, the belly fold, the maximum convexity of the buttocks and the breast are 1/2 to 1 square higher than in the later-style figures.[32]

Let us look first at three early style figures. The first one is from Boundary Stela S, dating to year 6 (Fig. 6.3).[33] The knee is on horizontal 6, the lower border of the buttocks on 10, the belly fold just above 10 1/2 squares above the baseline, the maximum convexity of the buttocks on horizontal 11, the navel just above 11,

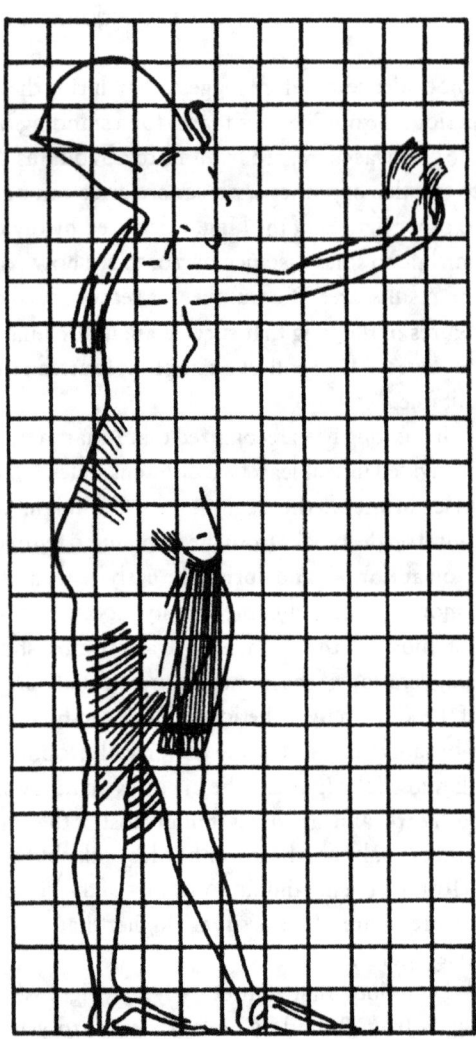

FIGURE 6.3

Standing figure of Akhenaton with hypothetical 20-square grid, Boundary Stela S, Amarna, eighteenth dynasty, after Davies 1908a, Plate 26.

the small of the back just above 14, the breast at 15 1/2, the junction of the neck and shoulders near 17 1/2, and the throat at 18 1/4.

The second figure from a small stela now in the Kestner Museum, Hanover,[34] again shows the top of the knee on horizontal 6, the lower border of the buttocks on 10, the belly fold around 10 1/2 squares up, the maximum convexity of the buttocks near horizontal 11, and the navel just above 11 (Fig. 6.4). The small of the back is slightly lower than in the first figure, at 13 1/2 squares. The nipple region is not clearly defined. The head proportions are closer to those on the slab from the royal tomb, with the junction of the neck and shoulders on horizontal 17, the throat on 18, and 19 running through the nose and ear.

The third figure shows the king in *sed* festival (jubilee) dress on a block now in the Fitzwilliam Museum, Cambridge (Fig. 6.5).[35] The knee is on horizontal 6, the lower border of the buttocks just below 10, the maximum convexity of the buttocks on 11, and the small of the back at about 14 1/2 squares up. The junction of the neck and shoulders is not clear, but the throat lies on horizontal 18.

A feature of some buildings at Amarna was a series of parapets and sloping balustrades, the latter running up the sides of ramps or steps, and these were decorated with scenes of the king and queen offering to the Aton.[36] Most are in a fragmentary or damaged condition, but two blocks, one from a balustrade and one from a parapet, preserve the figures of the royal couple reasonably well and are of interest, because although the proportions of the bodies correspond fairly closely with the three figures we have just examined, the heads are smaller.

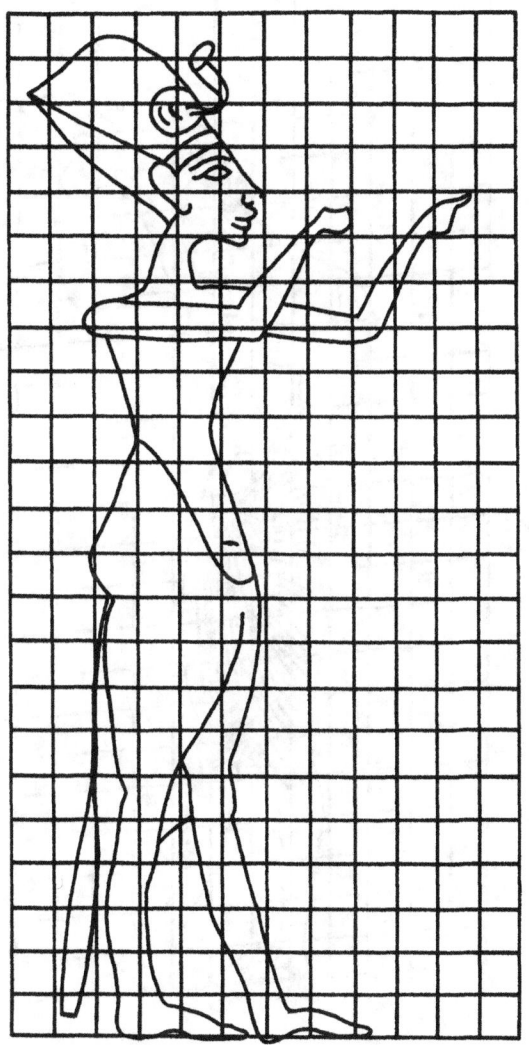

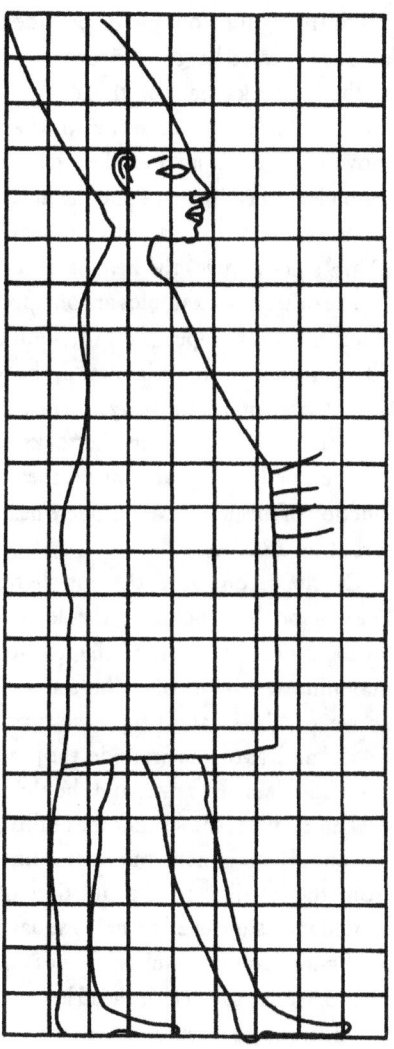

FIGURE 6.4
Standing figure of Akhenaton with hypothetical
20-square grid, stela, Amarna, Kestner Museum,
Hanover inv. no. 1570.22, eighteenth dynasty, after
photograph taken by John Baines.

FIGURE 6.5
Standing figure of Akhenaton with hypothetical
20-square grid, block from temple, Fitzwilliam Museum,
Cambridge acc. no. 2300.1943, eighteenth dynasty,
after museum photograph.

On the figure from the balustrade (Fig. 6.6),[37] the knee as expected lies on horizontal 6, the lower border of the buttocks on 10, the belly fold on 11, the maximum convexity of the buttocks and the navel just above 11, and the small of the back on 14. The breast region is pushed up to 16 and the junction of neck and shoulders is at 17 1/2 squares, while the throat at 18 1/2 squares gives the head its small appearance.

The other two examples are on opposite sides of the block from a parapet (Figs. 6.7–6.8).[38] On the first side, the knee is on horizontal 6, the lower border of the buttocks on 10, the belly fold just above 10 1/2, the maximum convexity of the buttocks and the navel on 11, the small of the back on 14, the nipple on 16, the junction of the neck and shoulders near 17 1/2, and the throat on 18 1/2.

On the second side, there is slight variation. The knee is on horizontal 6, the lower border of the buttocks near 10 1/2, the belly fold just below 11, the maximum convexity of the buttocks and the navel just above 11, the small of the back on 14, the nipple at 15 1/2, and, as on the first side, the junction of the neck and shoulders at 17 1/2, and the throat at 18 1/2.

This analysis shows that the bodily proportions are reasonably consistent but that sometimes the head from the hairline to the junction of the neck and shoulders is shortened by half a square. If we return to the figure that we examined first of all from Boundary Stela S, we can see that the head here is on the small side and bears some resemblance to the parapet and balustrade pieces.

To sum up, in these early figures the knee lies on horizontal 6, the lower border of the buttocks near 10, the belly fold between 10 1/2 and 11, the maximum convexity of the buttocks and the navel near or just

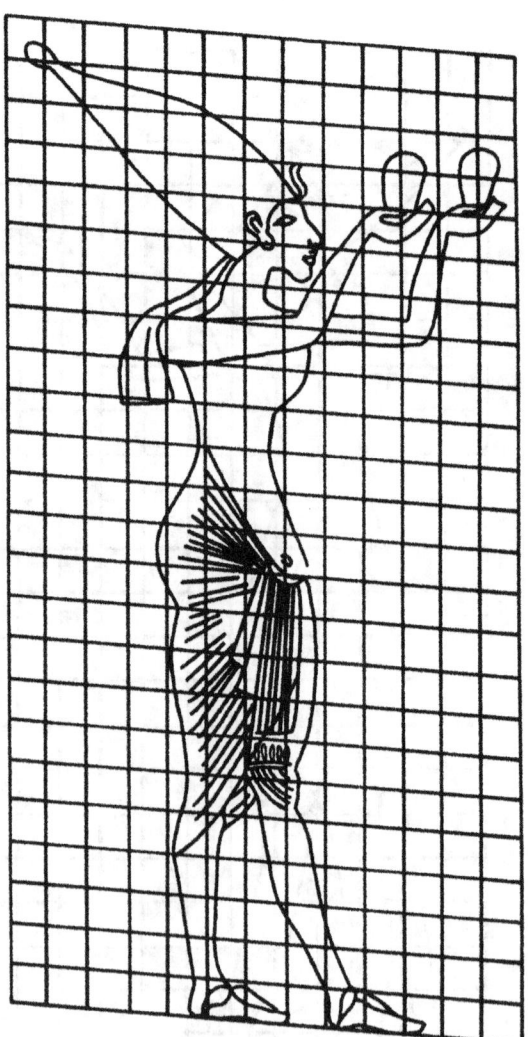

FIGURE 6.6

Standing figure of Akhenaton with hypothetical 20-square grid, block from balustrade, Amarna, eighteenth dynasty, Cairo Museum temp. no. 30/10/26/12, after Westendorf 1968, 138.

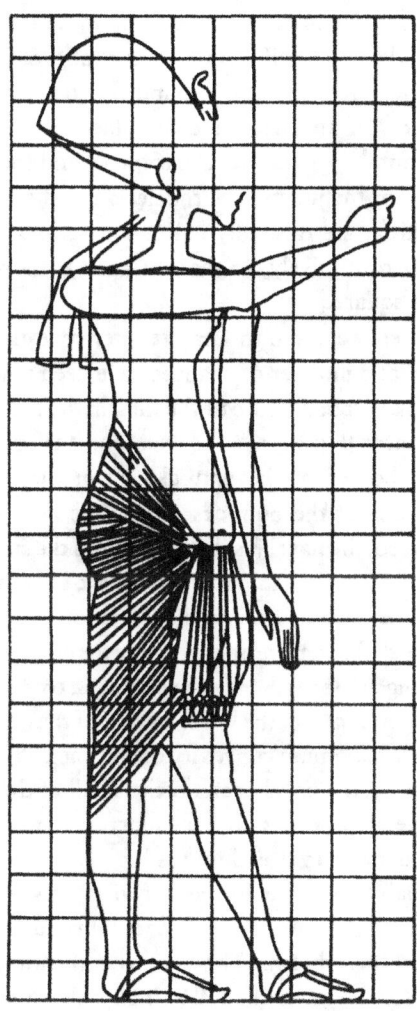

FIGURE 6.7
Standing figure of Akhenaton with hypothetical
20-square grid, block from parapet, Amarna,
eighteenth dynasty, Cairo Museum JE 87300, after
Roeder 1969, Plate 1.

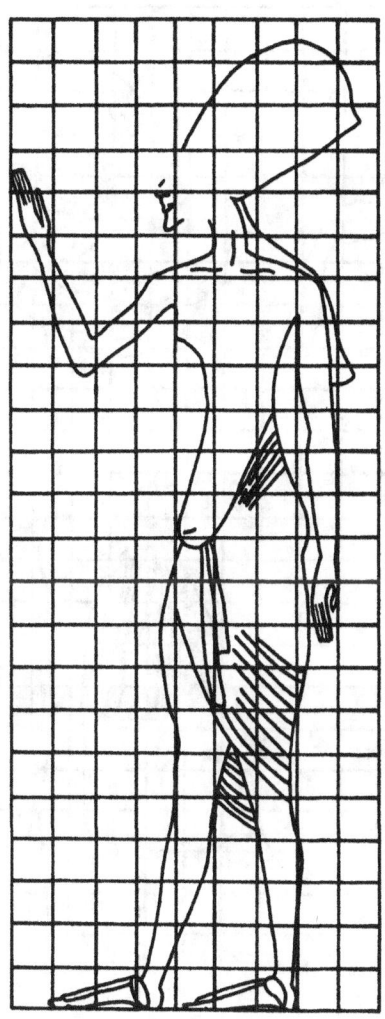

FIGURE 6.8
Standing figure of Akhenaton with hypothetical
20-square grid, block from parapet, Amarna,
eighteenth dynasty, Cairo Museum JE 87300, after
Roeder 1969, Plate 2.

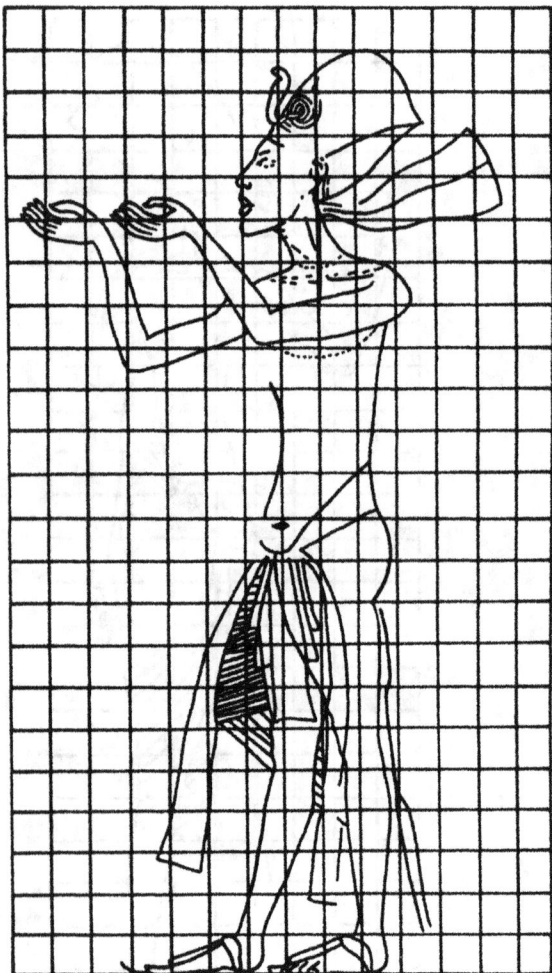

FIGURE 6.9

Standing figure of Akhenaton with hypothetical 20-square grid, tomb chapel of Apy, Amarna, eighteenth dynasty, after Davies 1906, Plate 31.

above 11, the small of the back somewhere around 14 (possibly up to half a square either above or below), and the breast region around 15 1/2 to 16. The junction of the neck and shoulders lies either on horizontal 17 with the throat on 18 and the hairline on 20, or the junction of the neck and shoulders and the throat are raised by half a square to 17 1/2 and 18 1/2 respectively, so that the head is shortened by half a square.

When we come to analyze later-style figures, we find that a number of changes have been made.[39] Let us look first at a figure of the king in the tomb of Apy at Amarna (Fig. 6.9).[40] The knee is on horizontal 6, the lower border of the buttocks on 9, the maximum convexity of the buttocks on 10, the belly fold just above 10, the navel just below 11, and the small of the back just above 12. The junction of the neck and shoulders lies on 17, and the throat on 18.

Much the same proportions are found on a figure of the king in the tomb of Merire I (Fig. 6.10).[41] The knee is on horizontal 6, the lower border of the buttocks on 9, their maximum convexity on 10, the belly fold just above 10, the navel near 11, the small of the back on 14, the nipple on 15, and the junction of the neck and shoulders on 17; the throat is lost.

Analysis of two further royal figures can be attempted by assuming that horizontal 18 runs along the level of their throats. The first, from the tomb of May (Fig. 6.11),[42] gives the following results: horizontal 6 runs through the top of the knee; 9 near the lower border of the buttocks; the belly fold is on 10; the maximum convexity of the buttocks at 10 1/2; the navel on 11; the small of the back at 13 1/2; the nipple near 15; and the junction of the neck and shoulders just above 17.

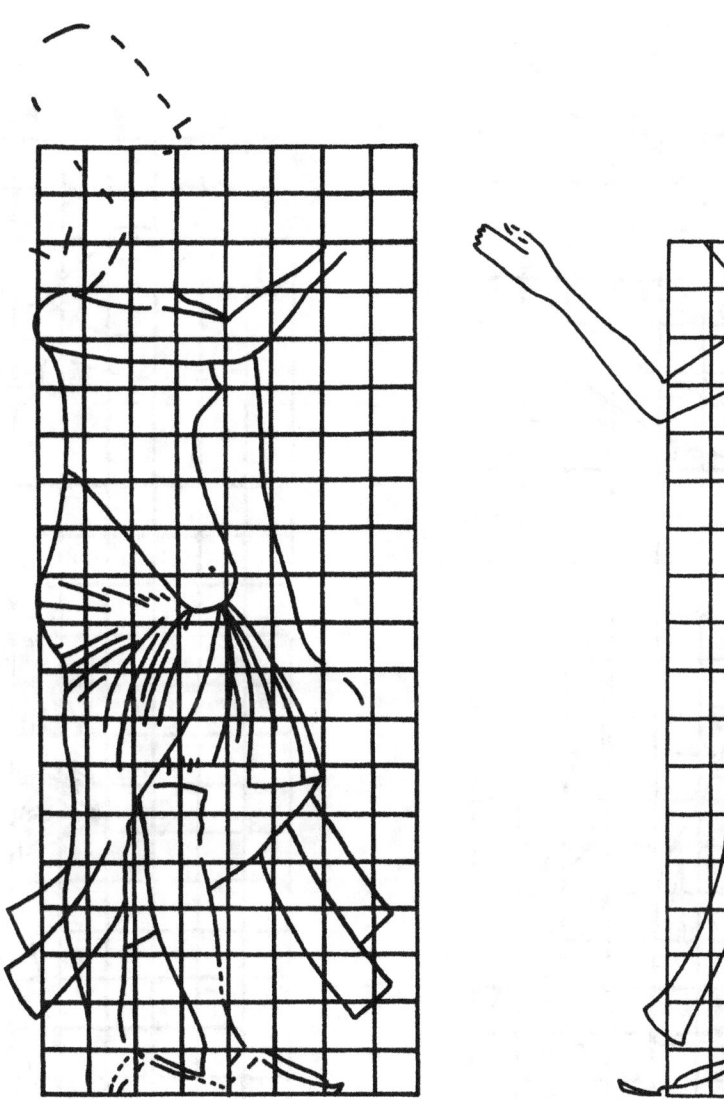

FIGURE 6.10
Standing figure of Akhenaton with hypothetical
20-square grid, tomb chapel of Merire I, Amarna,
eighteenth dynasty, after Davies 1903, Plate 22.

FIGURE 6.11
Standing figure of Akhenaton with hypothetical
18-square grid from throat to baseline, tomb chapel
of May, Amarna, eighteenth dynasty, after Davies
1908a, Plate 3.

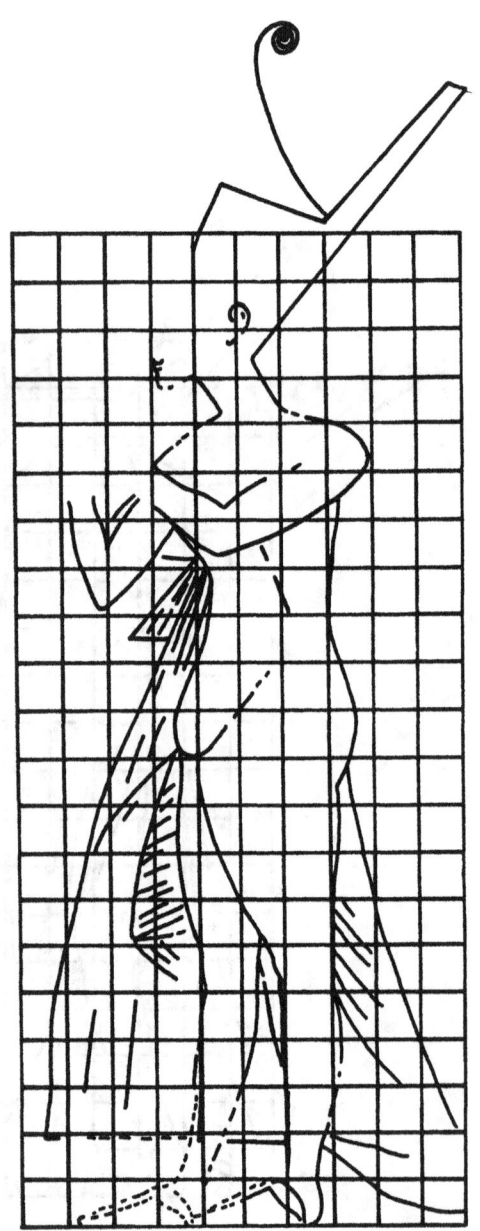

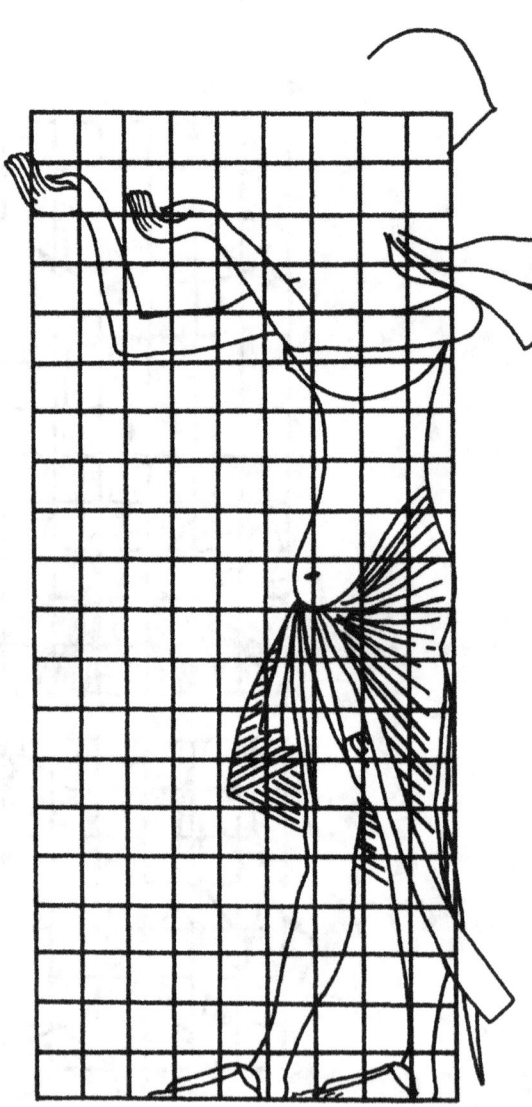

FIGURE 6.12
Standing figure of Akhenaton with hypothetical
18-square grid from throat to baseline, tomb chapel of
Panehesy, after Davies 1905a, Plate 12.

FIGURE 6.13
Standing figure of Akhenaton with hypothetical
17-square grid from junction of neck and back shoulder
to baseline, tomb chapel of Tutu, after Davies 1908b,
Plate 16.

The second figure, from the tomb of Panehesy (Fig. 6.12),[43] gives reasonably similar results: horizontal 6 again runs through the top of the knee; the lower border of the buttocks is about half a square above 9; the belly fold on 10; the maximum convexity of the buttocks at 10 1/2; the small of the back on 13; and the junction of the neck and shoulders near 17.

In a figure of the king from the tomb of Tutu,[44] which is missing the head, a hypothetical grid can be reckoned by taking the junction of neck and shoulders as the level of horizontal 17 (Fig. 6.13). This produces results consistent with the other later style figures. The top of the knee is again on horizontal 6; the lower border of the buttocks near 9 1/4; the belly fold on 10; the navel and the maximum convexity of the buttocks around 10 3/4; the small of the back on 13; the nipple on 15.

From this analysis we find that the levels of the lower border of the buttocks, the maximum convexity of the buttocks, the small of the back, and the nipple tend to be a half to a whole square lower than in the early style figures. Noting these changes in the vertical proportions helps to quantify the differences between the two styles. It is also possible to compare the horizontal proportions of various figures.

In the earlier figures where the width across the shoulders can be measured, it is about 4 1/2 to 4 3/4 squares, while in the later figures it is nearly 5 squares. The width at the level of the breast is 2 1/4 to 3 squares in the earlier figures, but 3 to 3 1/2 squares in the later ones. The width at the level of the small of the back is 1 3/4 to 2 squares in the early figures. In the later ones, it is 2 to 2 3/4 squares. However, in both types of figure the width at the level of the maximum convexity of the buttocks is similar, ranging from 3 1/4 to 4 squares. This analysis shows that the upper torso tends to be narrower in the early figures than in the later ones, but that the width of the buttock region did not change. When this is coupled with the higher small of the back in the early figures, the resulting proportions produce a short and narrow upper torso, so that the eye is drawn away from the relatively small upper part of the figure to the large buttocks, wide thighs, and prominent belly fold that occupy the region midway between the soles and the hairline. This effect is even greater on those figures where the head is small.

By contrast, in the later style figures, the widths across the shoulders, the nipple level, and the small-of-the-back level increase slightly, while the buttocks width remains the same. In addition, the level of the small of the back is often lowered, so that the upper torso is enlarged in proportion to the rest of the body and there is less contrast between the upper part of the body and the buttocks region.

Analysis on hypothetical grids also makes it possible to compare Amarna figures with traditional ones to see how the proportions have changed and where the extra 2 squares were added. In a figure of the reign of Amenhotep III, most commonly the knee would be on horizontal 6, the lower border of the buttocks on or near 10, the navel on or near 11, the small of the back on or near 12, the nipple on or near 14, the junction of the neck and shoulders on or near 16, and the hairline on 18 (Fig. 6.14).

In the early-style Amarna figure, the knee is still on horizontal 6, the lower border of the buttocks on 10, and the navel on or near 11. The nipple region, however, has risen to 15 1/2 or 16, while in some figures the junction of the neck and shoulders lies on 17 1/2, making at least 2 1/2 squares between the junction of the neck and shoulder and the hairline, instead of the traditional 2 squares. Half a square therefore has been added in the head region, while the other 1 1/2 squares are placed between the junction of the neck and shoulders and the navel, allowing space for the pendulous belly.

When the distance between the junction of the neck and shoulders and the hairline is 3 squares, then a complete square has been added in the head region, giving the typical long Amarna neck and drooping features. In this case, the addition to the torso is only 1 and not 1 1/2 squares.

In later-style figures, the extra square remains in the head region between the hairline and the junction of the neck and shoulders. The nipple on horizontal 15 lies 2 squares down from the junction of the neck and shoulders, as in traditional figures, but 4 squares above the navel on 11; in a figure from the reign of Amenhotep III, the distance between the navel on horizontal 11 and the nipple on 14 is 3 squares, showing that the extra square has been inserted between the navel and the nipple. Thus the vertical proportions of the lower half of the body are much the same as in traditional figures but the upper half is elongated. This means that while in traditional figures the lower leg to the knee is a third of the hairline height, in figures of Akhenaton it is only a third of the throat level, which is why the king appears to have short legs. In addition, the width of the shoulders and the small of the back is narrower than in traditional figures, while that of the buttocks is wider. The arms are also thinner, being less than a grid square wide, so that they appear to be very spindly.

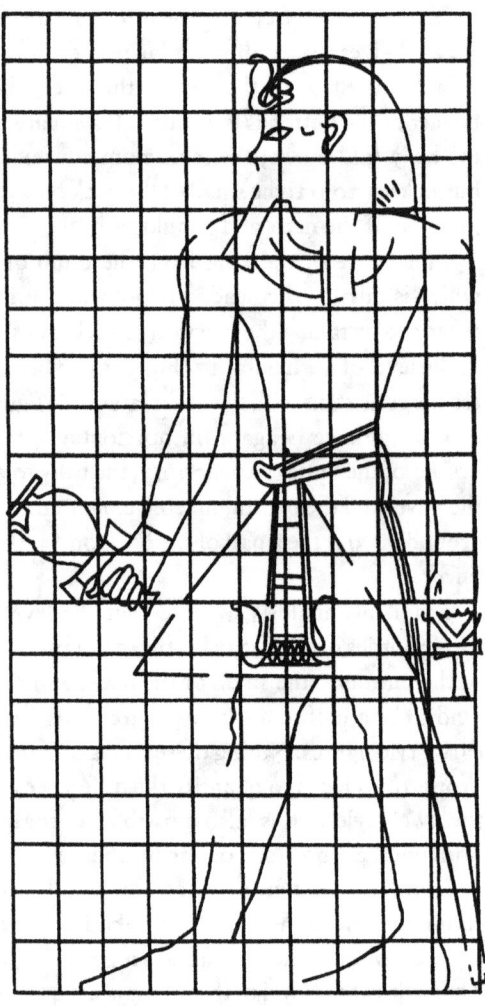

FIGURE 6.14

Standing figure of Amenhotep III with hypothetical 18-square grid, temple of Luxor, eighteenth dynasty, after Brunner 1977, Plate 163.

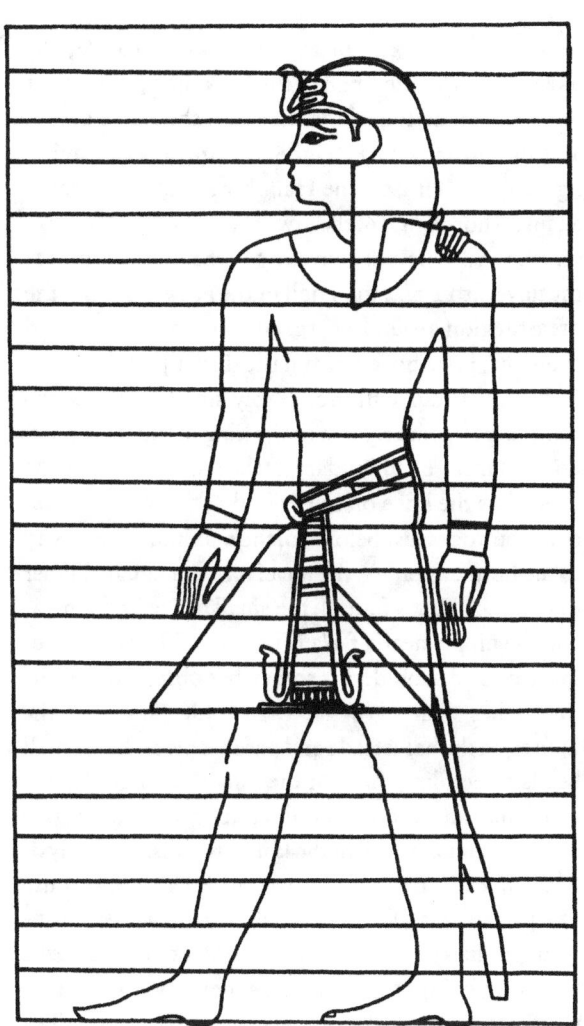

FIGURE 6.15

*Standing figure of Thutmose IV with grid horizontals
completed from surviving traces, KV 43, Thebes,
eighteenth dynasty, after author's photograph.*

A grid of 20 squares from soles to hairline is not entirely an Amarna innovation. One painted wall in the tomb of Thutmose IV (KV 43) has a series of standing figures of deities and the king drawn on a continuous 20-square grid.[45] Two extra squares have been added to various bodily regions, except in the case of the mummiform statue of Osiris, which stands on a base 1 square high and so acquires 1 extra square only. The treatment is anomalous, and the proportions and physique of the figures in no way foreshadow those done in the Amarna style (Fig. 6.15).

6.3. Standing Figures of the Queen

No complete figure of the queen survives with related grid traces, but the existence of one block that preserves her legs together with grid lines suggests that her figure could also be drawn on a grid.[46] Where the queen appears with the king, she is not drawn the same height as the king nor is she shorter by a fixed amount, so that it is unlikely that the king's grid was used to establish her proportions. Since we know that before the Amarna period both male and female standing figures were constructed on similar 18-square grids (Chap. 4.5), it seems a reasonable hypothesis that standing figures of Nefertiti were designed to fit a grid of 20 squares like those of the king.

If we analyze complete figures of the queen on hypothetical 20-square grids, we find that once again there are differences between the early and later styles.[47] If we look first at the queen's figure on the slab from the royal tomb,[48] we find that the knee is on horizontal 6, the lower border of the buttocks at 9 3/4, the

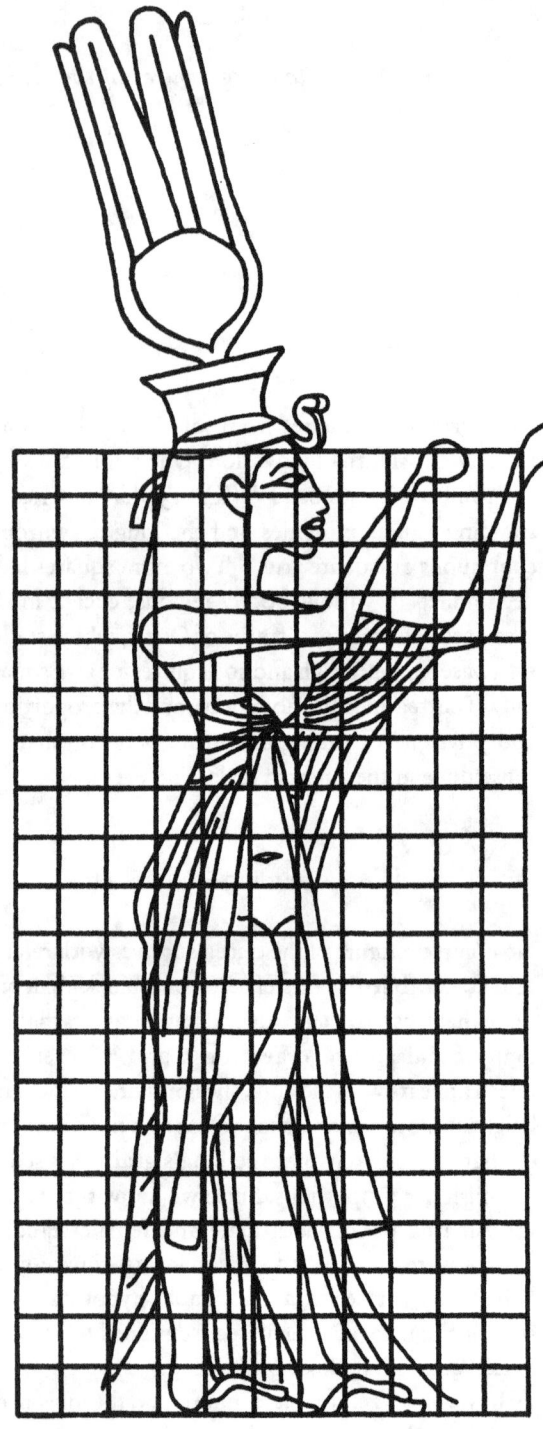

FIGURE 6.16

Standing figure of Nefertiti with hypothetical 20-square grid, limestone slab from royal tomb, Amarna, eighteenth dynasty, Cairo Museum 10/11/26/4, after Martin 1974, Plate 54 no. 395.

maximum convexity of the buttocks at 10 1/2, the navel at 11 3/4, the small of the back on 14, the breast on 15, the junction of the neck and shoulders on 17, and the throat on 18 (Fig. 6.16). In the companion figure to the king on the Hanover stela,[49] the knee is again on horizontal 6, the lower border of the buttocks on 10, the maximum convexity of the buttocks on 11, the navel at 11 1/2, the small of the back at 13 1/2, the breast region around 15, the junction of the neck and shoulders just above 17, and the throat just above 18.

Figures occur with noticeably small heads, corresponding to some figures of the king in the early style. For instance, on Boundary Stela S one figure of the queen has the knee on horizontal 6, the lower border of the buttocks just below 10, the maximum convexity of the buttocks on 11, the navel on 12 (1 square higher than on the king's figure), the small of the back on 14, and the nipple near 15 1/2 (Fig. 6.17). The junction of the neck and shoulders is somewhat obscured, but the throat lies nearer 18 1/2 than 18.[50] Similarly, the figures on the balustrade and parapet pieces have small heads resembling those of the king (Fig. 6.18).[51]

In the later style, modifications in proportions occur similar to those in the king's figures. An analysis of the queen's figure following the king's in the tomb of Apy (Fig. 6.19)[52] shows that horizontal 6 still runs through the knee but the lower border of the buttocks has dropped approximately a square to 9; the maximum convexity of the buttocks is on 10, the small of the back on 13, the junction of the neck and shoulders near 17, and the throat near 18. Similarly in the tomb of May (Fig. 6.20),[53] the figure of the queen has the knee on horizontal 6, the lower border of the buttocks near 9, the maximum convexity of the buttocks on 10, the navel on 11, the small of the back on 13, the breast

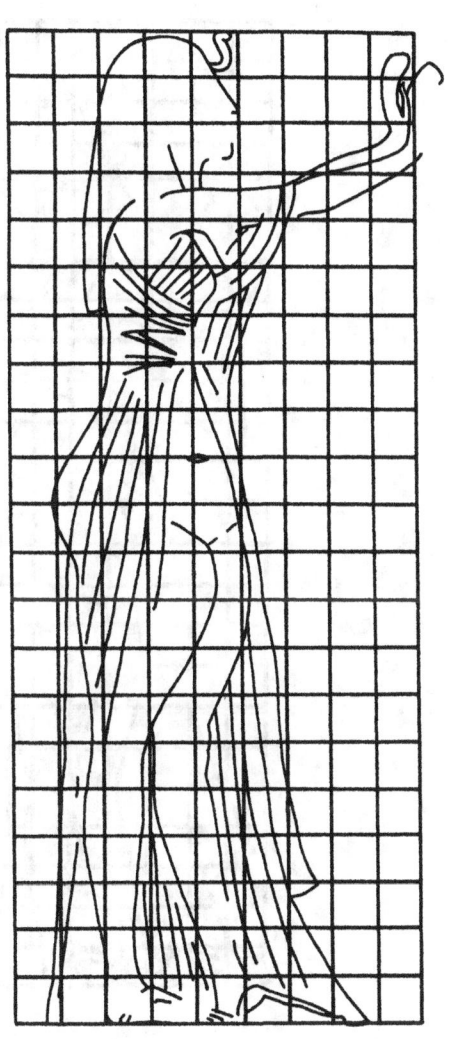

FIGURE 6.17
Standing figure of Nefertiti with hypothetical 20-square
grid, Boundary Stela S, Amarna, eighteenth dynasty,
after Davies 1908a, Plate 26.

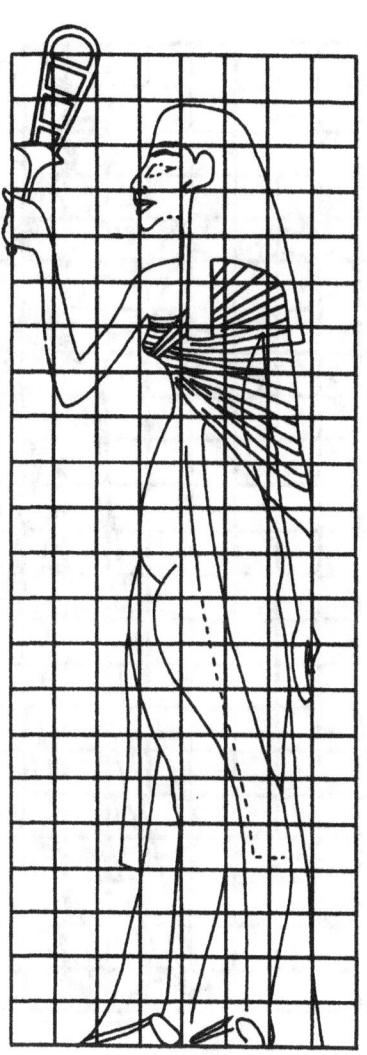

FIGURE 6.18
Standing figure of Nefertiti with hypothetical 20-square
grid, block from parapet, Amarna, eighteenth dynasty,
Cairo Museum JE 87300, after Roeder 1969, Plate 2.

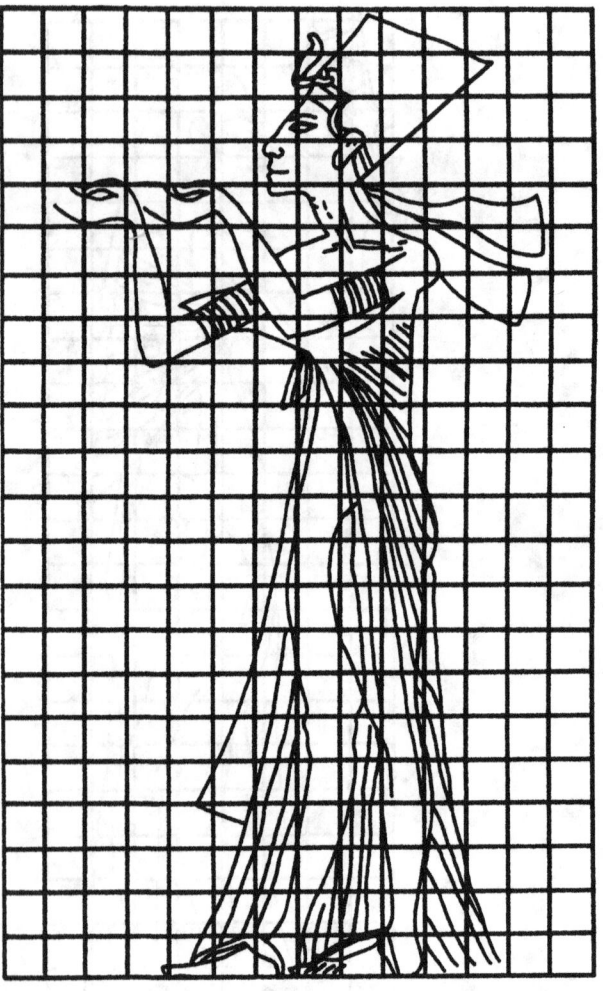

FIGURE 6.19
Standing figure of Nefertiti with hypothetical 20-square
grid, tomb chapel of Apy, Amarna, eighteenth dynasty,
after Davies 1906, Plate 31.

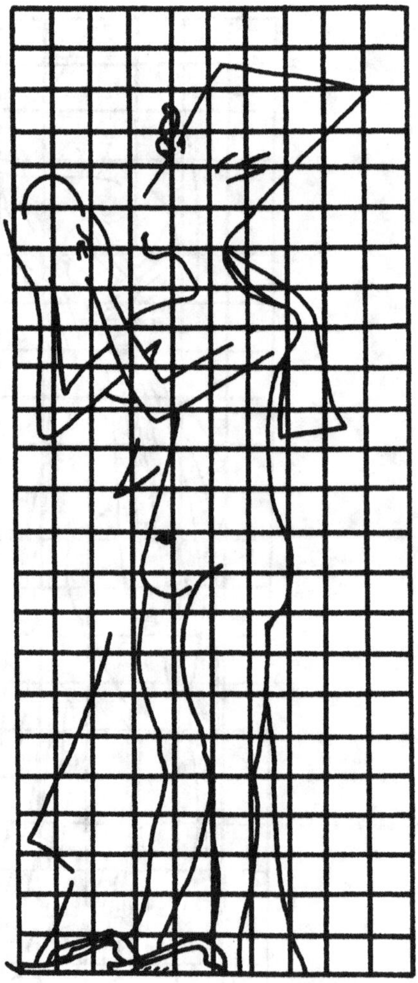

FIGURE 6.20
Standing figure of Nefertiti with hypothetical 20-square
grid, tomb chapel of May, Amarna, eighteenth dynasty,
after Davies 1908a, Plate 3.

near 15, the junction of the neck and shoulders near 17, and the throat near 18. However, just as in traditional figures, the queen's figure is usually more slender than that of the king. Another distinction seems to be the separation between the level of the navel and the level of the maximum convexity of the buttocks, which in almost all depictions of the royal couple together is greater in the queen than the king.[54]

6.4. Anomalies in the Tomb of Mahu

In considering the proportions of the king and queen so far, I have excluded two depictions of the royal couple from the tomb of Mahu,[55] contemporary with other figures in the later style. When Davies was recording this tomb, he noted that the proportions of the figures were bad.[56] It is interesting that grid analysis confirms that the figures have anomalous proportions and can quantify how they differ from other figures of the king and queen.

In the first scene,[57] the head proportions of the king's figure are normal with the throat near horizontal 18 and the junction of the neck and shoulders near 17, but the nipple is half a square lower than the usual 15, while the navel lies near 10 instead of 11, the belly fold near 9 instead of 10, and the lower border of the buttock a little below 9 (Fig. 6.21). The knee, however, still lies at 6.

On the accompanying figure of the queen, the anomalies are slightly different (Fig. 6.22). The throat level is lowered to horizontal 17 1/2 and the junction of the neck and shoulders to 16 1/2, and the breast is as low as 14. The lower border of the buttocks is still on 9, but horizontal 5 rather than 6 relates to the knee.

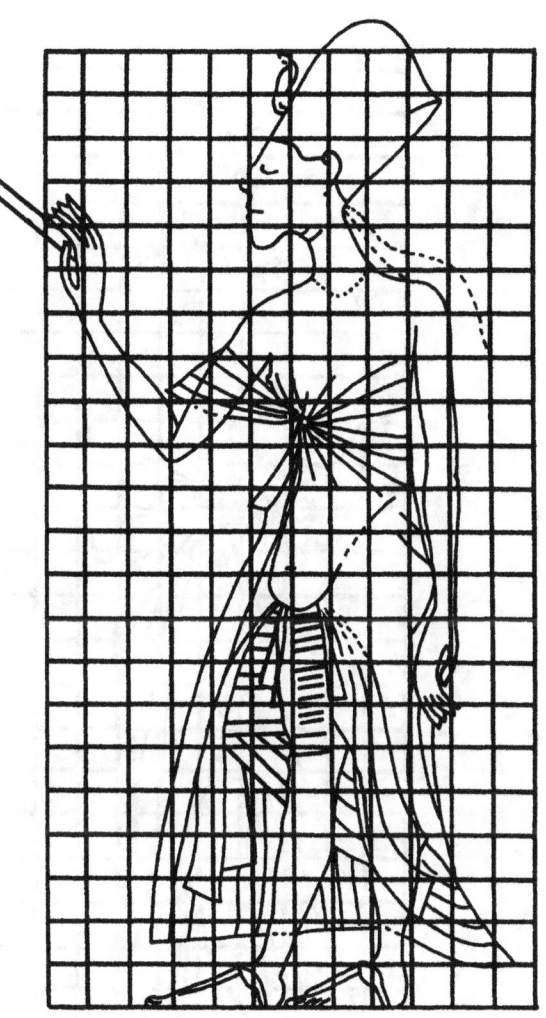

FIGURE 6.21
Standing figure of Akhenaton with hypothetical 20-square grid, tomb chapel of Mahu, Amarna, eighteenth dynasty, after Davies 1906, Plate 15.

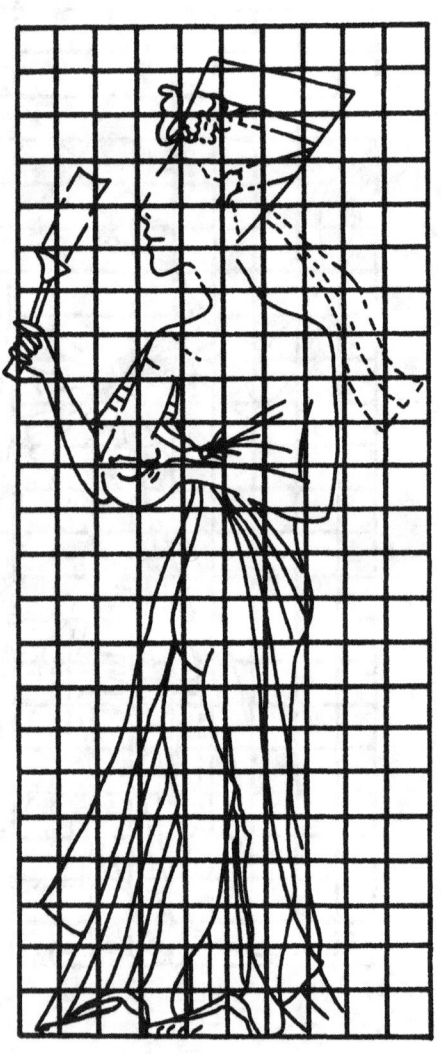

FIGURE 6.22
Standing figure of Nefertiti with hypothetical 20-square grid, tomb chapel of Mahu, Amarna, eighteenth dynasty, after Davies 1906, Plate 15.

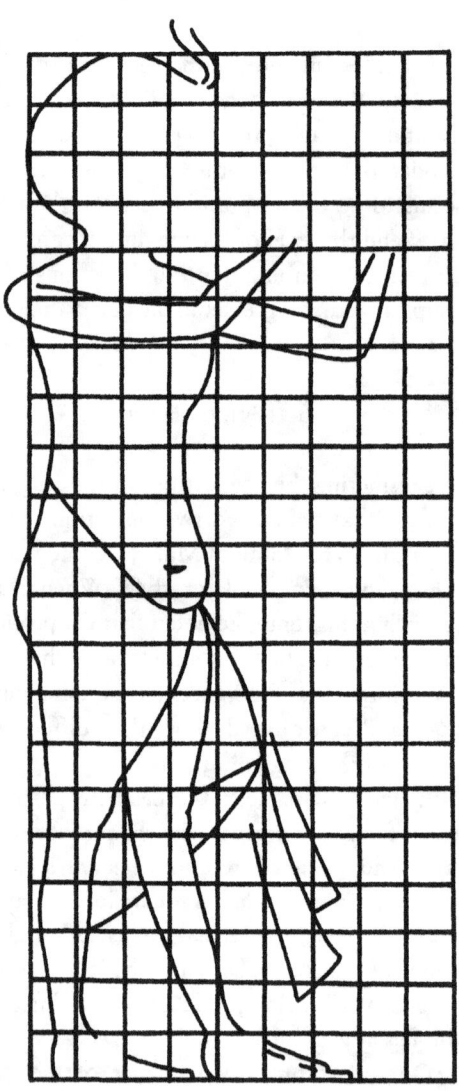

FIGURE 6.23
Standing figure of Akhenaton with hypothetical 20-square grid, tomb chapel of Mahu, Amarna, eighteenth dynasty, after Davies 1906, Plate 16.

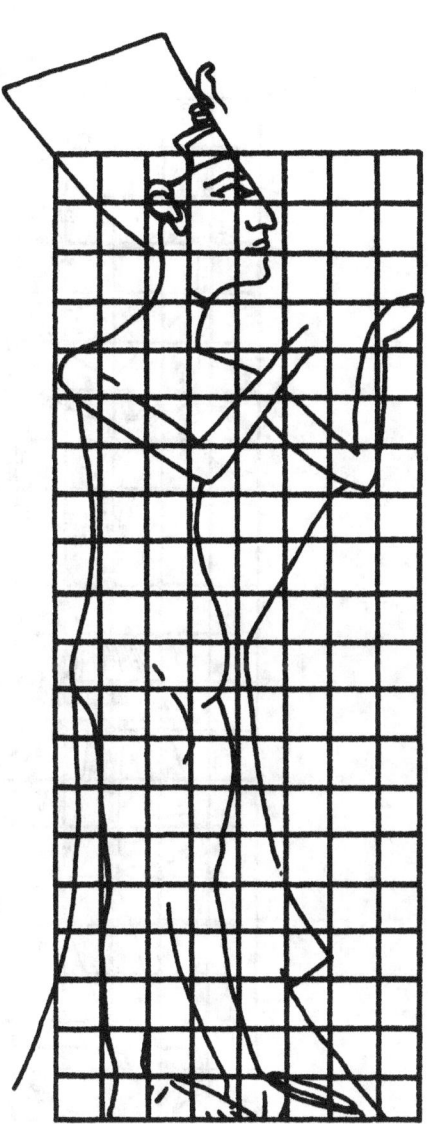

FIGURE 6.24
Standing figure of Nefertiti with hypothetical 20-square grid, tomb chapel of Mahu, Amarna, eighteenth dynasty, after Davies 1906, Plate 16.

In the second scene[58] the grid for the king has been calculated by taking the junction of the neck and shoulders as the level of horizontal 17 (Fig. 6.23). The breast region is then near 14 1/2, the navel at 10 1/2, the belly fold at 9 3/4, and the lower border of the buttocks at 8 3/4, with the knee still on 6. While the navel, belly fold, and lower border of the buttocks are not lowered as much as in the first figure of the king, they are still low compared to other figures.

·The companion figure of the queen is most surprising because of the size of the head, which is 4 squares from the hairline to the junction of the neck and shoulders instead of 3 squares (Fig. 6.24). If the breast were visible, it would lie almost as low as horizontal 14, and the lower border of the buttocks has dropped to 8 1/2, but the knee, unlike that of the other figure of the queen, is on 6. Thus the proportions of these figures in the tomb of Mahu, while not exactly the same in each case, all show some abnormality to a greater or lesser extext, the trend being to lower key points of the body, in some cases beyond what is found in royal figures portrayed in other private Amarna tombs.

6.5. Private Standing Figures

No grid traces survive on private standing figures, even those that are unfinished, so perhaps they were never drawn on grids. However, measurement shows they have a short lower leg like royal figures. In all cases, the hairline level on these figures is more than three times the height of the leg to the top of the knee. In the tomb of Ahmose,[59] the lower leg is a third of the height to the level of the throat, and the hairline is 2 squares higher on a 20-square hypothetical grid. On one figure, the lower border of the buttocks lies on horizontal 10, the belly fold on 11, and the junction of the neck and shoulders about a quarter square above 17 (Fig. 6.25). On the second,[60] the lower border of the buttocks lies approximately 9 1/2 squares above the baseline, the belly fold 10 1/2, and the junction of the neck and shoulders approximately 17 1/4 squares up (Fig. 6.26). On both figures, the width across the shoulders is less than 5 squares.

In the tomb of Panehesy, there is a figure of the tomb owner adoring.[61] It is bald-headed and so has no hairline, and the knees are hidden by an elaborate skirt. However, if a hypothetical hairline is selected by eye to run just above the top of the ear and a 20-square grid calculated, horizontal 18 runs through the chin between the lower lip and the throat, 17 through the junction of the neck and shoulder, 14 through the pronounced breast, and 10 through the belly fold (Fig. 6.27). Two figures of Pentu in his tomb are also bald-headed.[62] If, again, a hypothetical hairline is taken and a 20-square grid constructed, we find that the knee lies on horizontal 6 and the width across the shoulders is less than 5 squares (Figs. 6.28–6.29).

The wife of Merire I appears in her husband's tomb.[63] If her hairline height is divided by 20, horizontal 18 runs close to her throat, 17 through the junction of the neck and shoulder, her breast can be deduced to lie between horizontals 14 and 15, the lower border of her buttocks is about 9 1/4 squares above the baseline, and the top of her knees about 5 1/2 squares up (Fig. 6.30).

The analysis of these figures demonstrates clearly that the proportions adopted for royal figures were transferred to private ones. There is some variation, perhaps because these figures were drawn freehand,

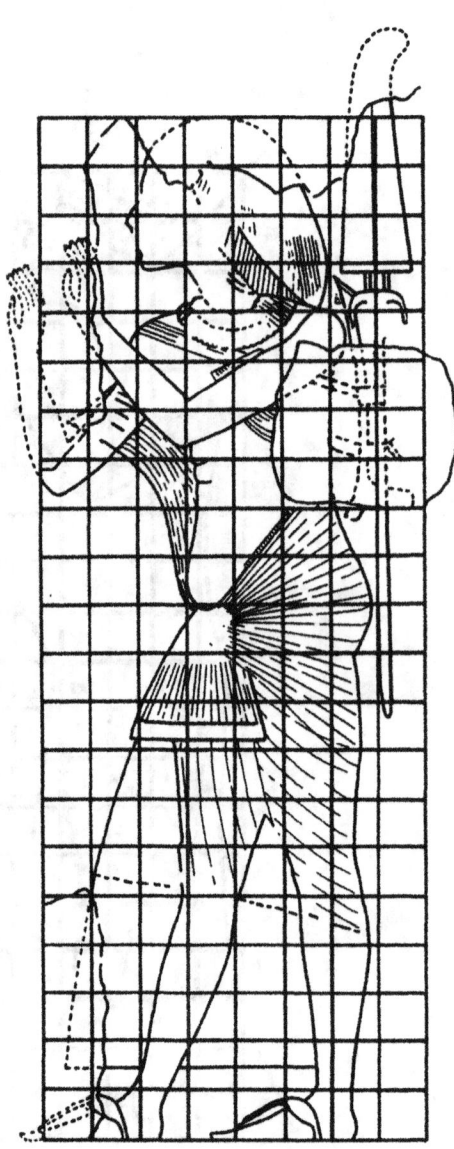

FIGURE 6.25
Standing figure of Ahmose with hypothetical 20-square grid, tomb chapel of Ahmose, Amarna, eighteenth dynasty, after Davies 1905b, Plate 29.

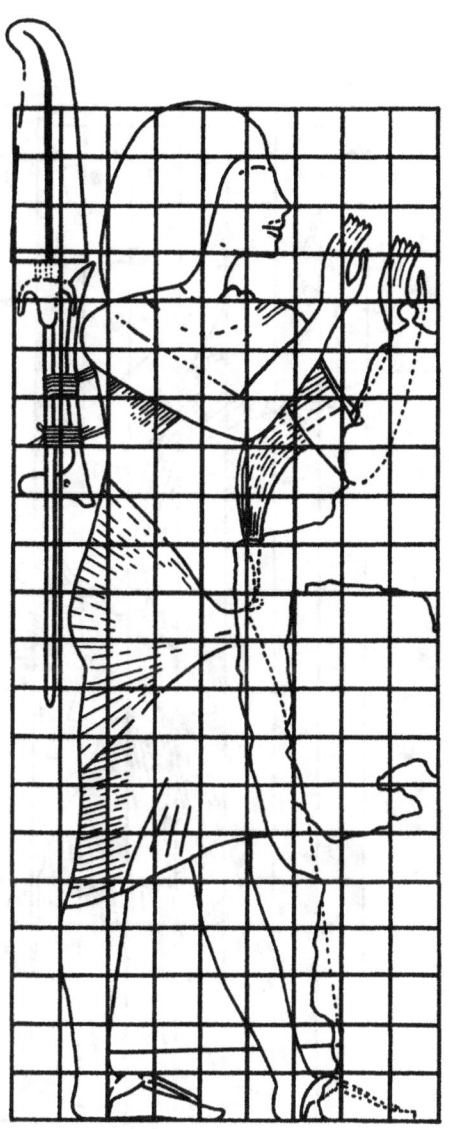

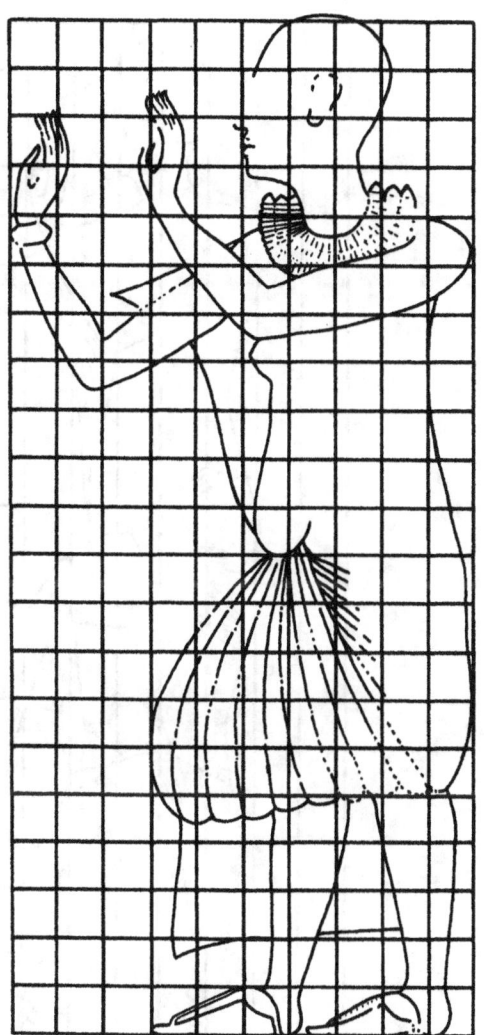

FIGURE 6.26
Standing figure of Ahmose with hypothetical 20-square grid, tomb chapel of Ahmose, Amarna, eighteenth dynasty, after Davies 1905b, Plate 28.

FIGURE 6.27
Standing figure of Panehesy with hypothetical 20-square grid, tomb chapel of Panehesy, Amarna, eighteenth dynasty, after Davies 1905a, Plate 22.

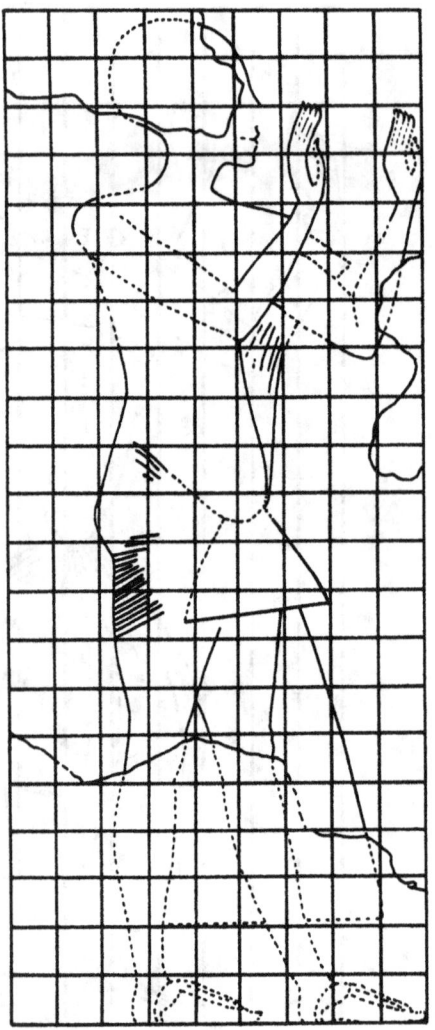

FIGURE 6.28
Standing figure of Pentu with hypothetical 20-square grid, tomb chapel of Pentu, Amarna, eighteenth dynasty, after Davies 1906, Plate 4.

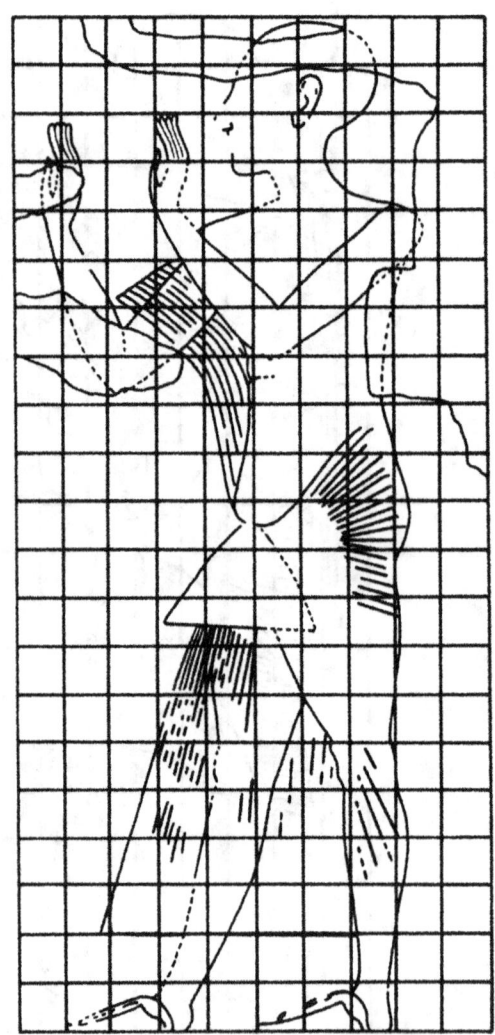

FIGURE 6.29
Standing figure of Pentu with hypothetical 20-square grid, tomb chapel of Pentu, Amarna, eighteenth dynasty, after Davies 1906, Plate 3.

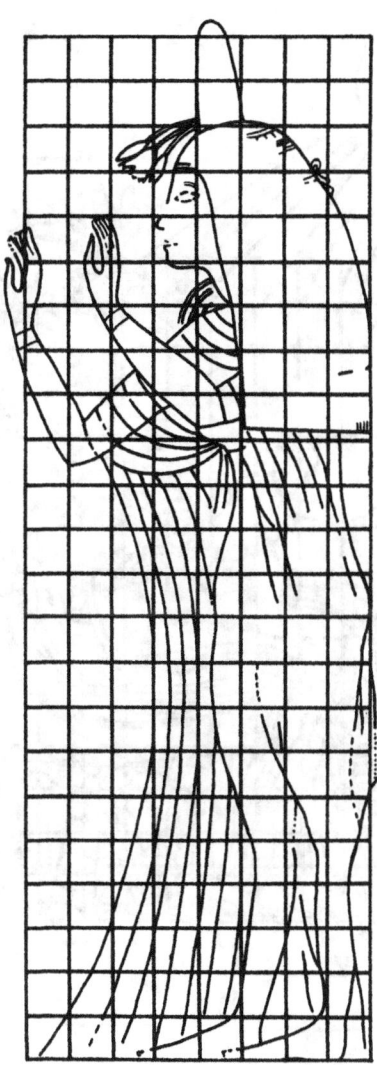

FIGURE 6.30

Standing figure of Senre, wife of Merire I, with hypothetical 20-square grid, tomb chapel of Merire I, Amarna, eighteenth dynasty, after Davies 1903, Plate 36.

but they have the short lower leg, narrow shoulders, and large head and neck associated with Amarna royal proportions.

6.6. Seated Figures

No Amarna seated figure survives with obvious grid traces, but we can attempt to deduce how seated figures might have fitted onto the Amarna grid system by comparing them with standing ones. Even if we are unable to arrive at a certain answer, we can still compare the proportions of seated figures if we analyze them on similar hypothetical grids, irrespective of whether these were used by the original artists or not.

There are two ways in which we can try to work out the number of grid squares in a seated Amarna figure. One approach is to take the height of the top of the knee above the baseline, since we know that in standing figures this distance is 6 squares. This gives a possible grid square size that can be divided into the height of the figure between base and hairline to give the total number of squares in the figure. Problems arise in many cases, however, because it is unclear exactly where the top of the knee lies. So, at best, this method can only yield approximate results.

A second approach is to attempt to relate seated Amarna figures to standing ones in the same way that traditional 14-square seated figures relate to 18-square standing ones (Sec. 4.4). In early Amarna standing figures, the lower border of the buttocks lies 10 squares below the hairline. If we assume that only 5 squares of the lower leg contribute to the height of the figure, as in 14-square figures, then seated figures would consist of $10 + 5 = 15$ squares. In testing this hypothesis, I have

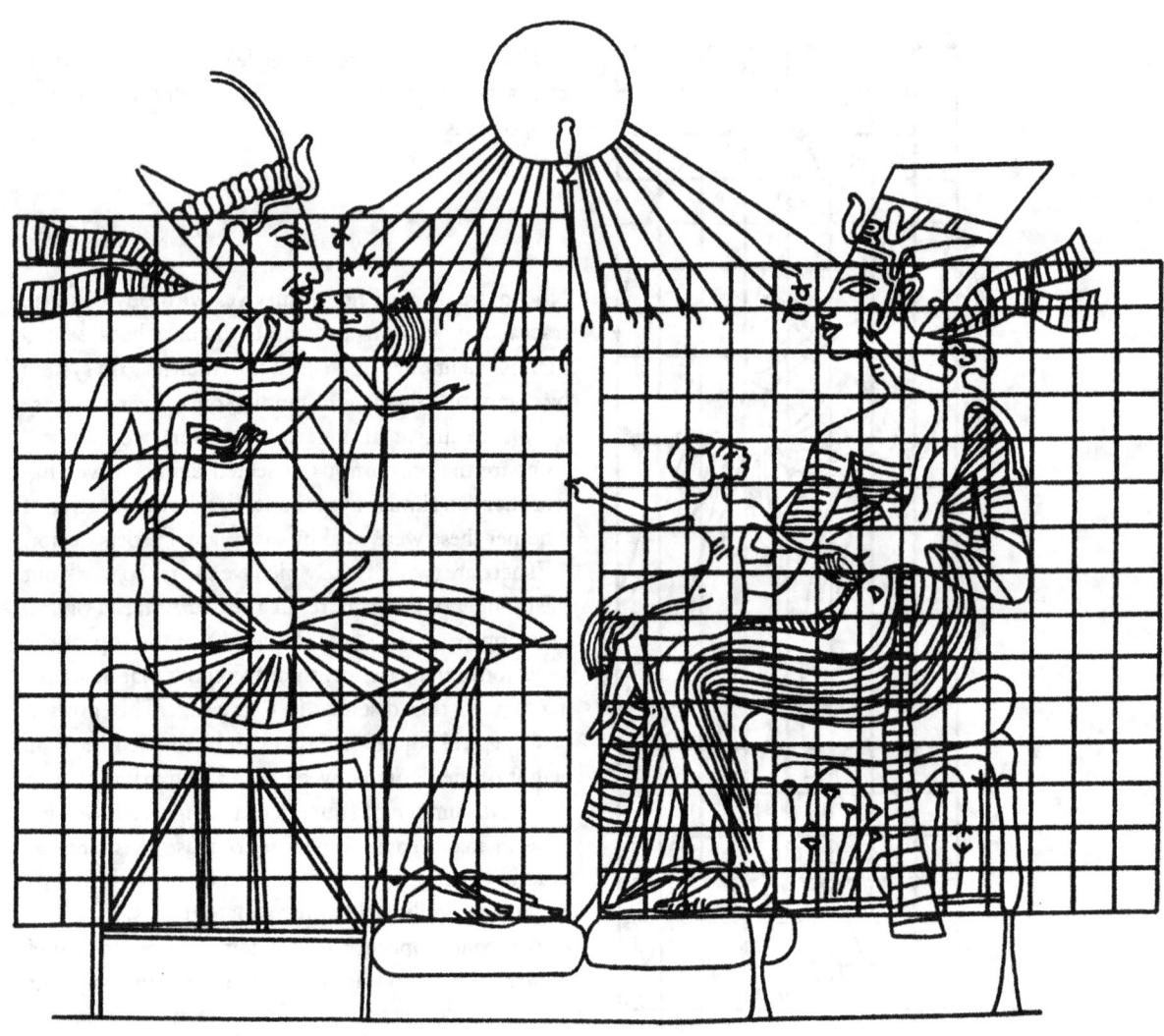

FIGURE 6.31
Seated figures of Akhenaton and Nefertiti with
hypothetical 15-square grids, stela, Amarna, Berlin
inv. no. 14145, eighteenth dynasty, after Aldred
1973, 102 no. 16.

found that in a number of cases the points of the body through which the horizontals of a 15-square grid pass on seated figures correspond very closely with the points of the body through which the horizontals of a 20-square grid pass on standing figures.

The best results are obtained from royal figures on private stelae (Figs. 6.31–6.32). For instance, on the Berlin stela[64] the first line below the hairline passes through the nose, the second runs through the throat, the third through the junction of the neck and forward shoulder, and the fifth through the breast region, just as in many standing figures. In standing figures, the navel is most often about 9 squares below the hairline and the belly fold 10 squares below. In seated figures, they are placed no lower than 8 and 9 squares below respectively and are often higher, presumably because they are pushed upward when the body is in a seated position; a similar effect occurs in 14-square seated figures. In addition, the royal buttocks often sag lower than horizontal 5, in contrast to traditional seated figures on a 14-square grid, where the lower border of the buttocks and bottom of the thigh run along the top of the seat in a straight line, commonly on the level of horizontal 5. At Amarna, royal personages sit on soft cushions into which the buttocks and thigh sink down in a curve, rising again to the level of the knees.[65]

Some of the royal seated figures in the private tombs at Amarna have proportions that correspond less well with those of standing figures.[66] Analysis on a 15-square grid shows that the distance from the hairline to the junction of the neck and shoulders is usually less than 3 squares, while the height of the knee is in most cases at least 6 1/2 squares above the base, giving a relatively small head and long leg. In addition, the frequent practice of placing the lower leg in seated

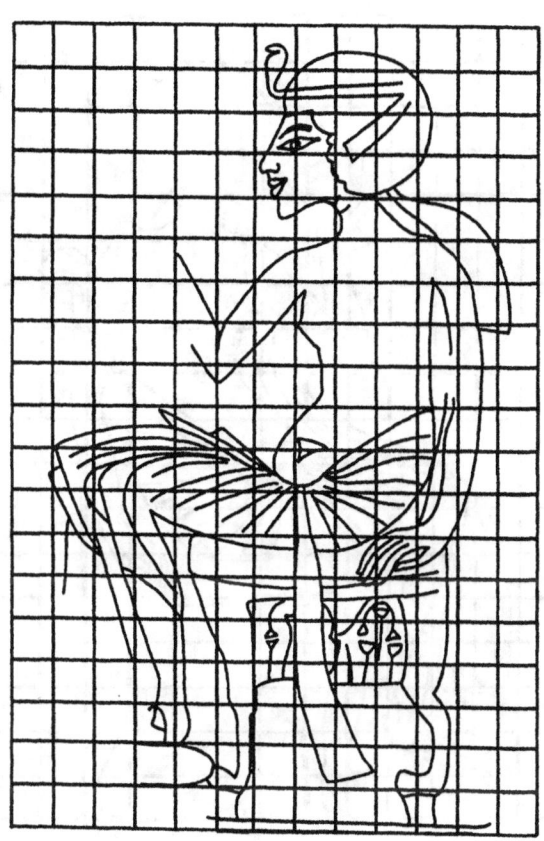

FIGURE 6.32
Seated figure of Akhenaton with hypothetical 15-square grid, stela, Amarna, British Museum EA 24431, eighteenth dynasty, after Edwards 1939, Plate 23.

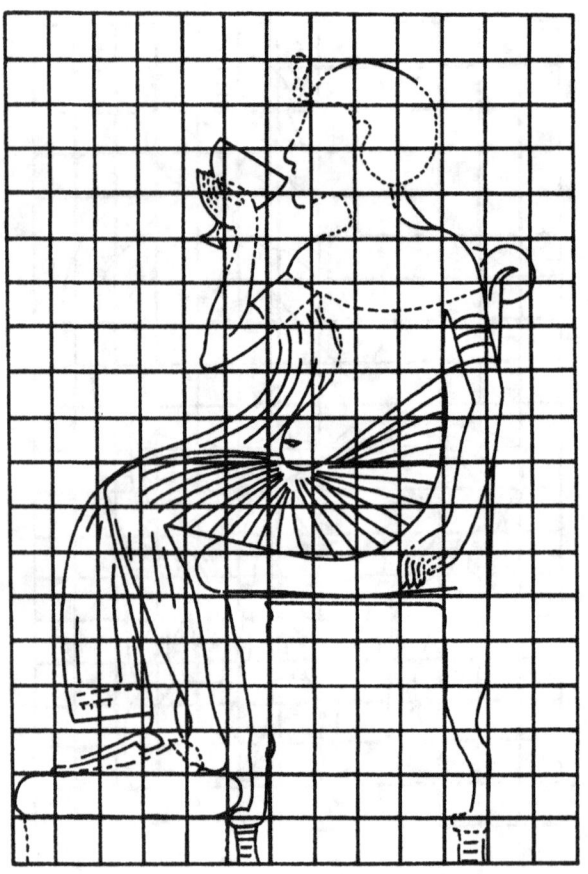

FIGURE 6.33

Seated figure of Akhenaton with hypothetical 15-square grid, tomb chapel of Huy, Amarna, eighteenth dynasty, after Davies 1905b, Plate 6.

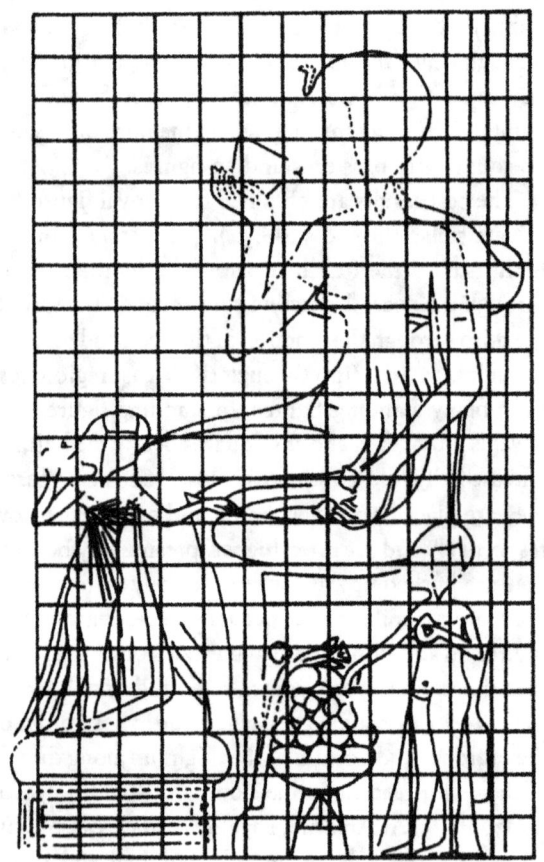

FIGURE 6.34

Seated figure of Nefertiti with hypothetical 15-square grid, tomb chapel of Huy, Amarna, eighteenth dynasty, after Davies 1905b, Plate 6.

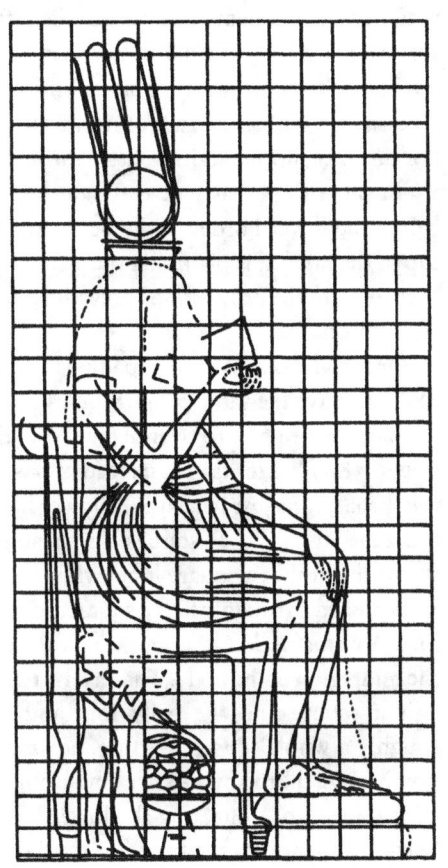

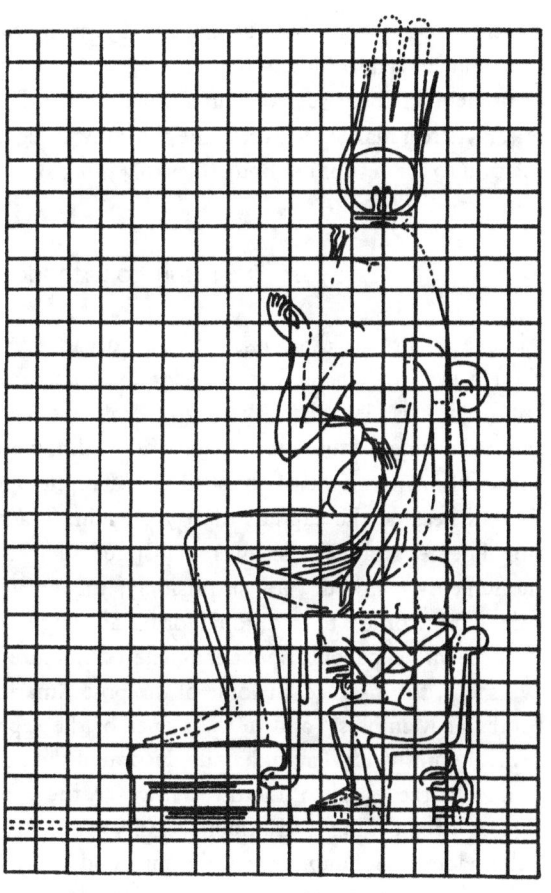

FIGURE 6.35
Seated figure of Teye with hypothetical 15-square grid,
tomb chapel of Huy, Amarna, eighteenth dynasty, after
Davies 1905b, Plate 6.

FIGURE 6.36
Seated figure of Teye with hypothetical 15-square grid,
tomb chapel of Huy, Amarna, eighteenth dynasty, after
Davies 1905b, Plate 4.

Amarna figures at an oblique angle makes it appear even longer. The result is that the leg is far more prominent in these seated figures than in standing ones, where a marked feature is the short lower leg in relation to the rest of the body (Figs. 6.33–6.36).

6.7. The Return to Orthodoxy

Akhenaton's reign lasted less than two decades. Although events at the end of the reign are somewhat confused, it is clear that Akhenaton's reforms were rejected during the subsequent reign of Tutankhamun. The city of Amarna was abandoned and Memphis and Thebes became the capitals of Egypt again. Traditional deities and their cults were reinstated and their monuments restored. Not surprisingly, the art returned more or less to traditional forms, although the Amarna influence could not be completely obliterated. We see it, for instance, in some of the post-Amarna tombs at Memphis[67] and in the scenes of the Opet festival with which Tutankhamun decorated the colonnade at the temple of Luxor.[68] However, the large figures of the king and Amun at the end of the colonnade[69] are indubitably traditional, and analysis shows that their proportions have returned to those generated by an 18-square grid. This return to orthodoxy can also be traced in the contents and decoration of Tutankhamun's tomb.

Among the statues found in the tomb were a pair of gilded figures of the king. In each the king is standing on the back of a panther, although the figures of the king and the panthers were made separately.[70] The one most frequently illustrated in the literature (no. 289b) is recognizably very much in the Amarna style with a long neck, prominent belly fold, and short legs. If the vertical height is divided into twentieths, the dividing lines pass through the same points as the horizontals of a 20-square grid on a figure of Akhenaton (Fig. 6.37). For instance, horizontal 18 passes through the throat, 15 through the breast, 11 through the navel, 9 just below the lower border of the buttocks, and 6 at the top of the knee. It is plain that the statue was designed according to the proportions prevailing in the reign of Akhenaton.

One might expect the companion to this statue (no. 289a) to have the same proportions, but a division of the hairline height into twentieths shows this is not so (Fig. 6.38). Horizontal 18, instead of passing through the throat, runs just beneath the lower lip; yet 17 is at the same level on both statues. As a result, in the first statue the neck is a square long, while in the second it is shortened to roughly half a square, so modifying the long Amarna neck. Other noticeable differences lie in the midregion of the body. The navel is raised by about half a square and the belly fold and buttocks by roughly a whole square. Further, horizontal 6 passes not through the top of the knee but through the bottom of the kneecap, elongating the lower leg. In fact, the height to the top of the knee is a third of the hairline height, and it is possible that this second statue was designed according to proportions generated by a traditional 18-square grid.

There are other details that differ between the two statues, confirming the impression that they were not originally made as a pair. The first has a typical Amarna crescent-shaped navel, while the navel of the second is round in the traditional manner. The kilt of the first statue has no belt and at the back it reaches to the bottom of the calf. The second statue has a wide

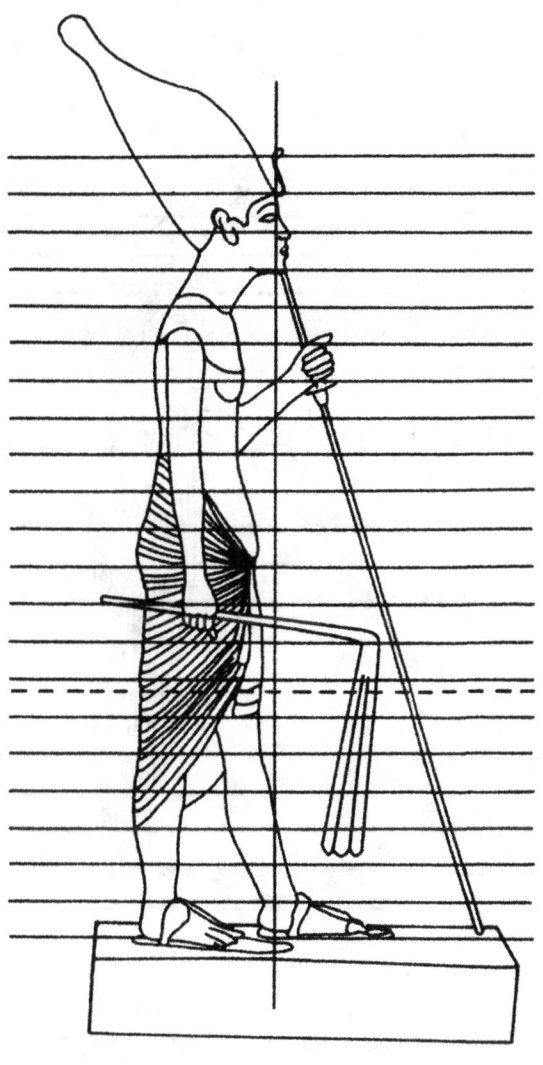

FIGURE 6.37
Standing statue of Tutankhamun on horizontals of
hypothetical 20-square grid, KV 62, eighteenth dynasty,
Carter no. 289b, after Burton photograph in Griffith
Institute Oxford C/B14 1519.

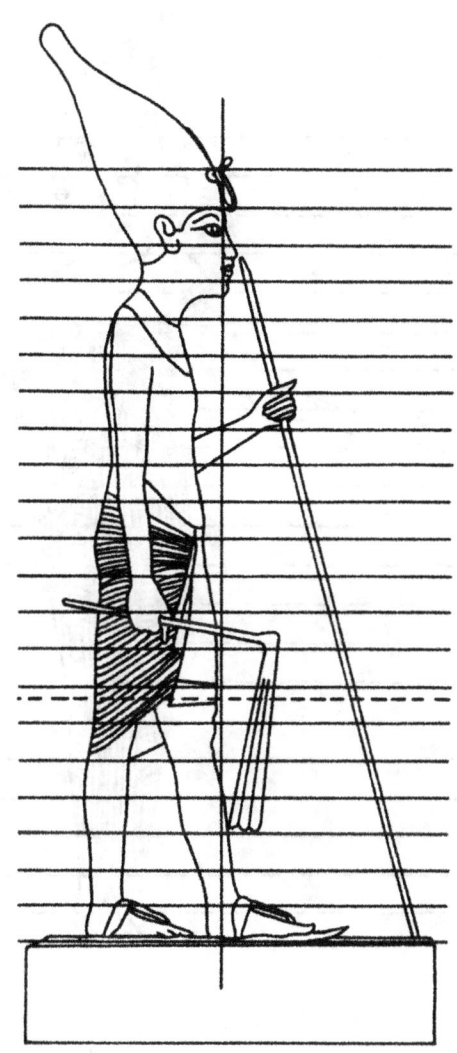

FIGURE 6.38
Standing statue of Tutankhamun on horizontals of
hypothetical 20-square grid, KV 62, eighteenth dynasty,
Carter no. 289a, after Davison 1979, 19.

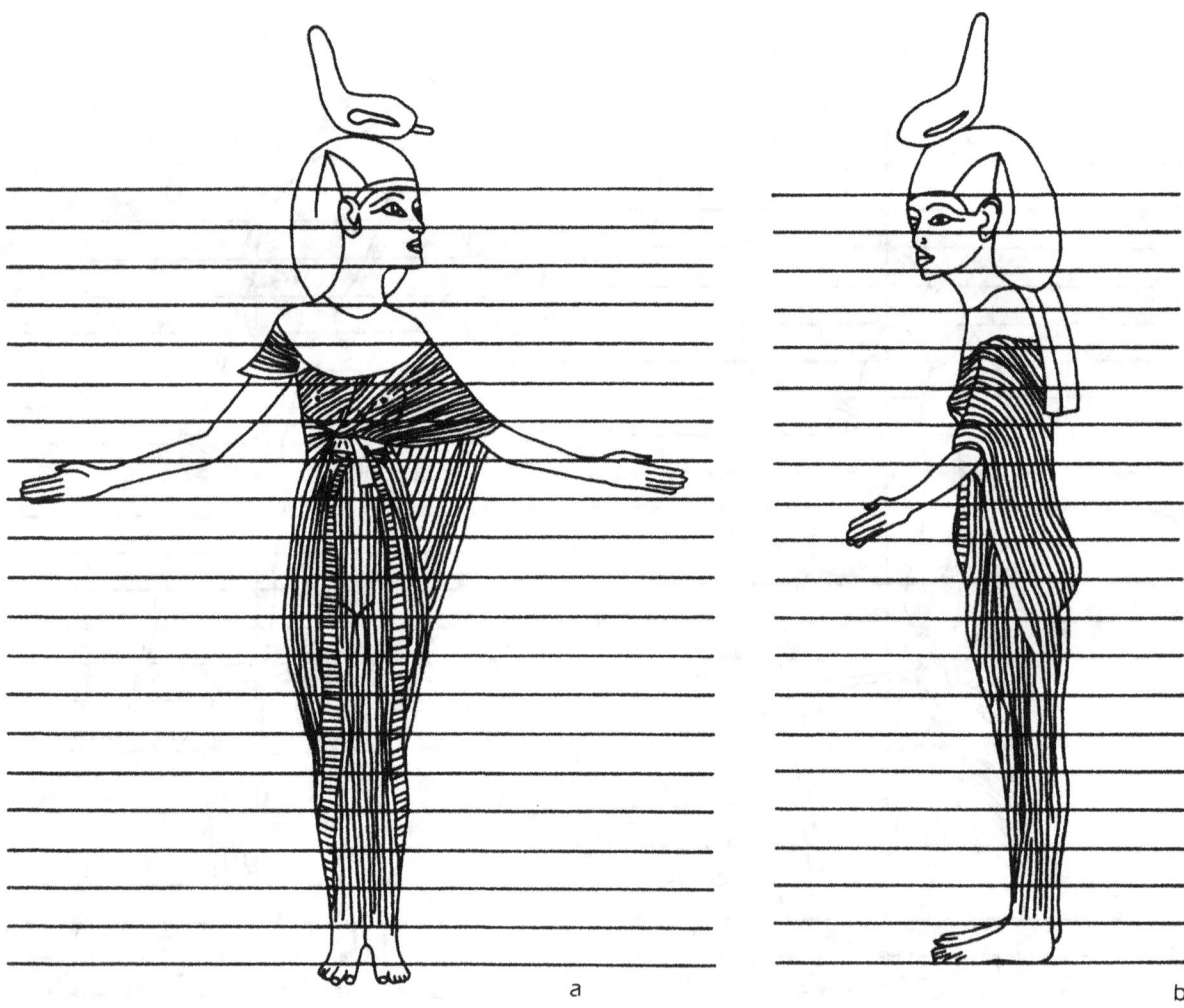

FIGURE 6.39
Standing statue of Selket on horizontals of hypothetical
20-square grid, KV 62, eighteenth dynasty: a, front
view, after Edwards 1976, Plate 25; b, side view, after
Davison 1979, 67 right.

belt and the kilt is shorter. Further, the eyes of the first statue have no cosmetic line and the eyebrows curve downward at the outer ends. In the second statue, the cosmetic line is pronounced and the outer end of the eyebrow turns to run parallel with it.

It is tempting to think that if the statues were not in fact created as a pair, the one with full Amarna proportions was made during Akhenaton's reign but left unused, and was later appropriated for Tutankhamun's funerary equipment. A companion would then have been made for it in Tutankhamun's reign according to the more traditional proportions that were being reintroduced. Since the panthers are separate from the royal statues, the Amarna style statue need not originally have been associated with the animal, if such symbolism were unsuited to the Aton religion.

Among some of the most beautiful objects in Tutankhamun's tomb were four gilded statues of the goddesses Isis, Nephthys, Selket, and Neith, which protected the king's canopic shrine.[71] Although the position of their knees is not completely clear, careful inspection of photographs seems to indicate that they have short lower legs. I have therefore analyzed them by dividing the distance between hairline and soles into twentieths and comparing them with figures of Nefertiti (Fig. 6.39a, 6.39b). In all four statues, the long Amarna neck of 1 square is present and the distance between the hairline and the junction of the neck and shoulders is 3 squares. Horizontal 18 runs along the throat and 17 through the junction of neck and shoulders; the nipples lie roughly at 14 1/2; the maximum convexity of the buttocks is near 10 and their lower border near 9. These levels agree closely with the proportions found in later figures of Nefertiti and were clearly designed according to the proportions used in later-style Amarna figures.[72]

However, since no statues of goddesses would have been made for royal use in the Amarna period, these four statues seem to show that Amarna proportions continued to be used without modification, at least in female figures, into the reign of Tutankhamun. On the other hand, the long pleated dresses and shawls draped around the figures are unexpected. This style of garment had appeared in the iconography of royal and private women in the reign of Thutmose IV, but it was neither then nor later adopted for goddesses, who right up to the end of the period of Roman occupation continued to wear the traditional straight, tight-fitting sheath dress that is sleeveless and ends just above the ankles. This is the dress worn by goddesses in all other representations in the tomb of Tutankhamun. Further, while the four statues wear the *khat* headdress (a cloth covering the hair), which in female figures is normally reserved for goddesses, it has been argued that in the Amarna period it was worn by queens taking the place of goddesses, who were of course excluded from the Aton cult.[73] The style of dress and the presence of the *khat* headdress, therefore, support the possibility that the statues originally represented an Amarna queen, and that the emblems of the goddesses worn on their heads were added later. The statues were probably left unused from the Amarna period and altered to make them suitable for use in the funerary equipment of the new king.

The majority of the items in the tomb equipment are decorated with figures that once more have traditional proportions, with the height of the lower leg to the knee one-third of the hairline height, although some Amarna traits survive. The four goddesses decorating

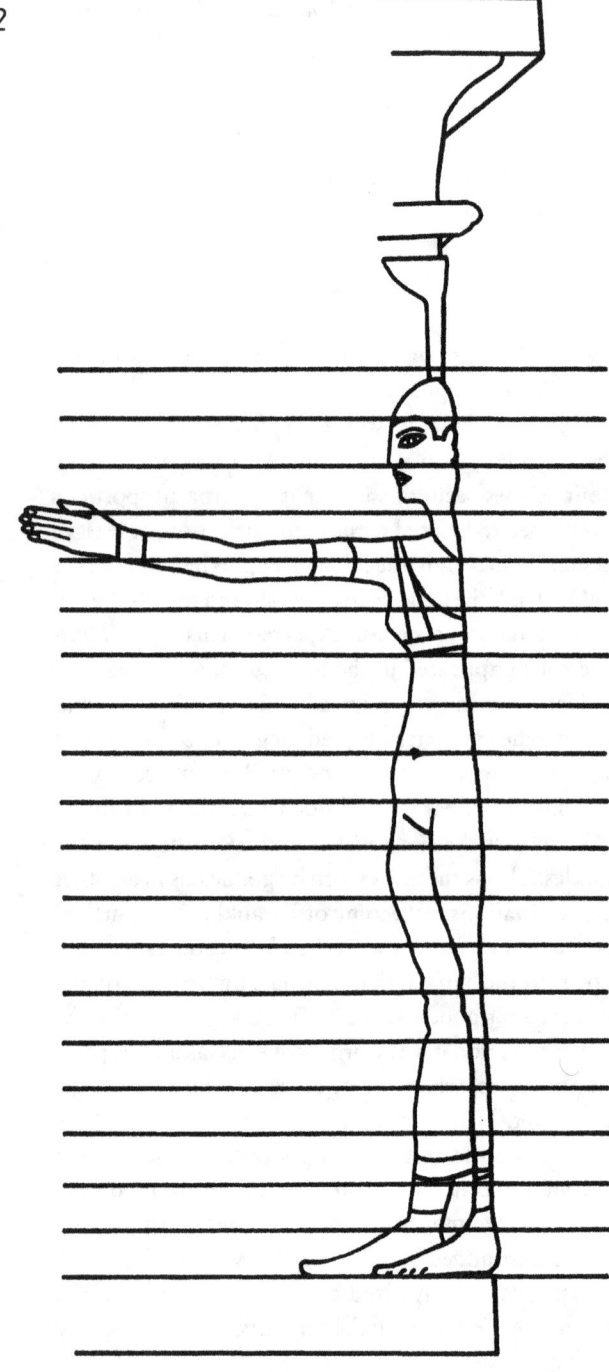

FIGURE 6.40
Standing figure of Nephthys in high relief on corner of sarcophagus with horizontals of hypothetical 18-square grid, KV 62, eighteenth dynasty, after Burton photograph in Griffith Institute Oxford C/B4 646B.

the sarcophagus of Tutankhamun[74] are clearly designed according to 18-square proportions, but it is interesting that the heads of Selket and Nephthys are 2 1/2 squares from the hairline to the junction of the neck and shoulders, not the traditional 2 squares (Fig. 6.40). This is perhaps a remnant of the larger head found in the Amarna canon.

The gold shrines that surrounded the sarcophagus are covered with figures whose leg and head proportions are clearly traditional.[75] However, the narrow width of the shoulders and limbs, which gives a look of delicacy to the figures, may be a remnant of the Amarna style. For some reason, the lower border of the buttocks lies on horizontal 9, not on 10 as in the proportions of the immediately pre-Amarna period (Figs. 6.41–6.42).

The proportions of the figures on the famous small gilded shrine[76] are also somewhat unusual. The height of the lower leg to the knee is always at least a third of the hairline height, justifying analysis on a traditional grid; one can also see by eye that the long Amarna neck is absent. However, in most of the figures the head is 2 1/2 squares from the hairline to the junction of the neck and shoulders, with horizontal 16 running through the throat, preserving the large Amarna head (Fig. 6.43). Further, the floating garments and streamers, the curves of draped limbs and of the buttocks and thighs in seated figures as they sink into soft cushions are all reminiscent of the Amarna style. So the decoration of the shrine would seem to be the work of craftsmen who were still steeped in the Amarna style but abandoned strict Amarna proportions in favor of more traditional ones.

On the foot of Tutankhamun's inner coffin, there is a kneeling figure of Isis, arms stretched wide in a

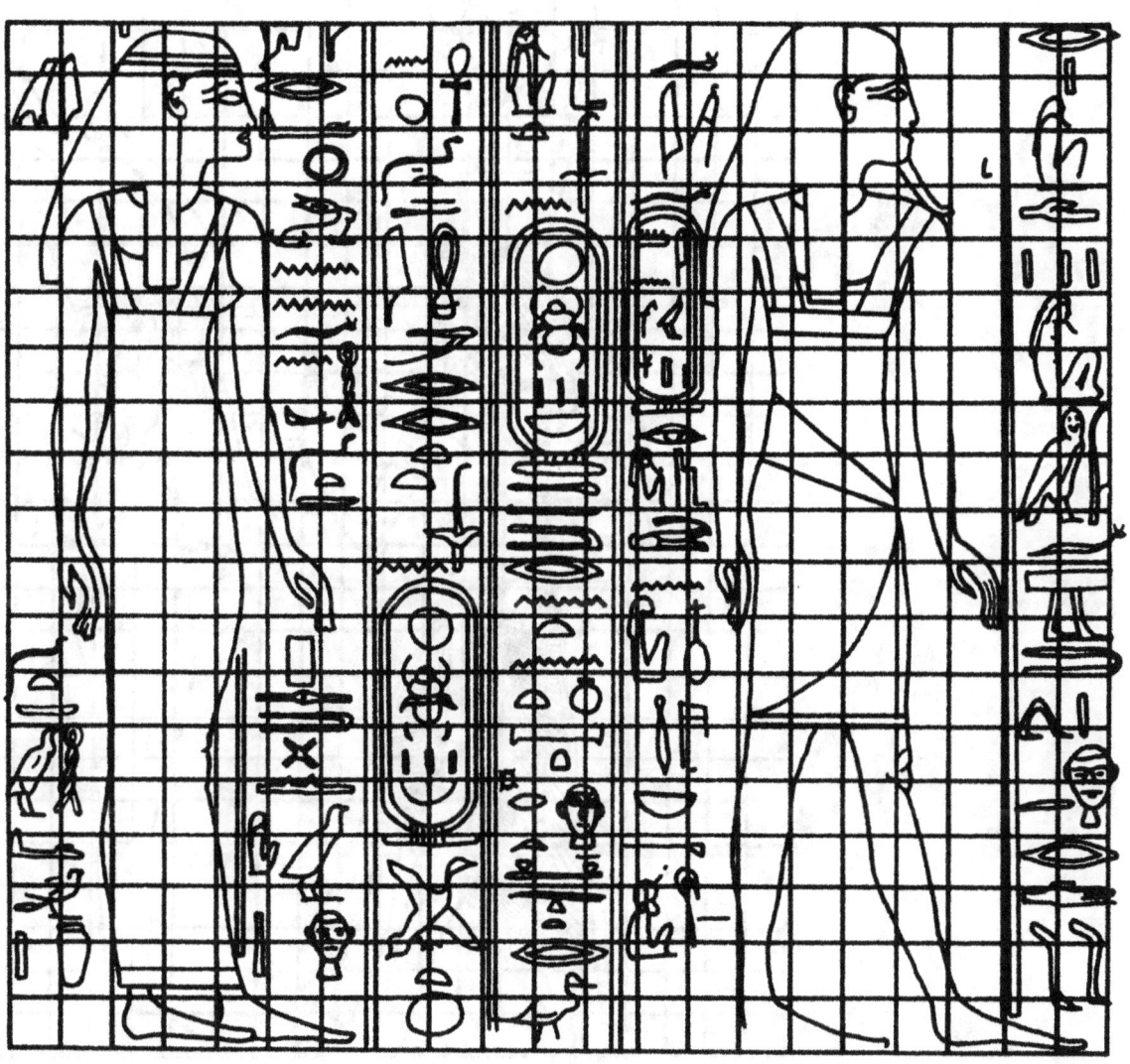

FIGURE 6.41
Standing figures with hypothetical 18-square grid,
shrine III, interior right panel, KV 62, after Piankoff
1955, Plate 27.

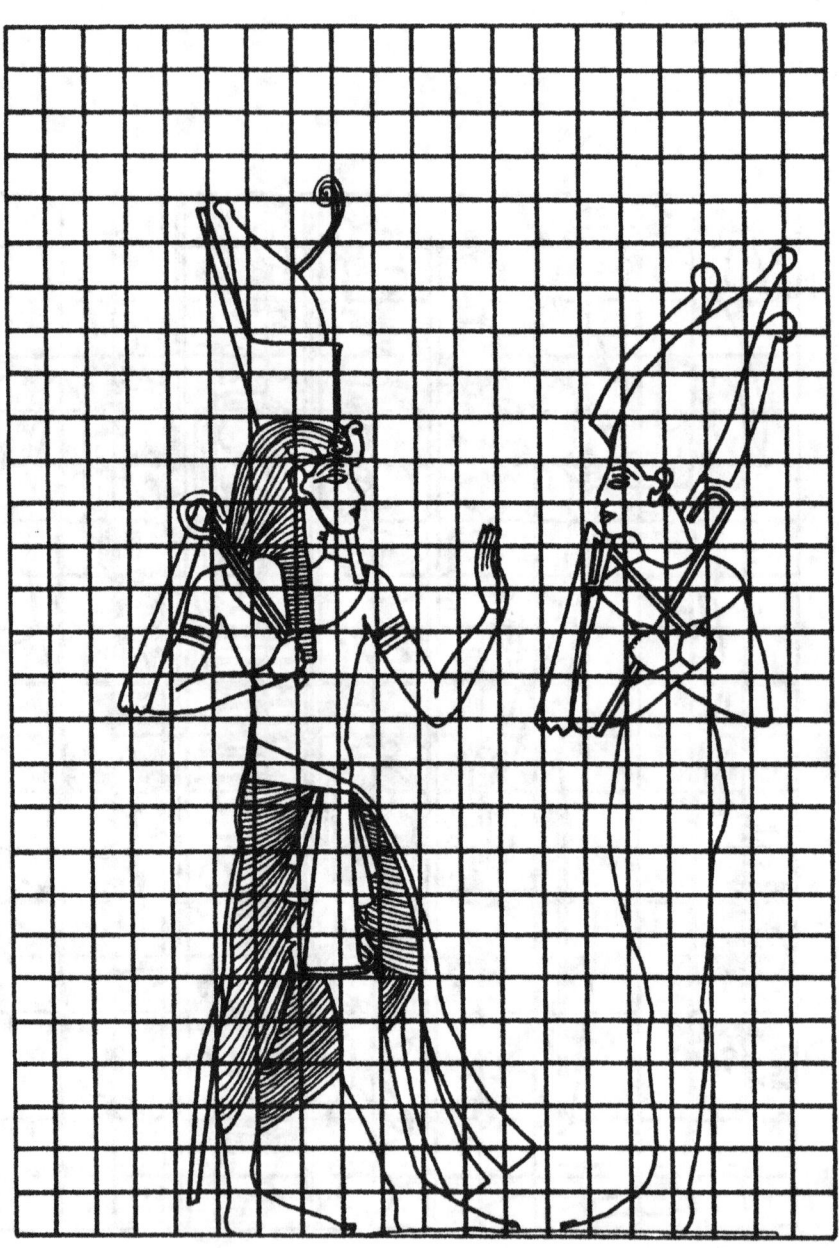

FIGURE 6.42
Standing figures of Tutankhamun and Osiris with hypothetical 18-square grid, shrine II, KV 62, eighteenth dynasty, after Kamal el-Mallakh 1978, Plate 27.

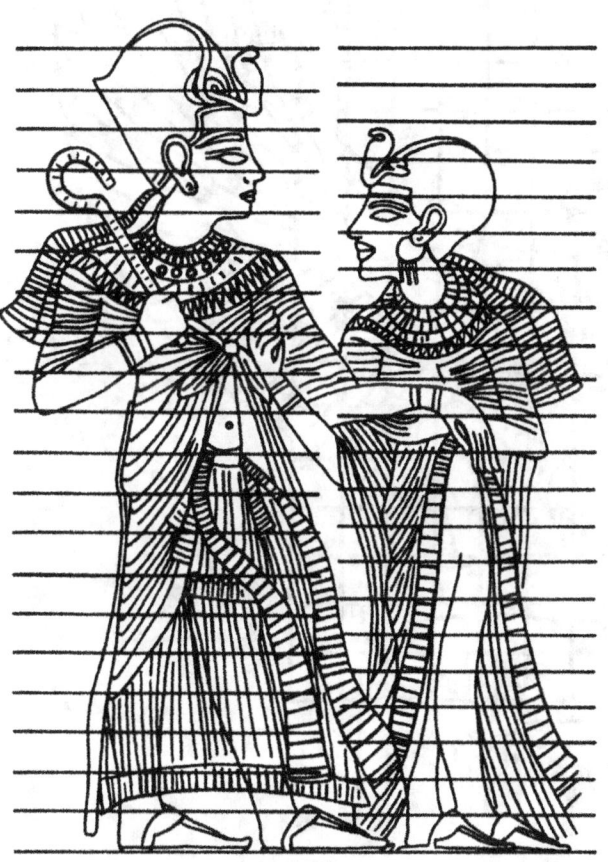

FIGURE 6.43

Standing figures of Tutankhamun and Ankhesenamun on horizontals of hypothetical 18-square grids, small gilded shrine, KV 62, eighteenth dynasty, after Eaton-Krauss and Graefe 1985, Plate 14 right.

gesture of protection,[77] and it would be hard to imagine a figure with more traditional proportions (Fig. 6.44). Figures who kneel in this fashion comprise 10 squares from hairline to baseline on a grid, with 9 squares to the lower border of the buttocks and 1 square for the width of the leg on which they sit (Sec. 5.4). In this figure, everything is traditional. The head from the hairline to the junction of the neck and shoulders is approximately 2 squares, and from there to the nipple is another 2 squares, while the lower border of the buttocks lies 9 squares below the hairline. The width across the small of the back is about 1 3/4 squares, which is common for female figures.

Amarna proportions, however, did not disappear completely in the reign of Tutankhamun, as is shown by an analysis of the figures on the walls of his tomb, no. 62 in the Valley of the Kings.[78] The plan of the tomb suggests that it was not designed for a royal burial, and it seems likely that when the young king died, probably unexpectedly, the work on his own tomb was not far enough advanced for it to be prepared in time for his burial. His successor Ay had therefore to order the use of another tomb. Possibly Ay as king then took Tutankhamun's intended tomb for his own, while the tomb in which he actually buried the young king may have been meant for himself as a private person. Certainly private people were buried in the Valley of the Kings. In any case, the decoration of Tutankhamun's final resting place must have been hastily executed between the king's death and burial, which may account for the unusual style of the figures on the walls.

If the proportions of the figures are analyzed, we find that they are not uniform on the south and north walls. On the south wall, the length of the king's lower

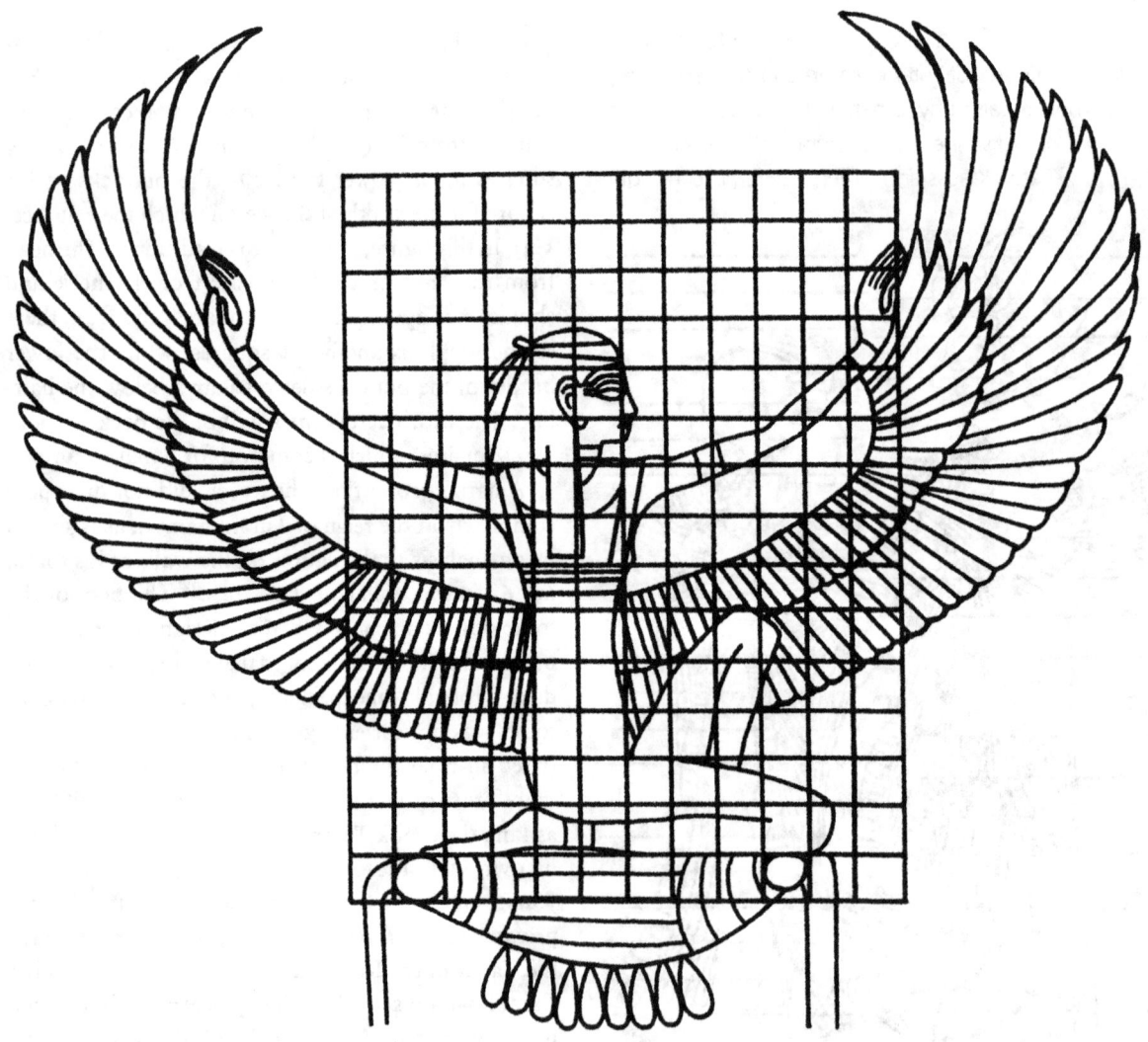

FIGURE 6.44
Kneeling figure of Isis with hypothetical 10-square grid,
foot of inner coffin, KV 62, eighteenth dynasty, after
Kamal el-Mallakh 1978, Plate 13.

leg to the top of the knee is unequivocally a third of the hairline height, suggesting that analysis on an 18-square grid would be appropriate (Fig. 6.45). The lower border of the buttocks is then just above horizontal 9, the maximum convexity on 10, and the small of the back a little above 12. The junction of the neck and shoulders is, however, 2 1/2 squares below the hairline.

On the north wall, the king and his *ka* at the left hand end of the row of figures plainly display their knees. They each have slightly different hairline heights, which is unusual in a row of figures, but in both cases the knee is only a third of the height to the chin and not to the hairline, suggesting proportions more appropriate to a 20-square grid (Fig. 6.46). The lower border of the buttocks is then near horizontal 9, the maximum convexity at 10 1/2, the navel on 11 1/2, the small of the back on or near 13, the nipple on 15, and the junction of the neck and shoulders on or near 17. The long Amarna neck is slightly shortened, so that 18 runs just higher than the level of the throat. These vertical proportions fall within the range of those found in figures of the Amarna king in the later style. Thus different teams of artists must have worked on the south and north walls, the former using proportions resembling traditional ones and the latter still using Amarna proportions.

More extraordinary is that the short lower leg is also found in the tomb of Tutankhamun's successor, Ay, where figures in many ways resemble those in Tutankhamun's tomb.[79] It is still present in the decoration of the tomb of Haremhab, the next king (Fig. 6.47),[80] and in that of his successor, Ramesses I,[81] although otherwise the figures and types of scenes in these last two tombs are completely traditional.

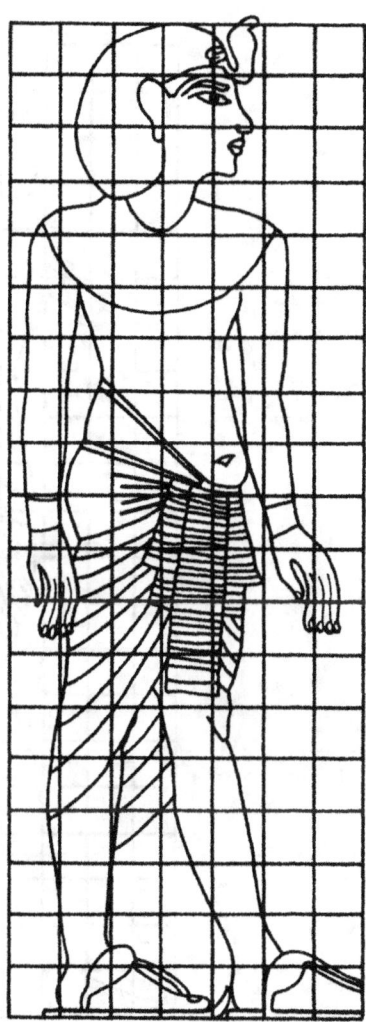

FIGURE 6.45
Standing figure of Tutankhamun with hypothetical 18-square grid, south wall, KV 62, eighteenth dynasty, after Desroches-Noblecourt et al. 1967, between pp. 140–141.

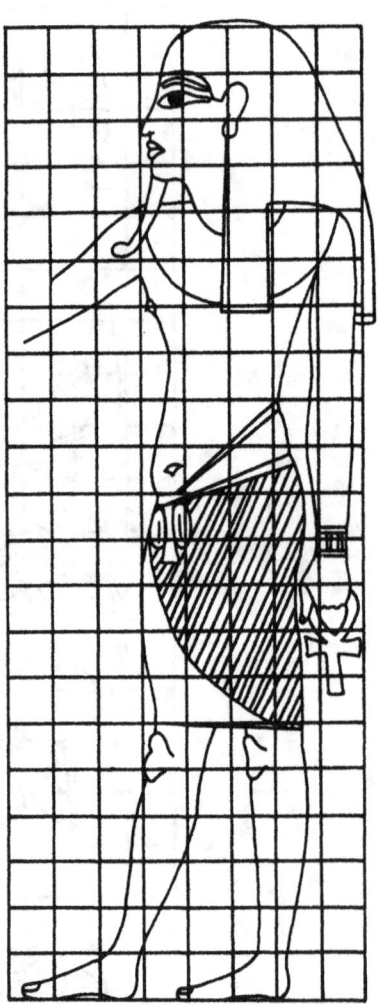

FIGURE 6.46

Standing figure of the ka of Tutankhamun with hypothetical 20-square grid, north wall, KV 62, eighteenth dynasty, after Desroches-Noblecourt et al. 1967, between pp. 140 and 141.

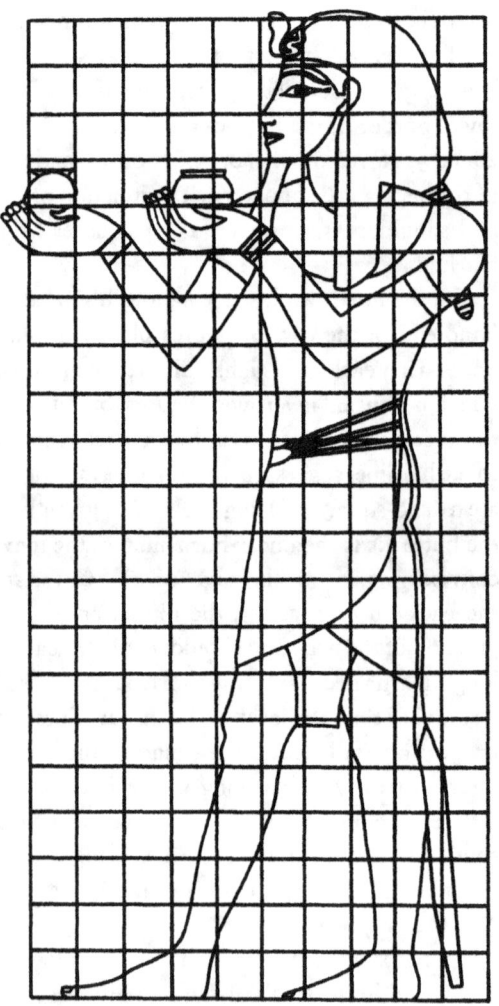

FIGURE 6.47

Standing figure of Haremhab with a hypothetical 20-square grid, KV 57, eighteenth dynasty, after Hornung 1971, Plate 7.

The survival of the short Amarna leg on royal material seems only to occur in the tombs of Tutankhamun, Ay, Haremhab, and Ramesses I; it has yet to be found on other royal monuments from these reigns. The workmen who excavated and decorated the royal tombs at Thebes lived in a special government community set up for this purpose. During the Amarna period, when there was no royal tomb built at Thebes, it is likely that this specialist work force was removed to the new capital at Amarna to work on the royal tomb there. In the reign of Tutankhamun, the situation must have gone into reverse; no more tombs were needed at Amarna, but a royal tomb was again to be built at Thebes. One can only suggest that this elite community of artists brought the short Amarna leg back to Thebes and continued to incorporate it in the figures of the tombs they decorated, in contrast to the artists working on other monuments who had returned to traditional leg proportions. It was not until the royal tomb of Sety I was decorated about 1300 BC that the leg proportions of figures returned to normal.

7

The Late Period and After

It was recognized by various scholars of the nineteenth century that a different grid system came into operation during the Late period and continued in use into the period of Roman occupation (Chap. 2). For a long time it was thought that the change to the later system took place in the twenty-sixth dynasty,[1] but there is in fact evidence that the new grid was already employed in the twenty-fifth dynasty. Grid traces on figures in the chapel of Amenirdis I, daughter of Kashta, at Medinet Habu, can only have been part of a 21 square grid to the upper eyelid, not an 18-square grid to the hairline.[2]

Although there can be no doubt that the later grid system was already in use by the twenty-fifth dynasty, a paucity of grid traces between the nineteenth and twenty-fifth dynasties makes it difficult to say exactly when the change took place. Bietak and Reiser-Haslauer have argued that the transition can be seen in the tomb of Montuemhat at Thebes, where two seated figures of Montuemhat and his wife, worked in high relief so as to be virtually statues, were apparently laid out on lines that form the horizontals of the earlier grid system, while elsewhere in the tomb an offering bearer has associated guidelines that relate to the later grid system.[3] Nevertheless, since evidence concerning the changeover from one grid to the other is scarce, we do not know whether the later grid was adopted all over Egypt at the same time or whether it might have been introduced into some areas before others. Nor can we tell at the moment whether the two grids were used side by side for any length of time.

7.1. Standing Figures in the Later Grid System

Although the later grid had undoubtedly been introduced by the time of the twenty-fifth dynasty, com-

plete figures associated with numerous grid traces do not survive from earlier than the twenty-sixth dynasty. One of the best known is a standing figure of Ibi, owner of Theban tomb 36.[4] Around the edges of the figure red lines from the original grid survive.[5] At some time in the past, these were completed in black to run across the relief-cut figure, from which all traces of the original grid had been removed by the working of the stone.[6] This restoration, which Mackay commented on in 1917,[7] is inaccurate and clumsy, with many of the black lines failing to meet up with the original red ones. It is, however, possible to reconstruct a grid for the standing figure based on the surviving traces (Fig. 7.1).[8]

From the same dynasty, there comes a limestone ostrakon showing a sketch of King Apries between two divine figures, one of which is falcon-headed; the second is almost lost.[9] The whole group is laid out on a grid (Pl. 7.1). Another figure on a grid dating to the Saite period, found in TT 223, was recorded by Lepsius (Fig. 7.2) and later by Prisse.[10] A later example associated with a grid is found on the sarcophagus of Takhos now in the Cairo Museum (Fig. 7.3).[11]

These examples show that in the later grid system, horizontal 21 passes through the upper eyelid (or root of the nose), 20 through the mouth, 19 through the junction of the neck and shoulders, 16 through or near the nipple, 13 through or near the small of the back, 11 through or near the lower border of the buttocks, 7 at the top of the knee, 6 below the bulge of the tibial tubercle, and 0 through the soles. An axial vertical runs through the ear dividing the neck and upper torso in two as in the old system. However, the armpits are now roughly 5 squares apart, that is, each lies 2 1/2 squares on either side of the axial vertical, so that they are placed between and not on grid verticals. The distance

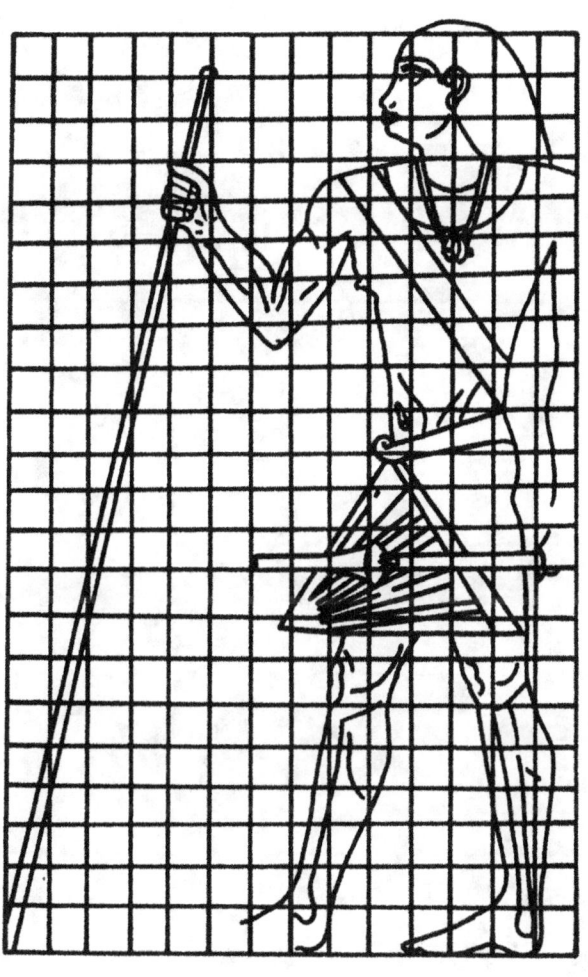

FIGURE 7.1
Standing figure of Ibi with grid completed from
surviving traces, TT 36, twenty-sixth dynasty, after
Kuhlmann and Schenkel 1983, Plate 31.

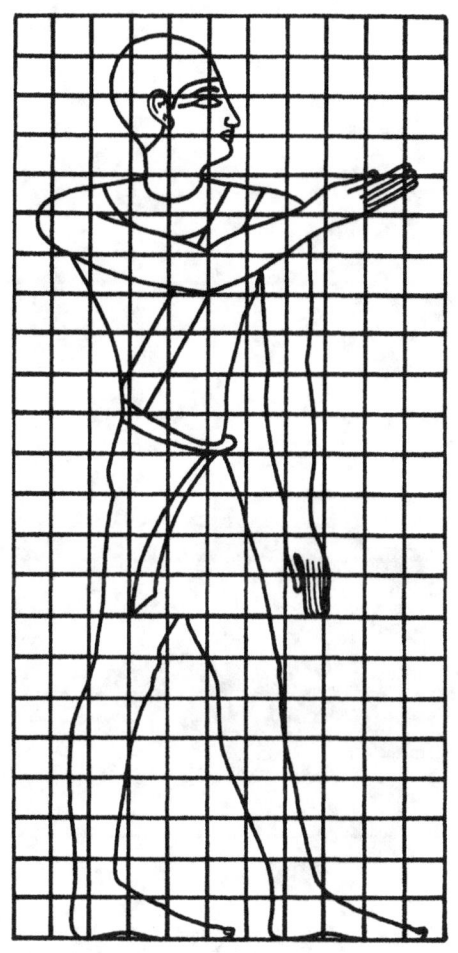

FIGURE 7.2
Standing figure on original grid, TT 223, twenty-sixth
dynasty, after LD 3, 282d.

PLATE 7.1
Figures of Apries and two deities on original grid,
ostrakon, twenty-sixth dynasty, Louvre, infrared
photograph provided by Le Laboratoire de Recherche
des Musées de France, reproduced by kind permission
of M.J.-L. de Cénival.

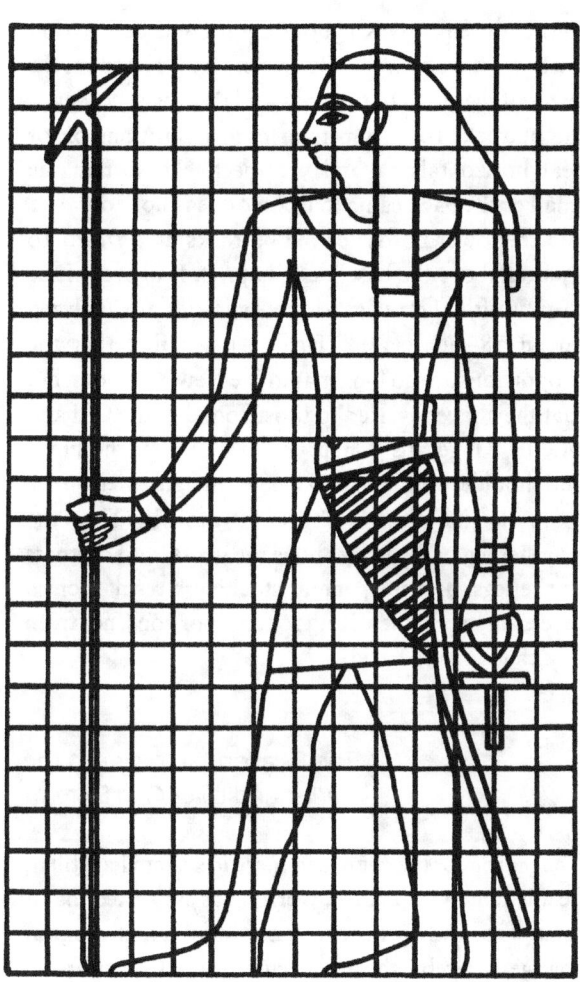

FIGURE 7.3

Standing figure on original grid, sarcophagus of Takhos, Cairo Museum, after Edgar 1905, 144 Figure 5.

across the shoulders along horizontal 18 is approximately 7 squares, so that the outer edges of the upper arms also lie between and not on verticals. The width across the body at the level of the small of the back is roughly 2 3/4 to 3 squares. The foot is variable, most commonly being between 3 1/2 to 4 squares long. The length of the forearm from elbow bone to fingertips measured along the long axis is often 6 squares.

Similar proportions continue into the Ptolemaic period, as can clearly be seen on blocks from a chapel of Ptolemy I Soter now in Hildesheim.[12] Later in the Ptolemaic period and during the Roman occupation, we find that there is a tendency for the lower border of the buttocks to drop to horizontal 10 from the earlier level of 11; the knee and the small of the back remain on or near 7 and 13 respectively.[13]

We have already seen that previous writers have disagreed over whether or not the change in grid system caused a change in proportions (Sec. 2.1). Blanc and Mackay both argued that it did. Mackay assumed that 3 1/3 extra squares had been added to the distance of 19 squares to the top of the head used in the early system. He even itemized them, saying that a third of a square had been added in the head region, 2 squares between the base of the neck and the waist, and 1 square in the legs. Thus the figure was made "long waisted" with an "apparent shortness of the lower part of the body, measured from the waist to the knees."[14] Even Prisse, who did not feel that proportions had been altered in any great way, thought that the later system led to stockier limbs and a certain clumsiness.[15]

The reason why these scholars felt that there had been a change in proportions as a result of the new grid system is surely because they were making compari-

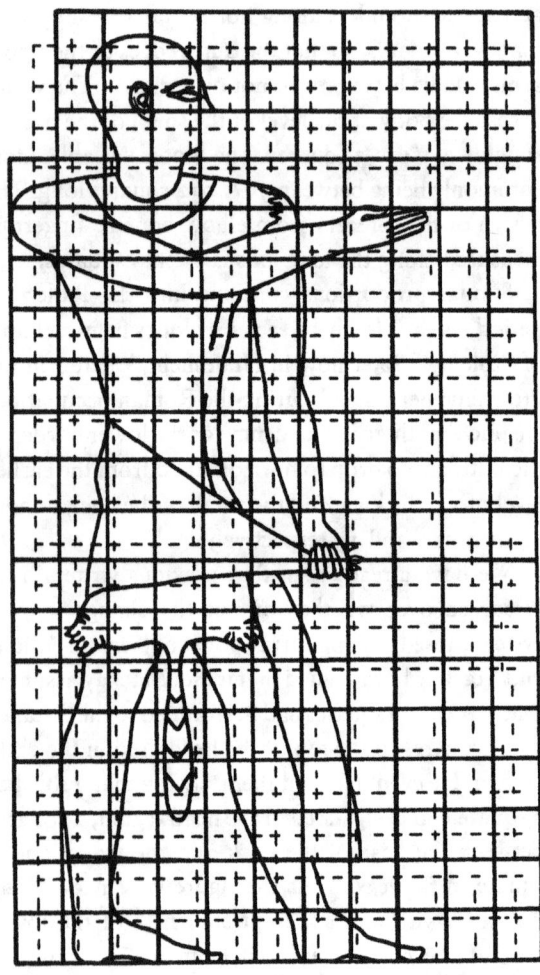

FIGURE 7.4

Standing figure on hypothetical 18-square grid (solid lines) and hypothetical 21-square grid (dotted lines), TT 414, twenty-sixth dynasty, after Bietak and Reiser-Haslauer 1982, Figure 109.

sons between New Kingdom figures and Late period ones. We have seen that during the New Kingdom the levels of the small of the back and the lower border of the buttocks rose from their earlier positions on or near horizontals 11 and 9 respectively, so that the small of the back came to lie on or near horizontal 12 and the lower border of the buttocks at 9 1/2 to 10 squares above the baseline (Chap. 5). If figures of the twenty-fifth and twenty-sixth dynasties are analyzed on an 18-square grid (Fig. 7.4), we find that the proportions are no longer as in the New Kingdom, but that they have reverted to those found in the Old and Middle Kingdoms (Chap. 4). In addition, the limbs and shoulder width in New Kingdom figures tend to be more slender than in the older models. Thus the lengthening of the body above the waist, the shortness of the legs, and the general stockiness result from a reversion to pre–New Kingdom proportions, not from any change in the grid.

7.2. The Relationship between the Earlier and Later Grid Systems

The reason for the change in the grid system has still to be adequately explained. Iversen has suggested that it related to, and was consequent upon, a metrological change whereby the royal cubit, equal to approximately 52.5 cm in modern units, came to be divided into 6 great palms, each equivalent to 8.75 cm, instead of the traditional 7 palms, each 7.5 cm; the small cubit, equal to six-sevenths of a royal cubit, or 45 cm, ceased therefore to be a standard unit of measurement.[16] He assumes that the royal cubit with its new divisions, often termed the "reformed" cubit, dates to the beginning of the twenty-sixth dynasty, when he believes the change in the grid system also took place. He cites no authority for this, and in fact it seems that no cubit rods divided into 6 great palms can definitely be dated so early.[17]

Because Iversen supposes that the length from elbow to fingertips is the equivalent of a royal cubit, he suggests that the grid system was changed in order to make the length of the forearm consist of 6 squares, each representing 1 great palm. However, I have already shown that if proportions in art reflect natural proportions, the living forearm from elbow to fingertips cannot be as long as a royal cubit or 52.5 cm, because it would produce figures of over six feet tall. On the other hand, a plausible stature results from assuming a living forearm length of a small cubit or 45 cm (Sec. 2.2.4).

Instead of assuming that the change in the grid system was the result of a change in the metrical system, it makes more sense to relate the change to the traditional system of metrological units. I have suggested that in the early grid system the basic length of the forearm from elbow to fingertips occupied 5 squares on the grid, so that the metrological length of the living forearm equal to 1 small cubit or 6 palms was represented by 5 grid squares. Thus the side of 1 grid square was the equivalent of 1 1/5 palms. Although this system had been in use for over a millennium, the grid system could have been changed in order to obtain a smaller square that would correspond to 1 palm or a sixth of a small cubit. In modern units, each new square would represent the 9 cm of the old square divided by 1 1/5, that is, 9 x 5/6 = 7.5 cm.

It would follow that the old hairline height of 18 squares would become equivalent to a height above the baseline of 18 x 6/5 = 21 3/5 squares, which would fall between grid horizontals. Not being an exact number of squares, this could no longer function as the upper point from which the proportions of the body were reckoned. Instead, new horizontal 21 immediately below at the level of the upper eyelid would have been used.

Whether or not this explanation of the purpose behind the change in the grid is correct or not, there is evidence to indicate that 5 old squares equal 6 new ones, since it seems that the basic length for the forearm in the twenty-sixth dynasty was 6 new squares.[18] Also, when hypothetical grids of 18 squares from hairline to soles and 21 squares from upper eyelid to soles are calculated for the same figure, horizontals 5 and 6, 10 and 12, and 15 and 18 coincide.[19]

Apparently, then, the grid square size in the later system has been obtained by multiplying the old square by five-sixths. It follows that we can multiply the horizontals of the old system by six-fifths to obtain their equivalent positions on the new grid:

Old Square	0	1	2	3	4	5	6
New Square	0	1 1/5	2 2/5	3 3/5	4 4/5	6	7 1/5

Old Square	7	8	9	10	11	12	13
New Square	8 2/5	9 3/5	10 4/5	12	13 1/5	14 2/5	15 3/5

Old Square	14	15	16	17	18	19
New Square	16 4/5	18	19 1/5	20 2/5	21 3/5	22 4/5

Only three levels above the baseline have exact equivalents in the two systems. Old horizontal 5, which often passes just below the tibial tubercle, becomes new horizontal 6. Old horizontal 10, which passes through some part of the buttocks and some-times through the knot of the belt, becomes new horizontal 12. Old horizontal 15 becomes new horizontal 18, but this level does not have a constant relationship with an obvious bodily feature.

Similarly there are other horizontals in the early grid system that in the classic proportions of the early Middle Kingdom and early eighteenth dynasty have no specific relationship with a part of the body. Horizontals 2, 3, 7, 8, 12, and 13 belong in this category; they all lie two-fifths or three-fifths of a square from a new grid line.

The grid horizontals in the early system that have a close association with a part of the body (in the early Middle Kingdom and early eighteenth dynasty) are 5 with the bottom of the tibial tubercle, 6 with the top of the knee, 9 with the lower border of the buttocks, 10 with either the top or the maximum convexity of the buttocks or with the knot of the belt, 11 with the small of the back, 14 with the nipple, 16 with the junction of the neck and shoulders, 17 with the bottom of the nose, and 18 with the hairline. From the table it can be seen that from the junction of the neck and shoulders down, two of these horizontals correspond with horizontals in the new system while, in the other cases, the old grid lines are only one-fifth of a square from a new grid line, so that a very small adjustment only would be needed in the position of these points of the body to bring them into conjunction with a new horizontal.

Such an adjustment seems to have been made in the case of the knee, the lower border of the buttocks, the small of the back, and the junction of the neck and shoulders, which in the new system lie on horizontals 7, 11, 13, and 19 respectively. The nipple, however, is

not moved from 16 4/5 to 17 but is lowered to 16,[20] which is only 13 1/3 squares above the baseline on the old grid. The reason for this may relate to the lowering of the junction of the neck and shoulders, which now lies on horizontal 19, although old horizontal 16 is the equivalent to new level 19 1/5. This pushes the level of the armpits down onto or very near new horizontal 17. The nipple therefore has to lie lower, and if it is to be on a grid line, it has to move down to 16 or 13 1/3 on the early grid.

Above the junction of the neck and shoulders, the differences between the old system and the new are not so easily adjusted. On the later grid, the bottom of the nose and the hairline lie almost halfway between horizontals; to adjust the drawing of the head to bring them to a grid line would noticeably alter proportions. Therefore, these points are no longer tied to grid lines in the later system. Instead, new points are used: the mouth lying on horizontal 20 and the upper eyelid on 21. The vertical proportions of the head remain unchanged, since the distance between the junction of the neck and shoulders and the mouth, and between the region of the mouth and the upper eyelid, is in both cases five-sixths of an old square or 1 new square (Fig. 7.5).[21]

The hypothesis can be tested by constructing hypothetical 21-square grids between the baseline and upper eyelid for Late period figures. These grids can then be turned into 18-square grids by expanding the squares by six-fifths (Fig. 7.6; solid lines mark the horizontals of the 21-square grid and dotted lines the horizontals of the derived 18-square grid). The results show that the bottom of the tibial tubercle lies on new horizontal 6 and generated old horizontal 5. New horizontal 7 passes across the tops of the knees which are thus 1 new square above the bottom of the tibial tubercle. Generated old horizontal 6 passes one-fifth of a new square higher, showing the slight adjustment that has been made between the tops of the knees in the early grid system and the later one. The lower border of the buttocks lies near new horizontal 11, which passes one-fifth of a new square above old horizontal 9, which marked the lower border of the buttocks in the traditional system, halfway between the soles of the feet and the hairline. New horizontal 12 coincides with generated old horizontal 10 and passes through or just below the knot of the belt. New horizontal 13 passes through the small of the back and through or near the top of the belt at the back. Generated old horizontal 11 passes one-fifth of a new square above, showing that the small of the back and the top of the belt have been lowered by one-fifth of a new square to coincide with a grid horizontal.

New horizontal 19 runs through the junction of the neck and shoulders while generated old horizontal 16 runs above it. Like the old knee horizontal 6, the position of the junction of the neck and shoulders has been lowered by one-fifth of a new square so that it can be placed on a grid line. However, the hairline lies noticeably lower than generated horizontal 18. This is because the proportions of the head above the shoulders remain as in the old system. The one-fifth of a new square that has been removed from below the junction of the neck and shoulders is not reincorporated above, so that the height of the figure to the hairline is now only equivalent to 17 5/6 old squares (1/5 new square = 1/6 old square). If the height of 2 old squares is measured from the new level of the junction of the neck

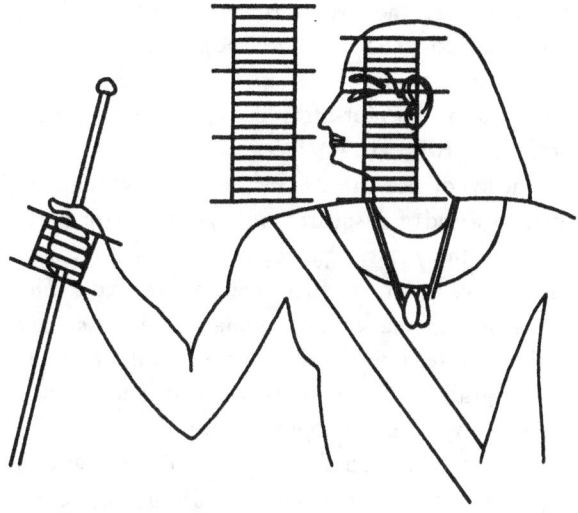

FIGURE 7.5

Upper part of figure of Ibi showing the proportions of the head in relation to old squares divided into sixths (in front of the face), and new squares divided into fifths (imposed on the face), the divisions of old and new squares being the same size.

and shoulders, they pass through the bottom of the nose and through the hairline. The greatest difference lies in the position of the nipple, for it lies on new horizontal 16, or four-fifths of a square below generated old horizontal 14.

The hypothesis can also be tested by reversing the method: a grid of 21 squares can be generated for a pre-twenty-fifth dynasty figure by diminishing the size of the squares of an 18-square grid by five-sixths (Fig. 7.7; solid lines mark the horizontals of the 18-square grid and dotted lines the derived horizontals of the 21-square grid). Generated horizontals 21 and 20 pass slightly lower than the upper eyelid and mouth respectively, but if horizontal 19 of the generated grid is raised to come into conjunction with old horizontal 16, generated horizontals 20 and 21 are pushed up to pass through the mouth and upper eyelid. Generated horizontal 13 lies below old horizontal 11, which passes through the small of the back and the top of the belt, and generated horizontal 11 lies above old horizontal 9, which passes through the lower border of the buttocks. Generated horizontal 7 lies below old horizontal 6, which marks the knee. Generated horizontal 16, on which the nipple lies in the later grid system, lies two-thirds of an old square below old horizontal 14, to which the nipple in the early system commonly relates.

Although the changes in proportions between Old and Middle Kingdom figures and those of the Late period, made in order to adjust the latter to the later grid system, are not major ones, they result in a slight lowering of the knees, small of the back, and junction of the neck and shoulders, and in a raising of the lower border of the buttocks, while the position of the nipple is readjusted more radically in a downward direction. Theoretically it should be possible, therefore, to tell on which grid any given figure was drawn, and an analysis

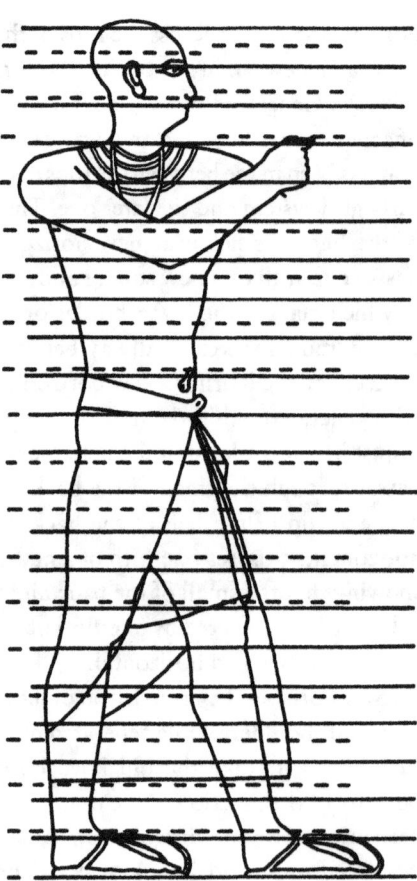

FIGURE 7.6

Standing figure of Ibi with solid lines marking the horizontals of a 21-square hypothetical grid between soles and upper eyelid; dotted lines indicate the horizontals of a second grid obtained by multiplying the first by six-fifths; horizontal 16 of the expanded grid has been lowered by one-fifth of a new square to run along horizontal 19 of the 21-square grid, TT 36, twenty-sixth dynasty, after Kuhlmann and Schenkel 1983, Plate 89.

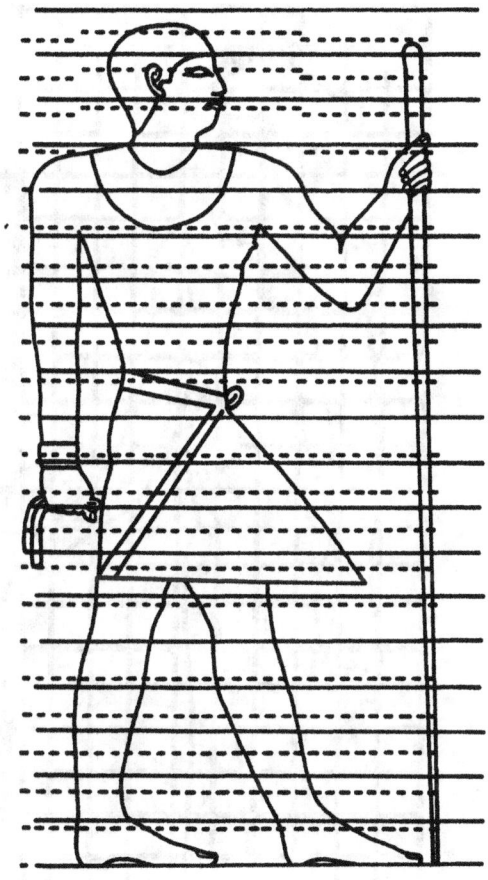

FIGURE 7.7
Standing figure of Mereruka with solid lines marking the horizontals of an 18-square hypothetical grid between soles and hairline; dotted lines indicate the horizontals of a second grid obtained by multipying the first by five-sixths; horizontal 19 of the diminished grid has been raised by one-fifth of a new square to run along horizontal 16 of the 18-square grid, as a consequence of which horizontal 21 passes through the upper eyelid, tomb chapel of Mereruka, sixth dynasty, after Iversen 1975, Plate 12.

on grids of twenty-fifth-dynasty figures might help elucidate the transition between the two systems. One has to remember, though, that in the early system key points of the body do not always fall exactly on the grid horizontal associated with them. For instance, in the Middle Kingdom and early eighteenth dynasty the lower border of the buttocks can fall anywhere between horizontals 9 and 9 1/2 and the small of the back between 11 and 11 1/2. Further, in relief the original drawn line is cut away and the new cut line may not always follow the drawn one exactly, so that slight changes may occur in the position of points of the body in relation to the original grid. If we allow for the same leeway in figures drawn on the later grid, it may not be possible to make clear-cut decisions from the levels of the knee, buttocks, small of the back, and junction of neck and shoulders concerning which grid was used.[22] The best means of distinguishing between figures drawn on the different grids might seem to be the level of the nipple, when this is visible, for theoretically it should be considerably lower in figures drawn on the later grid than in those drawn on the early one.[23] However, in the old grid system there are figures on which the nipple lies below horizontal 14, so that even the position of the nipple may not produce clear-cut evidence as to which grid was used when single figures are being considered.

7.3. Grids on the Stelae of Djoser

In room III under the step pyramid of Djoser, there are three stelae showing the king.[24] Two of these, the south and central stelae, preserve quite extensive grid traces.[25] The lines run across the cut relief showing that they are later "copyist's" grids. On these, one figure of the king is complete; the other figure is headless. The third stela was not gridded along with the other two because it could not be reached on account of a deep pit made by robbers in the floor just in front of it.[26] The particular interest of these pieces lies in the fact that the grids were put on so that there were 21 squares between the soles and hairline of the complete figure, and 19 squares between the junction of the neck and shoulders and the soles of the figure that had lost its head. In other words, the grids conform to the later grid system and are assumed to have been put on by Saite artists studying the earlier figures. The twenty-fifth and twenty-sixth dynasties were a period of archaization in art when artists looked to earlier times for their models. Other copyists' grids are known, but usually they do not conform to either the early or later grid system. Presumably they were simply used to aid copying and were not concerned with proportions.

7.4. Female Figures in the Later Grid System

Just as in the early grid system, so in the later, female figures consist of the same number of grid squares vertically as male ones, but otherwise there are a number of differences (Fig. 7.8). The small of the back lies higher, from around horizontal 15 to 16, and the body is more slender. The width across the shoulders at horizontal 17 is roughly 5 instead of 7 squares, and across the small of the back less than 2 1/2.[27] The breast may be adjusted so that its upper and lower borders lie roughly on horizontals 17 and 16 with the nipple between; in seated figures, which came to consist of 17 squares, these become horizontals 13 and 12 (Sec. 7.5).[28]

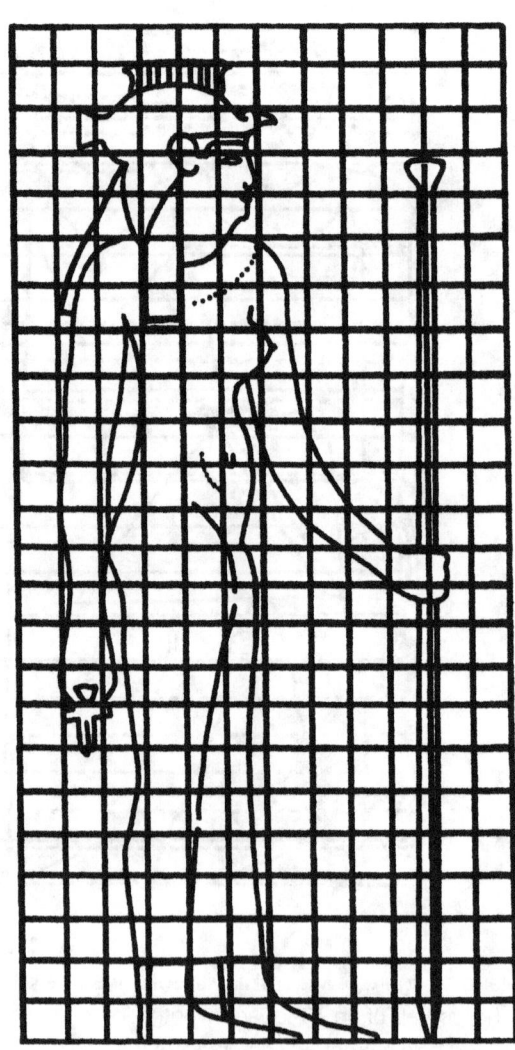

FIGURE 7.8
Standing female figure on grid completed from surviving traces, limestone ostrakon, Cairo CG 33412, Ptolemaic period, after Edgar 1906, no. 33412.

7.5. Seated Figures

Evidence from the Ptolemaic period shows that seated figures were drawn on a grid of 17 squares between the upper eyelid and the soles of the feet (Fig. 7.9).[29] Horizontal 16 runs through the mouth, horizontal 15 through the junction of neck and shoulders, horizontal 12 near the nipple when visible, horizontal 7 through or near the top of the knee, and horizontal 6 along the top of the seat.

In the early system, the top of the seat lay on horizontal 5—5 old squares being equivalent to 6 new ones—while the height of the figure was made up to 14 squares by adding the distance of 9 squares from hairline to buttocks, similar to the distance in standing figures. In the later grid system, the distance between the lower border of the buttocks and the upper eyelid is 10 squares. Logically one might then expect seated figures to consist of 16 (10 + 6) rather than 17 squares.

Scenes survive on the shrine of Taharqa from temple T at Kawa that show the standing king before a seated deity.[30] This monument is now in the Ashmolean Museum, Oxford, where it has been possible to make measurements on the figures.[31] On the west wall, the eye of the king is damaged, and his height was measured to the junction of the neck and forward shoulder to obtain 113.5 cm. The result was divided by 19 to arrive at an average grid square size of 5.97 cm. The seated figure of the ram-headed Amon-Re measures 83.5 cm from the junction of the neck and shoulders to the soles of the feet and sits on a dais 30 cm high. In terms of the king's calculated grid square size, the god would consist of 13.98 or approximately 14 squares between the junction of neck and shoulders and soles. An additional 2 squares would give the upper eyelid

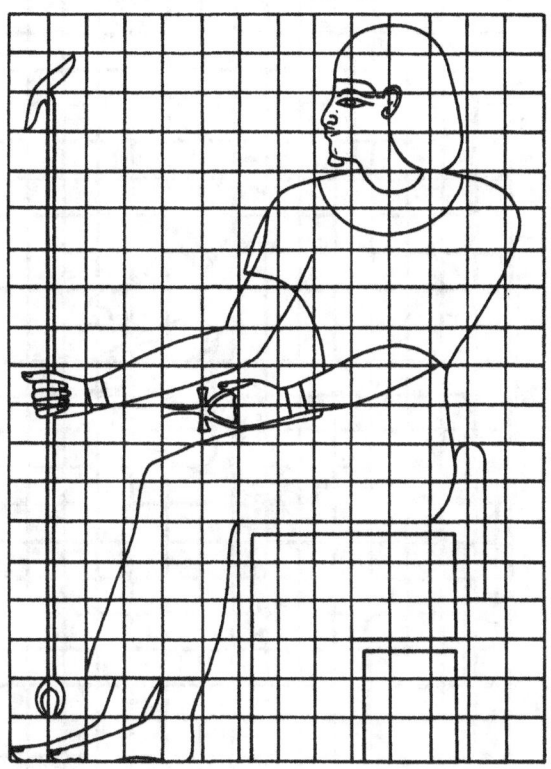

FIGURE 7.9
Seated male figure on original grid, temp. Ptolemy VII Euergetes II, after LD 4, 332 no. 6.

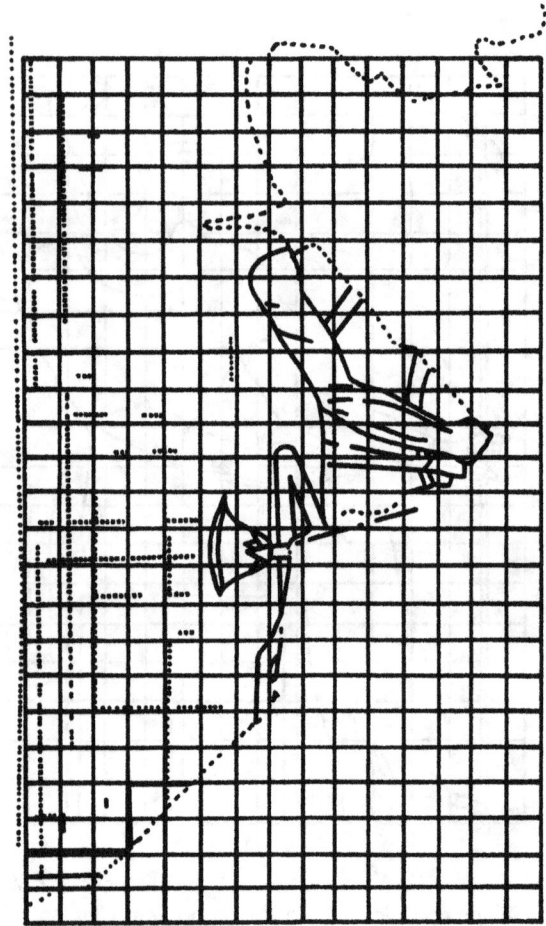

FIGURE 7.10

Seated male figure on hypothetical 15-square grid
between the grid horizontal trace on a level with the
shoulder and the top of the dais on which the chair
stands that forms the baseline. The surviving traces show
that the original grid was uneven; nevertheless, hypothetical horizontals 2,3, and 8 coincide with traces, as do
many of the hypothetical verticals, TT 36, twenty-sixth
dynasty, after Kuhlmann and Schenkel 1983, Plate 36.

height, making 16 squares in all. The dais has 5.02 or approximately 5 squares, bringing the seated god up to the height of the standing king.

On the east wall, the standing king measures 128.7 cm from upper eyelid to baseline, giving a grid square size of 6.12 cm. The seated figure of Amon-Re, which measures 97 cm from upper eyelid to baseline, would consist of 15.83 squares. The dais is lost. There is a possibility that the blocks on the reconstructed shrine do not now join exactly as they did, slightly altering measurements. It is clear, however, in these two scenes that the standing and seated figures could have been drawn on the same grid, but that the seated figures would have consisted of 16, not 17, squares.

In the tomb of Ibi, two seated figures survive with related grid traces. One is only fragmentary and the traces show that the grid was fairly uneven.[32] However, enough is left to suggest that the figure was drawn on a 17-square grid (Fig. 7.10). The second figure, which sits in front of a table of offerings, survives complete and is part of a larger scene, in which a standing figure faces the seated one.[33] The grid traces are again somewhat uneven but fit better with a 16-square grid for the seated figure rather than a 17-square one (Fig. 7.11). Further, traces in the published drawing of the scene (n. 33) give a distance of 3.2 cm for 7 squares. The upper eyelid level is 7.25 cm above the baseline, which would be equal to 15.86 squares. Allowing for the unevenness of the grid and the small scale of the drawing, this is close to 16 squares.

When other figures in the tomb are analyzed on alternative hypothetical grids, we find that if a 16-square grid is used, horizontal 6 runs along the top of the seat of the chair (Fig. 7.12). On a 17-square grid, horizontal 6 runs along the bottom of or below the seat

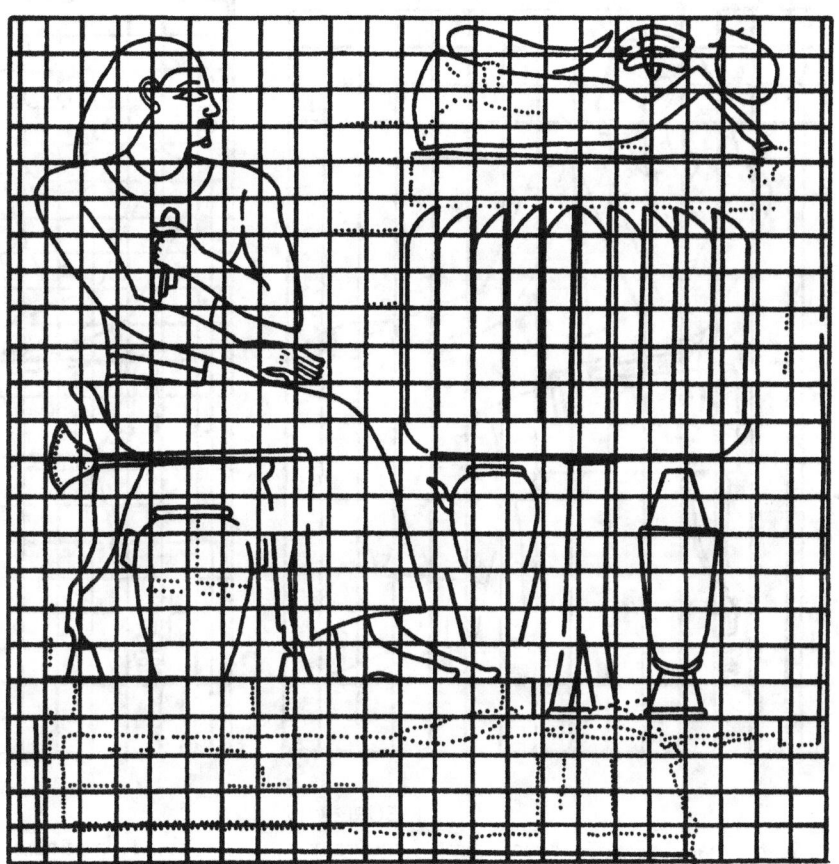

FIGURE 7.11
Seated male figure on 16-square grid completed from
surviving traces, TT 36, twenty-sixth dynasty, after
Kuhlmann and Schenkel 1983, Plate 37.

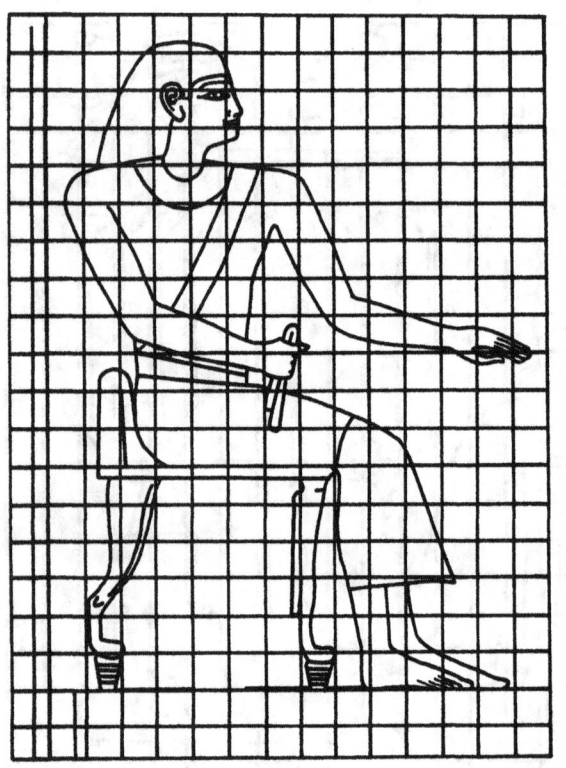

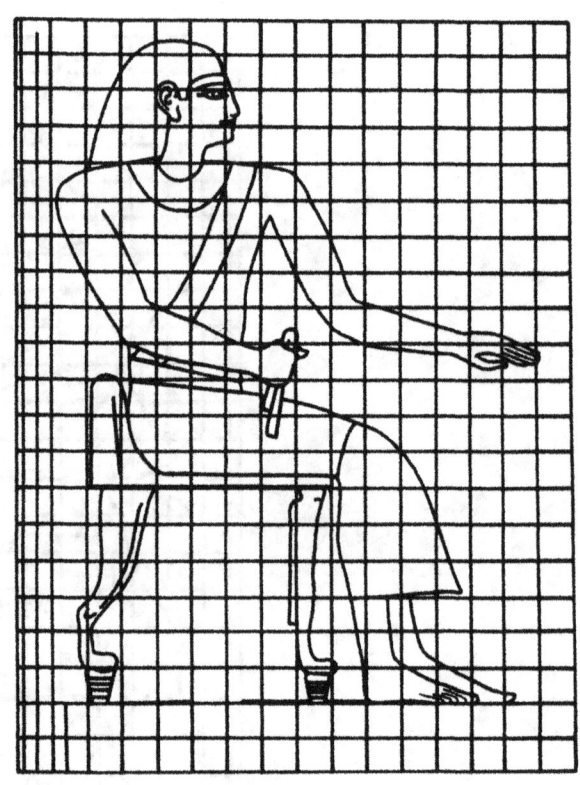

FIGURE 7.12
Seated male figure with hypothetical 16-square grid,
TT 36, twenty-sixth dynasty, after Kuhlmann and
Schenkel 1983, Plate 131a.

FIGURE 7.13
Seated male figure with hypothetical 17-square grid,
TT 36, twenty-sixth dynasty, after Kuhlmann and
Schenkel 1983, Plate 131a.

of the chair (Fig. 7.13). It follows that in many of the seated figures in the tomb of Ibi the proportions are not quite the same as those found in figures known to have been drawn on a 17-square grid, where horizontal 6 runs along the top of the seat.

Many Ptolemaic examples exist where seated figures can be deduced to have been drawn on a 17-square grid. For instance, in the tomb of Petosiris[34] or on the propylon of Ptolemy III Euergetes I at Karnak,[35] there are a number of composite scenes in which adjacent standing figures and seated figures raised up on daises with the same upper-eye level are apparently drawn to the same scale. If the presumed grid square size is determined by dividing the upper-lid height of the standing figures by 21, then the dais height is 4 squares, giving a 17-square height for the seated figures.

Similar proportions also occur on two twenty-fifth-dynasty blocks now in the Brooklyn Museum (Fig. 7.14).[36] In one scene, the goddess Mut stands behind a seated figure of Amon-Re; in the other, the divine adoratrice Amenirdis I stands before another seated figure of the same god. In both scenes, the dais is again 4 squares high on a hypothetical grid drawn for the standing figure, making the seated Amon-Re 17 squares to his upper eyelid. Evidently the 17-square system for seated figures was introduced early in the Late Period and was used alongside one of 16 squares. Later, 17 squares for seated figures seem to have become generally accepted.

In the tomb of Siamun at Siwa, a scene with a surviving grid shows the tomb owner before a seated figure of Osiris raised on a dais of 3 squares.[37] The tomb owner's figure consists of 21 squares to the upper eyelid. The figure of Osiris is badly damaged. The surviving fragment of the face is placed with the eye on the same level as that of Siamun, making a seated figure of 18 rather than 17 squares. It is unclear whether this fragment is in its original position or whether it has been replaced on the wall, but it clearly could not be lowered a square: not only would it be unsuitable to have the eye level of the deity lower than that of the tomb owner, but it would also bring the face too close to the crook held in the forward arm, of which the position is certain. A figure of Isis, now damaged, stood behind Osiris on the same grid. Thus the whole composition fitted on one grid, but for some reason the figure of Osiris was raised on a dais of only 3 squares, so that his seated figure comprised 18 and not 17 squares. Because of the damage to the god's figure, it is hard to see where the extra square was added. Horizontal 7 runs below and 8 above the point of the knee, which can be paralleled on other seated figures, so it seems likely that the extra square lies somewhere in the torso.

7.6. Kneeling Figures

In the same tomb at Siwa, grid traces survive on several other scenes. In one a figure of Nephthys kneels so that the goddess sits on her lower leg placed horizontally along the baseline.[38] The figure was originally drawn in red but has been corrected in black, in some places quite radically. In relation to the corrected figure, horizontal 12 runs at the level of the upper eyelid, 11 through the mouth, 10 a little below the junction of the neck and shoulders, 9 at the level of the bottom of the wig, 8 through the breast region, 7 at the level of the top of the dress, 6 through the elbow crease of the

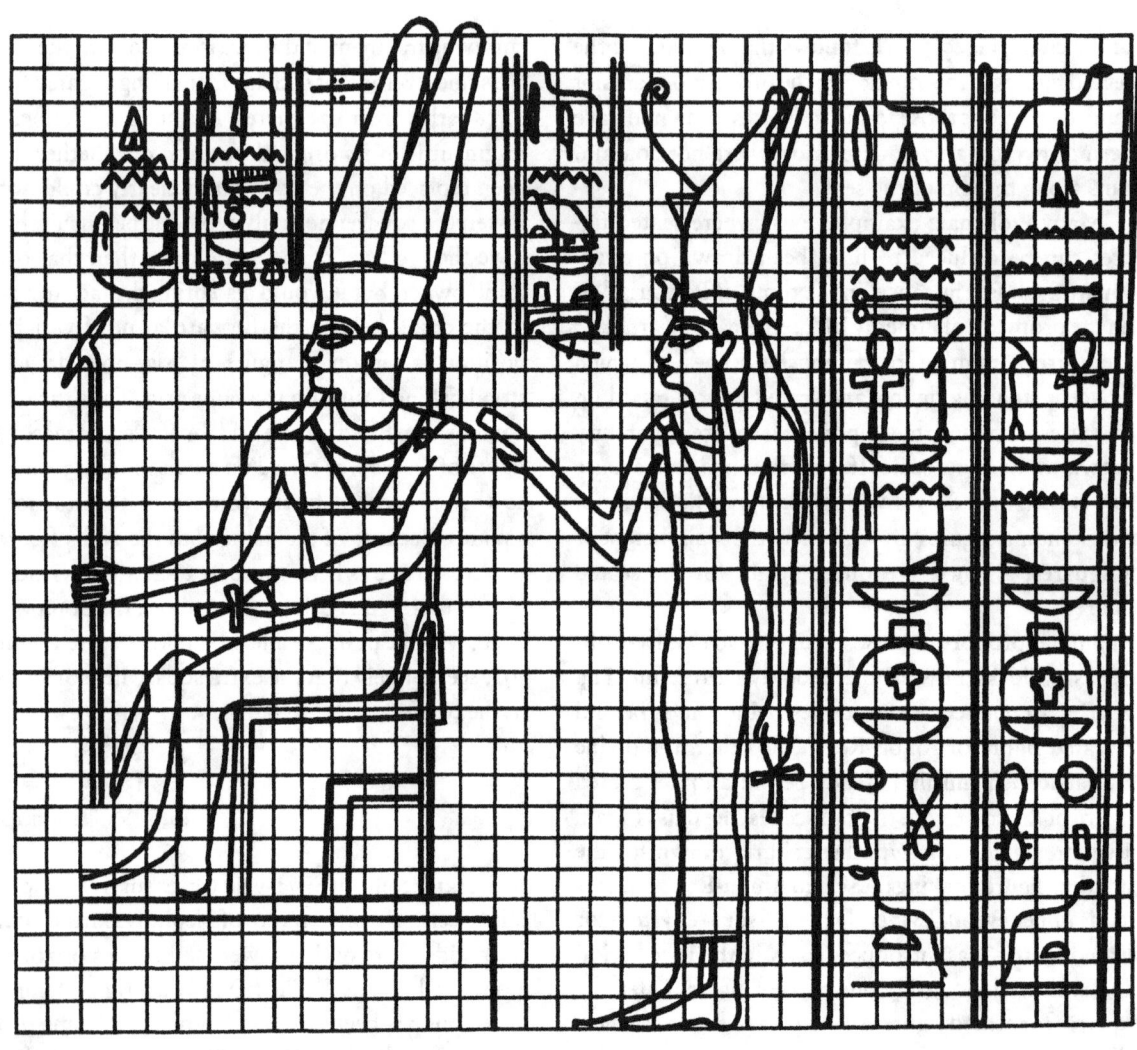

FIGURE 7.14
*Seated figure of Amon-Re and standing figure of Mut
with hypothetical 21-square grid, relief, Brooklyn
Museum acc. no. 87.184.2, twenty-fifth dynasty, after
museum photograph.*

forward arm, 4 through the junction of the stomach and thigh, 1 along the back of the lower leg, with 0 as the baseline. An axial vertical runs through the ear.

Somewhat similar proportions occur in the companion figure of Isis. Horizontal 12 runs through the eyebrow, 11 through the mouth, 10 through the junction of the neck and shoulders, 8 through the breast, 7 along the top of the sheath dress, 4 through the junction of the stomach and thigh. However, 0 seems to lie higher than the baseline on which the goddess kneels. I have shown in Chapter 5 that under the old grid system kneeling figures of this type were commonly drawn on 10-square grids. Decreasing the size of the grid square by five-sixths leads to an increase in the number of squares in the figure by six-fifths, which accounts for the 12-square grids seen, most clearly in the case of Nephthys, in this tomb.

7.7. "Sculptors' Trial Pieces"

One class of objects peculiar to the Late and Ptolemaic periods are the so-called sculptors' trial pieces or sculptors' studies. Their precise purpose is unclear; their often unfinished state together with the frequent survival of grid traces has led to the assumption that they were studies, practice pieces or perhaps models for apprentices to copy.[39] However, it has been argued that since many examples were discovered in temples or sacred animal cemeteries, they were in fact votive offerings.[40] It is possible that they do not even form a unified group, although it is convenient to treat them together.

The most common pieces worked in two-dimensions are limestone slabs, usually fairly small, deco-rated in relief on one or both sides.[41] Some are unfinished and show grid lines incised into the surface of the stone,[42] or less often applied in paint.[43] Even those that are finished may preserve at one or two of the edges a strip of stone showing the original surface level of the slab before it was cut away, and on this there sometimes remain traces of the grid lines.[44] The subject matter encompasses human figures, heads of a king or a goddess, and figures of animals, such as bulls, lions, rams, falcons, uraei, vultures, owls, and quail chicks, many of which are common hieroglyphs.[45] Although the animals were drawn on grids, there seems to be no specific number of grid squares associated with each type of animal. The human figures are drawn according to the later grid system.[46]

The sculpture in the round includes numerous royal busts, usually wearing the *nemes* headdress.[47] Many of the examples appear unfinished and retain traces of incised lines, especially on the back which is normally flat and preserves the side of the original block. These lines have been described and explained in detail by C.C. Edgar, who showed that they consisted of grid lines together with secondary lines added between the grid squares.[48]

In cutting one of these busts the sculptor would begin with a rectangular block which he would mark out with the appropriate lines. Just such a block is preserved in the Ägyptisches Museum, Berlin.[49] It is marked out on five of its six sides with incised lines; otherwise it is uncut (Fig. 7.15). The overall dimensions of the block are height 8.6–8.7 cm, width 8.5 cm, and depth 7.1–7.2 cm. The markings on the two faces that are almost square resemble those often found on the backs of some of the worked heads,[50] so that one side must have been the intended front and the other the intended back of the bust. The markings are similar except that two secondary horizontal lines, which other examples show were meant to mark the top of the forehead and the eyes, are absent from one, suggesting that it was to have been the back.

The block confirms Edgar's supposition that the fronts of the blocks were originally squared like the backs.[51] He was unable to demonstrate this because the fronts of the Cairo specimens that he studied were never preserved intact. However, the preparation of the blocks may have differed in detail from one to another; for instance, in many of the Cairo examples the sixth side or bottom of the block was marked as well,[52] while on the Berlin one it was left blank. Many surviving busts are 5 squares in height and include the bottom of the lappets of the *nemes*.[53] On others, the lappets are cut off short,[54] and this must have been intended with the Berlin block, because it is only just over 4 squares in height.

What may be termed the main incised lines, which were probably the first to be applied, form a squared grid organized around axial verticals and central horizontals that intersect near the middle of each side of the block, so as to divide it into approximate quarters. Further verticals and horizontals are for the most part placed at a distance of 2.1 cm from the axial vertical and central horizontal, yielding a basic grid square size of 2.1 cm, although the grid is not entirely regular.

The purpose of the various inscribed lines can be determined by referring to Edgar's analysis of the Cairo specimens,[55] where he was able to relate them to sculpted features. The axial verticals on the front and back are clearly to divide the intended head into symmetrical halves, and the paraxial verticals define the width of the face. The function of the axial verticals

on the lateral sides is less obvious, but they may be equivalent to the axial grid verticals used in two-dimensional art that commonly pass through the earhole or immediately in front of the ear. The central horizontals, as Edgar has shown, define the tip of the nose. This is an important difference between the squared grid of trial blocks for isolated heads and that used for complete statues and two-dimensional figures where, in the late system, grid horizontals pass through the mouth and the upper eyelid, not through the tip of the nose. Edgar suggested that the tip of the nose, being nearer to the original surface, was a more convenient starting-point than the mouth when the head was carved separately. A further reason for changing the orientation of the grid may have been that the tip of the nose is at the midpoint of the face, and it may, therefore, have been helpful to a sculptor to find it placed at a grid intersection at the center of his block.

Below the central horizontal related to the tip of the nose, the next grid horizontal defines the bottom of the chin, and shorter secondary horizontals mark the cleft of the mouth and the point of the chin. Short secondary verticals indicate the inner edges of the lappets of the *nemes* headdress. The first grid horizontal above the central one crosses the forehead between the eyebrows and the bottom of the front of the headdress, and is not related to any specific feature. The next grid horizontal up marks the top of the headdress. A secondary horizontal just above the central one crosses the whole front face of the block and is continuous with similar horizontals on the side face: this horizontal marks the bottom of the ears. Another secondary horizontal, higher up, marks the top corners or folds of the headdress. Shorter secondary horizontals define, from below upward, the bottom and top of the eyes, the

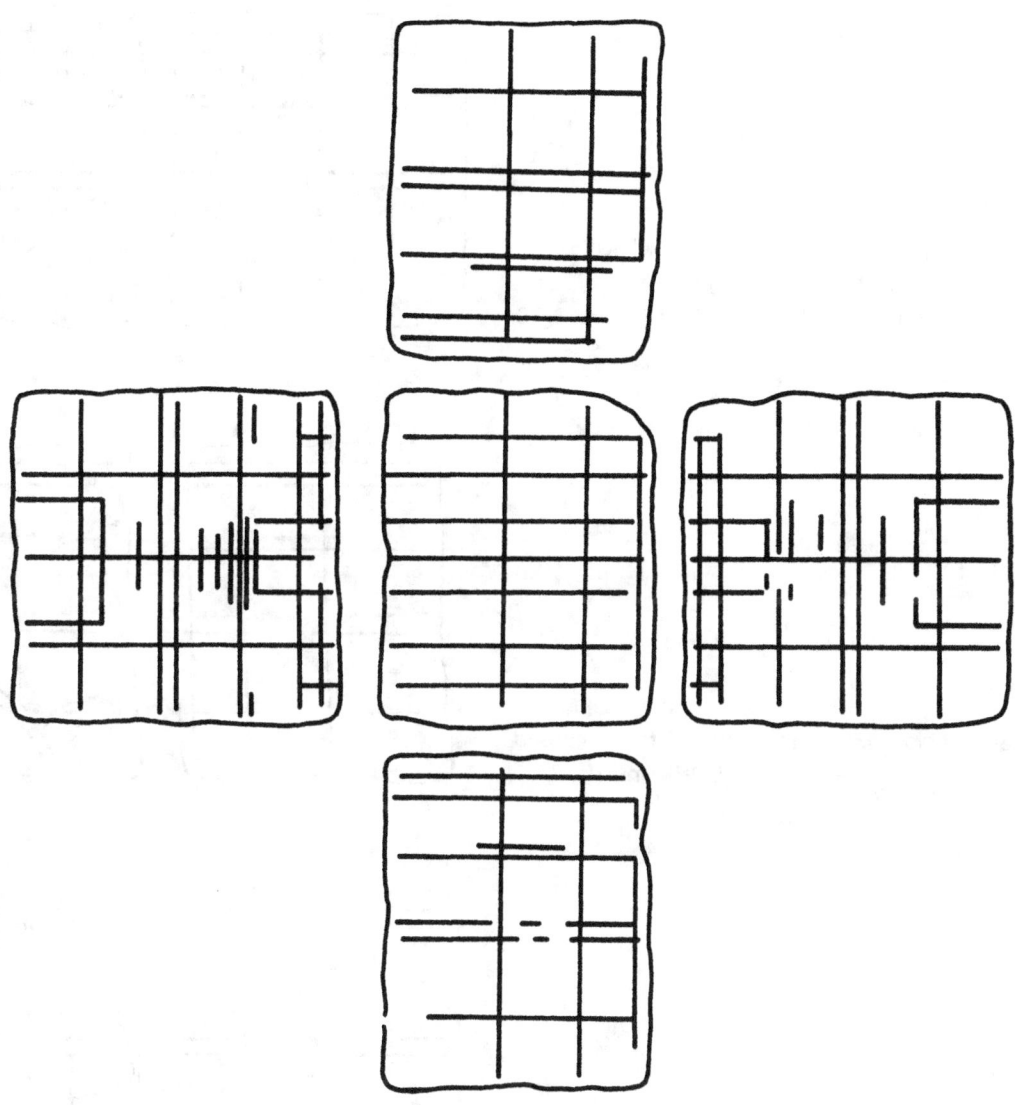

FIGURE 7.15
Block laid out for sculpture, Ptolemaic period, Berlin
inv. no. 3/70.

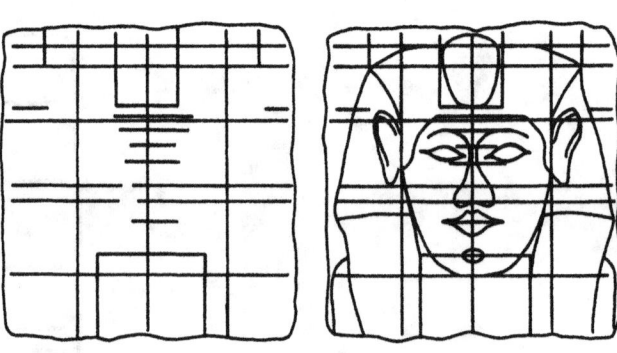

FIGURE 7.16
Front of block with sketch of front of statue
imposed, Ptolemaic period, Berlin inv. no. 3/70.

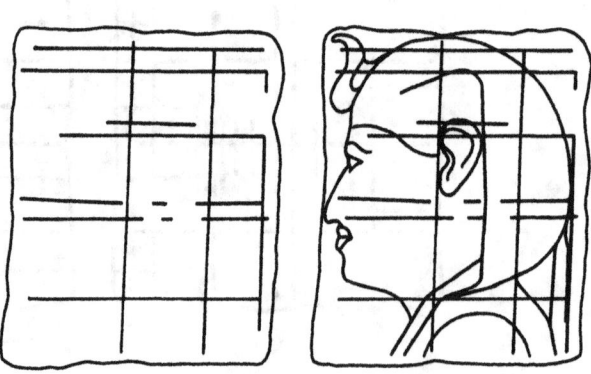

FIGURE 7.17
Side of block with sketch of side of statue imposed,
Ptolemaic period, Berlin inv. no. 3/70.

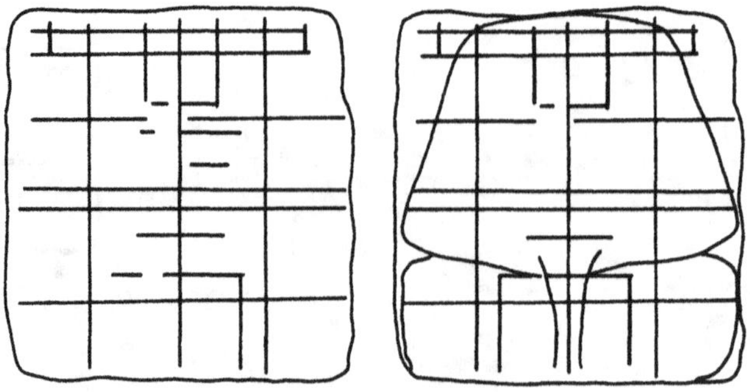

FIGURE 7.18
Back of block with sketch of back of statue
imposed, Ptolemaic period, Berlin inv. no. 3/70.

eyebrows, the top of the forehead (bottom of the front of the headdress), the top of the ears, and the bottom of the uraeus. Short secondary verticals bound the sides of the uraeus and, more laterally, intersect with the secondary horizontal to pinpoint the top corners of the headdress (Figs. 7.16–7.18).

The Cairo examples all have a flat back that is, in fact, one of the original sides of the block from which the head was cut; at the front, traces of grid lines are often still visible on the nose. Thus the distance between the flat back of these pieces and the tip of the nose represents the depth of the original block. In all the Cairo examples the ratio of the depth to height and width is much less than in the Berlin block. However, there exist other examples where the back of the head is fully modeled instead of being left flat. One such is found in the Fitzwilliam Museum, Cambridge, EGA 3209.1943, and the proportions of this piece are close to those of the Berlin block. It therefore seems likely that the Berlin block was the initial stage in the cutting of a royal head of which the back as well as the front was to be modeled.

The spacing of lines on the Berlin block bears out Edgar's observation that although in "trial pieces" of royal heads the grid horizontals were not placed at the same levels as in complete figures, the grid square size in relation to the size of the head was the same as in the late canon. The secondary horizontals defining the cleft of the mouth and the upper eyelid, which are traversed by grid horizontals 20 and 21 in a standing figure, are separated by a distance of 2.1 cm, which is the same as the predominant width of the grid squares on the block.

Composition and the Grid

8.1. Single and Multiple Grids in Composite Scenes

In this chapter I shall look at the various ways in which artists used grids to lay out composite scenes, that is to say, those containing figures of different heights and in different poses. My conclusions will be based on surviving grids and grid traces where these exist, using direct measurements made on site, and on hypothetical grids applied to photographs of scenes.

When the grid was first introduced, draftsmen made widespread use of it in tombs and occasionally on stelae, not only in drawing major figures but also in laying out registers of subsidiary figures.[1] To accommodate figures of varying sizes, different-sized grids were used appropriate to the desired height of each figure, as can be seen, for instance, in the well-preserved tomb chapel B2 at Meir.[2] Evidence in Theban tombs shows that this practice continued during the first half of the eighteenth dynasty (Pls. 1.1, 1.3, 5.4, 8.1), so that virtually all the walls to be decorated were first laid out with grids.[3] During the second half of the eighteenth dynasty it became usual to draw only major figures on grids and to sketch subsidiary ones either with the help of a few guidelines only (Pls. 5.5–5.7),[4] or else totally freehand (Pl. 1.5).[5] In the Theban tombs of the nineteenth and twentieth dynasties, I know of no examples of grid traces and it may be that the grid ceased to be used altogether.[6] If this was so for tombs it was not the case for temples, as surviving grids in the temples of Sety I and Ramesses II at Abydos show.

When a scene was laid out using grids, the draftsman had to make several choices. He could, as we have seen, change the grid square size every time the size of his figures changed, so that the major and subsidiary figures were each drawn on an appropriately sized grid (Pls. 1.1, 8.1).[7] On the other hand, he could put one grid over the entire scene appropriate to the major

figure only, and then add the smaller subsidiary figures freehand.[8] It is possible that each scene had already been worked out on a small scale on papyrus and that the noncanonical relationship of the subsidiary figures to the grid could be used in scaling up onto the wall, but this remains a matter of speculation because no such copybook layouts have been found. Sometimes different methods of working were used in the same tomb, suggesting perhaps that different draftsmen were at work.[9] At El-Kab in the tomb of Ahmose son of Abana, on the right end of the rear wall in the upper register, Ahmose and his wife sit in front of a table of offerings. Standing facing the couple is their grandson Paheri, who dedicates the offerings.[10] Grid traces show quite clearly on the seated couple and on Paheri's figure. The seated figures comprise the expected 14 squares from baseline to hairline. Paheri's baseline is 1 square below that of the seated couple because their chair is raised on a reed mat; his hairline is on a level with theirs, so that his figure occupies 15 squares on the grid, and is five-sixths the height of a standing figure on the same scale as the seated ones. Measurement shows that the figure is in proportion even though not drawn on its own grid. If the hairline height of 76.4 cm is taken as the equivalent of horizontal 18, then the junction of the neck and shoulders at 67.5 cm above the baseline lies at 15.90 (nearly 16) squares; the small of the back 50.2 cm above, at 11.83 (nearly 12) squares; the lower border of the back 42.6 cm above, at 10.04 (just over 10) squares; the point of the knee 25.7 cm above, at 6.05 (just over 6) squares.

A similar scene occurs on the west wall: a couple sit before a table of offerings that is dedicated to them by a standing figure.[11] The upper half of the couple is lost, but grid traces surviving on the offerings must belong

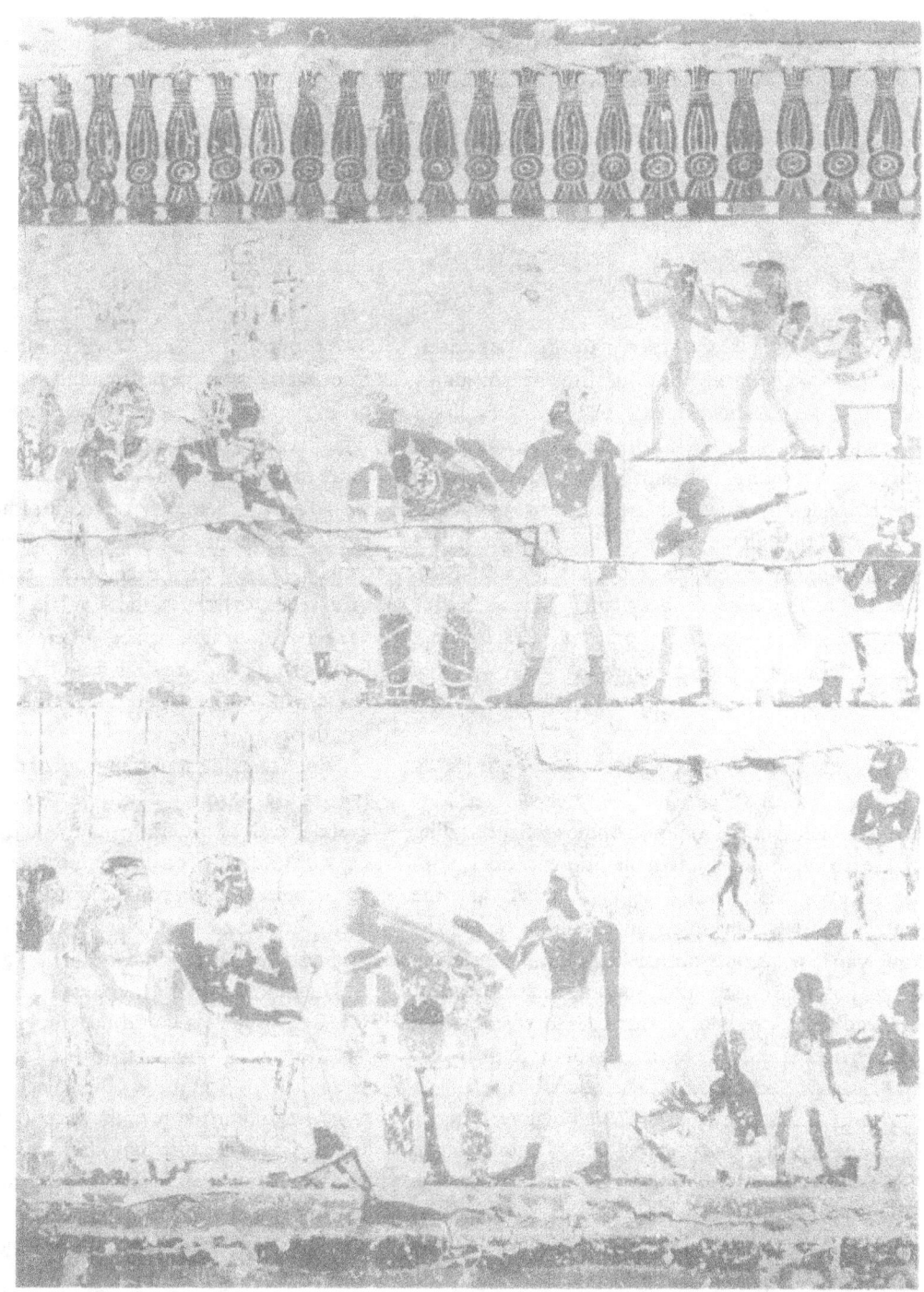

PLATE 8.1
Two registers with seated and standing figures on original grids, TT 22, eighteenth dynasty, MMA photo T 3408, photograph by the Egyptian Expedition, courtesy of the Metropolitan Museum of Art, New York.

to their grid, because the grid square size is approximately 3.1 cm and the position of the seated man's knee lies 18.6 cm above the baseline (3.1 x 6 = 18.6). The man offering to them also has associated grid traces on his figure. His hairline height is 49.4 cm, which divided by 18 would give a grid square size of 2.74 cm. Although the grid traces are slightly uneven, they are approximately 2.75 cm apart. So, unlike the first scene, the seated and standing figures in this second one were drawn on separate grids, each with a square size appropriate to its height.

8.2 Standing and Seated Figures on the Same Scale

In these scenes in the tomb of Ahmose, the standing and seated figures are drawn on different scales, with the standing figure being slightly smaller than the seated. In TT 42, the tomb owner stands before the king who is seated in a kiosk.[12] The figure of the tomb owner has been erased but the outline can still be seen; the head of the king is lost. Grid traces survive between the two figures and between the legs of the tomb owner and clearly fit both figures. The figure of the king is raised on a dais of 5 squares topped by a reed mat 1 square in height, so that its baseline is equivalent to horizontal 6 or the knee line of the tomb owner. The king's hairline must have lain 14 squares higher, 20 squares above the standing figure's baseline. Thus the hairlines of the two figures were not on the same level, unlike those in the tomb of Ahmose son of Abana. If the king had been raised only 4 squares on the grid, his hairline would have been on the same level as the tomb owner's. The extra elevation is surely deliberate to stress the relationship between ruler and subject.

By contrast, in temples where king and deity confront each other, they commonly have their hairlines or, in the case of the later grid, their eyelines on the same level. So when both figures are standing, they share the same baseline and hairline or eyeline, which would enable them to fit on to the same grid. This can be clearly seen in the chapel of Ptolemy I Soter from Tuna el-Gebel.[13] The decoration of the walls consists of a series of scenes showing the king performing various ritual acts before different deities. All the figures stand and are drawn on the same grid, which enables the draftsman to line up the figures along the length of each wall.

When the king stands in front of a seated deity, the two figures also usually have the same hairline or eyeline level, so the draftsman would have needed to use one grid only for the composition if he raised the god's figure 4 squares on the king's grid. While no such scene survives from the New Kingdom with associated grid traces, analysis on hypothetical grids shows that this method was in use in the eighteenth dynasty (Figs. 8.1–8.2).[14] This is confirmed by measurement on a small shrine of Thutmose III from el-Kab now in the Fitzwilliam Museum.[15] In the scenes on the two outer sides, a standing figure of the king occurs with a seated figure of a deity; their hairlines are on the same level and the seated figure is raised on a dais. On one side the hairline height of the king is 40 cm and that of the deity 31.2 cm; on the other the hairline heights are 39.9 cm and 30.9 cm respectively. Clearly the two scenes were meant to have been drawn on the same scale. If the two hairlines heights of the king are divided by 18 to obtain an average grid square size for each scene, then the first seated figure can be calculated to consist of 14.04 (just over 14) squares with a dais of 3.96 (just under 4)

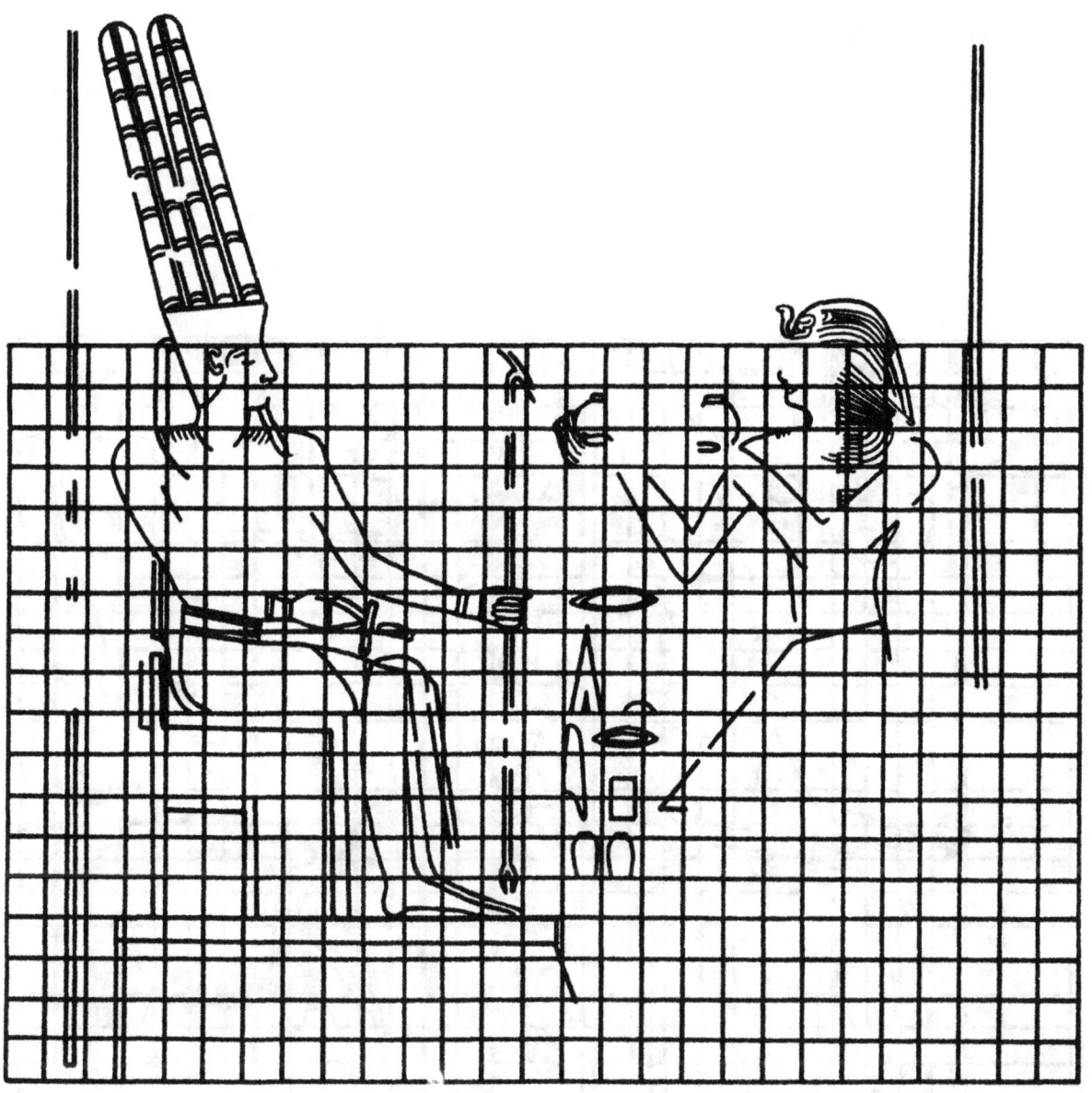

FIGURE 8.1
Standing figure of Amenhotep II offering to a seated
figure of Amon-Re on a hypothetical 18-square grid
calculated for the standing figure and drawn to run
over the seated one, alabaster shrine of Amenhotep II,
Karnak, eighteenth dynasty, after Van Siclen 1986,
Plate 41.

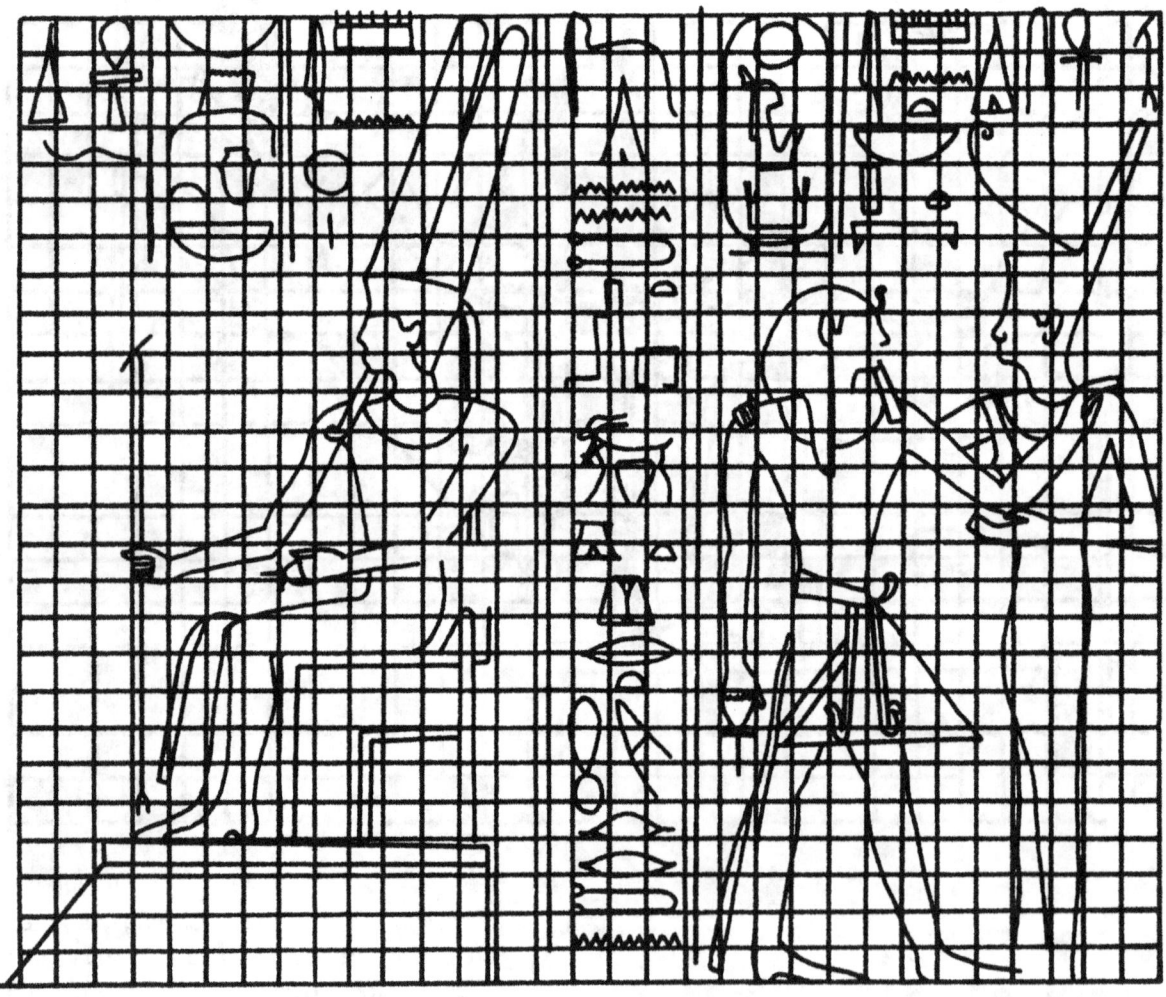

FIGURE 8.2
Block with hypothetical 18-square grid calculated for
the standing figures, chapelle rouge, vestibule, north
wall, course 5, detail of block 153, eighteenth dynasty,
after author's photograph.

squares, and the second one of 13.94 (just under 14) squares with a dais of 4.06 (just over 4) squares.

In the coronation scenes on blocks from Hatshepsut's *chapelle rouge*, standing, seated, and kneeling figures are all of a scale to fit one grid.[16] On a hypothetical grid the kneeling king and seated god, consisting of 11 and 14 squares respectively, are both raised 4 squares above the baseline of the standing goddess, whose identity varies in the different scenes. The two deities, whose figures frame that of the kneeling king, have the same hairline level, while that of the king who kneels to receive their benediction is 3 squares lower (Fig. 8.3).

For some reason, in the nineteenth and twentieth dynasties in scenes where the king stands before a seated deity, it becomes more usual to draw the two figures at slightly different scales. Hypothetical grids can easily be reconstructed for such scenes, and these show that while the hairlines usually remain on the same level, the figure of the deity is raised less than 4 squares on the king's grid. In fact, the baseline of the seated figure usually does not even coincide with one of the horizontals of the standing figure's grid. The result is that the deity's figure is on a slightly larger scale than the king's and would have needed its own grid, if drawn on one (Fig. 8.4). Scenes constructed in this way occur, for example, in the temple of Sety I at Abydos,[17] in the temple of Karnak,[18] in the temple of Ramesses II at Beit el-Wali,[19] in the temples of Ramesses III at Medinet Habu[20] and Karnak,[21] in the temple of Khonsu at Karnak,[22] and on the Bubastite portal at Karnak.[23] Even within one building, there is no fixed level for the deity's baseline in relation to the king's grid, and so no standard way of relating the two figures.

By contrast, in the small temple at Abu Simbel dating to the reign of Ramesses II, scenes showing Ramesses or his queen Nefertary standing before a seated deity are constructed with the two figures on the same scale.[24] If hypothetical grids are added, we find that the deity is almost always raised 4 squares on the standing figure's grid (Figs. 8.5, 9.7–9.8).[25] Thus the draftsmen at Abu Simbel employed a method that had been common in the eighteenth dynasty but which was no longer widely used in the nineteenth.

Why the older method should have been dropped is unknown but there must have been a good reason, because a relatively simple method of layout, involving the construction of one grid only, was replaced by one that would have necessitated the use of two separate grids. It is of course possible that only one grid was used on the wall and the second figure added freehand or perhaps squared up on the first figure's grid from a smaller sketch. Whatever the cause of the change, it is interesting to find that by the Late period and the Ptolemaic period, the older method had been reintroduced, although of course the later grid was now in use (Chap. 7). In the temple of Thoth at Qasr el-Aguz on the west bank at Thebes, which was built in the time of Ptolemy VII Euergetes II, some of the scenes preserve their grids. In one the king offers to a seated figure of Thoth with an ibis head and to a standing goddess behind; one grid goes across all figures. The king consists of 21 squares between the soles and upper eyelid, while Thoth comprises 17 squares from his soles to the top of his eye. The god's throne is placed on a dais that raises him 4 squares on the king's grid, so that the eyes of the two figures are on the same level. Two scenes recorded by Lepsius in the temple of Philae

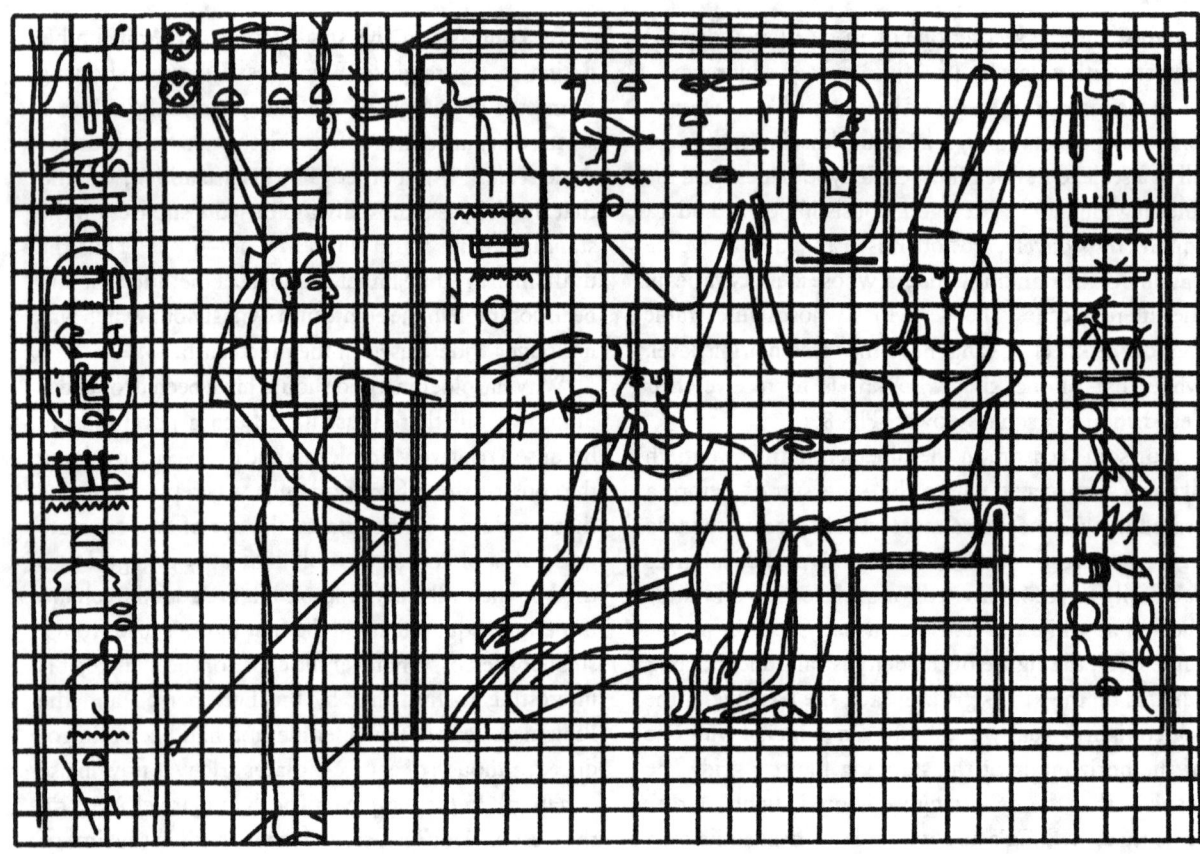

FIGURE 8.3
Block with hypothetical 18-square grid calculated for
the *standing figure, chapelle rouge, south facade,
course 7, block 145,* eighteenth dynasty, after author's
photograph.

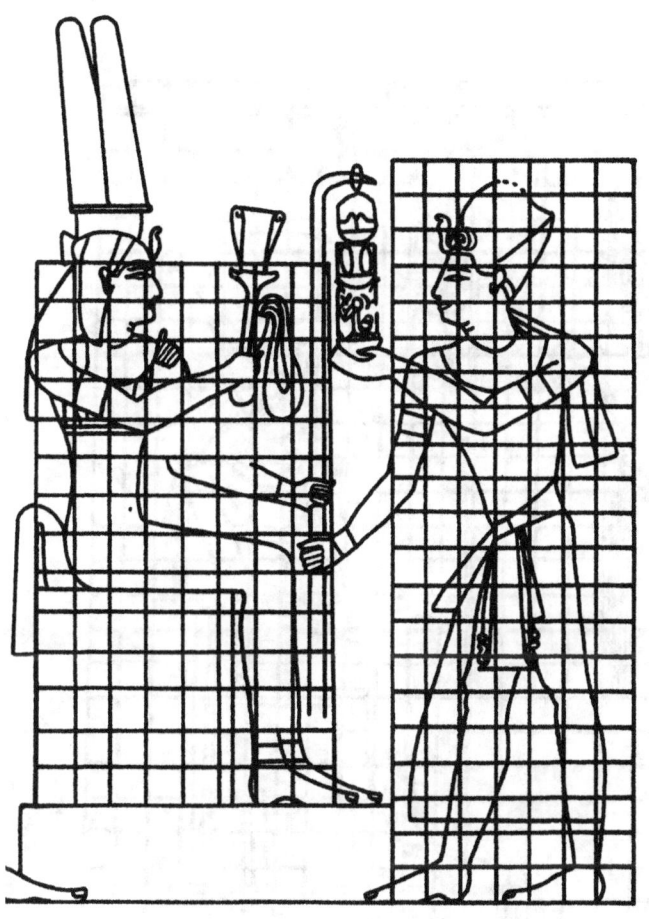

FIGURE 8.4

King offers to Isis with hypothetical 18- and 14-square grids calculated for the standing and seated figures respectively, temple of Sety I, Abydos, nineteenth dynasty, after Calverley 1938, Plate 45.

also show a standing figure of 21 squares before a 17-square seated figure raised on a dais of 4 squares.[26]

Although there are no remaining grid traces, the same layout can be demonstrated to have been in operation in the scenes decorating the screen walls in a building of Nectanebo I at Philae.[27] In one scene, for instance, the standing figure of the king is 74.5 cm from baseline to upper eyelid; that of Amon-Re, who is seated, is 60.5 cm from baseline to upper eyelid; while the dais on which he sits is 14 cm high. If a hypothetical grid size is calculated by dividing 74.5 cm by 21, then we find that the figure of Amon-Re comprises 17.05 (just over 17) squares and the dais 3.95 (just under 4) squares.

A similar system was also employed in the decoration of the tomb of Petosiris at Tuna el-Gebel. On the outside of the four screen walls are four scenes showing Petosiris before Thoth with either a baboon or ibis head.[28] In the two scenes to the right of the entrance, the eyes of the standing tomb owner and the seated deity are on a level. Measurement of the one where Thoth has a baboon's head shows that from soles to upper eyelid the figure of Petosiris is 61.8 cm (= 2.94 × 21), while Thoth from the soles to the top of his eye is 50 cm (= 2.94 × 17). Thus both figures would have an average grid square size of 2.94 cm. The dais is 11.8 cm high and thus comprises 4 grid squares, since 11.8 ÷ 2.94 = 4.01.

In the two scenes on the left hand side, the dais is still 4 squares high on a hypothetical grid drawn for the standing figure. However, the eye of the baboon is 17 1/2 rather than 17 squares above Thoth's baseline, while the eye of the ibis is slightly lower than the eye of Petosiris. The variations may be due to an uneven

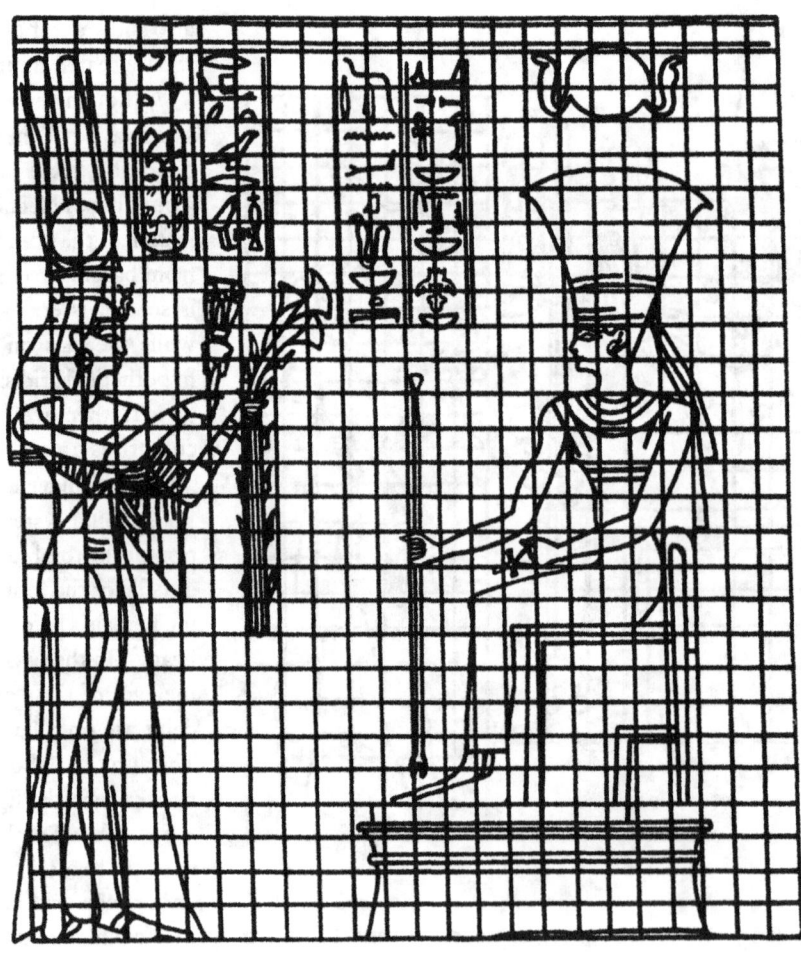

FIGURE 8.5
Nofretary Merenmut offering to Anuket with hypothetical 18-square grid calculated for the standing figure,
small temple of Abu Simbel, nineteenth dynasty, after
Desroches-Noblecourt and Kuentz 1968, Plate 44.

original grid or to changes that occurred during the cutting of relief, although there is no way of proving this. Inside the same tomb other groups of standing and seated figures are found that would fit onto one hypothetical grid with the seated figures raised on a dais of 4 squares.

8.3 Kneeling Figures on the Same Scale as Standing and Seated Figures

When kneeling figures occur together with standing or seated ones in one scene, they can easily be accommodated on the same grid. In the early system the kneeling figure with a vertical foot will occupy 11 or 12 squares (Sec. 5.4) on the grid of the other figure; the hairlines will not be on the same level. So in tomb chapel B2 at Meir, kneeling and standing figures appear side by side on the same grid, both on the same baseline.[29] Seated and kneeling figures occur together on some of the blocks from the *chapelle rouge* (Fig. 5.12);[30] hypothetical grids for the seated figures would fit the kneeling ones also.

In the temple of Sety I at Abydos there are a number of scenes where the king kneels between two seated deities, all three figures sharing the same baseline.[31] A hypothetical grid calculated for the seated figures also fits the kneeling one (Fig. 5.13). However, when the king kneels before a seated deity whose figure is raised on a dais, it is no longer possible for one grid to fit both figures, for the baseline and hairline of the seated figure rarely relate to horizontals on the hypothetical grid of the kneeling king.[32]

8.4 Ithyphallic Mummiform Figures

One type of figure that is almost always raised above the main baseline of a scene is the ithyphallic mummiform figure originally associated with the god Min but taken over by the god Amon-Re. Because the figure is normally shown as a cult statue, it stands on a statue base. In scenes where the king confronts this type of figure, both hairlines are most often on the same level, as in other scenes of the king and deities, but in this case the figures have different baselines. One might have expected draftsmen to have developed a standard relationship between the king and the ithyphallic figure, to aid the layout of the composition. For instance, the statue base could always have been 1 square high on the king's grid with a square dropped from the god's figure, as sometimes happened with other mummiform figures (see below). This last may have been the case in the scenes on the shrine of Philip Arrhidaeus at Karnak where surviving traces show that the king and ithyphallic Amon-Re were on the same grid.[33] The bottom of both figures is lost, but the small of the back and lower border of the buttocks lie 1 square higher on the figure of Amon-Re than that of the king, while the junction of neck and shoulders and eye levels lie on the same grid horizontals. This suggests that the figure of Amon-Re has been raised 1 square on the grid that runs over several scenes on the shrine, but that it lost 1 square from the torso to keep the eye level the same as the king's. If so, the whole figure would have consisted of only 20 and not 21 squares. On the propylon of Ptolemy III Euergetes I at Karnak,[34] on the other hand, ithyphallic figures of Amun do not have the same eye level as the king.[35] The draftsman has simply drawn the figures on the same scale as the king and raised them on a pedestal 1 square high, so that they comprise 21 squares on the king's grid.

Neither of these, however, was the usual method of layout used in earlier times. Analysis of examples from the reigns of Senwosret I,[36] Amenhotep I,[37] Hatshepsut,[38] Sety I,[39] and Herihor,[40] for instance, show that the statue base of the ithyphallic figure rarely coincides with a horizontal of the king's hypothetical grid, nor does it lie at a particular height on the king's grid, varying from less than 1 square in examples in the temple of Khonsu to nearly 2 squares in the chapel of Senwosret I, and within any one building at a given period the level is not constant. Usually the hairline heights of the king and divine image are level, although occasionally they differ by a small amount; this may be the result of the relief cutting and not of the original layout. On many pre-Amarna monuments, the ithyphallic figures of Amon-Re as they now exist are post-Amarna restorations that usually fail to follow the outline of the original figure.[41]

8.5 Analysis of Composite Scenes on a Single Grid

In the temple of Ramesses II at Abydos, there is a complex scene whose original grid can still be seen, giving an idea of how it was laid out.[42] The composition shows the deified king enthroned in a bark that is dragged toward a figure of Thoth by the souls of Pe and Nekhen, who are divided into two registers. Behind the king stands the figure of a goddess who embraces him while another goddess stands behind the bark. One grid covers the whole scene with a grid square size of approximately 9.2 cm, appropriate to figures that are life-sized or a little taller (19 × 9.2 = 174.8 cm). This grid fits the standing figure of Thoth and the goddess behind the bark, so that they are 18 squares to their hairlines. It also fits the seated king, who is 14 squares from soles to hairline but whose throne is raised 6 squares above the major baseline of the scene, placing his hairline on a higher level than the two deities who stand at either end of the scene. The souls of Pe and Nekhen and the goddess embracing the king are drawn on a smaller scale and do not fit the grid. The falcon-headed figures occupy 10 grid squares to their eyes, but measurement shows that their proportions are canonical for the period. The grid clearly plays an important part in the layout of this scene but does not obviously control all the elements in it.

Also at Abydos but in the temple of Sety I, a scene shows Ramesses II dragging a sled toward the figures of Thoth and the deified Sety I.[43] Grid traces that survive between the legs of Ramesses can be shown to have formed part of an 18-square grid relating to the king's figure. If it is extended to run over the figures of Thoth and Sety I, we find that Sety I has the same hairline level as Ramesses II and relates in a regular way to the grid. The figure of Thoth, however, is raised exactly 1 square on the grid, so that his knees, lower border of the buttocks, small of the back, and junction of the neck and shoulders lie 1 square higher than on the other figures (Fig. 8.6). If the figure of Thoth is raised because of the god's divine status, we need to explain why the deified king does not share the dais. The reason for Thoth's elevation seems in fact to be compositional. The god is shown with a bare ibis head that occupies approximately 2 squares from the junction of the neck and shoulders to the top of the head, whereas a human head at this period occupies 2

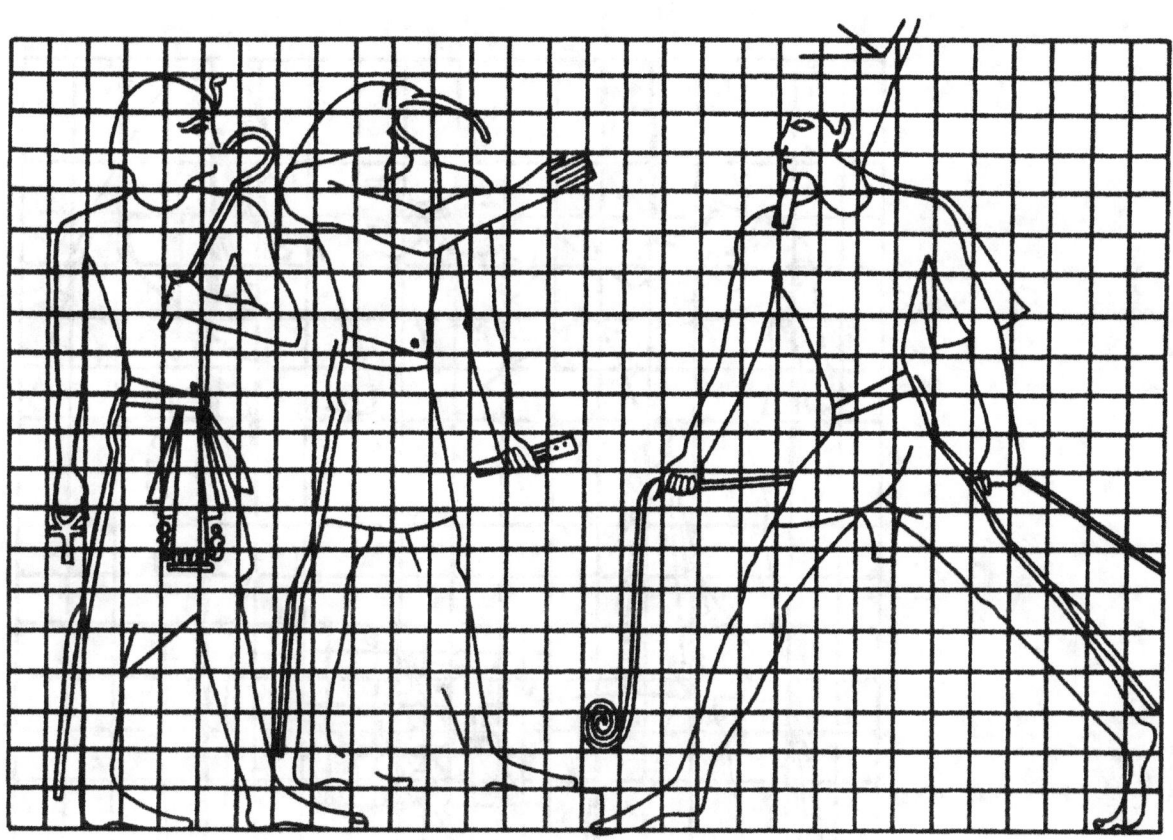

FIGURE 8.6
Ramesses II dragging sled to Thoth and deified Sety I
with 18-square grid reconstructed from traces between
the legs of Ramesses II, temple of Sety I, Abydos,
nineteenth dynasty, after author's photograph.

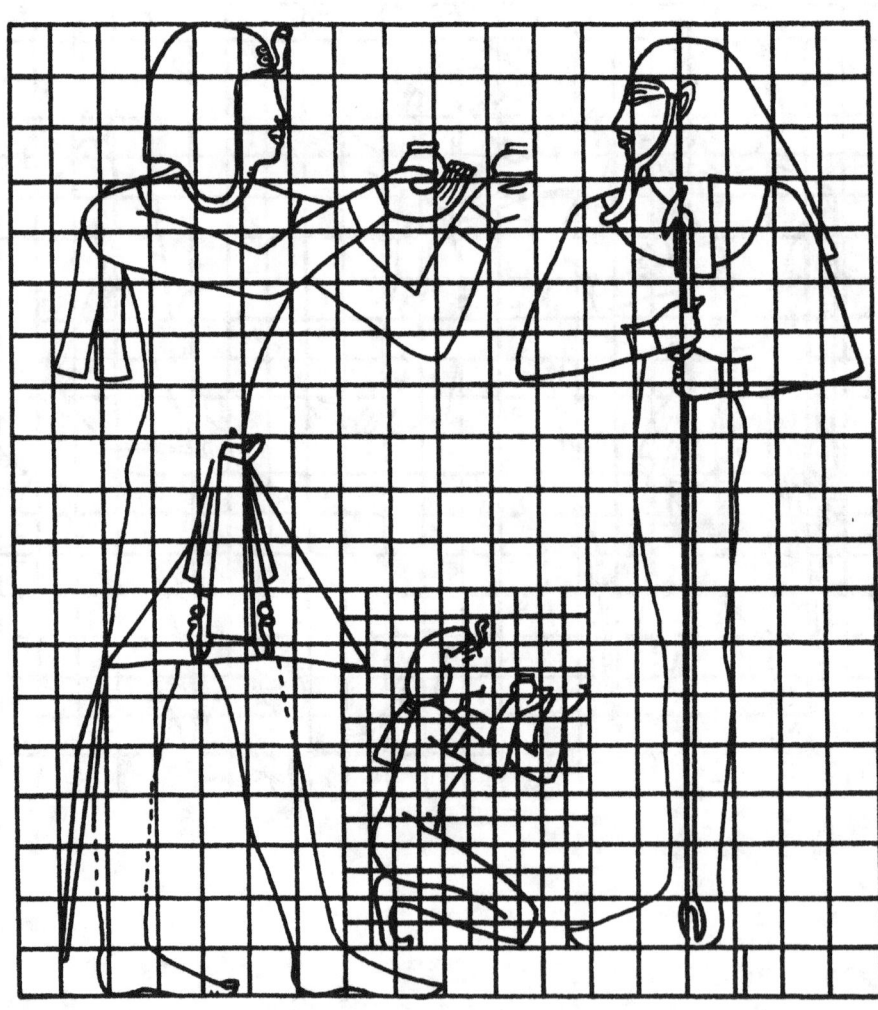

FIGURE 8.7
King offering to mummiform deity with hypothetical 18-square
grid calculated for king's figure, temple of Sety I, Abydos,
nineteenth dynasty, after Calverley 1938, Plate 16.

squares from the junction of the neck and shoulders to the hairline with another square to the top of the head. In other words, where Thoth is shown with an ibis head, he has no proper hairline and the bird's head is a square shorter than a human head.[44] If the god and king were standing side by side with their feet at the same level, the god would be a square shorter than the king. The draftsman has therefore chosen to place the tops of the heads of the two figures at about the same level by raising Thoth's baseline a square above that of Sety I.

Other scenes that include more than one figure can be analyzed on hypothetical grids to gain an insight into their composition. Another scene in the temple of Sety I at Abydos shows a group of three figures that can apparently be related to one such grid.[45] Sety I offers to the statue of a mummiform deity, which is raised on a statue base on which a small figure of a king also kneels. If a hypothetical grid, calculated for the king's standing figure, is placed over the group, it shows that the top of the statue base lies on horizontal 1, and the hairline, junction of the neck and shoulders, and lower border of the buttocks of the king and deity are at the same level; the knee of the deity is 6 squares above the top of the statue base and 1 square above the level of the king's knee (Fig. 8.7). Although it cannot be proved conclusively, it is possible that the draftsman constructed the mummiform figure on the king's grid simply by dropping a square from the thigh region. The kneeling figure has its baseline on horizontal 1 and its hairline roughly on horizontal 7. In other words it is 6 squares high. A kneeling figure at this period consists of 12 squares on its own grid (Sec. 5.4), so the draftsman may have treated each square of the

king's grid as 2 squares in relation to the kneeling figure. It must be said that in most cases, small figures in this temple do not relate this neatly to the grids of nearby large figures. Often the hairline does not even lie on a grid horizontal, while the number of larger grid squares relates in no obvious way to the total number of squares expected for the pose of the smaller figure. This kneeling figure, therefore, appears to be exceptional. It is tempting to think that its construction was intentional, but if so it was not a method that was widely copied.

In the small temple of Abu Simbel, Ramesses II stands between the raised figures of Horus and Seth who crown the king.[46] If a hypothetical grid is constructed for the king's figure, horizontal 2 runs along the baseline for the two gods, so that each dais is 2 squares high (Fig. 8.8). The equivalent of the hairline for each god lies 18 squares higher, 2 squares above that of the king, so that the two divine figures use the same grid as the king. It is interesting to note that the poses of the gods are not quite symmetrical. Seth's raised hand is slightly higher than that of Horus and his *renpet* (notched palm-rib) staff runs close to a vertical 2 squares in front of his belt, while Horus' staff is only 1 1/2 squares in front of his belt. The variation is probably deliberate, for while Egyptian artists aimed at balance, they avoided absolute mirror images.

Similar scenes exist elsewhere, but few have been published in a form that can be analyzed.[47] However, three such scenes are found in the mortuary temple of Ramesses III at Medinet Habu.[48] In two of them, the figures of the king and the gods are drawn on the same scale and the gods are raised up on a dais 1 square high on a hypothetical grid.[49] In the third, the figures are on

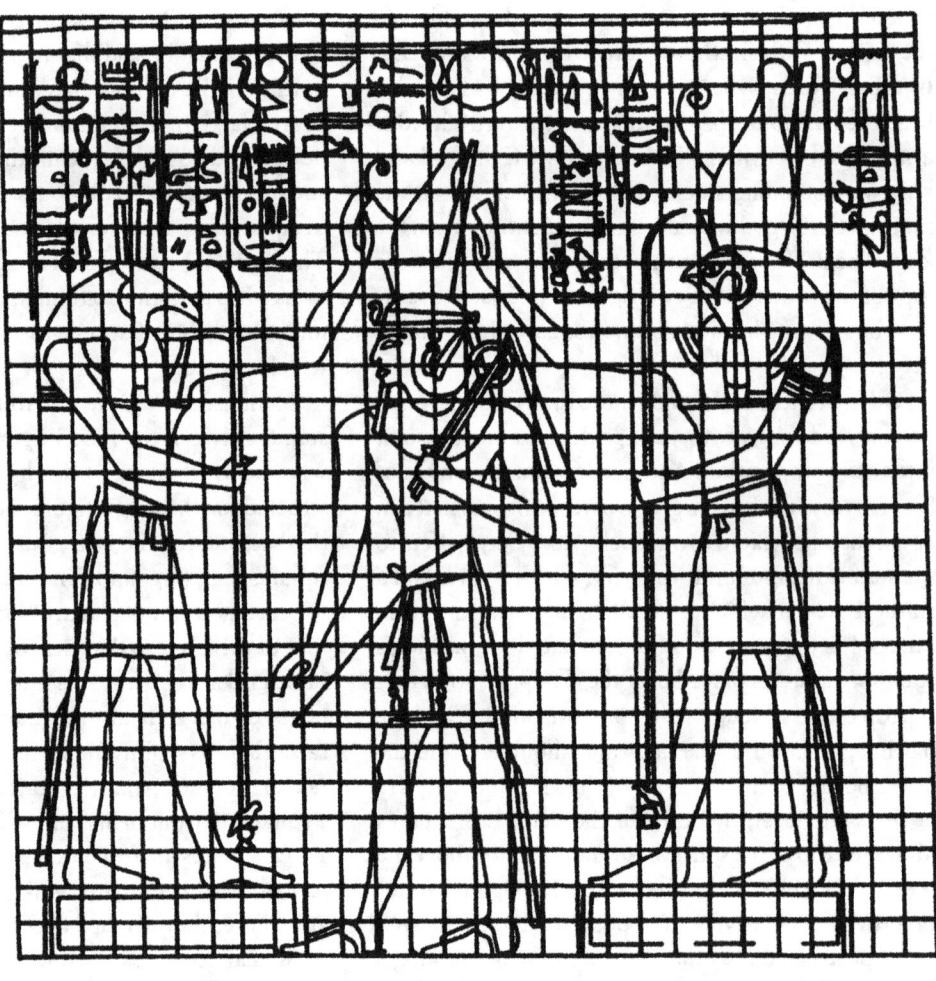

FIGURE 8.8
King being crowned by Horus and Seth with hypothetical 18-square grid calculated for king's figure, small
temple at Abu Simbel, nineteenth dynasty, after
Desroches-Noblecourt and Kuentz 1968, Plate 42.

a different scale with the figures of the gods smaller than the figure of the king, so that they could not all have been drawn on the same grid.

A scene of similar composition dating to the twenty-fifth dynasty is found on the edifice of Taharqa at Karnak.[50] Here the king stands between the raised figures of Thoth and Horus who purify the king. The head of the king, the head and shoulders of Thoth, and the head and torso of Horus are now missing, but a hypothetical grid can be reconstructed for the king's figure by dividing the distance between the soles and the junction of the neck and shoulders by 19 (Fig. 8.9). Horizontal 7 runs through the knee, 11 through the lower border of the buttocks, and 13 near the small of the back, as would be expected on the later grid. The verticals are placed so that the outer edges of each upper arm and each armpit lie between grid lines with an axial vertical dividing the upper torso. The figures of the gods are raised exactly 2 squares, so that their baseline is the same as horizontal 2 on the king's grid. Their knees lie 7 squares up, and the lower border of buttocks and small of the back on Thoth's figure lie 11 and 13 squares up respectively. The eyes of the two figures must originally have lain 2 squares above the king's horizontal 21. The two columns of hieroglyphs in front of the gods' figures are 2 squares wide. On my hypothetical grid, with the verticals placed according to the king's figure, they are bounded by grid verticals, while the streams of *ankh* (life) and *was* (dominion) hieroglyphics, which the gods pour over the king, also run down vertical lines.

In a later scene in the temple of Kom Ombo, the king is purified by Horus and Thoth. The king's eye level survives and, if the scene is analyzed on a hypothetical grid, we find this is on the same level as the junction of the neck and forward shoulders of the gods (Fig. 8.10). The bodies of the three figures are similarly proportioned, but those of the gods are raised 2 squares on the king's grid.

A scene of similar type at Kalabsha shows Augustus purified by Thoth and Horus. Although no grid lines show on the photograph published by Henri Gauthier,[51] and presumably they were washed off after the construction of the Aswan dam, Lepsius recorded the scene with a grid over the king's figure,[52] which makes it clear that the top of the dais of the raised gods lies on horizontal 2 of the grid. If the grid is completed to cover the whole scene, horizontal 9 runs through the gods' knees and 12 through the lower border of the buttocks. The small of the back lies between horizontals 15 and 16, while 21 runs through the junction of the neck and shoulders. In other words, the proportions are normal for this time with the knee on horizontal 7, the lower border of the buttocks on 10 (Sec. 10.7), the small of the back between 13 and 14, and the junction of the neck and shoulder on 19. Horizontal 23 of the king's grid runs at the bottom of Horus' eye, but it runs through the ibis neck below the small head on the figure of Thoth. Horizontal 24 runs through Thoth's eye and through the top of the head. Although Thoth's ibis head may, on other monuments, consist of 2 squares between the junction of his neck and shoulders and the top of the head, rather than 3 squares as here, in a scene of Ptolemy VII Euergetes II at Qasr el-Aguz,[53] this distance comprises 3 squares as at Kalabsha.

Behind the figure of Horus in the Kalabsha scene stands another falcon-headed figure, that of Harsiese, whose feet are on a level with those of the king, while

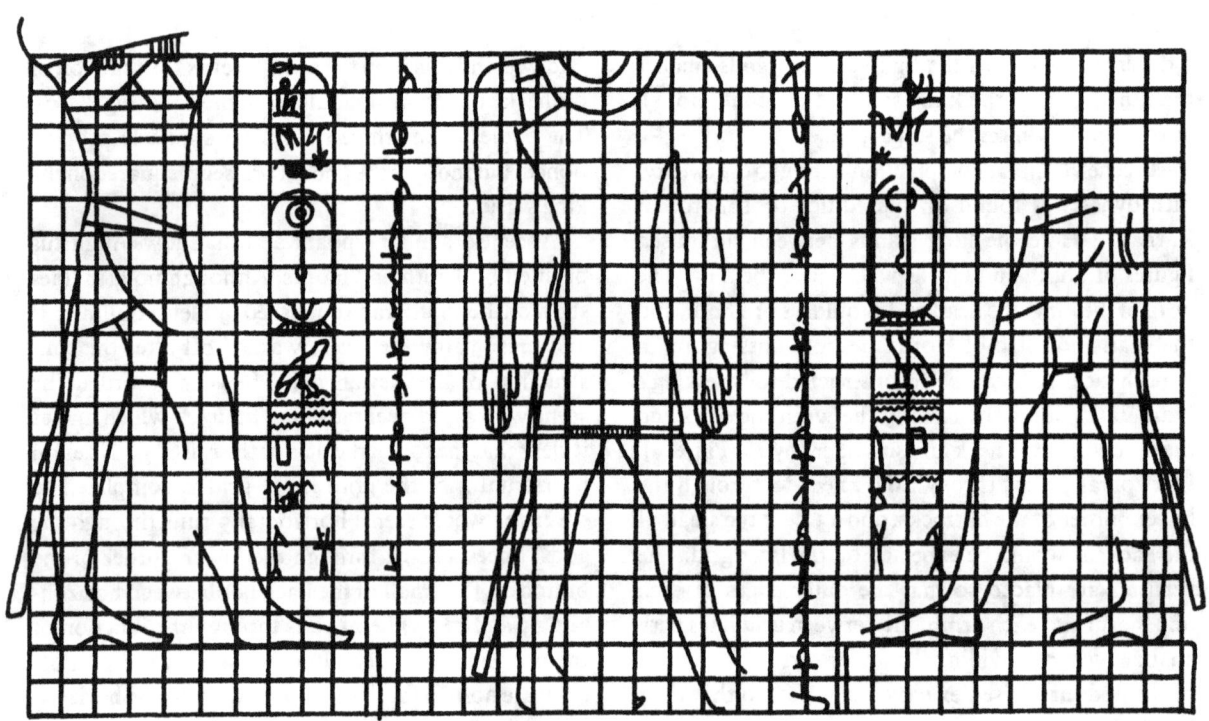

FIGURE 8.9
King being purified by two deities with hypothetical
19-square grid from the junction of neck and shoulders
to the soles calculated for the king's figure, building of
Taharqa by sacred lake at Karnak, twenty-fifth dynasty,
after Parker et al. 1979, Plate 7.

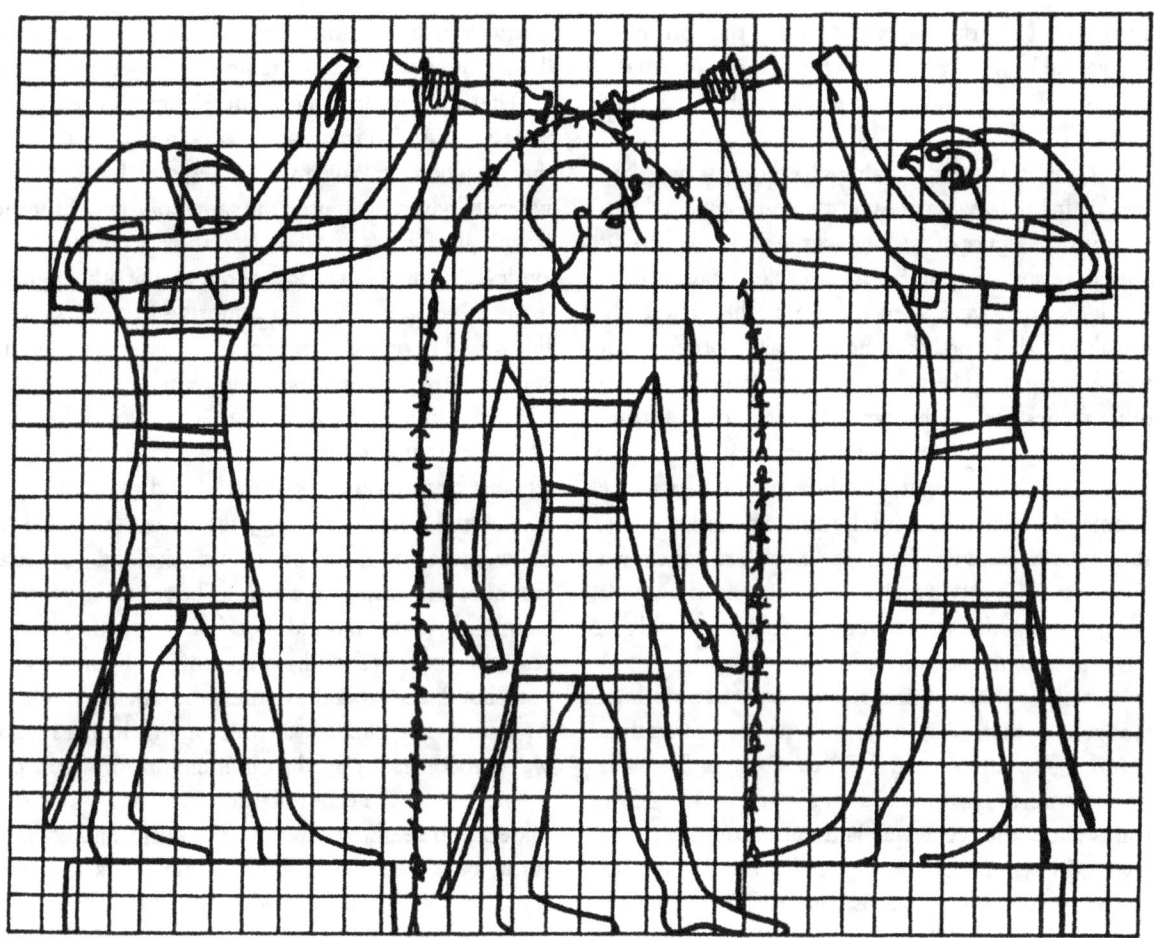

FIGURE 8.10
King being purified by Thoth and Horus with
hypothetical 21-square grid calculated for the king's
figure, temple of Kom Ombo, Ptolemaic period, after
author's photograph.

horizontal 21 of the king's grid runs at the bottom of his eye and horizontal 22 at the top of his head. All the figures could probably have been laid out on the same grid.

Lepsius' draftsman has almost certainly squared up the grid in his drawing of Augustus and completed it to run over the figure of the king, as the grid traces could only have survived on the uncut background, not on the figures that were worked in sunk relief. There is a possibility, therefore, that the scene as recorded is not totally accurate. The similarity in composition to the other scenes of the same type suggests, however, that the copy is probably essentially correct.

By contrast, the figures in three such scenes in the temple of Khonsu at Karnak showing Ramesses IV, Ramesses XI, and Herihor respectively are not drawn on the same scale.[54] In each case, the figures of the gods are slightly smaller than that of the king and could not have fitted onto the same grid.

In a scene in the shrine of Amenirdis I at Medinet Habu, in which Shepenwepet II drives four calves before figures of Osiris and Horus, Osiris is shown as a mummiform figure raised on a statue base.[55] Grid traces show the scene was laid out according to the later grid system. Shepenwepet and Osiris have the same shoulder and eye levels, but Osiris' baseline lies on horizontal 1 of Shepenwepet's grid. The top of his knee is placed correctly 7 squares above his baseline, but the lower border of his buttocks is on a level with that of Horus, 11 squares up in the case of the latter but only 10 squares up on Osiris' figure. So we may again speculate that the mummiform deity was constructed on the same grid as its neighboring figures by dropping a square from the thigh region, as in the example described above from the temple of Sety I at Abydos.

The mummiform figure of Khonsu raised on a pedestal was also treated this way in a few scenes on the propylon of Ptolemy III Euergetes I,[56] but elsewhere the draftsman used the same solution as for the ithyphallic figures of Amun (see above). He raised the eye level of Khonsu a square above that of other figures in the scene, so that Khonsu comprises a full 21 squares but would fit on a grid appropriate to the figure of the standing king and deities in the scene.[57]

In the tomb of Siamun at Siwa, a mummiform figure of Amset that survives on a grid comprises only 20 squares between the upper eyelid and the baseline.[58] Horizontal 19 runs through the mouth and 12 just below the lower border of the buttocks, and 7 as usual just above the top of the knee. The resulting proportions give a long thigh and short back. Thus they do not resemble those of the other mummiform figures examined, but the fact that the figure is drawn on 20 and not 21 squares may indicate a tradition in which a square was sometimes dropped from mummiform figures.

More analysis needs to be done on a wide sample of material to see how often mummiform figures on a statue base are related to another figure's grid in this way. We have already seen that the ithyphallic mummiform figure of Min or Amon-Re rarely shows this relationship to the figure of the king that normally confronts it. The reason why this should be is unclear. To the modern viewer it would seem that the draftsman rejected a simple solution, involving the use of one grid onto which both figures would fit, and instead adopted a more complicated layout.

Nonhuman Elements and the Grid

9.1. Offerings, Scepters, Calves, Sky

Although when a scene is drawn on a squared grid the main purpose of the grid is to help obtain the proportions of the major figures depicted, the very presence of the grid raises the possibility that nonhuman elements in the scene might also be laid out with reference to the vertical and horizontal grid lines.

A common item to relate to a grid line is the table of offerings. When a seated figure sits in front of such a table, one of the grid horizontals sometimes defines either the top or bottom of the table. There is no rule governing the exact relationship, and we find the top of the offering table on horizontals 7 (Fig. 9.1, Pl. 1.3),[1] 6 (Pl. 8.1, upper register),[2] 5 (Pl. 8.1, lower register),[3] and 4[4] of surviving grids. Elsewhere the bottom of the offering table may fall on a horizontal (Pl. 1.2).[5] There may be variations within individual tombs. In TT 89, a sketch in the upper register shows the bottom of the offering table drawn along horizontal 5, with the top of the pile of offerings on horizontal 12 (Pl. 5.2). In the lower register, which repeats the theme of a seated figure in front of offerings, the offering table falls between horizontals 5 and 6 without touching either, and the pile of offerings just tops horizontal 12 (Pl. 5.3).[6] In TT 22, two scenes, one above the other, have the top of the offering table on horizontal 6 of the grid for the seated couple in one, and on horizontal 5 in the other (Pl. 8.1).[7] In tomb chapel B2 at Meir, there is one scene showing the tomb owner before a table of offerings with reed leaf loaves, in which horizontal 6 defines the top of the offering table and horizontal 10 marks the top of the loaves.[8] A more complex composition of offerings is found on a grid in TT 229.[9] The tops of the three mats on which the offerings are placed all relate to grid horizontals, while the arrangement of the offerings in horizontal layers would seem, to a certain degree, to be grid-influenced.

Traces of grids survive on a twelfth dynasty stela belonging to a sculptor called Userwer.[10] A double scene in one register shows on the left a woman, facing left, offering to a seated couple facing right, and on the right a man, facing right, offering to a seated couple facing left; both couples sit before an offering table. The bottom of the offering table in the left half of the scene relates to horizontal 5 of the standing figures, who share a grid, while on the right hand side it is the top of the offering table that relates to the same horizontal (Pl. 1.2). In TT 74, there is a scene with surviving grid traces where horizontal 18 of a standing figure forms the baseline of a reed mat with offerings placed to the left of the figure.[11]

In Meir tomb chapel B2, a figure on a grid carries two baskets containing animals that are suspended from a yoke (Fig. 9.2).[12] The flat tops of the semicircular baskets lie exactly along horizontal 10 of the figure, and the rounded bottoms touch horizontal 8 two squares below. Three female standing figures are still to be found on their grids in the tomb of Sarenput II at Aswan.[13] Two of the figures hold a lotus in front of them.[14] The long stems of the flowers coincide with the fifth grid vertical in front of the axial line (Fig. 4.13). All the figures also carry in their rear hands flowers whose stems relate to the third vertical behind the axial line. When standing figures hold a scepter horizontally at their sides, the handles of the scepters frequently run along horizontal 8 (Pl. 1.1; Fig. 9.3).[15] In the fishing and fowling scene in TT 92, the central papyrus clump is grid-related. The stems of the taller papyrus umbels are placed on every second grid verti-

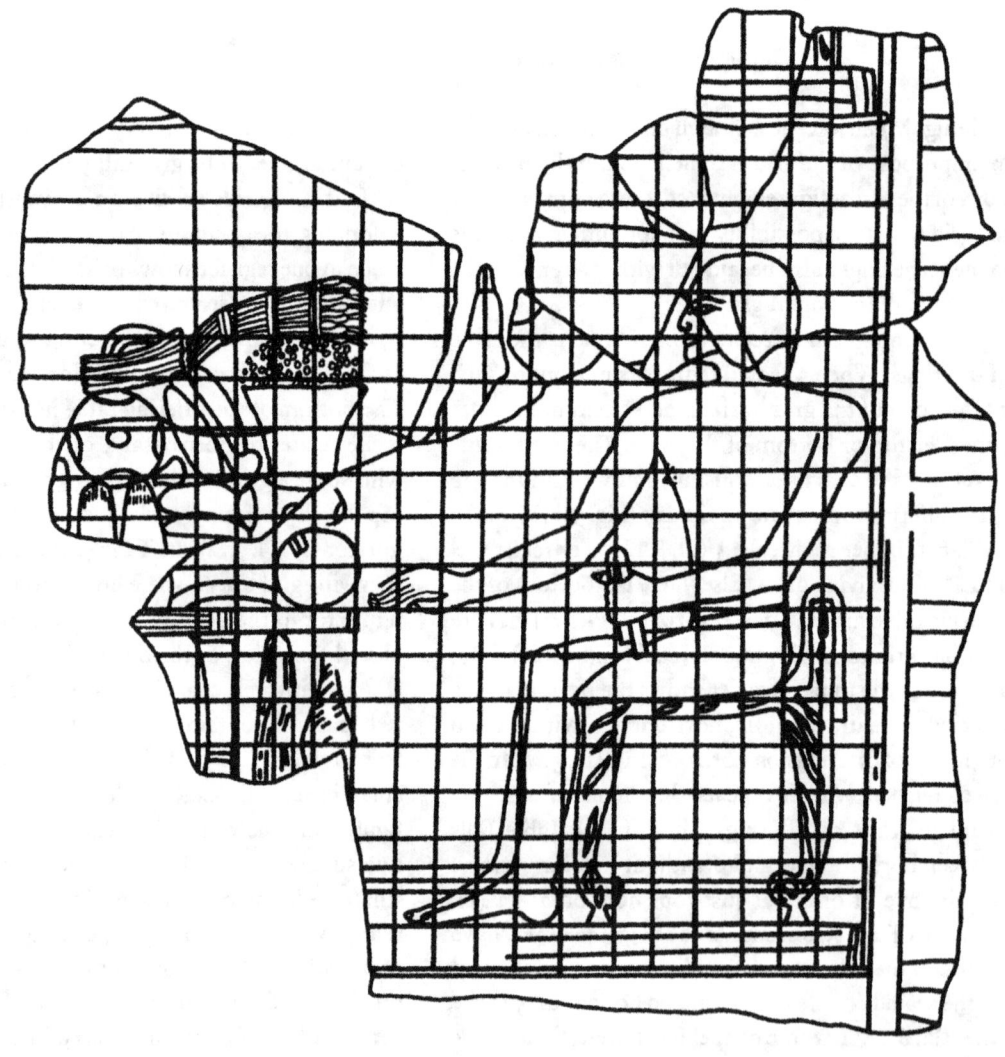

FIGURE 9.1
Seated figure on a fragment of wall painting with
surviving grid traces, British Museum EA 43467,
eighteenth dynasty, after museum photograph.

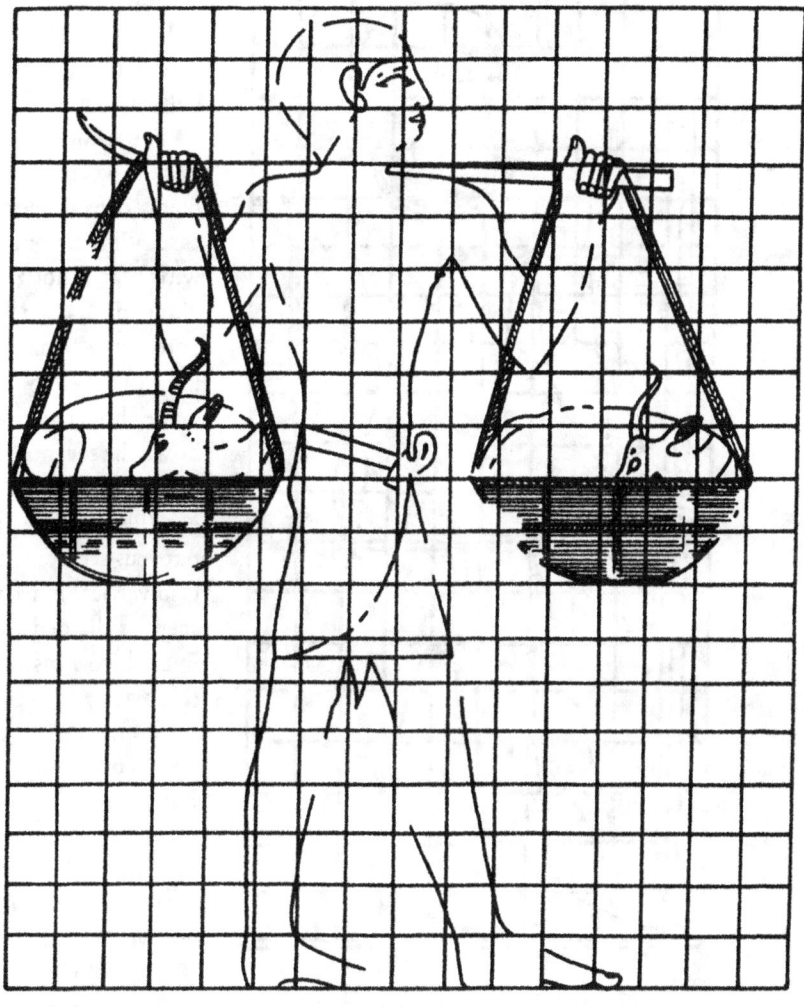

FIGURE 9.2
Figure carrying two baskets containing animals on an
original grid, tomb chapel Meir B2, twelfth dynasty,
after Blackman 1915a, Plate 11.

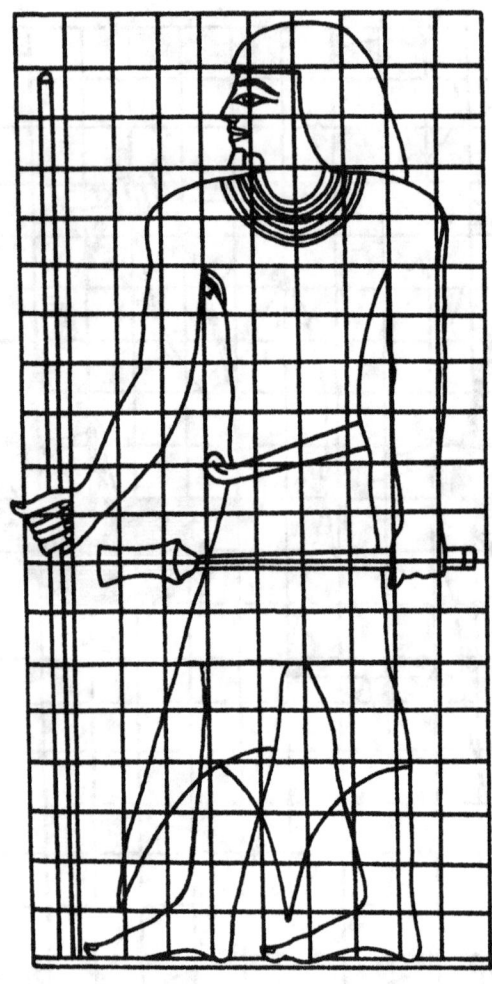

FIGURE 9.3

Standing figure of Sarenput II carrying a scepter with grid completed from surviving traces, Qubbet el-Hawa, twelfth dynasty, after Müller 1940, 84b.

cal, and those of the shorter ones on each grid vertical in between. The shorter closed buds are placed halfway between the stems of the open umbels, and so halfway between the verticals.[16]

The straight line that marks the bottom of the kilt or skirt worn by men may lie on a grid line,[17] although plenty of examples occur in which this is clearly not the case. Whether or not such lines were made to coincide with a grid horizontal was perhaps left to the individual draftsman to decide. In the chapel of Ptolemy I Soter from Tuna el-Gebel, a series of scenes shows the king offering to different deities. Some of the male deities hold a *was* scepter, the right side of which runs down the seventh grid vertical in front of the axial line, that is, the vertical line relating to the position of the ear (Pls. 9.1–9.2).[18] A figure of a goddess holds a papyrus scepter which in her case runs down the sixth grid vertical in front of the axial line (Pl. 9.3).[19] Each scene is divided from the next by an incised vertical line which runs in the middle between two verticals (Pl. 9.3).[20]

A figure of a goddess holding a papyrus scepter occurs on a sculptor's trial piece published by Edgar.[21] Remains of the incised grid can be completed to show that the scepter ran down a vertical grid line 6 squares in front of the axial line (Fig. 7.8). In tomb Meir B2, the tomb owner's wife holds a papyrus scepter so that a grid vertical runs directly down the center of its stem (Fig. 4.10).[22]

A representation of a statue of Thoth in the form of a baboon squats on a pedestal in the chapel of Ptolemy I Soter.[23] The top of the pedestal coincides with grid horizontal 6. In addition, the long censer held by the king runs along horizontal 19 and the offering stand is placed between two grid verticals. In another scene the

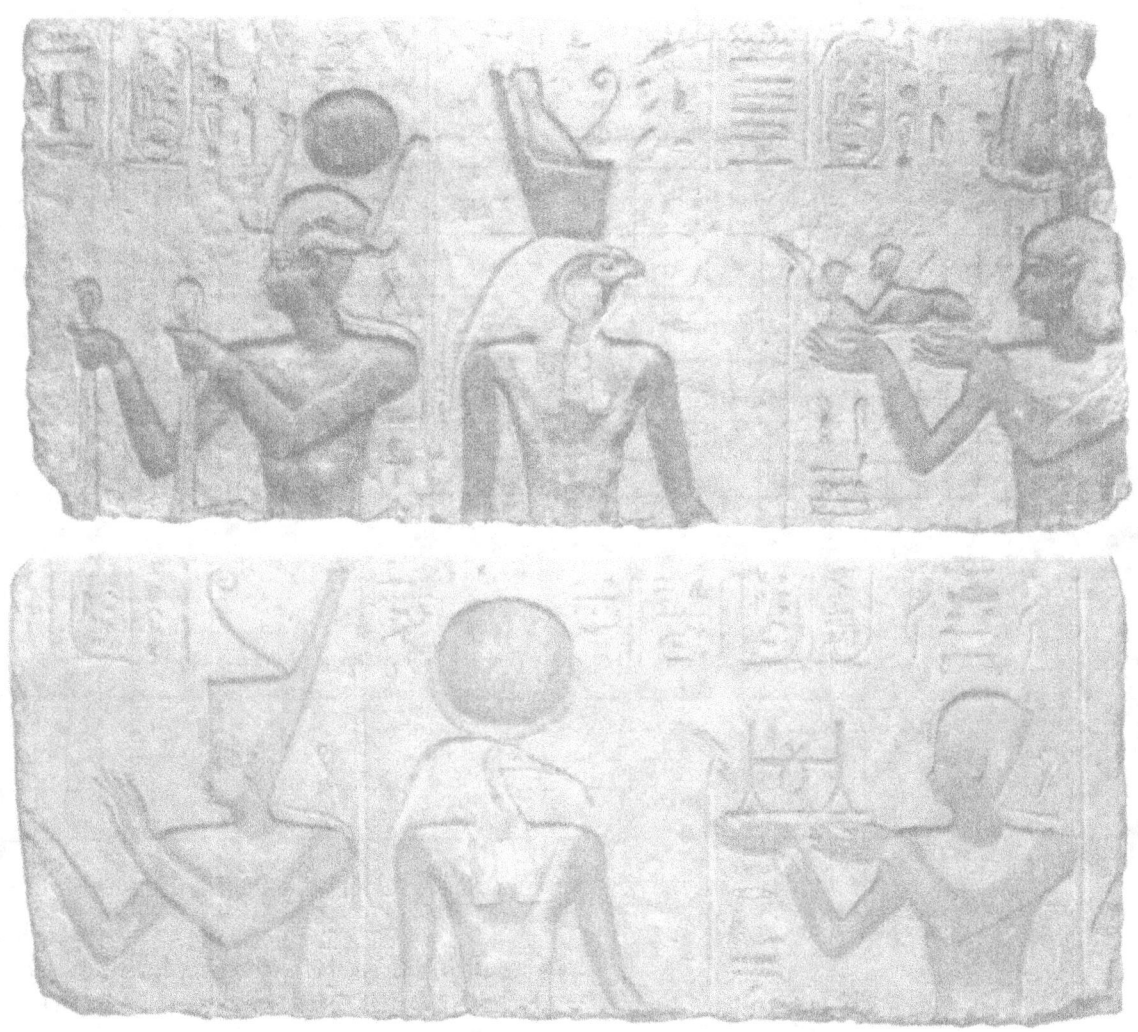

PLATE 9.1
Detail of scene in the chapel of Ptolemy I Soter from
Tuna el-Gebel, Pelizaeus-Museum Hildesheim inv. no.
1883, photograph by permission of Pelizaeus-Museum
Hildesheim.

PLATE 9.2
Detail of scene in the chapel of Ptolemy I Soter from
Tuna el-Gebel, Pelizaeus-Museum Hildesheim inv. no.
1883, photograph by permission of Pelizaeus-Museum
Hildesheim.

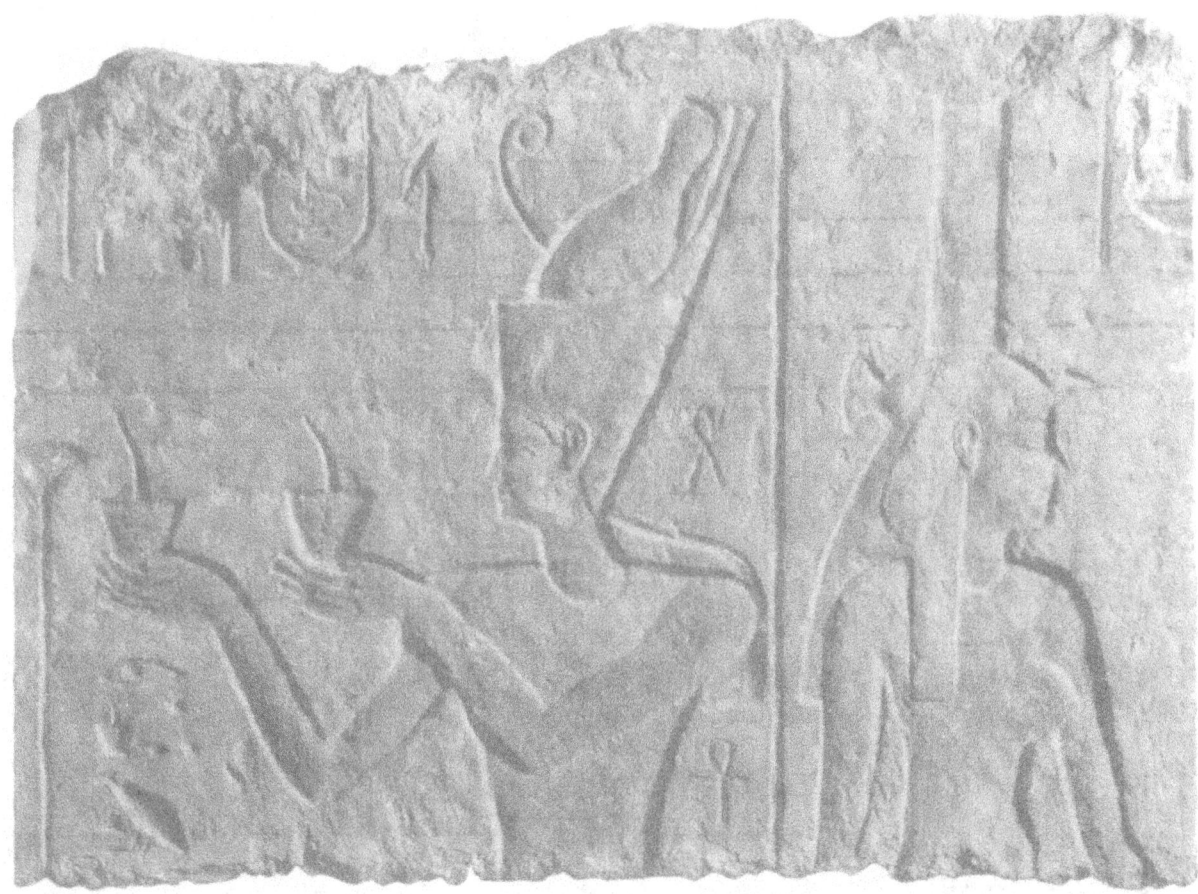

PLATE 9.3
Detail of scene in the chapel of Ptolemy I Soter from
Tuna el-Gebel, Pelizaeus-Museum Hildesheim inv. no.
1883, photograph by permission of Pelizaeus-Museum
Hildesheim.

king offers the combined signs of *shes* (vessels of alabaster) and *menkhet* (clothes).[24] The bottom of the *menkhet* sign relates to horizontal 19 and its crossbar lies on 21 (Pl. 9.2).

A scene on the alabaster shrine of Amenhotep I, now in the open-air museum at Karnak, shows a standing figure of Thutmose I offering four calves to Amon-Re.[25] No grid traces survive, but if a hypothetical grid is placed on the figure of the king it enables us to see how the calves are spaced in relation to the king's figure (Fig. 9.4). The lowest calf shares the baseline of the king. The baseline of the second calf lies halfway between horizontals 4 and 5 on the king's grid. The third calf stands on horizontal 9, and the fourth has its baseline between horizontals 13 and 14. The head of each calf lies roughly half a square below the baseline above. The top of the fourth calf's head lies half a square below horizontal 18. Clearly in composing this scene, the draftsman took the distance in squares between the baseline and hairline of the standing king and divided it by 4 to obtain 4 1/2, and each calf was fitted into 4 1/2 squares.

In the mortuary temple of Hatshepsut at Deir el Bahri, part of a similar scene survives, recorded by Edouard Naville, showing the king driving four calves.[26] The head and shoulders of the king's figure are lost, but the top of the belt at the back is clear. If this is taken as horizontal 11, a grid square size can be calculated for the figure in Naville's plate. The baselines of the second, third, and fourth calves would then lie 4.01, 8, and 11.99 squares above the baseline respectively. Each calf almost touches the baseline of the calf above, so that the top of the fourth calf, which is now lost, should have lain near horizontal 16. Thus it is likely that this scene was laid out so that the calves stood on

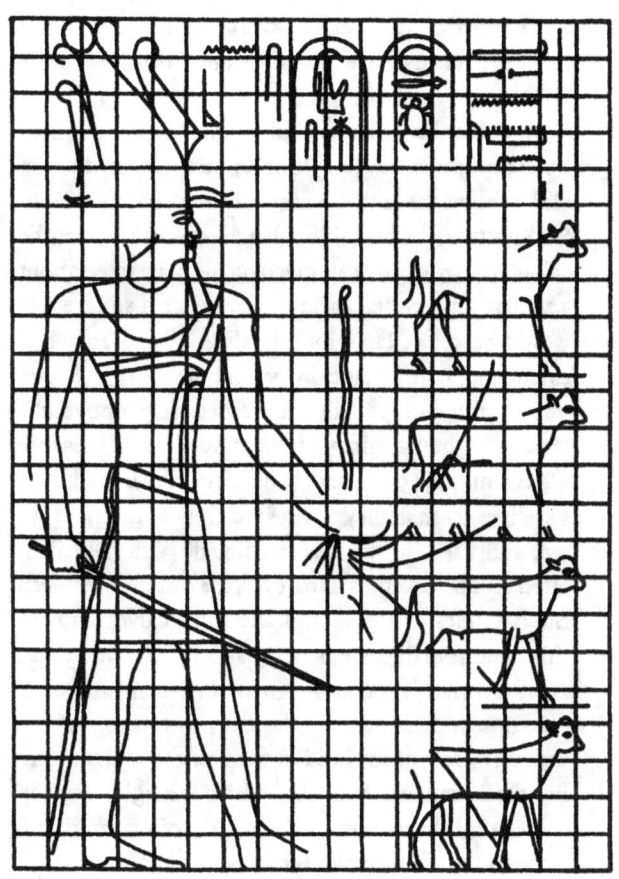

FIGURE 9.4

Figure of Thutmose I driving four calves to Amon-Re on a hypothetical 18-square grid, alabaster chapel of Amenhotep I, Open Air Museum at Karnak, eighteenth dynasty, after author's photograph.

horizontals 0, 4, 8, and 12 of the king's grid. What filled the space above the calves and horizontal 16 is now lost.

A similar scene in the Epigraphic Survey publication of the mortuary temple of Ramesses III at Medinet Habu shows the king driving four calves before Amon-Re Kamutef.[27] The hairline height of the king can be calculated from the scale given on the plate to be about 177.207 cm, so that the appropriate grid square size would be 9.845 cm. Horizontals 4, 8, and 12 when calculated mathematically would lie at 39.38 cm, 78.76 cm, and 118.14 cm respectively above the baseline. The baselines of the calves in fact measure 38.24 cm, 77.45 cm, and 116.67 cm above the king's baseline, so that they are respectively 1.14 cm, 1.31 cm, and 1.47 cm too low to coincide with the calculated grid horizontals. However, the distance between the baselines of the second and third calves and the third and fourth calves is 4 squares (39.21 cm, 39.22 cm respectively) and the height of the second and third calves is approximately 3 squares to the top of the head. The top of the head of the first calf is damaged, but the animal was probably the same height. The top calf is slightly smaller, perhaps to avoid coming too close to the hieroglyphs above.

It seems possible, therefore, that the calves were laid out on the grid used for the king's over-life-size figure, but that the grid was slightly uneven, so that horizontals coinciding with the calves' baselines ran lower than on a mathematically accurate grid. The discrepancies are over a centimeter, and as much as 1.5 cm for horizontal 12, but similar divergencies can be found on surviving grids of this size at Amarna and Abydos. We cannot brush aside the possibility, therefore, that the calves were spaced out by placing them on horizontals 0, 4, 8, and 12 of the king's grid. The solution would be slightly different from the one used in the alabaster shrine, but similar to the layout at Deir el-Bahri in that a spacing of 4 rather than 4 1/2 squares is used. The space above the calves, between horizontals 16 and 18, is filled by a caption reading "driving calves to his father." It must be remembered that since the original grid has been lost, it can never be conclusively determined whether this reconstruction is correct or not.

A similar composition in the twenty-fifth dynasty chapel of the divine adoratrice Amenirdis I at Medinet Habu shows Shepenwepet II driving four calves before figures of Osiris and Horus (Sec. 8.5). It was drawn on the later grid of 21 squares between the soles and upper eyelid.[28] If the few surviving grid traces are completed to run over the whole scene, we find that the calves are placed every five lines on horizontals 0, 5, 10, and 15, with each calf roughly 4 1/2 squares to the top of its head. The draftsman has taken a distance of 20 squares and divided that by 4 to produce 5 squares for each calf.

Another scene of this type occurs on the propylon of Ptolemy III Euergetes I.[29] Measurement on the publication shows that the four calves lie about 0, 4.9, 9.8, and 15 squares respectively above the baseline. Clearly the baselines of the calves can be regarded as coinciding with horizontals 0, 5, 10, and 15, just as in the twenty-fifth dynasty scene at Medinet Habu.

In the Ptolemaic temple of Hathor at Dendera, grid traces survive on the east and west entrance jambs of the Nut shrine.[30] On the east thickness five figures carrying offerings are placed one above each other.[31] Over each figure is the sky hieroglyph. The same grid is used all the way up the jambs. In each case the bottom of the sky hieroglyph lies 29 squares above the figure's baseline, the top of the sky is 1 square higher, and the soles of the next figure another square up. The surviving grid traces show that in some instances the baseline of the figures is cut slightly above the corresponding grid horizontal. In some other monuments where scenes are topped by a sky hieroglyph but where there are no surviving grid traces—for example, in the *chapelle rouge* of Hatshepsut and the propylon of Ptolemy III at Karnak—hypothetical grids suggest that the top or bottom line of the sky, or sometimes both, may have been placed so as to coincide with a grid horizontal.

9.2. The Placement of Hieroglyphs

The question now to be considered is whether in gridded scenes the hieroglyphs were placed in such a way as to fit into the grid. In fact, there seems to be no hard and fast rule followed by draftsmen. In tomb chapel B2 at Meir, where grids survive on a number of scenes, the grid lines were not extended to cover the surrounding lines of hieroglyphs,[32] while text placed within the areas covered by grids is contained within extra lines that are not part of the grid.[33] In a number of eighteenth-dynasty tombs, guidelines were laid out to take lines or columns of text that do not relate to any grid (Pls. 1.3–1.5).[34] By contrast, in the unfinished tomb of Ahmose son of Abana at el-Kab, at the top of the upper register on the rear wall the text was clearly laid out on the same grid as the seated figures of Ahmose and his wife.[35] The text was written in columns, each of which is 2 grid squares wide. Only three column dividers had been put in before work stopped. The hieroglyphs were placed with their right edge against a vertical, so that the divider had to be cut to

the right of the vertical. One can see that there could have been problems with marking the divisions between some of the other columns because little space has been left between the hieroglyphs. It is clear looking at this text that the horizontals also played a role in its layout, helping to line up the tops and bottoms of hieroglyphs on the same level.[36]

Columns of hieroglyphs have also been aligned by means of the grid in the chapel of Ptolemy I Soter from Tuna el-Gebel.[37] Horizontal 24 marks the bottoms of the columns at the tops of the scenes along the two walls (Pls. 9.1–9.3).[38] This helps to produce an even alignment. Some irregularities still occur, as for instance, in scene VIII where the bottom of the king's cartouche drops below the horizontal, while in scene VII the column writing the name of Horsiese finishes above the horizontal leaving a slight gap (Pl. 9.1).[39] However, there can be no doubt that horizontal 24 was used as the marker for the bottoms of the columns. In addition, the width of the columns is grid related. The single royal cartouche preceded by the title *nesu bity* "King of Upper and Lower Egypt" is usually 2 squares wide[40] and followed in the next 2 squares without a divider by the phrase *di ankh djed was mi ra* "given life, stability, and dominion like Re" (Pls. 9.1–9.3).

The various deities' inscriptions have a slightly different layout. The columns of text each occupy 2 squares width, but are separated by the width of a square with a column marker running down the middle between the two verticals (Pls. 9.1–9.2).[41]

In some of the scenes, the deity holds a *was* scepter, which acts as the right-hand marker of a column of hieroglyphs running between the fist and the foot. We have already seen that the scepter lies on a grid vertical.

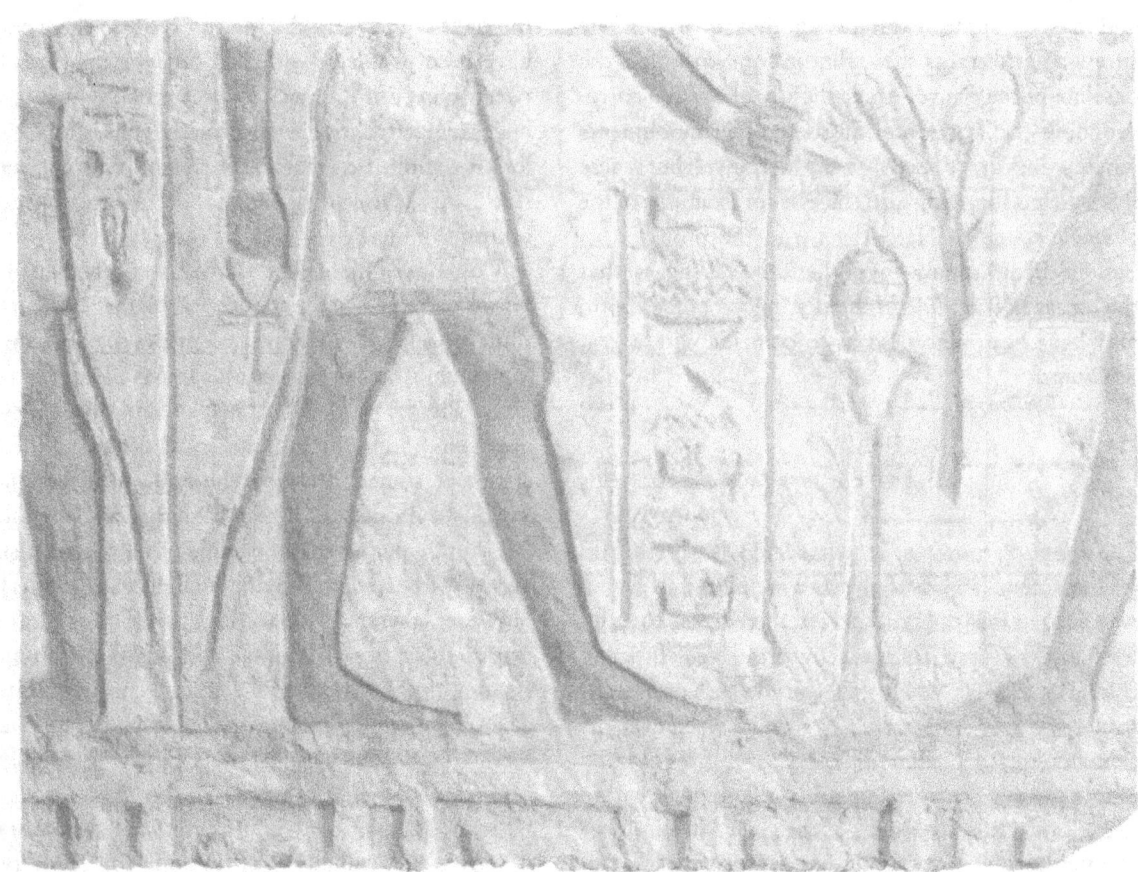

PLATE 9.4
Detail of scene in the chapel of Ptolemy I Soter from
Tuna el-Gebel, Pelizaeus-Museum Hildesheim inv. no.
1883, photograph by permission of Pelizaeus-Museum
Hildesheim.

The left-hand column marker lies on a grid vertical 3 squares from the scepter (Pl. 9.4).[42] The hieroglyphs, therefore, have a different relationship to the grid than do the ones at the top of the scene. There the signs are bounded by grid verticals 2 squares apart with a marker a half square to either side. Below, the signs center on a square but extend half a square to either side with the two markers lying half a square away, each on a vertical. Thus in each case the width of the column is 3 squares, but the columns are placed differently on the grid.

Other texts are fitted in without column markers, but the very presence of the grid would help orient them and keep them aligned. There can be no doubt that the grid which was placed on the walls of the chapel to aid in drawing the figures was also used to help in the layout of the texts.

When it comes to analyzing scenes on hypothetical grids to see if the hieroglyphs were grid-related, we run into several problems. First, we cannot be sure that we have exactly duplicated the position of the horizontals and verticals of the original grid assuming that the scene being analyzed was drawn with the aid of a grid. In addition, because grids were so often uneven, the further we get away from the figure that generated the grid, the less likely it is that the grid lines correspond to the originals. Secondly, where there are no grid traces, we cannot know if there was one grid over the whole scene or several different-sized grids relating to figures drawn at different scales. If the latter is the case, we are still ignorant of where exactly the change occurred and to which grid any particular text might have related; and if a text runs above figures drawn at different scales, we do not know what happened at the possible transition between grids.

In practice when it comes to analyzing scenes on hypothetical grids, we find that sometimes the hieroglyphs appear to fit into the grid in such a way as to suggest it governed their layout, while at other times there seems to be no relationship at all, except for the fact that lines and columns of texts usually have horizontal and vertical properties like the grid lines. Thus the grid could have been used to orient the hieroglyphs, although sometimes the columns and their dividers are not at right angles to the baseline and so presumably not parallel with grid verticals.

Even if the layout of hieroglyphs in a scene appears to be unrelated to grid lines, it is worthwhile calculating the width of columns or lines of text in grid squares, because this dimension differs on different monuments and contributes to the overall style of a piece.

In the open-air museum at Karnak, there is a gateway originally built at Medamud by Senwosret III but with decoration added by Sekhemrewadjkhau Sebekemsaf I of the seventeenth dynasty.[43] In one scene the king offers to Montu. Both figures are standing and fit the same hypothetical grid, if we assume that Montu's hairline runs at the top of his falcon head (Fig. 9.5). The columns of hieroglyphs, including one divider, that are placed above the figures are approximately 2 squares wide. As I have placed the grid, a vertical runs down or near the right side of each divider and defines the left edge of the hieroglyphs. The right edge of the signs is defined by the left edge of the divider. Below the hands of the king to the right of Montu's *was* scepter, there is a column of hieroglyphs without any markers that fit into 2 grid squares, with the edges roughly defined by grid verticals. Running down behind Montu are more hieroglyphs. These are slightly smaller and cramped in their arrangement

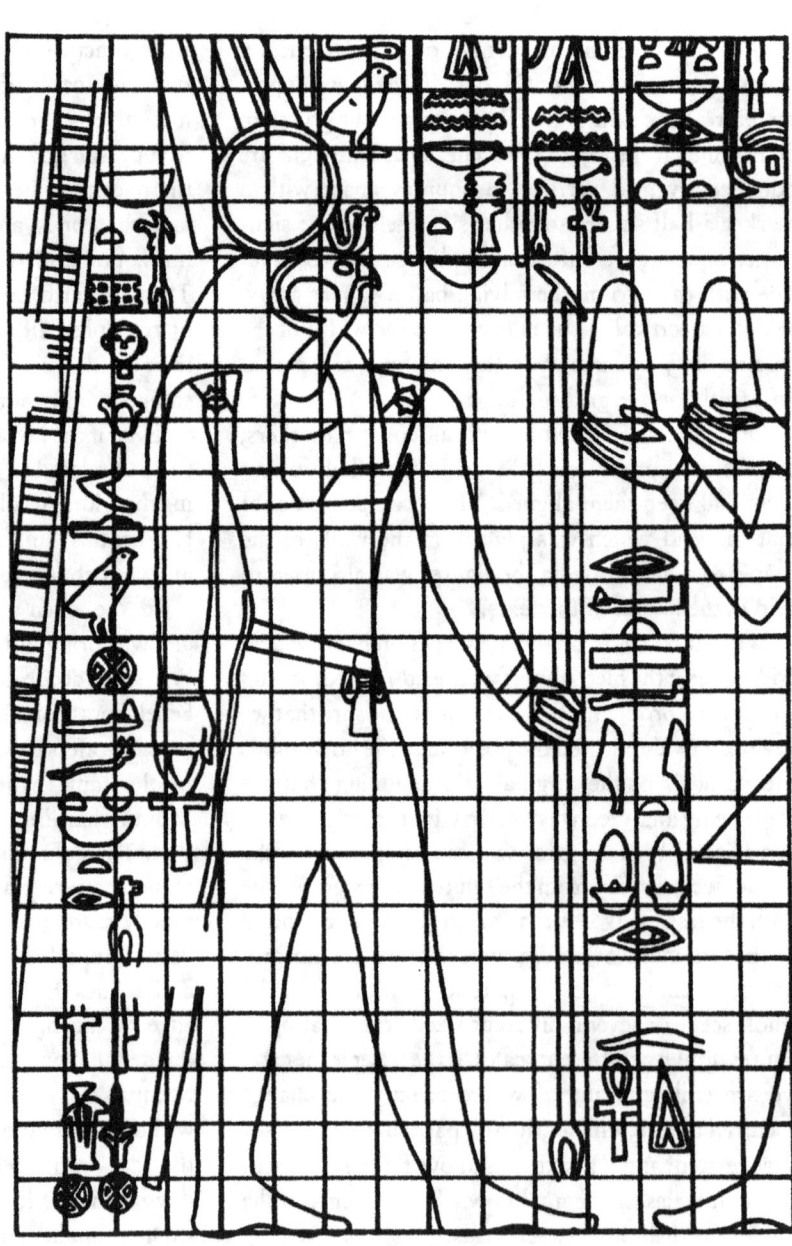

FIGURE 9.5
King offering to Montu with
hypothetical 18-square grid,
gateway decorated by
Sekhemrewadjkhau
Sebekemsaf I, Open Air
Museum at Karnak,
seventeenth dynasty, after
author's photograph.

because they have to fit between the oblique border of the scene and the god's figure, which is too narrow for a column covering 2 full squares.

To the right of the king's figure is a separate scene preserving a smaller figure of Montu facing right.[44] The right half of the scene is lost. If we place a hypothetical grid over what survives based on a division of Montu's figure into 18, we find that the first column of hieroglyphs that survives on the right is approximately 3 squares wide, if we include one column marker. As I have placed the grid, a vertical runs down the right edge of the hieroglyphs and another down the left side of the marker on the left of the column (Fig. 9.6). The next column, however, is only 2 1/2 squares wide including the marker on the left hand side. The hieroglyphs are 2 squares wide, bounded on either side by a grid vertical. The next two columns are once again 3 grid squares wide, including one column marker. So we have a case of four adjacent columns of hieroglyphs, of which three are 3 squares wide and one is narrower at only 2 1/2 squares. We do not have to look far to find the reason. The second column has had to be reduced by half a square to avoid overlapping the head of Montu's *was* scepter and his hand, which cannot be drawn closer to the body if there is still to be space to write *neb waset* "Lord of Thebes" between his scepter and thigh. Further, if all the columns were a full 3 squares wide, the final one would be unattractively close to Montu's double feathers.

From the reign of Hatshepsut numerous blocks survive belonging to her *chapelle rouge*.[45] When hypothetical grids are added we find that in many instances the columns of hieroglyphs are 3 squares wide with a grid vertical bordering both edges (Figs. 8.2–8.3).

Where there are column markers, these often lie half a square to the left or right of the edge of the hieroglyphs between two verticals. The tops of the columns usually lie on or close to grid horizontal 26 of the standing figures.

These blocks, apart from those of the top course, are all approximately the same height, although their width may differ, and they were probably all meant to be laid out with the same size grid. A study of all the surviving blocks would probably tell us a lot about the composition of the scenes. On a sample of fourteen blocks I found that the height of the standing figures, excluding ithyphallic figures of Amon-Re on a statue base, ranged from 35.7 cm to 37 cm, a difference of only 1.3 cm, with an average height of 36.5 cm (most 36.6 cm). The grid square sizes appropriate to these figure heights would range from 1.98 cm to 2.06 cm, with a difference of 0.08 cm. The variations could be accounted for by inaccurate grids and the cutting of relief, which might not precisely correspond to the original sketch on the grid. Measurement showed that the tops of the columns of hieroglyphs came very close to hypothetical line 26. If we divide the distance to the tops of the columns above the baseline by 26 and multiply by 18 the results are not far from the actual hairline height, differing in most cases by a few millimeters only.

There is no doubt in my mind that the grid played a large part in the compositional layout of the blocks of the *chapelle rouge*. Because of the unusually small size of each scene and the fact that the building was dismantled, the blocks are easier to study and measure than larger scenes with life-size figures in temples and tombs. However, work on the latter can be done by using published photographs and line drawings, where

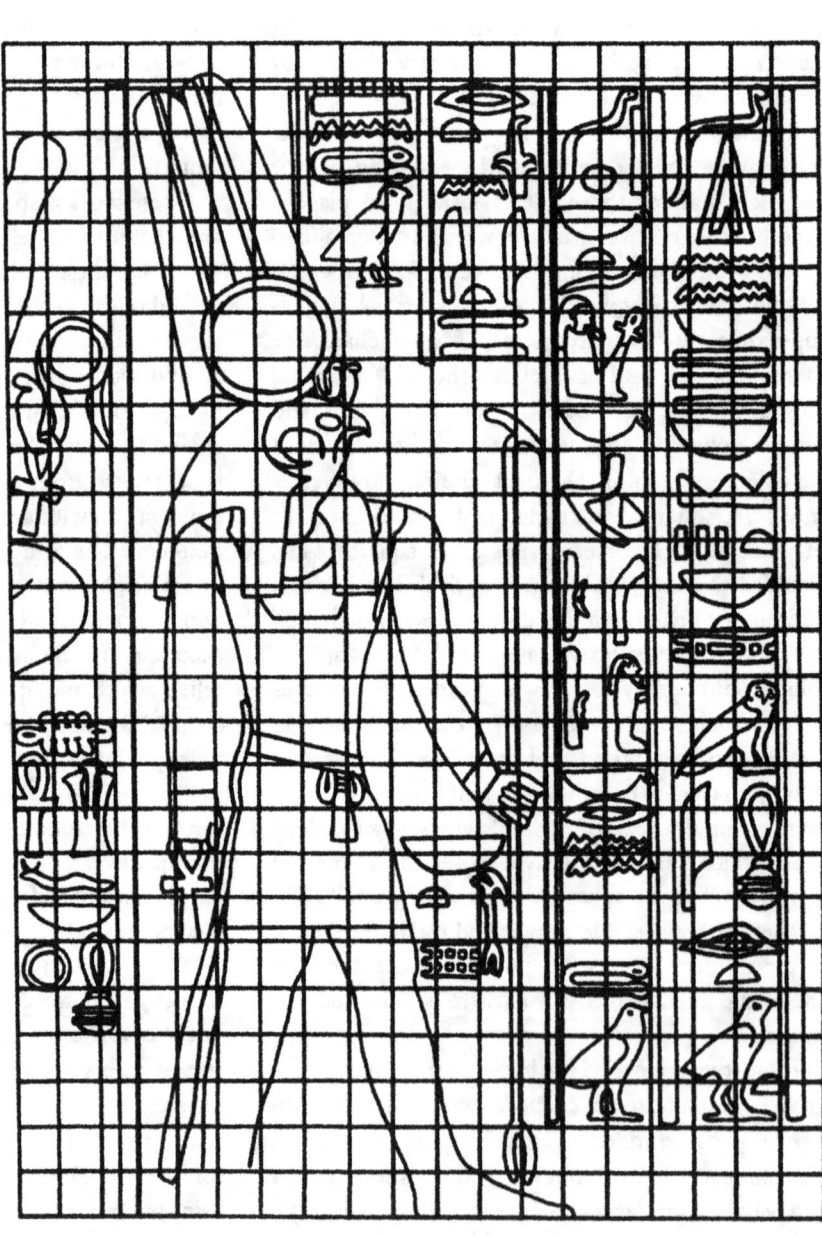

FIGURE 9.6
Figure of Montu with
hypothetical 18-square grid,
gateway decorated by
Sekhemrewadjkhau
Sebekemsaf I, Open Air
Museum at Karnak, seven-
teenth dynasty, after
author's photograph.

they exist, provided they are accurate. The temple of Sety I at Abydos is an obvious case in point, with its splendid publication sponsored by the Egypt Exploration Society and the Oriental Institute Chicago.[46]

The high quality of workmanship in the temple is plain to see. We have already examined two composite scenes where one grid probably governed the layout of several figures (Sec. 8.5). We have also seen that in the predominant scene type of king standing or kneeling before a seated god raised on a dais, the royal and divine figures are on different scales and would not fit one grid, unlike, for instance, the compositions in the *chapelle rouge*. Now we have to ask whether in this temple hieroglyphs relate in any obvious way to the grid. What we find in any one scene is that the width of the columns is usually constant but cannot be expressed in whole numbers of grid squares or even in half squares. If we postulate that many scenes employed more than one grid to obtain the differently scaled figures, then to have used the grids to lay out the hieroglyphs might have meant changing the widths of columns across scenes. For instance, one scene shows the king adjusting the crown of Atum.[47] The columns of hieroglyphs above the scene are the same width above both figures. They consist of a grid square on Atum's grid but just over a square on the king's, so they may all have been laid out on the god's grid. However, such a relationship between hieroglyphs and grid in this temple is not common, and it may be that the draftsmen who worked in this temple preferred to measure out the hieroglyph columns separately. Even so we can see that there is a different ratio between the size of the hieroglyphs and the grid square size appropriate to neighboring figures in this temple and in, for example, the *chapelle rouge*, for at Abydos the columns are often less than 2 squares wide, even when calculated according to the smaller grids appropriate to the king's figures.

In the small temple of Ramesses II at Abu Simbel,[48] the columns of hieroglyphs are often approximately 2 squares wide (Figs. 8.5, 9.7–9.11),[49] although in some scenes there is no obvious fit between the hieroglyphs and the hypothetical grids. The column markers do not, however, always coincide with the hypothetical verticals.[50] In the scene described above where Ramesses II is crowned by Horus and Seth (Sec. 8.5),[51] the hypothetical grid appears to relate to some extent to the width of the hieroglyph columns (Fig. 8.8). Those above Seth and the king are 2 squares wide and are divided from one another by grid verticals. The two columns in front of Horus, on the other hand, are not divided by grid verticals, since their edges fall halfway between lines. If they are measured, though, their width still equals 2 grid squares. We cannot be sure, of course, that the hypothetical grid verticals correspond with the originals. I have placed them in relation to the king's body, so that the outside of the forward upper arm touches a vertical; the next one to the right passes through the forward armpit; the next through the eye; the next forms the axial line; the second vertical behind passes through the rear armpit; and the next one touches the outer edge of the upper arm. This we know from standing male figures on surviving grids is the usual way of positioning a standing male figure on the grid (Sec. 4.3).

If the grid verticals correspond roughly to the originals, we find that between the right uraeus on the sun disk and the curl of the double crown worn by Horus, there would not be room for two columns of hieroglyphs each 2 squares wide, using grid verticals to

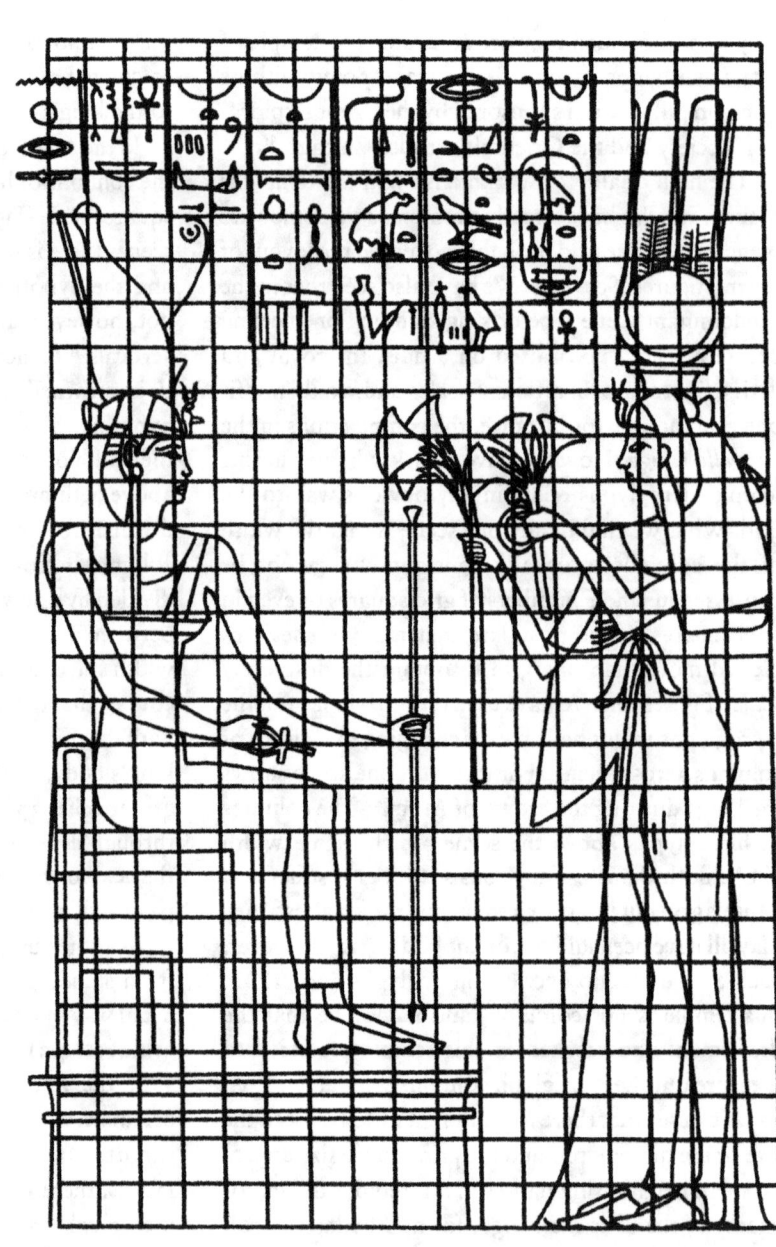

FIGURE 9.7
Nofretary Merenmut offering to Mut
with hypothetical 18-square grid
calculated for standing figure, small
temple at Abu Simbel, nineteenth
dynasty, after Desroches-Noblecourt
and Kuentz 1968, Plate 58.

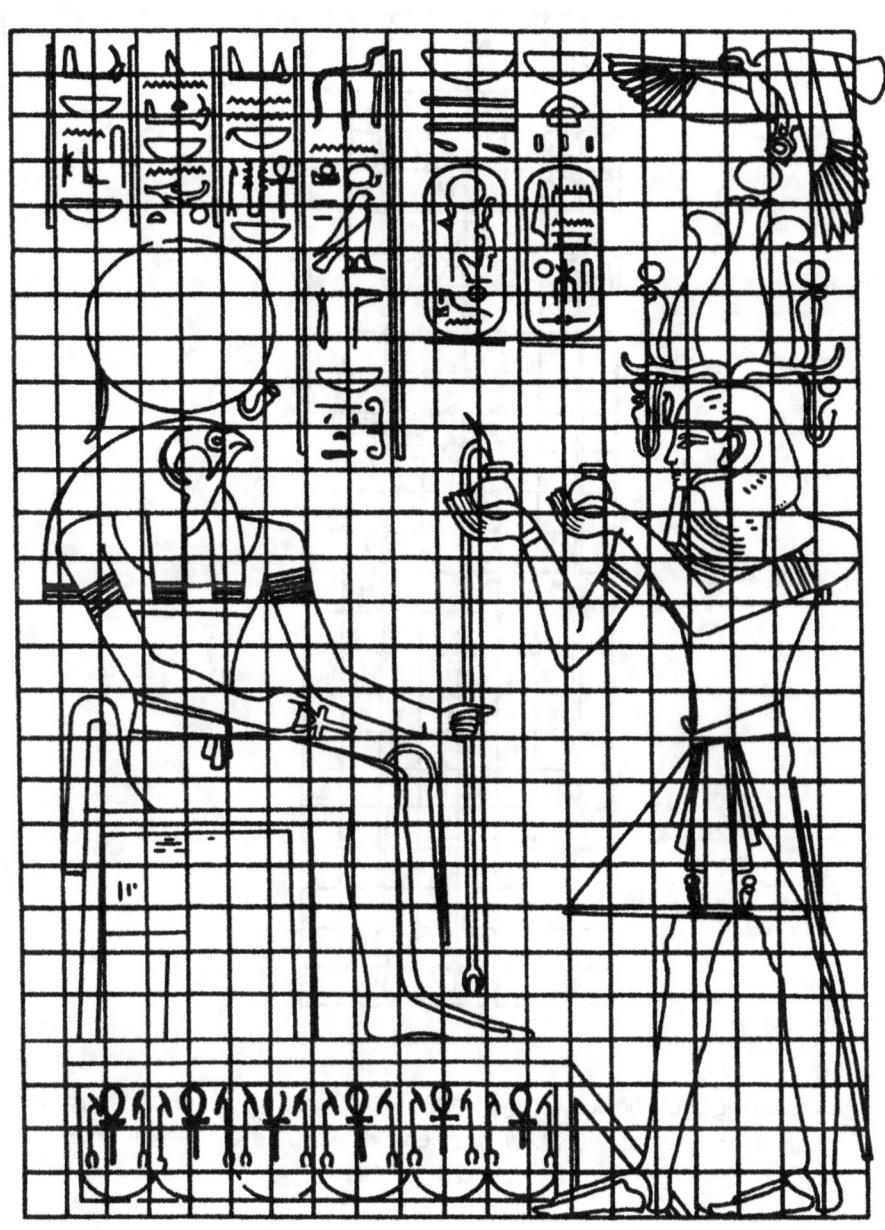

FIGURE 9.8
Ramesses II offering to
Re-Harakhte with hypothetical 18-square grid calcu-
lated for standing figure,
small temple at Abu Simbel,
nineteenth dynasty, after
Desroches-Noblecourt and
Kuentz 1968, Plate 56.

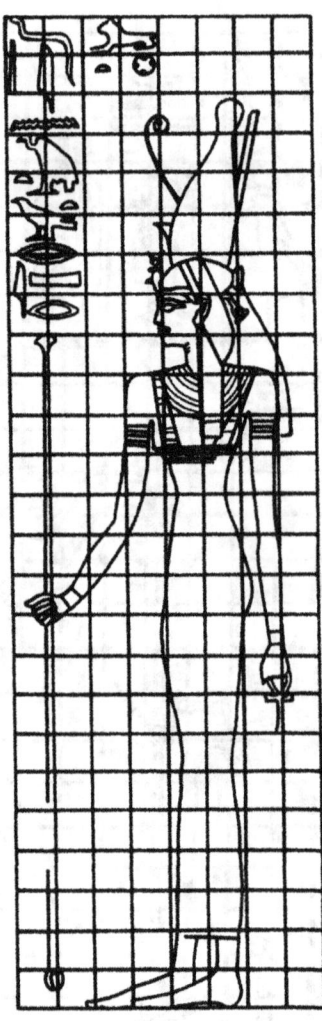

FIGURE 9.9

Standing figure of Mut with hypothetical 18-square grid, small temple at Abu Simbel, nineteenth dynasty, after Desroches-Noblecourt and Kuentz 1968, Plate 80.

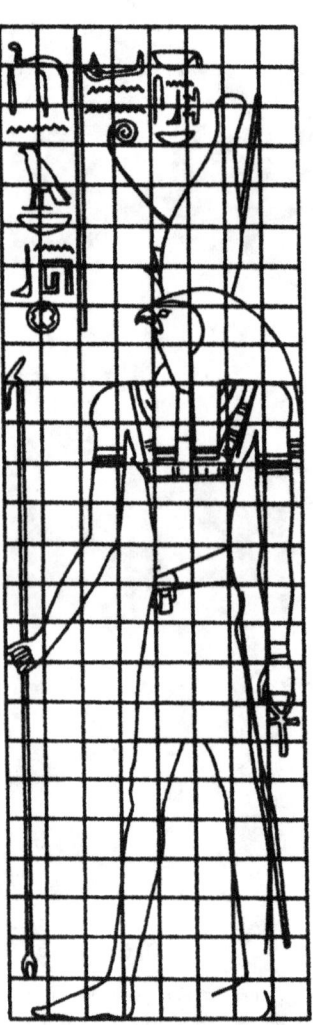

FIGURE 9.10

Standing figure of Horus, lord of Buhen, with hypothetical 18-square grid, small temple at Abu Simbel, nineteenth dynasty, after Desroches-Noblecourt and Kuentz 1968, Plate 70 left.

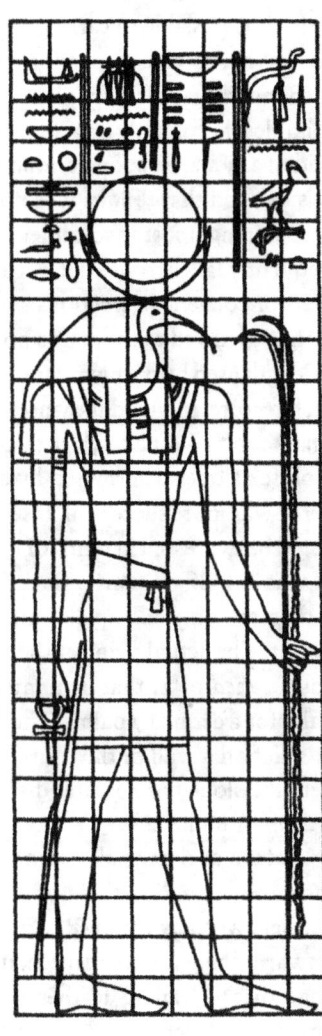

FIGURE 9.11

Standing figure of Thoth, lord of Hermopolis, with hypothetical 18-square grid, small temple at Abu Simbel, nineteenth dynasty, after Desroches-Noblecourt and Kuentz 1968, Plate 70 right.

mark their edges. To maintain the balance with the other columns of hieroglyphs, the width has been retained by adjusting the position of the columns by half a square. The final column behind Horus is again bounded by two verticals, though here the hieroglyphs run right up to the right-hand vertical. The marker has been moved further out and rather carelessly added so that it is not quite vertical.

Relationships between hypothetical grids and hieroglyphs are far harder to see in the temples of Ramesses III at Karnak and Medinet Habu.[52] The columns within scenes are usually less than 2 grid squares wide, although sometimes they may approximate to a width of 2 grid squares. However, column markers rarely coincide with verticals on the hypothetical grids, as they do in some other temples.

9.3. Ruled Lines

A striking aesthetic feature of Egyptian two-dimensional art is the contrast or tension that can develop between the flowing lines of the contours of limbs and bodies, and the often boldly ruled straight lines of various objects related to them, such as staffs, fishing spears, or scepters held in the hand; the front of the kilt or apron; the back of the red or double crowns; and the edges of the tall falcon feathers worn on the head by Amon-Re and other deities. Sometimes these ruled straight lines are horizontal, as in the case of the *sekhem* scepter, normally held in the right hand, and the tops and bottoms of seats and offering tables already considered (Sec. 9.1). We have seen that these horizontal elements in the scene are often related to horizontals of the grid. In other instances the ruled straight lines are vertical, as with many staffs and often the *was* scepter. Whether these items were commonly placed in direct relation to grid verticals is harder to determine, since they are seldom present in scenes with surviving grids. However, papyrus and *was* scepters on the walls of the chapel of Ptolemy I Soter can be seen to relate to grid verticals (Sec. 9.1; Pls. 9.1–9.4). If a hypothetical grid is constructed and positioned in a manner that seems appropriate for other considerations—that is, with an axial vertical, or verticals through one or both armpits, or adjacent verticals defining a hanging arm in a male figure—it is often found that a vertical of the grid coincides with one or other edge of a vertically orientated object. One may conclude, therefore, that the draftsman was often influenced by the location of a predrawn grid in his placement of vertical as well as horizontal elements in the design.

The question then arises whether obliquely ruled straight lines were also grid-influenced, the aim being to give them a predetermined slope by drawing them through selected grid intersections. It is certain that the Egyptians as a nation of pyramid and pylon builders were keenly aware of slope or batter in architecture and had their own way of measuring it, which was in terms of the *seked* or the lateral displacement in palms or fractions of a palm for a drop of a royal cubit of 7 palms. Various pyramid problems involving a *seked* of 5 1/4 are contained in the Rhind mathematical papyrus.[53]

One approach to the problem of slope in two-dimensional art would, therefore, be to determine the lateral displacement in selected units for a particular drop, measured in the same units. Obviously, such units could have been grid squares. Since the slope is a ratio, it is possible to carry out an investigation without having to construct appropriately sized grids for each individual case, simply by superimposing onto a suitable photograph or accurate drawing a standard grid of any size. It soon became apparent by the use of this method that 7 units was not the correct drop for determining most two-dimensional slopes, since it frequently failed to yield lateral displacements of whole units or convenient fractions such as halves and quarters. It occurred to me at this point that, since the unit of length used by the Egyptians for purposes other than architecture and land measurement was probably the small cubit of 6 palms,[54] it might be more fruitful to look for slopes determined by a drop of 6 units, and here I was more successful. It seemed that many slopes could be expressed in terms of the lateral displacement of whole, half, or quarter units for a drop of 6 units. A rather striking example is found in the temple of Luxor. The actual pylon at the entrance to this temple has a *seked* of 1, that is, a lateral displacement of 1 palm for a drop of 7 palms. The same pylon is depicted in relief on a wall of the courtyard of the temple, and here the slope has a lateral displacement of 1 unit for a drop of 6 units.[55]

A drop of 6 units also seems to work well in many instances to define the slopes of the double falcon feathers worn by Amon-Re. From the twelfth dynasty onward, there are frequent examples where the front edge of the leading feather has on measurement a lateral displacement of 1 unit for a drop of 3 units, which may be termed a slope of 2, that is, 2 units for a drop of 6 units, and the back edge of the trailing feather has a lateral displacement of 1 unit for a drop of 4 units, giving a slope of 1 1/2. Examples of feathers with these slopes occur in the bark chapel of Senwosret

I (Fig. 9.12),[56] and the *chapelle rouge* of Hatshepsut at Karnak (Figs. 5.12, 8.2).[57]

In the temple of Ramesses III at Karnak, this same combination of slope is common (Fig. 9.13) but sometimes the feathers are steeper.[58] When this is so, the lateral displacement at the front is often 1 unit for a drop of 4 units, giving a slope of 1 1/2, and at the back, 1 for a drop of 6 units, giving a slope of 1 (Figs. 9.14–9.15). In most instances, the reason for this seems to be lack of space, as when the figure is on a narrow pillar, or when the back of the feathers abuts onto a column of hieroglyphs or the rear wall of the shrine in which the figure is depicted.[59]

In the temple of Sety I at Abydos,[60] where there are many examples of double feathers, measurement shows more variety in the slopes, and suggests that drops of 5 and 7 units may have been used, as well as drops of 6 units. It is interesting in this temple to compare the slopes of the feathers of Amon-Re with the much more upright ones of Isis. The favored slope for the front feather of Isis is 1, steeper than for the feathers of Amon-Re, apart from one instance in which the god stands in a narrow shrine and the feathers are cramped for space.[61] The back feather of Isis most often has a slope of 1/2, which is steeper than any slope found with the feathers of Amon-Re.

Also in the temple of Sety I at Abydos, measurement revealed an interesting difference in the slopes of the back of the red and double crowns worn by the king, Horus, and other deities, according to whether the crown is worn close-fitting to the head, as by Atum, Re-Harakhte, Wadjit, and sometimes the king, or whether it is perched on a wig or headdress, as with Horus and Mut and with the king at times. The close-fitting crown tilts backward, the favored slope being 2.

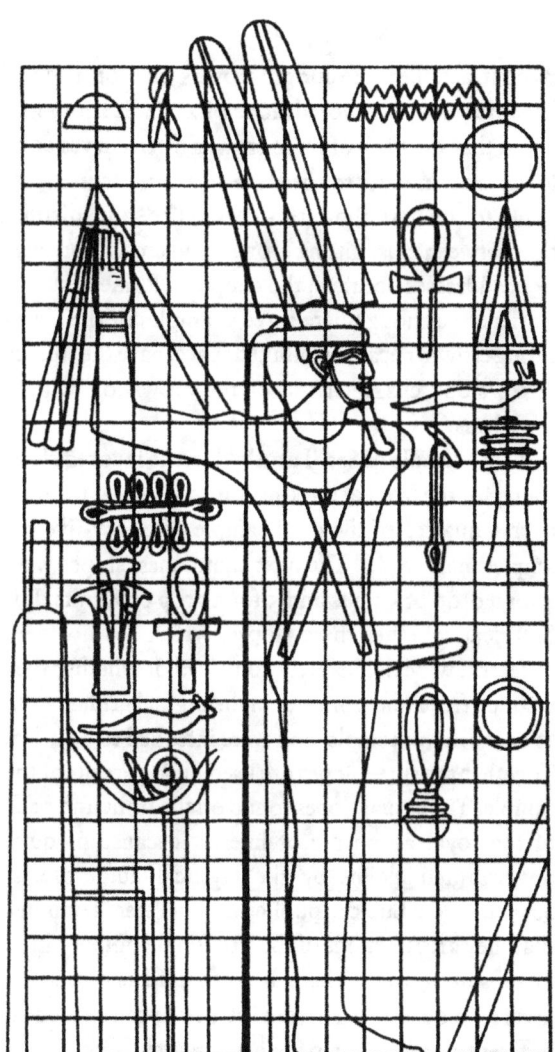

FIGURE 9.12
Standing figure of Amon-Re with hypothetical 18-square grid, bark chapel of Senwosret I, Open Air Museum at Karnak, twelfth dynasty, after author's photograph.

By contrast, the more upright crowns worn on a wig or headdress have a favored slope of 1 1/2. It should be noted that the back of these crowns often curves at its lower end inward toward the head; measurements apply to the part above this curve. The same distinction between close-fitting crowns and crowns on wigs or headdresses occurs in the temple of Ramesses III at Karnak,[62] although here three examples of the close-fitting crown, because of limited space, have the steeper 1 1/2 slope characteristic of the crown on wig or headdress.[63]

In the temple of Sety I at Abydos, the favored slope found for the front of the king's apron is 4 1/2, forming over a quarter of the total sample of eighty-five examples measured.[64] The next commonest slopes were 4 for a drop of 5 units and 5 for a drop of 7 units. It is not clear whether these slopes, which are not very different, were deliberately contrived or whether they resulted from unevennesses in the orginal grid, known to occur in this temple, and were intended to be 4 1/2. Together the three slopes are used in 60 percent of the sample. The actual slopes found on the front and back of the royal apron are of interest because of quite unwarranted claims by the mystical numerologist Schwaller de Lubicz, publicized by Peter Tomkins, that they are functions of the irrational number phi or of its square root. There is some evidence that the favored slope for the front of the apron varied at different periods,[65] but further research is needed to confirm this.

So far I have been considering the slopes of oblique ruled lines as obtained by measurement on material lacking surviving grids. The obvious way, however, to check my hypothesis that slopes were determined by reference to a grid is to examine scenes where grids or

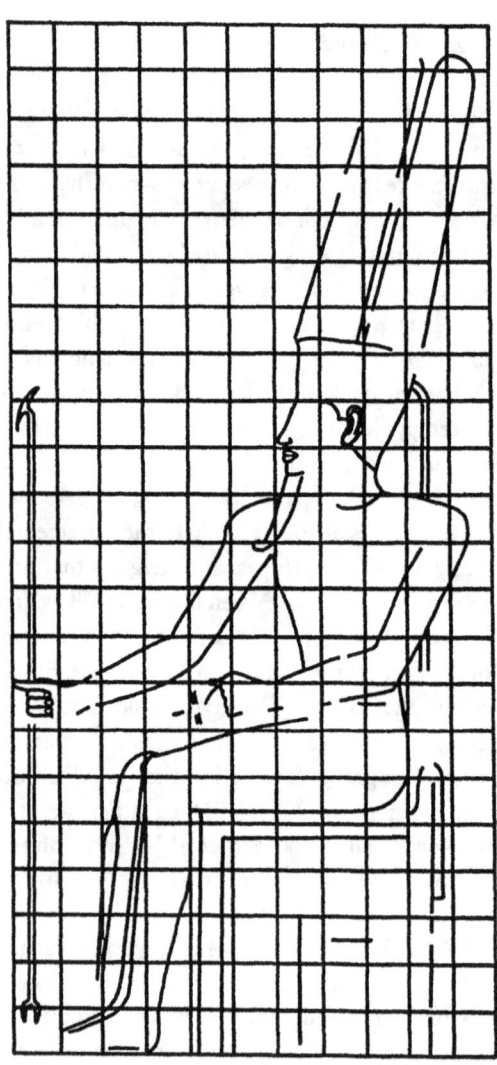

FIGURE 9.13
Seated figure of Amon-Re with hypothetical 14-square grid, temple of Medinet Habu, twentieth dynasty, after Epigraphic Survey 1930, Plate 45F.

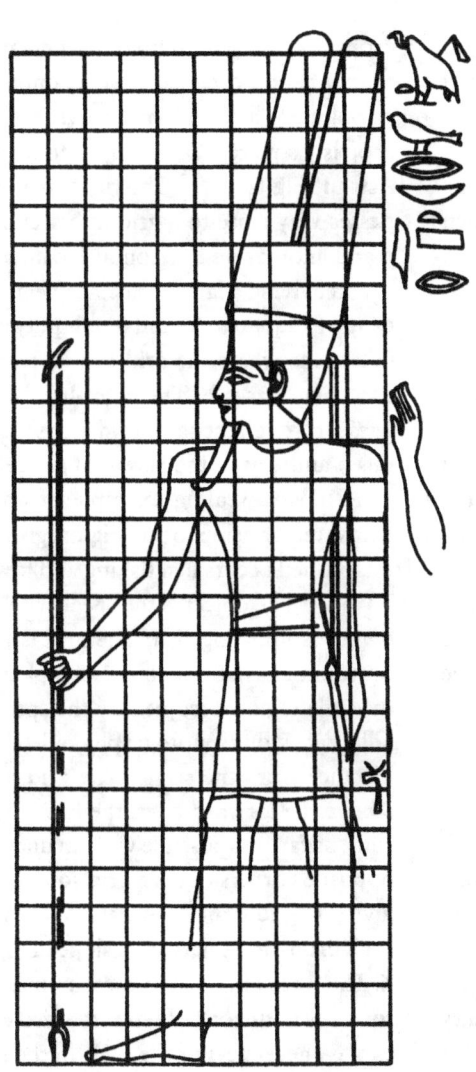

FIGURE 9.14

Standing figure of Amon-Re with hypothetical
18-square grid, temple of Medinet Habu, twentieth
dynasty, after Epigraphic Survey 1930, Plate 45D.

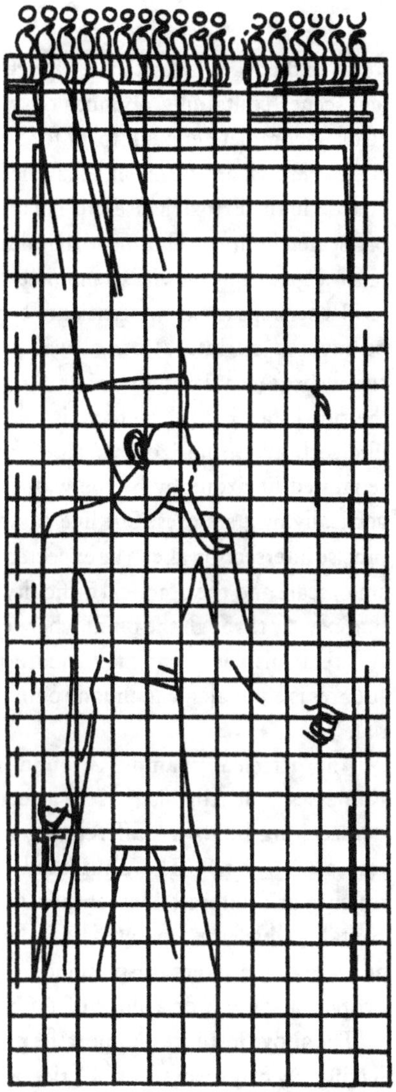

FIGURE 9.15

Standing figure of Amon-Re with hypothetical
18-square grid, temple of Medinet Habu, twentieth
dynasty, Epigraphic Survey 1932, Plate 105I.

traces of them are still present. Unfortunately there are few scenes containing obliques on which a grid survives in complete enough form for such a test. However, there is an excellent example on a "drawing board" in the British Museum. This shows the outline of a seated figure of Thutmose III holding a staff drawn onto a grid that survives complete (Pl. 5.1). It is a model perhaps for an apprentice to copy or possibly to be squared up into a formal wall scene, and it has clearly been very carefully drawn. The left-hand side of the ruled staff below the hand is related to three grid intersections on horizontals 10, 6, and 2, which are separated horizontally by the width of 1 square and vertically by 4 squares. The line passes as close to the precise intersection as can be expected, considering the small scale and the practical difficulty of ruling a third line exactly through the point where two others cross. A lateral displacement of 1 square for a drop of 4 squares is equivalent, as already pointed out, to a slope of 1 1/2.

Another clear example is found in the temple of Ramesses II at Abydos.[66] Here a seated figure of the deified king holds a staff relating to surviving grid traces (Fig. 9.16). The right-hand side of the staff touches grid intersections on horizontal 9 and horizontal 5, which are separated horizontally by 1 square, again giving a lateral displacement of 1 square for a drop of 4 squares or a slope of 1 1/2.

The above instances support the notion of obliquity having been measured on a grid using a drop of 4 squares and giving a result that can be conveniently expressed as the displacement for a drop of 6. I have already mentioned that measurements in the temple of Sety I at Abydos have suggested that sometimes other

drops may have been used, particularly 5 and 7, that cannot be so expressed. Two examples can be cited of an obliquely held staff on a surviving grid in which the drop is 5 squares. One is in the tomb of Sarenput II at Aswan (Fig. 4.11).[67] The right-hand side of the staff passes very close to a grid intersection on horizontal 9 and another on horizontal 4 with a separation of 1 square, giving a lateral displacement of 1 square for a drop of 5 squares. A similar obliquity is found in TT 92 in a scene where the grid can be reconstructed from surviving traces.[68] The right-hand side of the staff passes through the same grid intersections on horizontals 9 and 4 as in the Sarenput figure.

A most revealing example of an oblique object whose relationship to the original grid can be definitely established occurs in a fishing and fowling scene from TT 92.[69] The object is the spear with which the tomb owner is impaling fish. The grid is present as traces only, but I have been able to complete it in its entirety over the region occupied by the spear by using three adjacent Mond photographs, all taken at the same distance from the scene. The grid is far from even. Above the forward hand the lower edge of the spear runs, as far as is possible with an uneven grid, through opposite corners of each grid square that it traverses, giving in grid terms a lateral displacement of 1 square for a drop of 1 square, or a slope in my terminology of 6. The slope obtained by measurement with a protractor is the flatter one of 6 1/2, the discrepancy being due to the unevenness of the grid. In the part of the spear below the hand, it is the upper edge that traverses the opposite corners of each grid square, again giving the grid-determined slope of 6. The two parts of the spear are approximately aligned spatially, but because of the

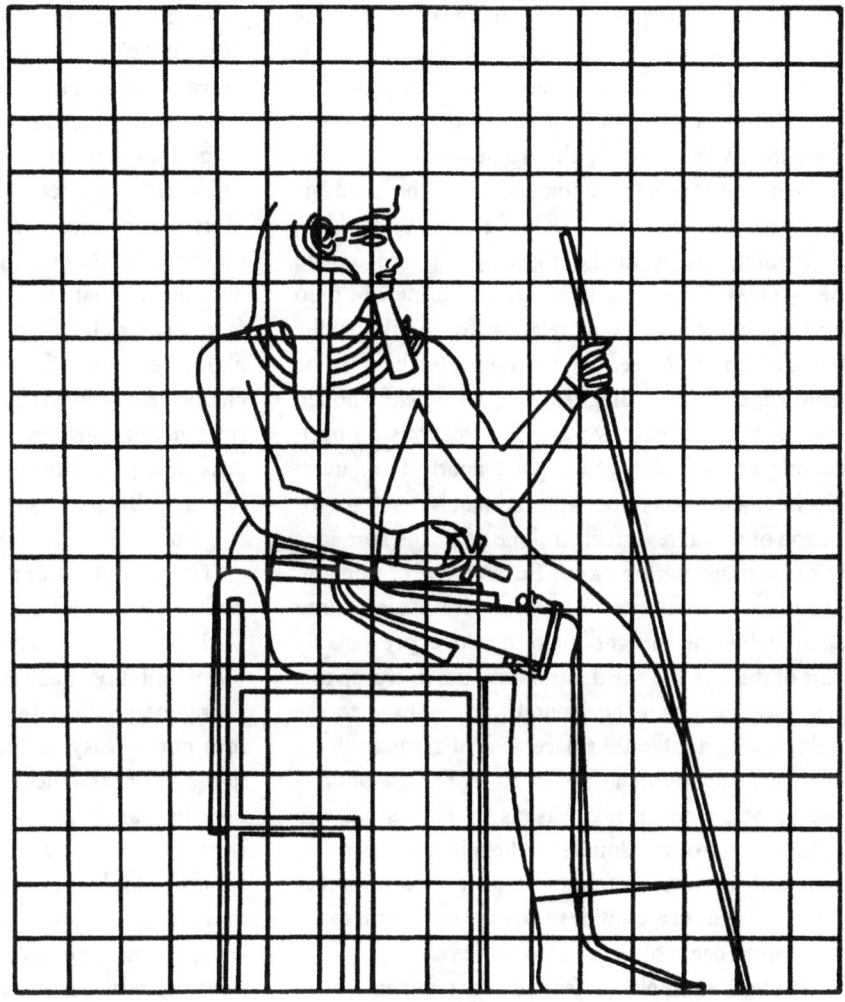

FIGURE 9.16
Seated figure of king with grid completed from
surviving traces, temple of Ramesses II, Abydos,
nineteenth dynasty, after author's photograph.

irregularity of the grid, the squares traversed by its lower part are not in line diagonally with those traversed by its upper part but are immediately to their left. There can be little doubt, I think, that the draftsman's intention in this scene was to give the spear a one-for-one obliquity and that he used his imperfect grid to achieve this end as best he could.

Turning now to the later grid system, reasonably clear traces of a grid survive on the shrine of Philip Arrhidaeus at Karnak in relation to an ithyphallic figure of Amon-Re wearing the double feathers.[70] The front edge of the leading feather passes near, though not exactly through, two grid intersections on horizontals 25 and 28 1 grid square apart. The lateral displacement is therefore approximately 1 square for a drop of 3 squares, giving a slope of 2. The rear edge of the trailing feather passes through a grid intersection on horizontal 27. The top of the feather is cut into a curve, but the straight line of the edge, presumably part of the original ruled line, continues in red up to a grid intersection on horizontal 31, 1 square to the right, giving a lateral displacement of 1 square for a drop of 4 squares, or a slope of 1 1/2. The use of these two slopes, 2 and 1 1/2, was, as we have seen, also characteristic of the double feathers in other periods. This and the other examples support the notion that the grid was used as a guide to give the proper tilt to the two components of the double feathers.

Another example of feathers that appear to be related to grid intersections can be seen on a gridded papyrus from the Ägyptisches Museum, Berlin.[71] It shows a seated king wearing a crown of paired ostrich feathers supported by a ram's horns. The feet and base of the throne, and so the baseline of the grid, are missing. The grid itself shows some peculiar features. While it is clearly drawn according to the later and not the early system, its upper limit is not the upper eyelid but the hairline, while the relationship of the features to grid horizontals resembles that of three-dimensional "trial" pieces (Sec. 7.7) rather than that typical of two-dimensional Ptolemaic art. Nevertheless, a number of orthodox characteristics are present, most notably an axial vertical that passes between the two feathers, through the junction of the ram's horns, and along the front of the lappet. The point of the forward elbow lies neatly on a grid intersection. With regard to the grid relationships of the feathers, their outer edges pass close to grid intersections that are 1 square apart horizontally and 6 squares apart vertically, giving a slope of 1.

The fact that in some of the examples considered the obliques pass close to but not precisely through certain of the grid intersections does not necessarily exclude the possibility that they were intended to relate to those intersections. In practice, as I mentioned above, it is not so easy to draw a line exactly through an intersection, and there is no reason to suppose that the ancient draftsmen were concerned with extreme accuracy. Their aim was more likely to have been to get things to look approximately right. This does, however, raise a major problem to be faced in examining obliques and their relationship to the grid. When a line does not pass neatly through a grid intersection, can we assume that this was due to inaccurate ruling or is the position near the intersection simply due to chance? This is an important consideration when it comes to trying to measure obliques where there is no surviving grid. If the draftsmen were often not exact, how can we discover if there was indeed an intended slope? Further, even if the slope of an oblique was fixed by the grid, since grids were often uneven, a mathematically calculated grid may not duplicate the original. Finally, in the cutting of relief, lines may be changed slightly, so that either the baseline, used to orientate the hypothetical grid, or the oblique line may no longer be precisely as the draftsman originally drew it. It may, therefore, be impossible to determine whether or not draftsmen regularly related oblique lines to the grid. However, the application of hypothetical grids will give an idea of whether artists preferred to use roughly the same slopes for particular items, whether they varied them, deliberately or at random, and whether the same items were given similar or different slopes at different periods. These points are of interest because they relate to style.[72]

Changing Proportions
and Style

10.1. The First Three Dynasties

There can be no doubt that the proportions of the figures associated with the grid in the twelfth dynasty are similar to those of figures of the fifth and sixth dynasties, although, so far as we know, the grid had not been developed for use with figures in the Old Kingdom (Chap. 4). This serves to underline the fact that the proportions are not dependent on the grid, and that the grid was simply adopted as an aid to obtaining them. The question then arises as to when these proportions were first introduced into Egyptian art. I shall investigate this problem by applying hypothetical grids to early dynastic figures.

In the art of the predynastic period, the human figure had not yet taken on the characteristic form that would be used throughout pharaonic times. One of the earliest monuments to show this form is the palette of King Narmer.[1] Here the face of the king is in profile with a full-view eyebrow, eye and ear, and a half-mouth; the shoulders and chest are full-view, the buttocks and limbs in profile; the two feet, seen from the inside, are undifferentiated. Analysis on hypothetical 18-square grids, however, shows that the two figures of the king do not yet have classic Old Kingdom proportions (Figs. 10.1–10.2). The lower legs from the soles to the knee are longer than a third of the hairline height; the lower border of the buttocks lies on or above horizontal 10; the small of the back lies on or above horizontal 12. On the figure wearing the red crown, the armpits are on horizontal 14 and lie about 3 squares apart, while the width across the shoulders is just over 5 squares; horizontal 16 passes under the chin. On both figures the neck is so short as to be almost nonexistent. The royal figure on the so-called scorpion macehead, which may in fact belong to

Narmer, also exhibits long lower legs, narrow shoulders, and a short neck.[2] A figure with similarly long legs is found on an early royal monument from Gebelein.[3] The small figure of King Den smiting an enemy on an ivory label has a thinner waist and higher buttocks than those found in traditional proportions.[4] However, unlike that of Narmer, the figure is bent forward in the act of smiting.

None of these early figures, then, has attained the classic proportions of the Old Kingdom. On the other hand, in the third dynasty a series of stelae showing Netjerikhet Djoser was set up in his pyramid complex at Saqqara in which the figures of the king conform closely to such proportions (Fig. 10.3).[5] The junction of the neck and shoulders is on or near horizontal 16, the small of the back on or near 11, the lower border of the buttocks on or near 9, and the top of the knee on or near 6. The shoulders are 6 squares wide, the distance between the armpits is 4 squares, and the width of the body at the level of the small of the back is approximately 2 1/4 squares. The neck, however, is still very short.

From the same dynasty come three figures of Djoser's successor, Sekhemkhet Djoser-Teti, cut into the rock at Wadi Maghara in Sinai.[6] Two of the figures stand upright, one wearing the white crown and the other the red crown. Overall they come close to classic proportions, but it is interesting to note that the two figures are not identical (Fig. 10.4). On the one wearing the white crown, the elbow crease of the rear arm lies on horizontal 12, the small of the back is just above horizontal 11, but the top of the belt at the back lies below this line. In the second figure, the elbow crease of the rear arm falls below horizontal 12 but the small

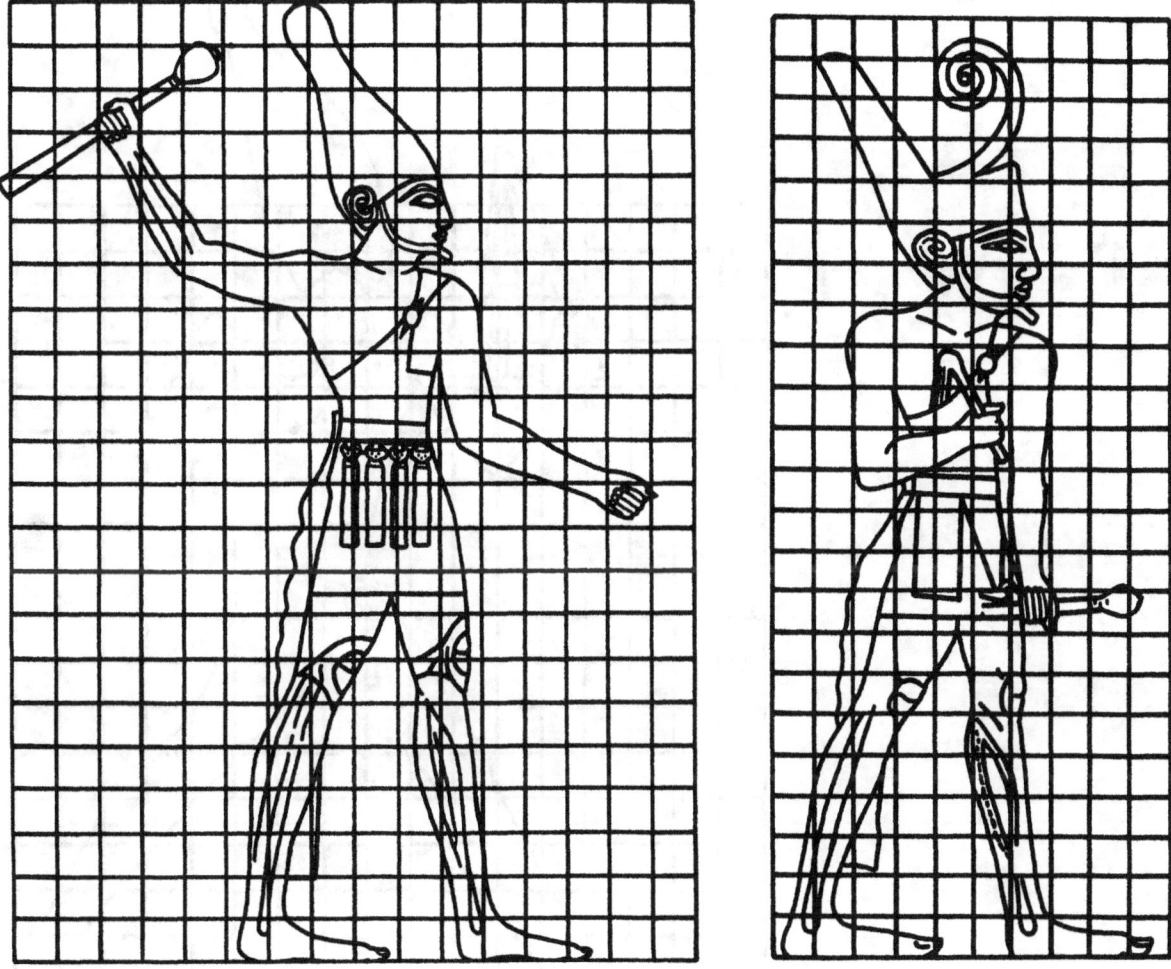

FIGURE 10.1

Standing figure of king on hypothetical 18-square grid, Narmer palette, first dynasty, after Iversen 1975, Plate 15.

FIGURE 10.2

Standing figure of king on hypothetical 18-square grid, Narmer palette, first dynasty, after Iversen 1975, Plate 16.1.

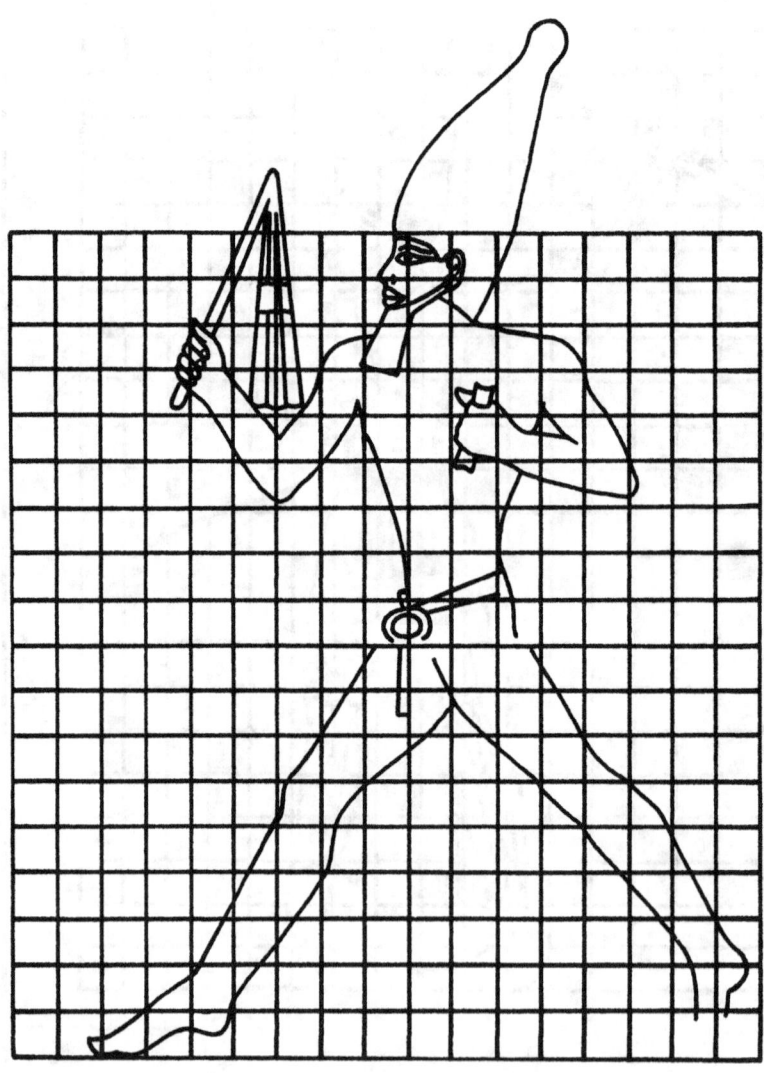

FIGURE 10.3
Running figure of king on hypothetical 18-square grid,
northern stela, south tomb, funerary complex of Djoser,
Saqqara, third dynasty, after Firth and Quibell 1935, Plate 42.

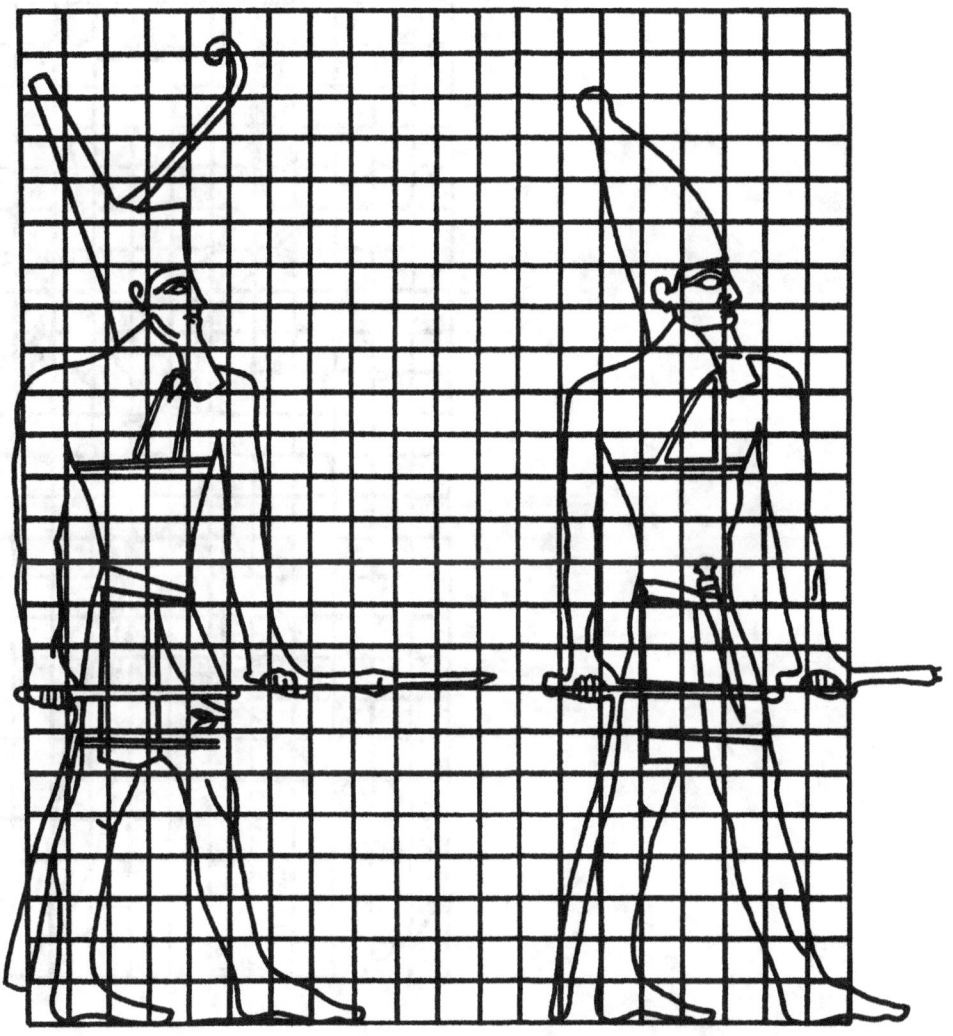

FIGURE 10.4
Two standing figures of Sekhemkhet Djoser-Teti on
hypothetical 18-square grid, Wadi Maghara, Sinai, third
dynasty, Gardiner et al. 1955, Plate 1 no. 1a.

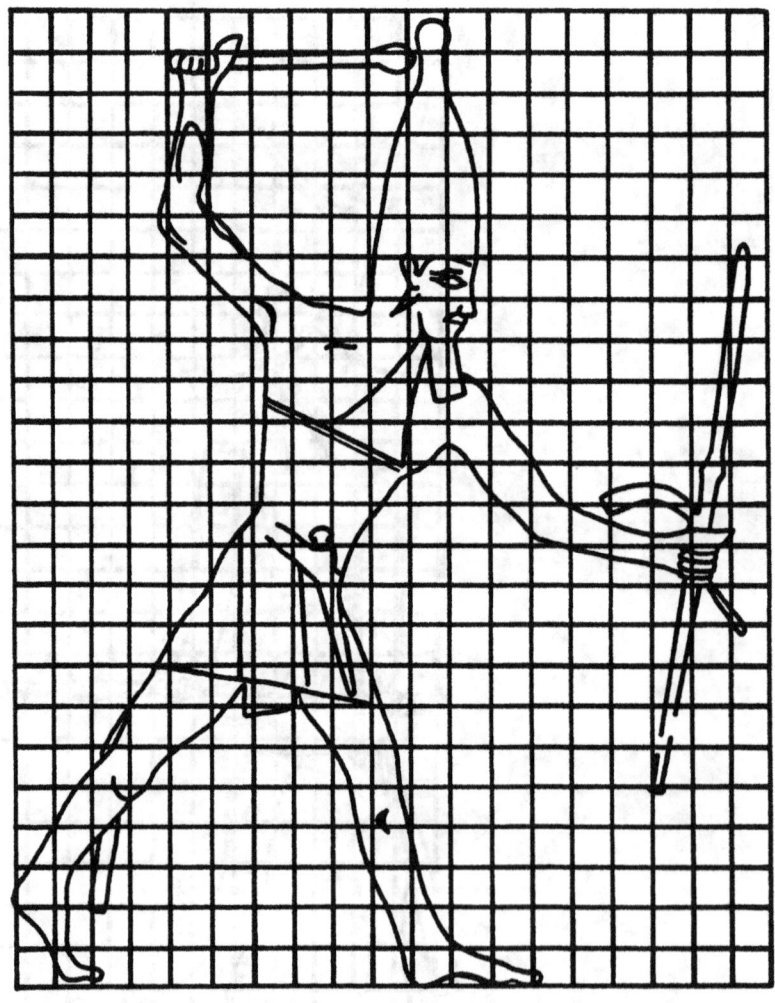

FIGURE 10.5
Smiting figure of Sekhemkhet Djoser-Teti on hypotheti-
cal 18-square grid, Wadi Maghara, Sinai, third dynasty,
Gardiner et al. 1955, Plate 1 no. 1a.

of the back and the top of the belt coincide on horizontal 11. Both figures have the short necks we have already seen in earlier figures.

The third figure shows the king smiting an enemy (Fig. 10.5). As in the Den figure, the front shoulder is dropped and the rear one raised, so as to bend the figure forward. The nipple region lies on horizontal 13, rather than the traditional 14, because the body is bent. Correspondingly, the small of the back is raised a square to horizontal 12 and the lower border of the buttocks to 10. This smiting posture, in which the body is bent forward by lowering the front shoulder and nipple and raising the rear shoulder, small of back and buttocks, is found repeatedly from now on; one may compare, for instance, a figure of Snofru, also from Wadi Maghara, from the beginning of the next dynasty.[7]

Private material from the first three dynasties comes from tombs mostly in the form of niche stones, which usually show the deceased seated on the left facing right before funerary offerings. If such figures are analyzed on a 14-square grid, we find a variety of proportions. One male figure on a niche stone from Saqqara has virtually classic vertical proportions, with the junction of the neck and shoulder near horizontal 12 and the top of the knee on 6 (Fig. 10.6).[8] The top of the chair seat, however, lies above horizontal 5 and the thigh is raised even higher by the height of the cushion on which the figure sits. By contrast, the horizontal proportions of this figure are very narrow, being less than 5 squares across the shoulders and less than 1 3/4 squares at the level of the small of the back, while the outstretched forearm is long at about 5 3/4 squares from elbow to fingertips.

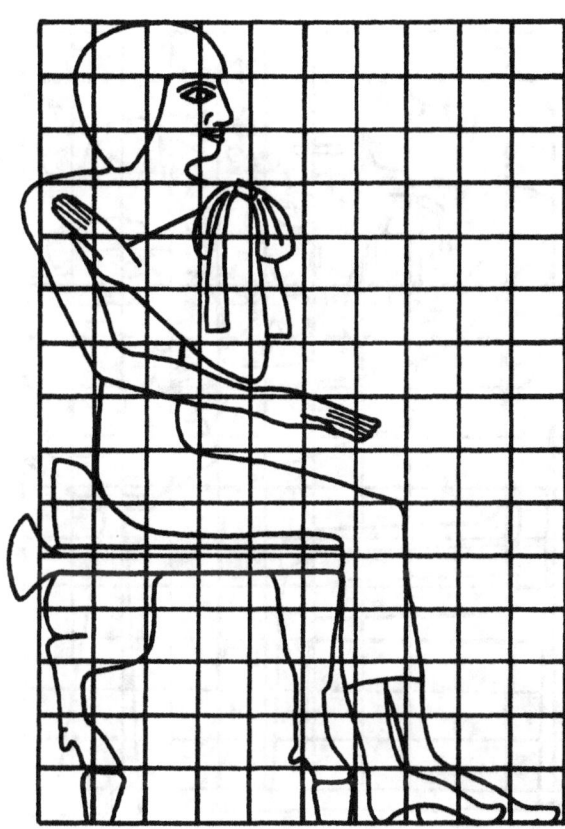

FIGURE 10.6

Seated figure on hypothetical 14-square grid, niche stela, Saqqara, second dynasty, after Smith 1981, 49 Figure 32.

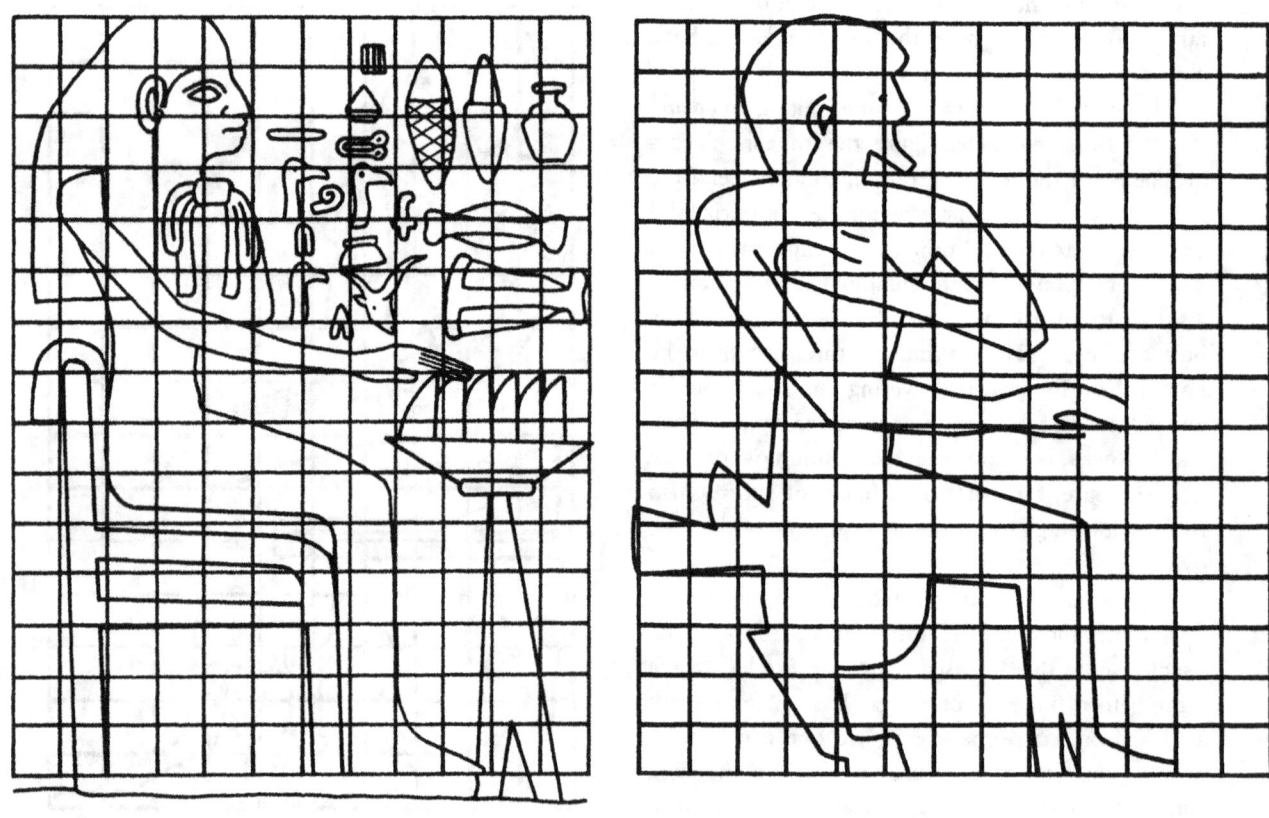

FIGURE 10.7
Seated figure on hypothetical 14-square grid, niche
stela, second dynasty, Quibell 1923, Plate 27.

FIGURE 10.8
Seated figure on hypothetical 14-square grid, after
Kaplony 1963, Plate 147 no. 853.

We may compare this figure with a similarly dated female figure (Fig. 10.7).[9] The top of the seat is near horizontal 5, the knee near 6, and the junction of the neck and shoulder on 12. The forearm is approximately 6 squares long. The width across the shoulders is 4 squares, and at the level of the small of the back just under 2 squares. Here the narrowness of the figure would be perfectly acceptable for a woman in later times.

Other figures show considerable variation in proportions. A male figure has the junction of neck and shoulders near horizontal 12 with shoulders almost 6 squares wide, but the knee lies on horizontal 5 and the top of the seat on 4, so that the legs are shorter than in classic figures (Fig. 10.8).[10] Another male figure also has short legs, with the knee over half a square below horizontal 6;[11] the shoulders are only just over 4 squares wide (Fig. 10.9). By contrast, there is another figure where the top of the seat is on horizontal 6, while the knees lie higher at more than 6 1/2 squares above the baseline (Fig. 10.10).[12]

Some of the finest work of the third dynasty is found on the wooden panels from the tomb of Hesire at Saqqara.[13] Accomplished as the work is, we find that the proportions differ from those found in Djoser's figures. In the standing figures of Hesire on panel CG 1427, the top of the knee is near horizontal 6, the lower border of the buttocks a little above 9, the small of the back a little above 11, and the junction of the neck and shoulders on 16 (Fig. 10.11). The width across the shoulders is about 4 3/4 squares wide and between the armpits about 3 1/4 squares, so that the width of each upper arm is only about three-quarters of a square. At the level of the small of the back, the body is approxi-

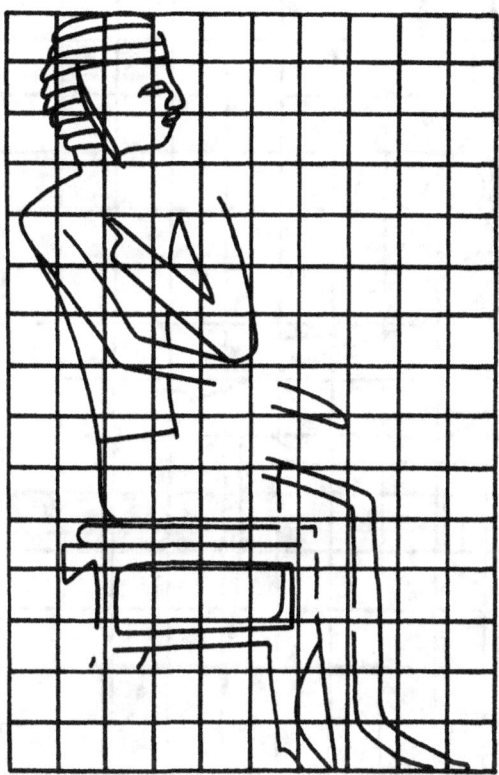

FIGURE 10.9
Seated figure on hypothetical 14-square grid, third dynasty, after Kaplony 1963, Plate 138 no. 833.

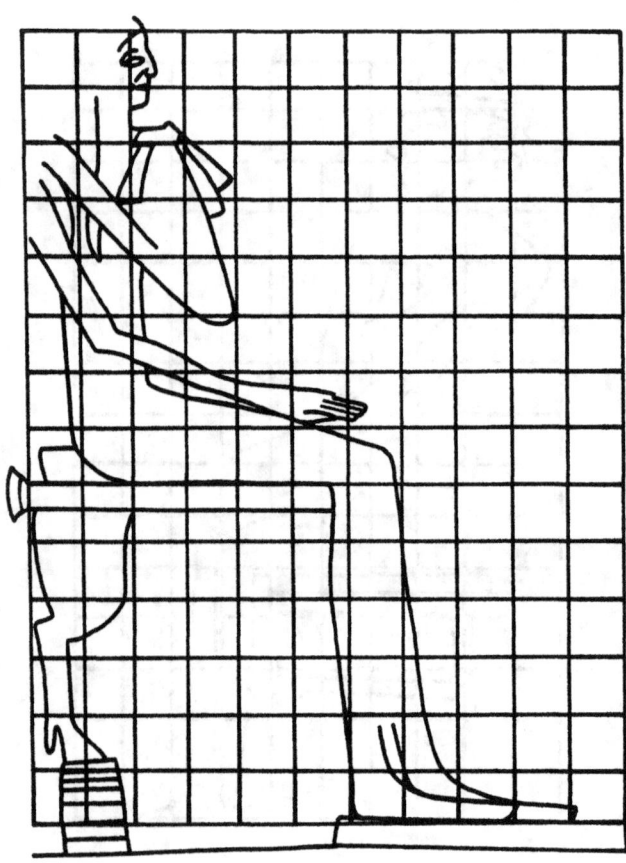

FIGURE 10.10

Seated figure on hypothetical 14-square grid, third
dynasty, after Kaplony 1963, Plate 139 no. 838.

mately 2 squares wide. Thus the proportions are more
slender than in classic Old Kingdom figures. In the
seated figure on panel CG 1426, the junction of the
neck and shoulders is on horizontal 12, the top of the
knee near 6, and the top of the seat on 5, but the figure
is again narrow across the shoulders at about 5 squares
(Fig. 10.12).

These examples show that during the first three
dynasties proportions in the human figure were far
from standardized. What were to become the classic
Old Kingdom proportions are found in the royal
figures of Djoser and his successor, but not in the
private figures of Hesire, apart from the heights of the
knee and the junction of the neck and shoulders.

10.2. The Fourth to Sixth Dynasties

In the fourth dynasty, proportions in the tomb of
Khafkhufu I (G 7140) come very close to the classic.[14]
In the seated figures, though, the tops of the knees tend
to lie below horizontal 6, with the top of the cushion
on which the figure sits below horizontal 5 (Fig.
10.13). A female figure from the same tomb demonstrates female proportions (Fig. 10.14). The junction
of the neck and shoulder lies on horizontal 16 and the
nipple on 14, but the small of the back is raised to 12
and the lower border of the buttocks to 9 1/2. The
figure is just under 5 squares across the shoulders and
3 squares across the armpits. The lower legs are
lengthened, with the tops of the knees lying roughly
6 1/2 squares above the baseline.

Slightly different proportions are found in the female figures of Mersyankh III.[15] In most of these,

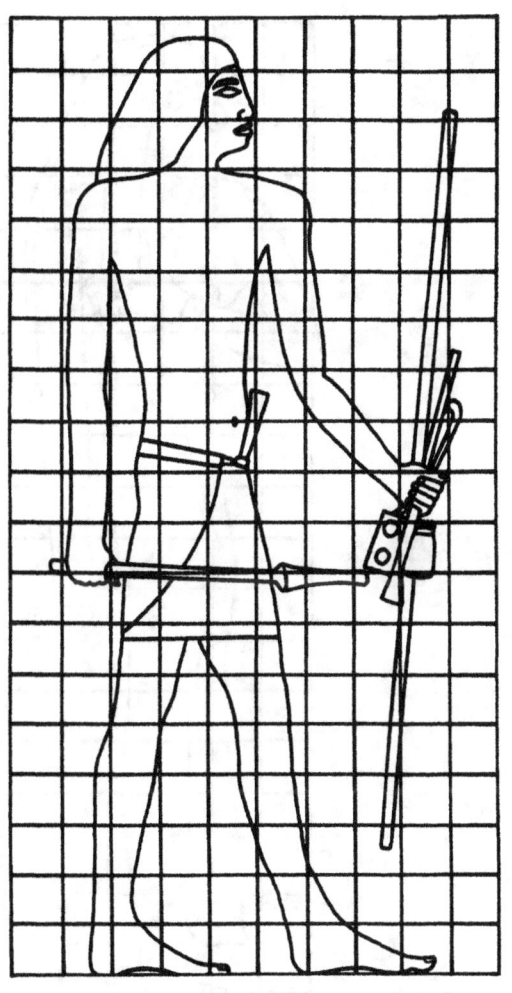

FIGURE 10.11

Standing figure on hypothetical 18-square grid, tomb of
Hesire, Saqqara, third dynasty, after Donadoni 1969, 54.

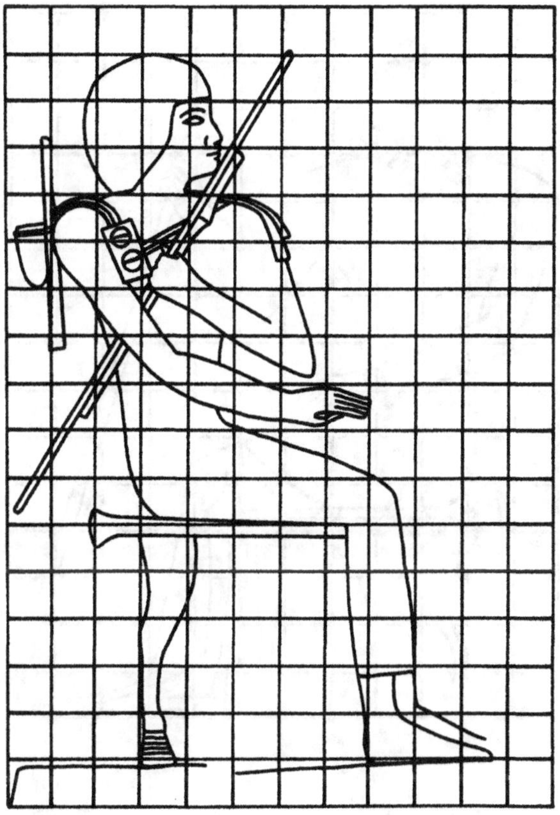

FIGURE 10.12

Seated figure on hypothetical 14-square grid, tomb of
Hesire, Saqqara, third dynasty, after Lange and Hirmer
1961, Plate 19.

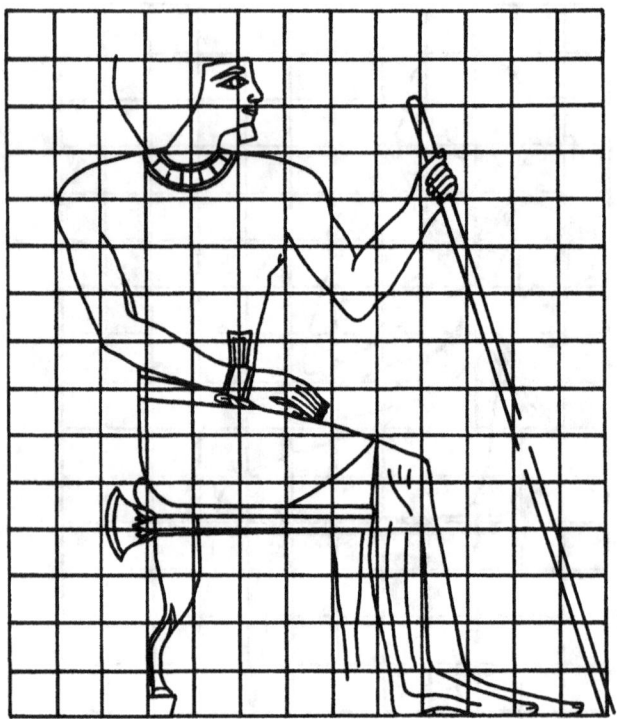

FIGURE 10.13
Seated figure on hypothetical 14-square grid, tomb chapel of Khafkhufu I, Giza, G7140, after Simpson 1978, Figure 30.

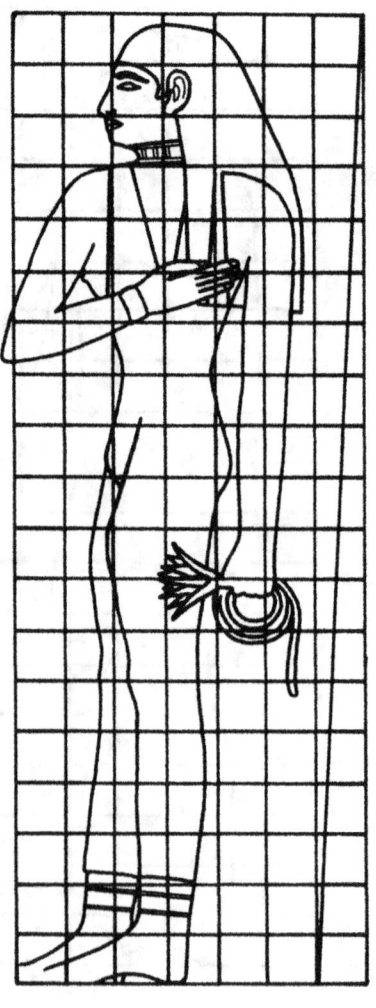

FIGURE 10.14
Standing female figure on hypothetical 18-square grid, tomb chapel of Khafkhufu I, Giza, G7140, after Simpson 1978, Figure 34.

horizontal 16 runs along the level of the chin, so that the junction of the neck and shoulders is depressed by a quarter of a square or more. As a consequence, the level of the breast is lowered below horizontal 14 and the small of the back is somewhere around 11 1/2 or, in one instance, 11 (Fig. 10.15). The buttocks are spreading and in some figures have no obvious lower border; elsewhere the lower border falls on horizontal 9. The width between the armpits is about 3 1/2 squares.

By the fifth dynasty, there is no lack of classically proportioned standing and seated figures (Figs. 10.16– 10.23). Good examples are to be found in the mastabas of Ptahhotep and Akhtihotep,[16] Ti,[17] Mereruka,[18] and Khentika called Ikhekhi.[19] Although the majority of figures now follow similar proportions, not all do so. In the mastaba of Qar, we find a seated figure with the armpits on horizontal 11, the nipple at 10 1/2, the knees at 6 1/2, and the top of the seat at 5 1/2.[20] In the same mastaba, two other seated figures are considerably more slender than is now normal, being about 5 squares across the shoulders, 3 1/2 squares between the armpits, and less than 2 squares across the back.[21]

Alongside classically proportioned figures in the tomb of Ti (Fig. 10.23), two seated figures have short lower legs, so that the tops of the knees are almost on a level with the top of the seat.[22] If these figures are analyzed on a 14-square grid, the junction of the neck and shoulders lies above horizontal 12 and the nipple above horizontal 10. Measurement shows that the distances from the junction of the neck and shoulders to the hairline and to the nipple are each one-third of the knee height, just as in a classically proportioned figure. However, the distance between the nipple and the top of the knee is five-sixths of the knee height

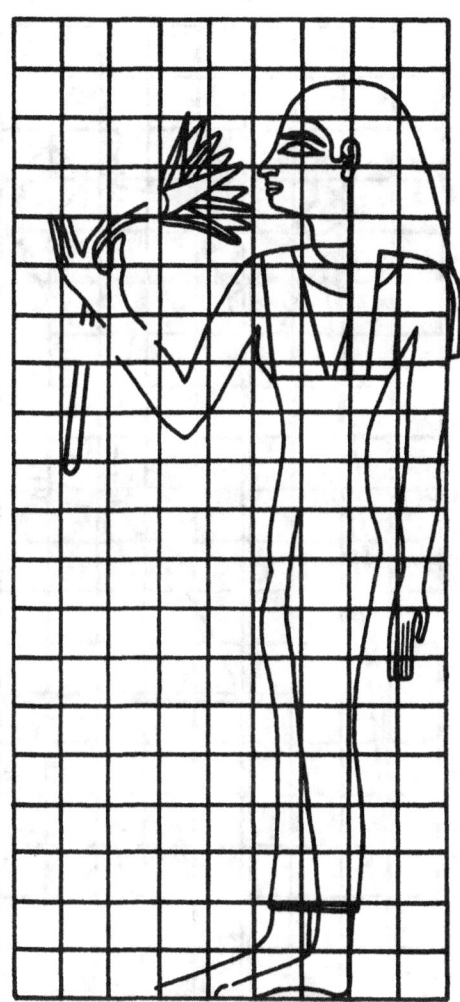

FIGURE 10.15

Standing female figure on hypothetical 18-square grid, tomb chapel of Mersyankh III, Giza, G7530, fourth dynasty, after Dunham and Simpson 1974, Figure 3b.

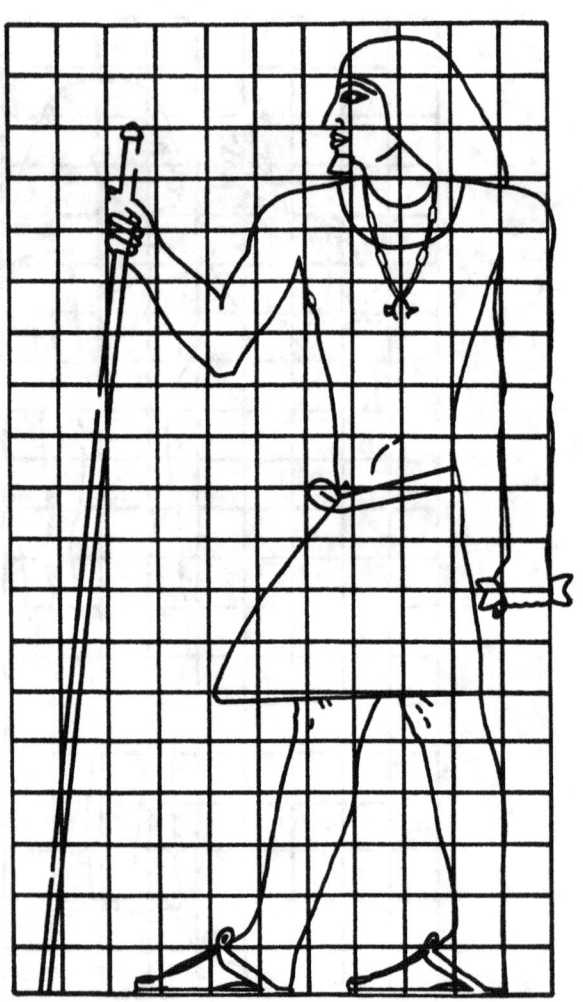

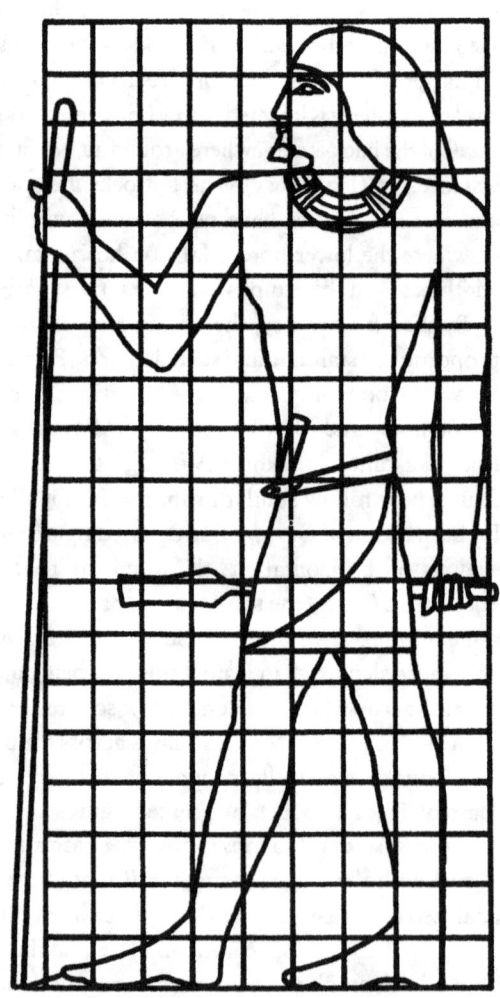

FIGURE 10.16
Standing male figure on hypothetical 18-square grid,
tomb chapel of Ti, Saqqara, fifth dynasty, after Wild
1966, Plate 171.

FIGURE 10.17
Standing male figure on hypothetical 18-square grid,
tomb chapel of Ti, Saqqara, fifth dynasty, after Epron
and Daumas 1939, Plate 20.

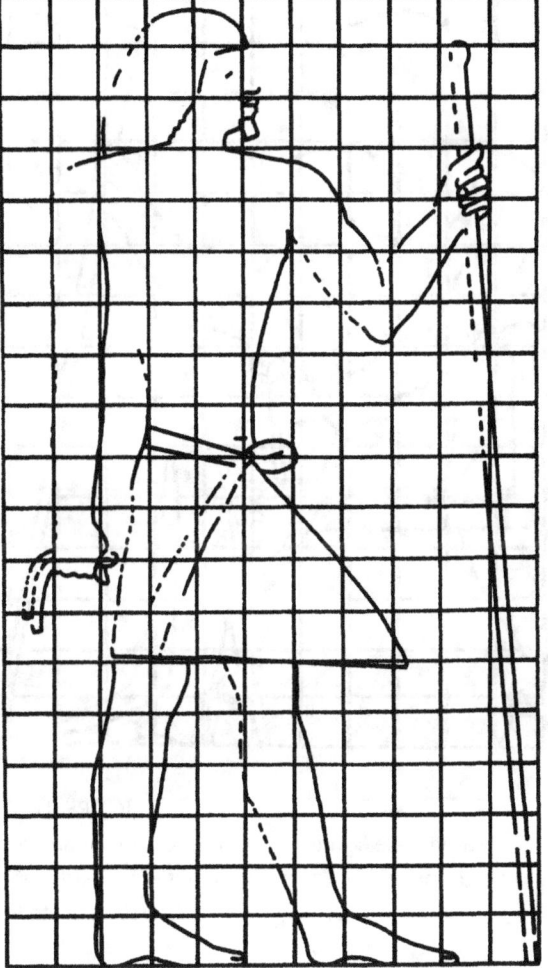

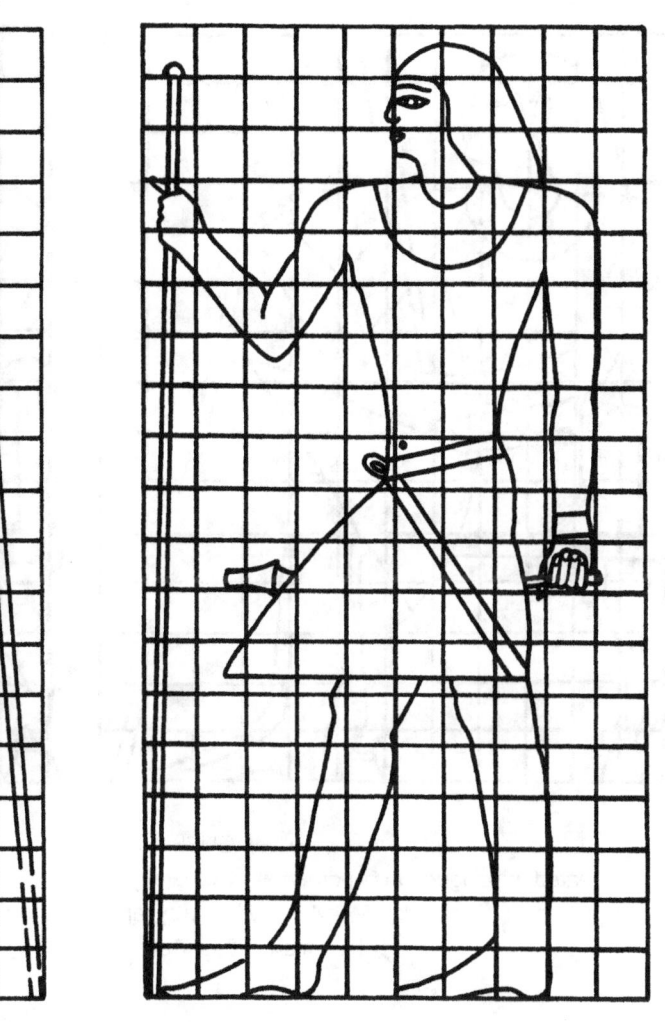

FIGURE 10.18
Standing male figure on hypothetical 18-square grid, tomb chapel of Ti, Saqqara, fifth dynasty, after Epron and Daumas 1939, Plate 60.

FIGURE 10.19
Standing male figure on hypothetical 18-square grid, tomb chapel of Mereruka, Saqqara, early sixth dynasty, after author's photograph.

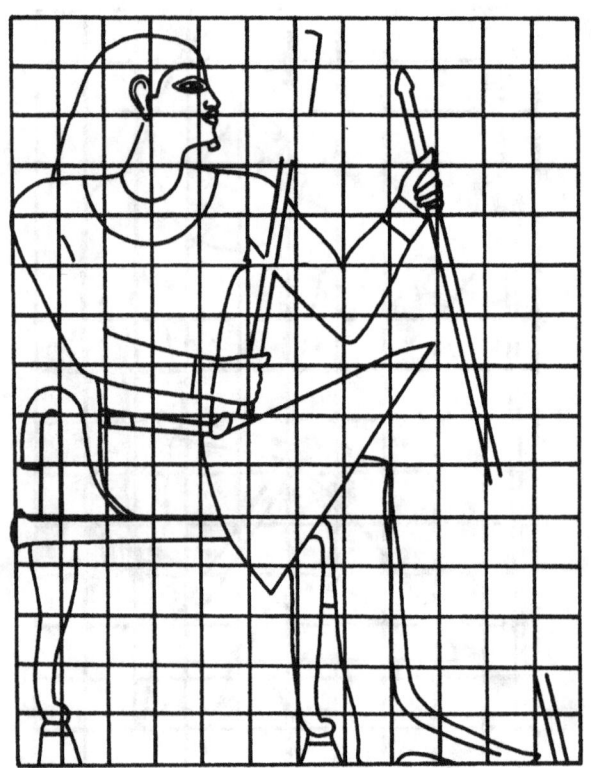

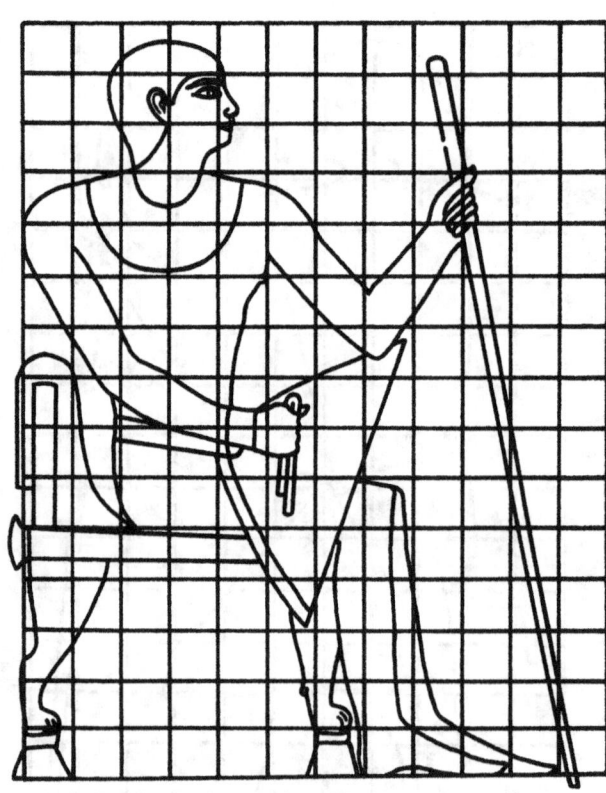

FIGURE 10.20
Seated male figure on hypothetical 14-square grid,
tomb chapel of Pepiankh, Meir A2, sixth dynasty, after
Blackman 1953a, Plate 29.

FIGURE 10.21
Seated male figure on hypothetical 14-square grid,
tomb chapel of Mereruka, Saqqara, sixth dynasty, after
Duell 1938, Plate 96.

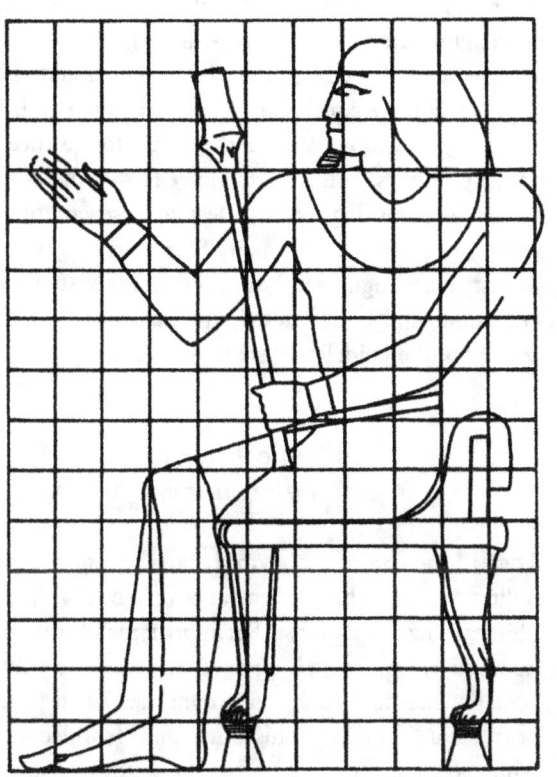

FIGURE 10.22
Seated male figure on hypothetical 14-square grid,
tomb chapel of Khentika, Saqqara, sixth dynasty, after
James 1953, Plate 6.

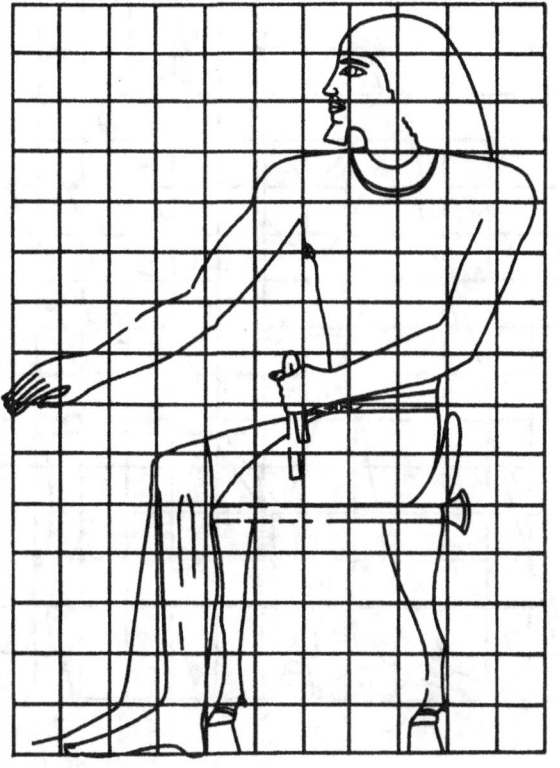

FIGURE 10.23
Seated male figure on hypothetical 14-square grid,
tomb chapel of Ti, Saqqara, fifth dynasty, after Wild
1966, Plate 161.

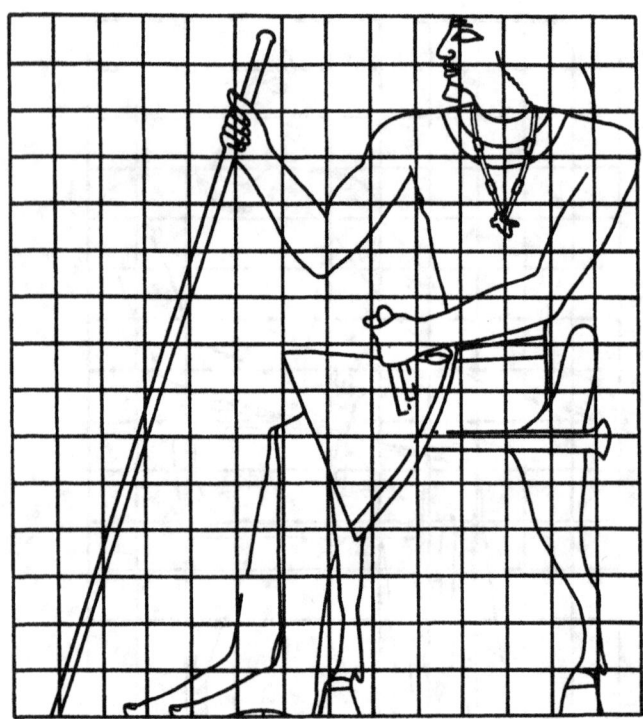

FIGURE 10.24
Seated male figure on hypothetical 15-square grid,
tomb chapel of Ti, Saqqara, fifth dynasty, after Wild
1966, Plate 149.

instead of four-sixths (or two-thirds). In other words, if the figures are analyzed on 15-square grids, from the hairline to the junction of the neck and shoulders is approximately 2 squares, from there to the nipple is also roughly 2 squares, from the nipple to the knee is about 5 squares, and from the knee to the sole of the foot is 6 squares (Fig. 10.24). Despite these variations, what is noticeable in the many fifth- and early sixth-dynasty major figures is the considerable constancy of key points and body widths, apparently outside the control of the guideline system (Sec. 4.1).

10.3. The First Intermediate Period and the Preunification Theban Style

Toward the end of the sixth dynasty, economic and political troubles hit the central government at Memphis, causing it to collapse. For approximately the next hundred years, Egypt was split into various power centers. The ninth and tenth dynasties ruled in the north, not from Memphis but from Herakleopolis, while power came to be held in the south by a line of rulers in Thebes who would later take the titles of kings and form the eleventh dynasty. Other local rulers held sway over their own districts, although they did not use royal titles. There was no longer one artistic center for the country, as there had been during the Old Kingdom when the royal residence was located at Memphis. While the Memphite tradition continued in the north, provincial regions to the south, which had already begun to produce monuments during the sixth dynasty, were now cut off from the Memphite center and, to judge by their output, from a supply of trained, competent artists. As a result, local workshops at the various provincial centers of power struggled to produce the monuments demanded by their employers. The work was frequently inept, showing bad draftsmanship and clumsy cutting of relief. This can already be seen in the late sixth-dynasty tombs at Aswan. A series of stelae from tombs at Naga ed-Der range in quality from poor to accomplished work.[23] Among the material from the first Intermediate period we begin to see individual styles developing, and gradually more accomplished and confident work was produced alongside the inept, as though a new supply of competent artists was emerging trained in the developing styles.[24]

When the line of Theban rulers came to dominate the south, they were able to command the best artists available. These were trained in a distinctive local style which they took to great heights, producing work of the highest artistic standards in composition, draftsmanship, and relief-cutting.[25]

Along with changes in style there occur changes in the proportions of figures. When figures are analyzed on appropriate hypothetical grids, we find that the heads are often less than 2 squares between the hairline and the junction of the neck and shoulders (Figs. 10.25–10.27). In many seated figures, the lower legs from the soles to the tops of the knees are longer than the classic 6 squares (Figs. 10.25–10.28). In standing male figures, the levels of the small of the back and the buttocks are often raised to horizontal 12 and 10 respectively (Fig. 10.27), and sometimes even higher (Fig. 10.25), while the width across the shoulders may be narrowed (Fig. 10.28).[26]

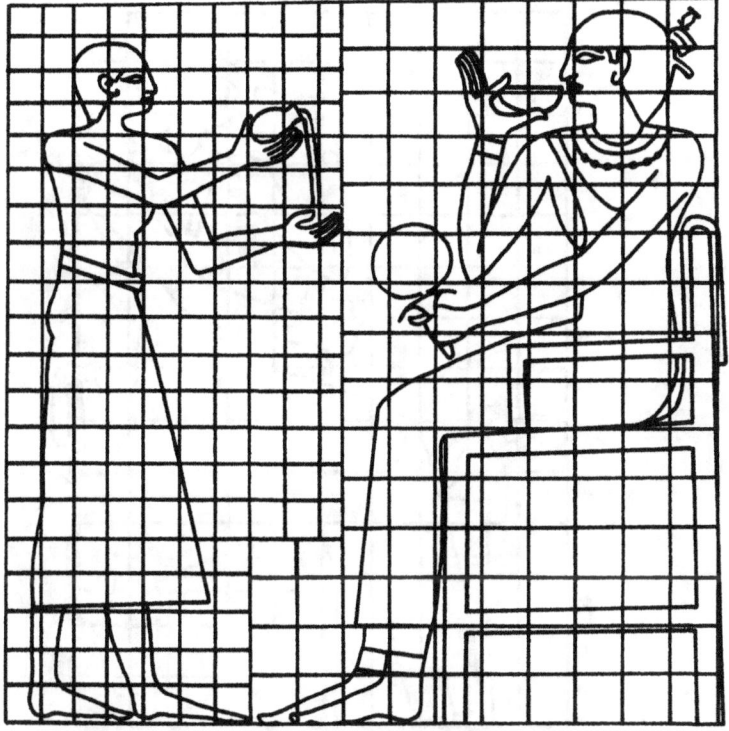

FIGURE 10.25
Standing and seated figures on hypothetical 18- and 14-square grids respectively, coffin of Kawit, Thebes, Theban eleventh dynasty, Cairo JE 47397, after Lange and Hirmer 1961, Plate 83 top.

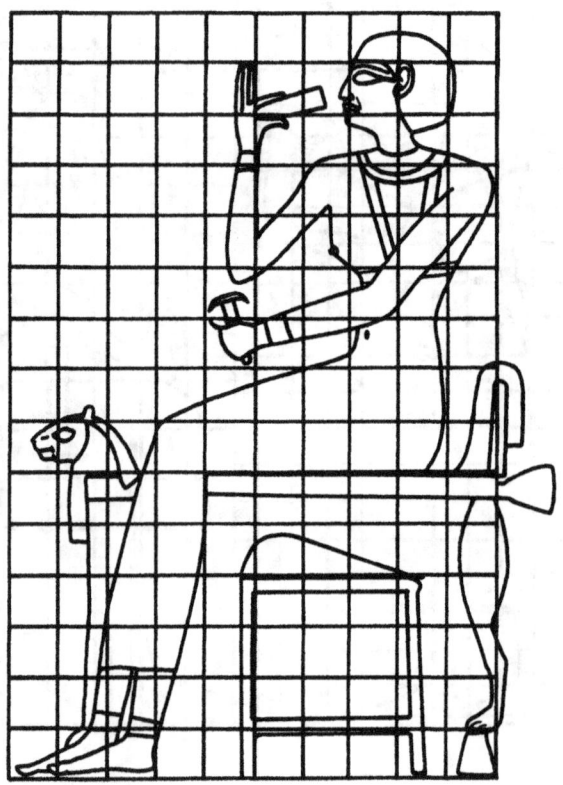

FIGURE 10.26
Seated female figure on hypothetical 14-square grid,
coffin of Aashit, Thebes, Theban eleventh dynasty,
Cairo JE 47267, after Aldred et al. 1978, 235 no. 226.

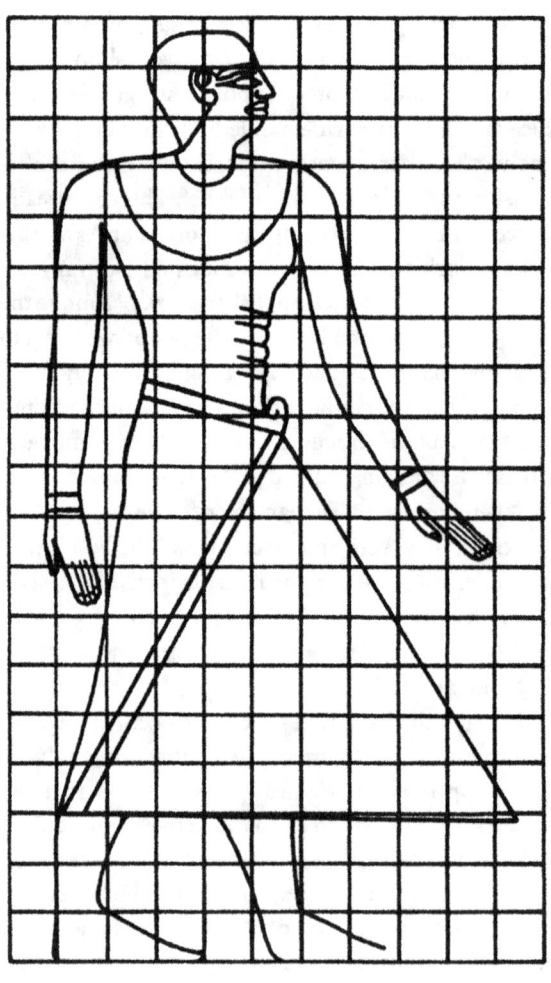

FIGURE 10.27
Standing male figure on hypothetical 18-square grid,
stela of Tjetji, Theban eleventh dynasty, British Museum
EA 614, after James and Davies 1983, Figure 23.

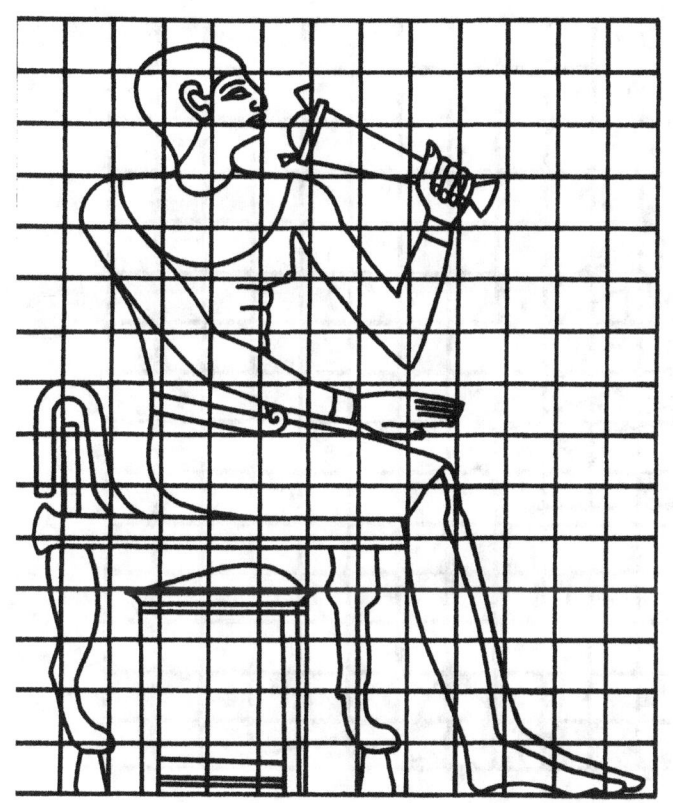

FIGURE 10.28
Seated male figure on hypothetical 14-square grid, stela
of Maaty, Thebes, Theban eleventh dynasty, MMA
14.2.7, after author's photograph.

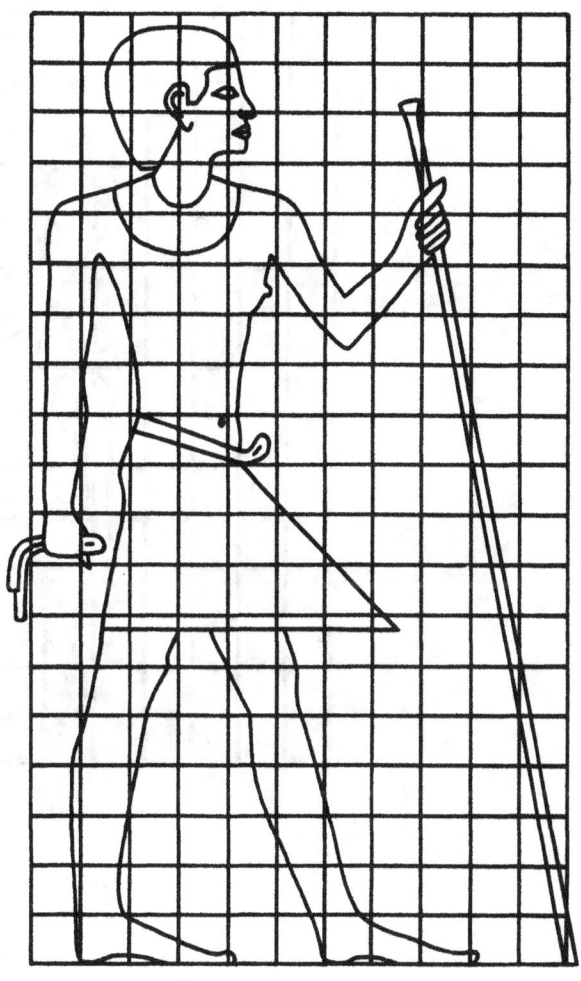

FIGURE 10.29
Standing male figure on hypothetical 18-square grid,
stela of Amenemhat Nebuy, Abydos, late twelfth
dynasty, Fitzwilliam Museum, Cambridge E.207.1900,
after Bourriau 1988, no. 39.

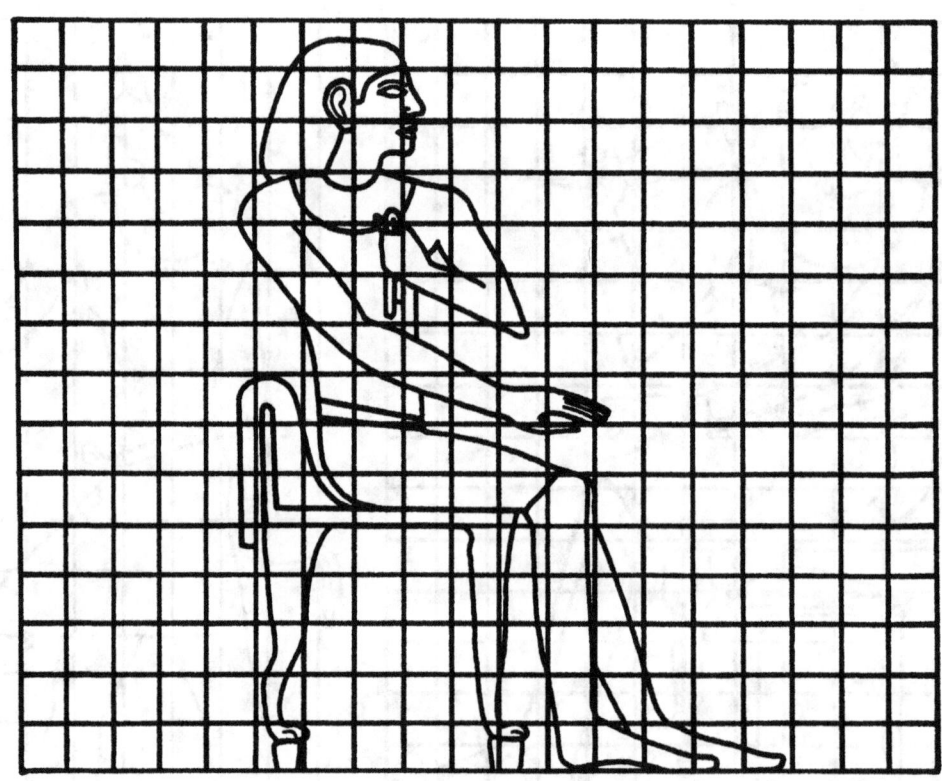

FIGURE 10.30
Seated male figure on hypothetical 14-square grid, stela
of Amenemhat Nebuy, Abydos, late twelfth dynasty,
Fitzwilliam Museum, Cambridge E.207.1900, after
Bourriau 1988, no. 39.

10.4. The Middle Kingdom

The fourth king of the Theban line, Nebhepetre Montuhotep II, finally overcame the tenth dynasty at Herakleopolis in the north and reunited Egypt once more under a strong central government. Although the royal residence and necropolis remained in the south, the north with its separate artistic tradition and Old Kingdom monuments became accessible again to the southerners. In addition, Montuhotep took into his service artists working in the Memphite tradition who had previously served the Herakleopolitan kings.[27] He seems to have deliberately ordered the adoption of the Memphite style of art, the reason no doubt being political, based on a desire to emulate the last period of strong centralized rule in Egypt, before its order collapsed into chaos. As a result, the proportions of figures after the reunification closely resemble the classic proportions of the Old Kingdom.

These proportions remain relatively stable throughout the first half of the twelfth dynasty, until about the reign of Senwosret III, when private figures begin to undergo changes.[28] The greatest alteration lies in the increasing narrowness of the body. The width across the shoulders is usually reduced from 6 squares, sometimes to 5 squares or even less, in standing, seated, and kneeling male figures (Figs. 10.29–10.35). In a classically proportioned figure, the length of the lower leg is roughly the same as the shoulder width. Now the shoulders are much narrower, giving figures a curiously elongated appearance. In addition, the width of the body at the level of the small of the back is often only 2 squares or less, increasing the slenderness of the figures (Figs. 10.31–10.32, 10.34–10.35).

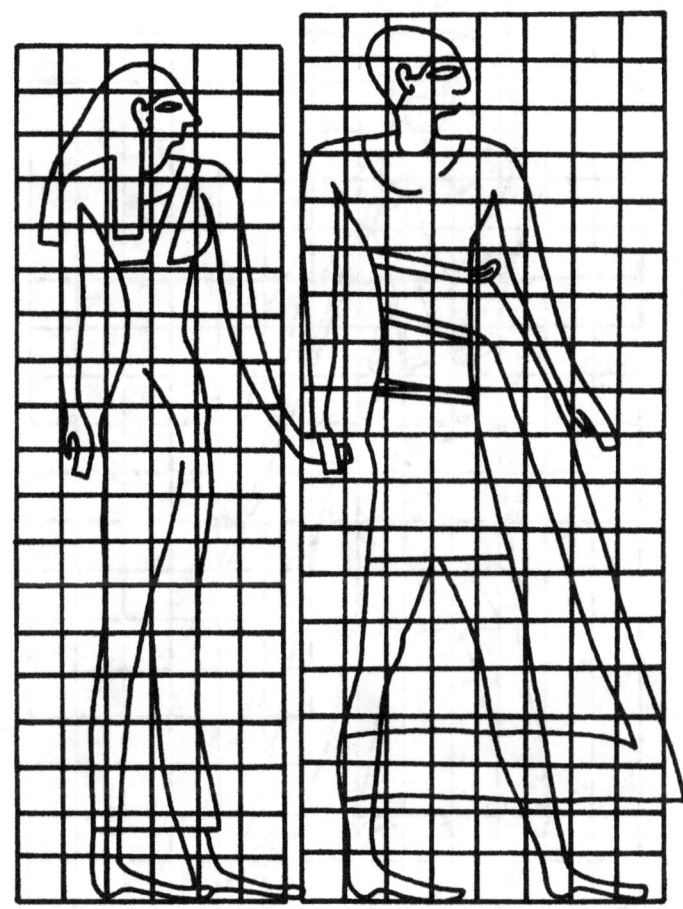

FIGURE 10.31
Standing male and female figures on hypothetical 18-square grids, stela of Renisonb, Abydos, twelfth–thirteenth dynasty, MMA 63.154, after Simpson 1974, Plate 81 top left.

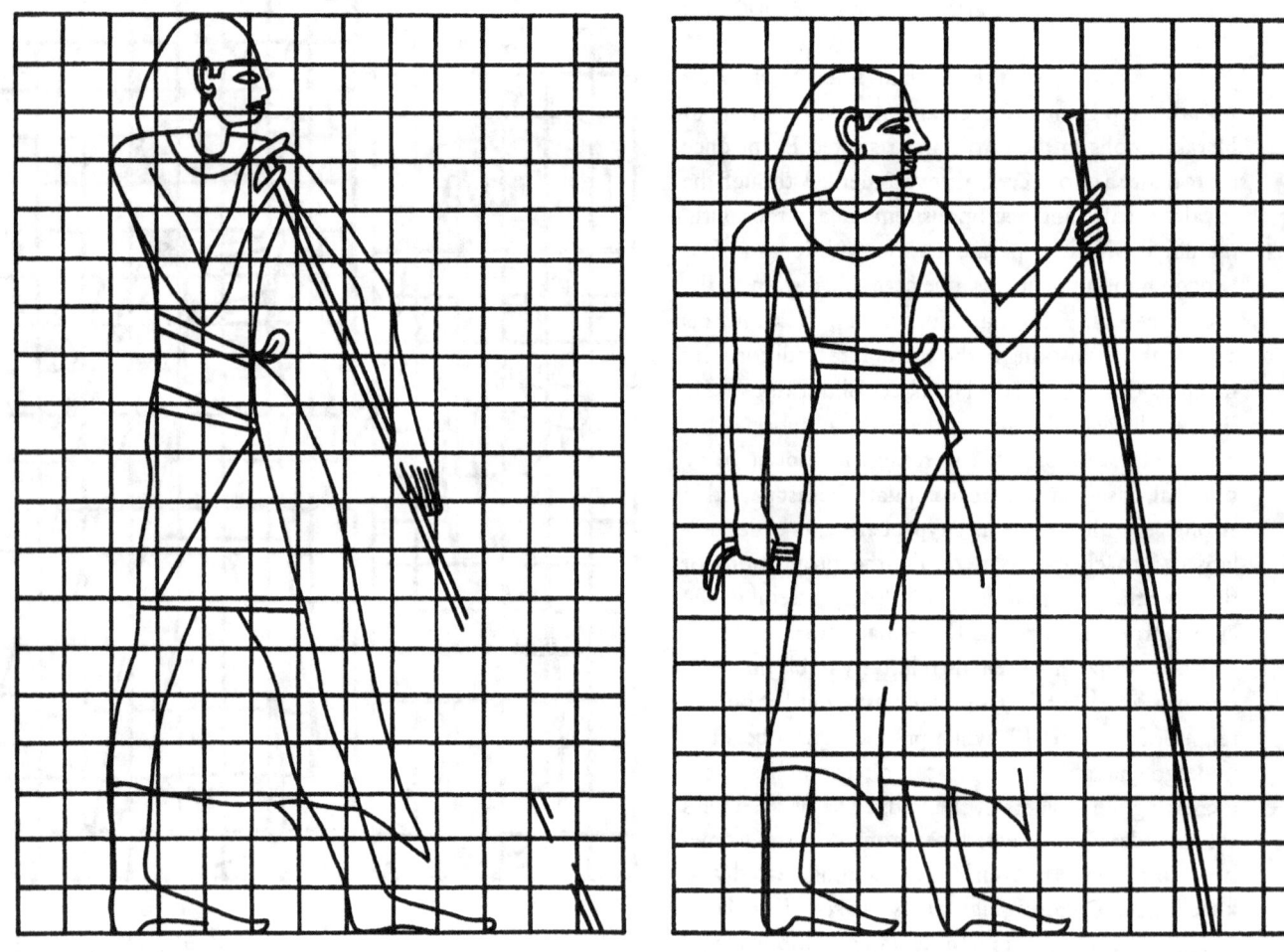

FIGURE 10.32
Standing male figure on hypothetical 18-square grid,
stela of Senwosret, Abydos, twelfth–thirteenth dynasty,
Louvre C18, after Simpson 1974, Plate 70 bottom.

FIGURE 10.33
Standing male figure on hypothetical 18-square grid,
stela of Renefsonb, twelfth–thirteenth dynasty, Florence
inv. no. 7598, after Bosticco 1959, Plate 40.

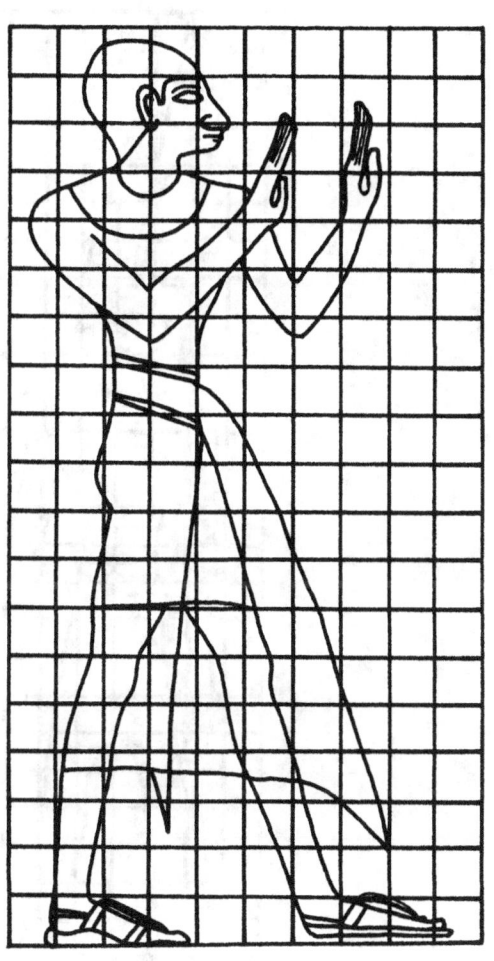

FIGURE 10.34
Standing male figure on hypothetical 18-square grid,
stela of Amenisonb, Abydos, thirteenth dynasty,
University of Liverpool, Department of Egyptology E.30,
after Bourriau 1988, no. 48.

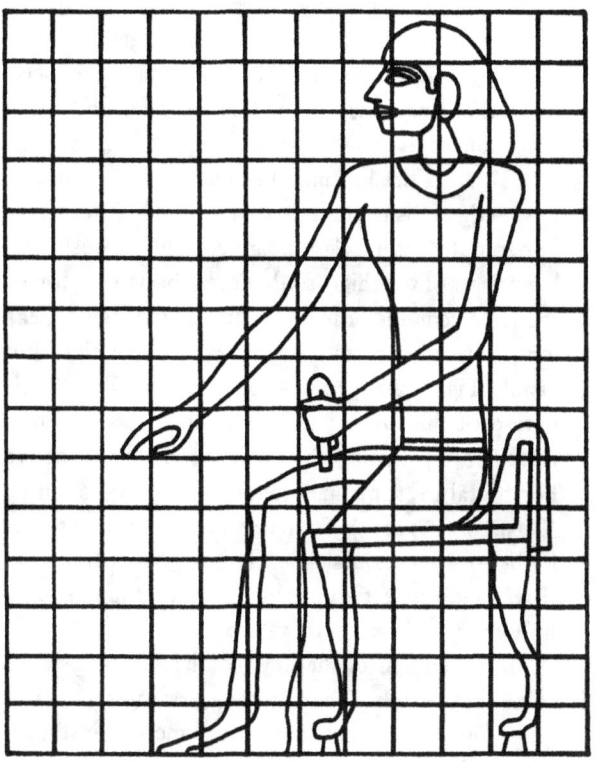

FIGURE 10.35
Seated male figure on hypothetical 14-square grid, stela
of Senwosret, Abydos, twelfth–thirteenth dynasty,
Louvre C16, after Simpson 1974, Plate 71 left.

Two other factors may further enhance the effect in some figures. The distance between the hairline and the junction of the neck and shoulders may be reduced to less than 2 squares, thus making the trunk and lower limbs longer in proportion to the head (Figs. 10.31–10.33). Also the kilt may be shortened, so that the lower edge falls nearer horizontal 7, rather than near horizontal 6 as in classic figures. This exposes the lower part of the thigh, so that even though the top of the knee remains near horizontal 6, the legs appear longer because of the greater expanse of the limb visible (Figs. 10.29, 10.31–10.32, 10.34). This domination of the lower part of the body is sometimes increased by raising the small of the back above horizontal 11, sometimes to the level of horizontal 12 (Figs. 10.31–10.34). To match the diminished torso, limbs are often more slender than in a classic figure, so that, for instance, the upper arms are less than a square in width (Figs. 10.31–10.32, 10.35).

In seated figures, the length of the lower leg shows some variation. In some examples it remains 6 squares long (Fig. 10.30), but there are numerous instances where it is up to nearly a square shorter or longer (Fig. 10.35).[29] The lower leg is often short in kneeling figures, forming a narrow base from which the slender torso rises, which causes the same elongated effect found in other figures.[30]

Much of the art of this period is not of a high standard, due to the number of fairly humble officials who now had the resources to commission monuments, mainly stelae, and it is likely that many of the figures were drawn freehand without grids. Proportions, as at any other period, are not uniform even on one monument. Nevertheless, the general narrowing

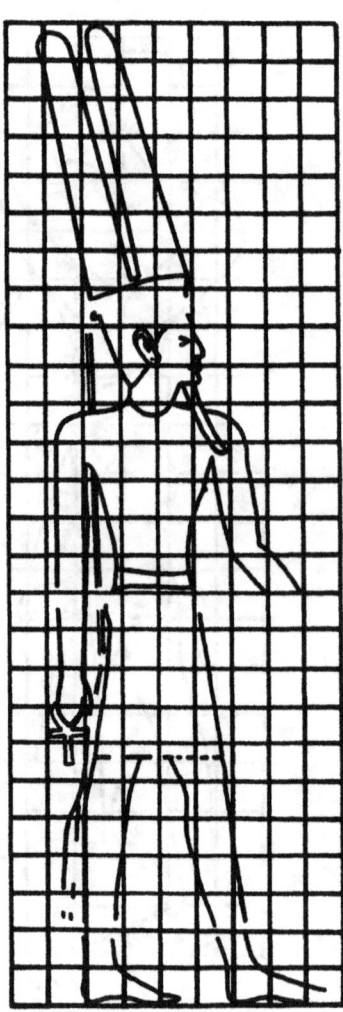

FIGURE 10.36
Standing male figure on hypothetical 18-square grid, temple of Ramesses III, Karnak, twentieth dynasty, after Epigraphic Survey 1936b, Plate 107F.

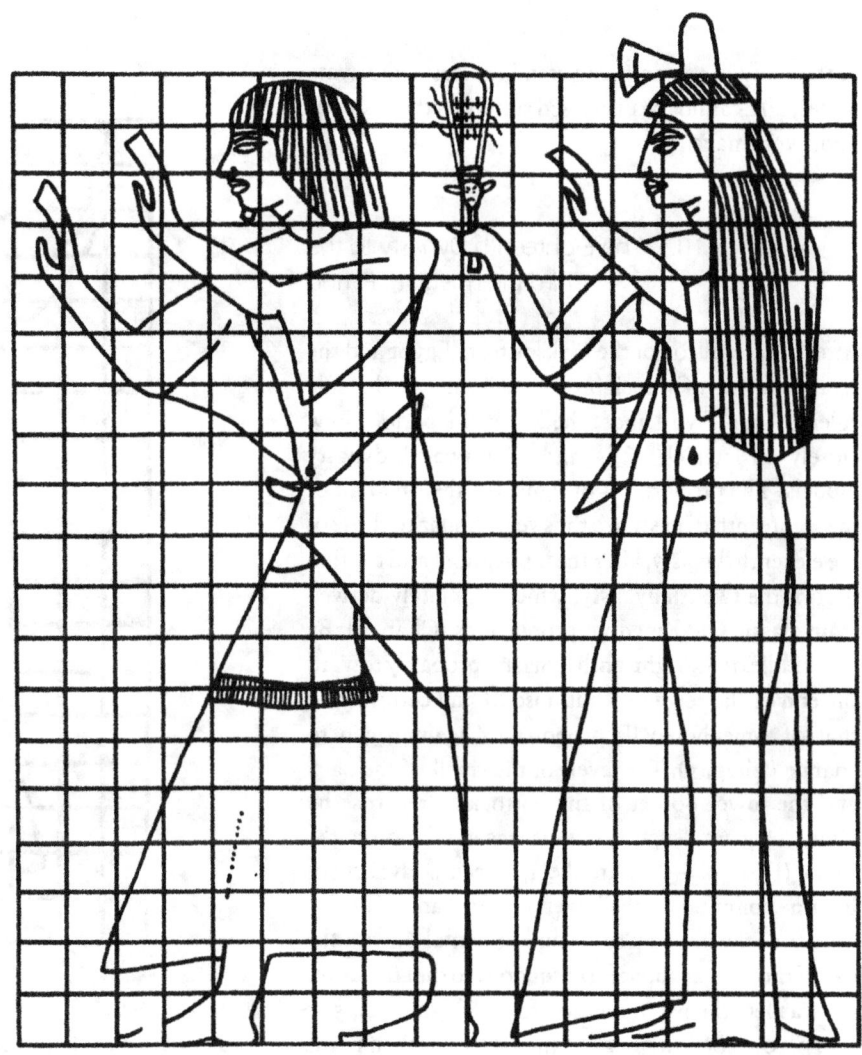

FIGURE 10.37
Standing figures of Maya and Tey on hypothetical
18-square grid, block from tomb of Maya, Memphis,
Ramesside period, Stockholm, Medelhavsmuseet NME
23, after Martin 1987, Plate 38 no. 105.

of the body is a widespread trend, at least on private
pieces, and cannot be dismissed simply as the result of
poor workmanship.

10.5. The Eighteenth Dynasty to the Third Intermediate Period

After the expulsion of the Hyksos from Egypt and the
establishment of the eighteenth dynasty as the sole
rulers of the Two Lands, the art of the period drew
closely on later eleventh- and early twelfth-dynasty
models. The proportions of figures in the first half of
the eighteenth dynasty are thus very similar to those of
the eleventh dynasty, after the unification, and the first
part of the twelfth dynasty, which ultimately derived
from classic Old Kingdom proportions (Chap. 5). By
the middle of the eighteenth dynasty, probably toward
the end of the reign of Thutmose III and certainly by
that of Amenhotep II, proportions again began to
change (Chap. 5). The levels of the small of the back
and the lower border of the buttocks often rose by
about a square, lengthening the legs in relation to the
torso (Figs. 5.3–5.4). In the nineteenth dynasty it
became common for the lower, rather than the upper,
border of the kneecap to lie on horizontal 6, with the
top of the knee at about 6 1/2 squares, so that the lower
leg was lengthened in relation to the thigh (Figs. 5.5,
9.8, 9.10). The lower leg continued to lengthen in the
twentieth dynasty, so that the top of the knee was often
pushed up to 6 3/4 (Figs. 5.6, 9.14). At the same time
the width across the shoulders was reduced from 6
squares (Figs. 9.14–9.15), and sometimes the width of
the upper arms was reduced to less than 1 square (Fig.

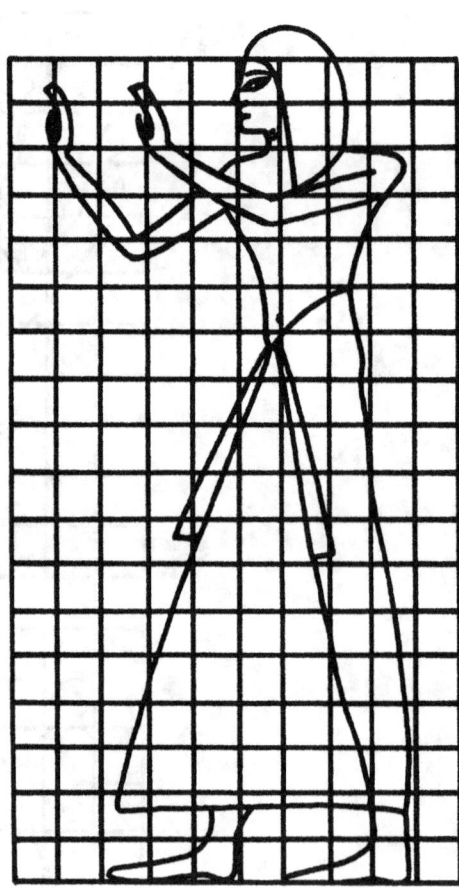

FIGURE 10.38
*Standing male figure on hypothetical 18-square grid,
stela of Wenennefer, nineteenth dynasty, British
Museum EA 154, after James 1970, Plate 27.*

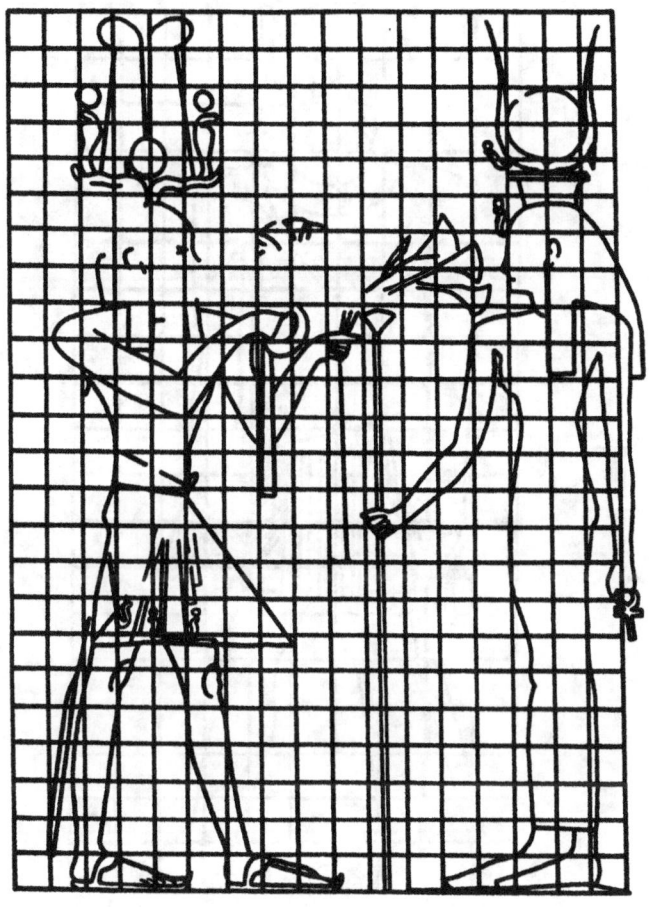

FIGURE 10.39

*Standing male and female figures on hypothetical
18-square grid, small temple at Abu Simbel, nineteenth
dynasty, after Desroches-Noblecourt and Kuentz 1968,
Plate 25.*

10.36). In some private figures, the small of the back rose as high as horizontal 13, making a small upper part of the body in relation to the long lower part (Figs. 10.37–10.38).

All these changes had the effect of feminizing male figures. In a man and a woman of the same height, the small of the back tends to be higher in a woman. The woman is also narrower across the shoulders and more slender of limb than the man. Male figures of the New Kingdom, in contrast to those of the Old Kingdom and early, postunification Middle Kingdom, usually show little or no musculature.[31] This feminization of the male goes hand in hand with an elaboration of costume in which male figures, both private and royal, wear layers of loose pleated garments tucked about the body in a more or less complicated fashion.[32] Women also wear flowing pleated dresses sometimes tied with sashes, but on the whole their costume tends to be less elaborate than the more extreme male costume. As male figures become feminized, female ones become more exaggeratedly feminine, so that the level of the small of the back becomes even higher, the shoulders become narrower, and the limbs more slender (Figs. 8.5, 9.7–9.9). The contrast is plainly seen when male and female figures are depicted together, so that the natural differences between the two sexes are generally maintained (Fig. 10.39).

What is perhaps strange to our way of thinking is that this trend of feminization began under the military kings Thutmose III and Amenhotep II and continued in use during the reigns of Sety I, Ramesses II, and Ramesses III, all warriors who decorated the walls of Egypt's temples with the records of their military campaigns.[33] Since the making of war was clearly considered a male occupation in ancient Egypt, as in many cultures, it is surprising that the masculine is not emphasized in the art of this period, as for instance in that of the military neo-Assyrian empire.[34]

10.6. Archaism in the Twenty-fifth and Twenty-sixth Dynasties

The feminizing style of the New Kingdom continued into the third Intermediate period. It can be seen, for example, in the scenes of Herihor in the temple of Khonsu at Karnak, and on the Bubastite portal at Karnak decorated in the reigns of Sheshonq I, Osorkon I, and Takelot III. Toward the end of the period, however, we find figures with completely different proportions. A good example is a plaque of King Iuput II.[35] Analyzed on an 18-square grid, the tops of the knees are on horizontal 6, the lower border of the buttocks falls below 9, and the small of the back lies on 11. The width between the armpits is just over 4 squares and across the shoulders just over 6 squares. The upper arms are about a square wide (Fig. 10.40). In other words, the proportions have returned to classic Old Kingdom models. In addition, the costume is deliberately archaizing and can ultimately be traced back to monuments of the first dynasty.

Iuput II was contemporary with the early twenty-fifth dynasty which conquered Egypt from Nubia. The monuments of these Nubian kings also employ an archaizing style of art, based on Old and Middle Kingdom models. The elegant feminizing forms of the later New Kingdom are abandoned. The human figure returns to classic proportions with broad shoulders, a

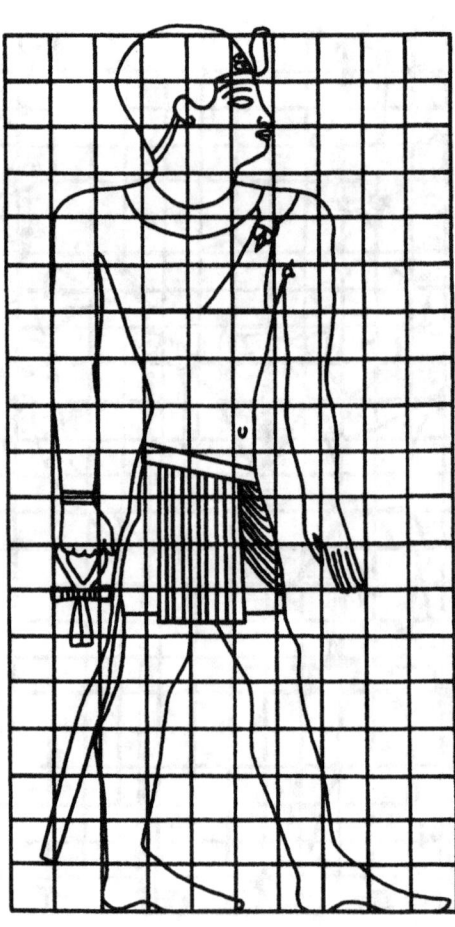

FIGURE 10.40
Standing male figure on hypothetical 18-square grid, plaque of Iuput II, twenty-third dynasty, Brooklyn 59.17, after Fazzini 1975, cat.89.

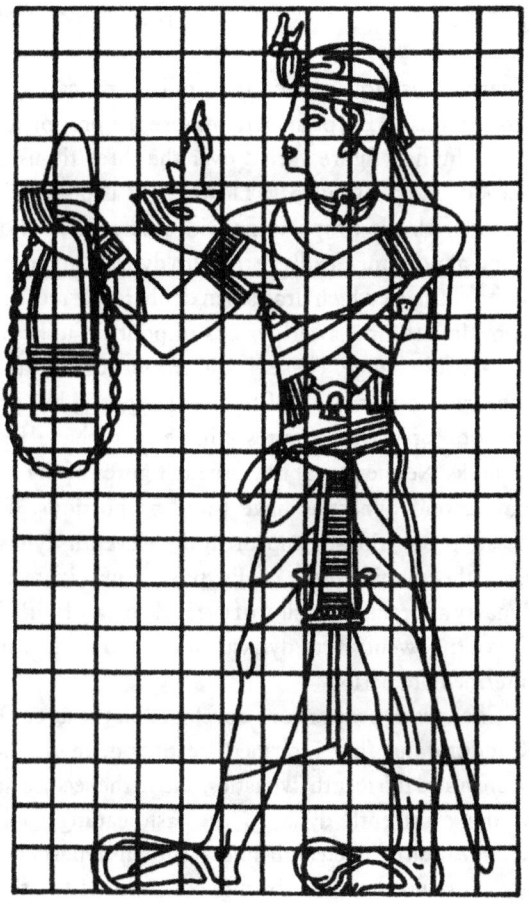

FIGURE 10.41

Standing male figure on hypothetical 18-square grid, shrine of Taharqa, temple T, Kawa, twenty-fifth dynasty, Ashmolean Museum Oxford 1936.661, after Macadam 1955, Plate 17e.

lower small of the back and buttocks, a shorter lower leg and stocky limbs (Figs. 8.9, 10.41). These are all masculinizing traits.

It is tempting to attribute this archaization and return to classic proportions to the conquering Nubian dynasty, but there is some evidence that it may in fact have begun in the north. However, too little representational material is known from the second half of the third Intermediate period to trace the precise location where this archaizing trend developed. Nor is there sufficient evidence to connect the adoption of the later grid system with the introduction of the archaizing style, although at the moment this would seem a plausible assumption.

10.7. The Ptolemaic Period and the Roman Occupation

There is evidence that the later grid system continued to be used during the Ptolemaic period and the Roman occupation.[36] On the whole, the basic proportions established in the twenty-fifth dynasty persist, yet there develops at this period a new and quite unmistakable style. Often attributed to Greek influence, the beginnings of the style can already be seen in the work of the last native rulers of Egypt and have their roots based firmly in ancient tradition.[37] Within the relief-cut outline, the body is roundly modeled to give full cheeks in the face and swelling breasts, stomach, and buttocks on the body. The elaborately worked vulture headdress and wig with drilled locks worn by Isis on a block of Nectanebo II in the Louvre is in its treatment a forerunner of countless Ptolemaic goddesses and queens. On the scenes of Nectanebo I at Philae, we see already the beginnings of the characteristic arrangement of hieroglyphs found in Ptolemaic scenes in which vertical columns and horizontal lines are uncompromisingly juxtaposed at right angles around the crowns of figures to leave a stark rectangular space.[38] This effect is less readily found in earlier work where crowns and hieroglyphs are much more closely integrated.

The development and maturation of the characteristic style of art found in Ptolemaic Egypt and continuing into the Roman occupation still needs further investigation. The trend is toward increasing complexity in iconography, more extensive rendering of detail in relief, and growing exaggeration in the modeling of the body, exemplified by the gross elongation of the female breast which bulges out to overlap the upper arm. Despite the three-dimensional effect of the high modeling of the body, the basic principles of Egyptian two-dimensional art are not abandoned. There is no attempt to incorporate the illusion of depth into the flat drawing-surface, as in Greek art, and the human figure is still rendered in its traditional composite form. A full analysis of vertical and horizontal proportions over the whole period would show the extent to which proportional changes also occurred. One such change is found in the temple of Kom Ombo among the figures dated to Ptolemy VI and Ptolemy VIII. The characteristic small tight buttocks of the Ptolemaic figures are lowered a square, so that their lower border lies on horizontal 10 instead of 11 (Fig. 8.10). The small of the back and top of the belt remain on or near horizontal 13.

10.8. Conclusions

Clearly it is not correct to ascribe one canon of proportions to Egyptian art, because the proportions of the human figure varied over the three thousand years of Egyptian history. However, it is possible to speak of classic proportions with reference to those found almost universally in the fifth dynasty and much of the sixth, to which draftsmen deliberately returned from time to time after periods of political upheaval and artistic change. These classic proportions began to appear in royal figures of the third dynasty, but proportions of private figures still seem to have been variable. Neither royal nor private figures of the first and second dynasties have these proportions. The classic proportions reappear in the eleventh dynasty after the reunification of Egypt, in the eighteenth dynasty after the expulsion of the Hyksos, and with the rise of the twenty-fifth dynasty at the end of the third Intermediate period.

Changes in proportions developed in the later Old Kingdom and first Intermediate period, in the late twelfth and thirteenth dynasties, and in the second half of the eighteenth dynasty, the last leading to the feminization of nineteenth- and twentieth-dynasty male figures that continued throughout most of the third Intermediate period. These changes clearly affect the style of figures, though other factors are also involved in making the overall style of any given period, such as differences in the cutting and modeling of relief, characteristics of facial features, shape of the head, the rendering of individual parts of the body, and costume. The changes in style of figures in the thirtieth dynasty and early Ptolemaic period are unmistakable but are less obviously linked to changes in proportion.

From the Middle Kingdom onward draftsmen often drew human figures on a squared grid that had a fixed relationship to the height of the figure. Three different systems were used at different times. From the twelfth dynasty to probably the end of the third Intermediate period and excluding the Amarna period, standing figures occupied 18 squares from soles to hairline and seated figures 14 squares. From the twenty-fifth dynasty, standing figures were 21 squares from soles to upper eyelid and seated figures 17 (or sometimes 16) squares. For a short time in the Amarna period, standing figures were drawn on a grid of 20 squares from soles to hairline. Before the Middle Kingdom from at least the fifth dynasty, figures were drawn not on a grid but on a set of guidelines.

While a change in proportions could coincide with a change in the grid, as in the Amarna period, this was not necessary. The early grid system continued to be used as proportions changed during the New Kingdom, while figures with proportions very close to the classic were drawn on the later grid system. This shows quite clearly that the grid system is not the same as the canon of proportions, and that the two terms should not be used interchangeably.

Further, we must remember that canons of proportions and their expression on the grid are not rigid. Not only do proportions and therefore the relationship of key points of the body to the grid change over time, but they may vary within limits on the same monument. The grid was only a guide and draftsmen did not count from line to line as they drew, but sketched their outlines with flowing strokes, producing figures that approximated the ideal proportions of the period but often included small variations. Thus, for instance, although the male fist is frequently the width of a grid square, it can be greater or smaller. In analyzing changes in proportion over time, we are concerned with general trends in the material, since individual figures at any given period may not conform totally with an "ideal" for that period.

The skill of Egyptian draftsmen is demonstrated in their freehand work. For instance, in the tomb of Sety I large figures of the king and deities embracing in an unfinished room are only sketched in.[39] There is no sign of grids, yet the proportions of the figures conform closely to the ideal for the period. Human figures sketched on ostraka are also usually drawn without a grid.[40]

The grid was not, then, a straitjacket that forced all figures to be identical. When a figure differs slightly from ideal proportions, it is not because it was produced by a bad draftsman but because there was room for some variation. There can be no doubt that early scholars were right when they saw the grid as a guide rather than a device to control every last detail in the drawing of the human figure.

Abbreviations

ASAE	*Annales du Service des Antiquités de l'Egypte.* Cairo.
BIFAO	*Bulletin de l'Institut Français d'Archéologie Orientale.* Cairo.
CdE	*Chronique d'Egypte.* Brussels.
CG	*Catalogue générale des antiquités égyptiennes du Musée du Caire.*
DE	*Discussions in Egyptology.* Oxford.
GM	*Göttinger Miszellen.* Göttingen.
JARCE	*Journal of the American Research Center in Egypt.* New York.
JEA	*Journal of Egyptian Archaeology.* London.
LD	Lepsius, K.R. 1849–1859. *Denkmäler aus Aegypten und Aethiopien 1–12.* Berlin.
MDAIK	*Mitteilungen des Deutschen Archäologischen Instituts Abteilung Kairo.* Mainz.
PM	Porter, B., and Moss, R.
RT	*Recueil de travaux relatifs à la philologie et à l'archéologie égyptiennes et assyriennes.* Paris.
SAK	*Studien zur Altägyptischen Kultur.* Hamburg.
TT	Theban tomb.
ZAS	*Zeitschrift für Ägyptischen Sprache und Altertumskunde.* Berlin.

1. Introduction

1. Osborne 1970, 840–861; for a survey of different drawing systems, see Dubery and Willats 1972.
2. Osborne 1970, 230, 840.
3. Ibid., 839.
4. Russman 1980.
5. E.g., Caminos and James 1963, Pl. 15.

2. Previous Work on the Grid and Proportions

1. Prisse 1879, 122–129.
2. Blanc 1876, 229–230.
3. Wilkinson 1880, 270–271; 1890, 266–267.
4. Lepsius 1897, 233–238.
5. Lepsius 1884, 1.
6. Maspero 1887, 162–163.
7. Edgar 1905.
8. Mackay 1917.
9. Baud 1935, 44–58.
10. Iversen 1955, 16.
11. Ibid., 11.
12. Ibid., 12.
13. Ibid., 13.
14. Ibid., 14.
15. Lepsius 1865; 1884.
16. Lepsius 1884, 8.
17. Ibid., 8.
18. Iversen 1955, 21.
19. Ibid., 21.
20. Lepsius 1897, 237.
21. Lepsius 1884, 1.
22. Iversen 1955, 37.
23. Ibid., 39.
24. Ibid., 41.
25. Hanke 1959.
26. Iversen 1971.
27. Robins and Shute 1986.
28. Bietak and Reiser-Haslauer 1982, 225–226.
29. Iversen 1975, 38.
30. Piankoff and Hornung 1961, Pl. 27.1.
31. Iversen 1975, 43.

32. Ibid., 44.
33. Ibid., 53.
34. Ibid., 31.
35. Ibid., 71.
36. Ibid., 32.
37. Ibid., 6–7.
38. Ibid., 31.
39. E.g., Blackman 1915a, Pl. 2.
40. E.g., Robins 1986, Fig. 21.
41. Iversen 1975, 45.
42. Ibid., 46.
43. Ibid., 58. In fact, the fingers of the hand are slightly curved back but not significantly bent.
44. Ibid., 47.
45. Ibid., 48.
46. Ibid., 58.
47. Ibid., 44.
48. Ibid., 44, n. 2.
49. Ibid., 24.
50. Ibid., 43.
51. Ibid., 55.
52. Ibid., 62.
53. Edgar 1905, 146.

3. Methods

1. Davies 1903, 8.
2. Equipment kindly lent by Dr. Nigel Strudwick.
3. Shedid 1988, 25–27, Pl. 4; Baud 1935, Fig. 23.
4. Monneret de Villard 1927, Figs. 65–68.
5. Newberry 1893a, 1893b, 1896, 1900.
6. Newberry 1893a, Pl. 10.
7. LD 2, 152g–152h.
8. Newberry 1893a, Pls. 17–18.
9. Evidence from the eleventh dynasty tomb of Inyotef at Thebes shows that guidelines, not grids, were used there, Jaroš-Deckert 1984.
10. Blackman 1914, 1915a, 1915b, 1924, 1953a, 1953b.
11. Blackman 1953a, Pl. 65 (view of serdab); Pls. 63b–64 (later decoration).

12. Ibid., Pls. 42–43.

13. Ibid., Pls. 63b, 64a.

14. Ibid., Pls. 37–38.

15. Davies 1903, 1905a, 1905b, 1906, 1908a, 1908b.

16. Davies 1908b, Pl. 40.

17. PM 4, 209–230.

18. Davies 1903, 7–8; 1905a, 9–13, 33–34; 1906, 2.

19. Davies 1906, Pl. 15.

20. Davies 1908b, Pl. 40.

21. Edgar 1906, no. 33412; Mackay 1917, Pl. 16.7.

22. Erman 1909, Fig. 125; Hildesheim 1959, 38 Fig. 14.

23. Hodjash and Berlev 1982, 232–233 no. 161; Erman 1909, Fig. 125; Kayser 1971, cover; Hildesheim 1959, 38 Fig. 14.

24. E.g., Blackman 1915a, Pl. 10 bottom right; British Museum EA 579, Bourriau 1988, no. 20; TT 353, MMA photos M8C 189–191. See also Müller 1940, 84 left and middle.

25. E.g., Bietak and Reiser–Haslauer 1982, 225–226.

4. Proportions in the Old and Middle Kingdoms

1. I would like to thank Ms. Gabriele Wenzel for lending me a copy of her master's thesis, "Struktur- und Hilfsliniensysteme in ägyptischen Wandbildern." My section on Old Kingdom guidelines was written before I saw this, and it was never my intention to discuss the subject in great detail. For a very full and meticulous treatment, the reader should now go to the work of Wenzel.

2. E.g., Davies 1901, Pl. 17 bottom; Quibell 1909, Pl. 66 no. 1, p. 24; Williams 1932; Smith 1946, 247 Fig. 95.2; LD 2, Pls. 65, 68; Fischer 1963, Pls. 2,3, and frontispiece; Davies 1902, frontispiece and Pl. 6; Saleh 1977, Pl. 17; Fisher 1924, Pls. 53, 55; Blackman 1953a, Pl. 37.

3. Dunham 1937, Pl. 28 no. 1.

4. Jaroš–Deckert 1984, 120–124, foldout 4.

5. For an exception, see Quibell 1909, Pl. 66 no. 1.

6. Davies 1902, frontispiece and Pl. 6.

7. CG 20131, Lange and Schäfer 1902a, 154–155, Pl. 108 top.

8. Fisher 1924, 16–17, Pl. 55.

9. Lepsius 1897, 233–238; 1884 appendix.

10. Prisse 1879, 123.

11. Lepsius 1897, 233–235.

12. Smith 1946, 247, 251 Fig. 95 no. 5; Wild 1953, Pl. 119; Duell 1938, Pl. 11; Brewer and Friedman 1989, Figs. 2.19, 2.22–2.24, 2.27a,–2.27b (all from tomb of Khnumhotep and Niankhkhnum).

13. Iversen 1975, Pl. 1.1.

14. Davies 1900, Pls. 20, 20a.

15. British Museum EA 67153, Emery 1958, Pl. 97, p. 84; Spencer 1980, cat. no. 16. My thanks to John Baines for drawing attention to the block.

16. Williams 1932, 10 n. 31; Smith 1946, 247 n. 1.

17. Iversen 1975, 29, 60.

18. Dunham 1937, stelae 5, 9, 14, 59, 77.

19. Jaroš–Deckert 1984, 120–124, foldout 4.

20. Müller 1940, 82–88, Pls. 32a–32b, 36.

21. Petrie 1930, Pls. 25–27, p. 14.

22. B2, Blackman 1915a, Pls. 2–4, 10, 11, 15; B4, Blackman 1915b, Pl. 17; C1, Blackman 1953b, Pls. 18, 19, 21, 25, 29, 39.

23. LD 2, Pl. 152g–152h; Newberry 1893a, Pl. 10.

24. PM 3² ii, 551(2). The scene is recorded in Firth and Gunn 1926, Pl. 54, cf. vol. 1, pp. 283–284[4], but the grid traces are omitted. However, in situ inspection shows that red traces remain where the background has not been cut away to the left of the owner's head. Completion of the grid shows that it fits the figure perfectly.

25. Lange and Schäfer 1902b, Pls. 118–119; Clère and Vandier 1948, 2 no. 2; Schenkel 1962, 59; Fischer 1973, 23 n. 45; Brunner 1965, Pl. 8; Freed 1984, 21, 82–89, including a discussion of the problems involved.

26. Compare, e.g., the male standing figures on surviving grids in tomb B2 at Meir, Blackman 1915a. The lower border of the buttocks lies on horizontal 9 on the figures in Pl. 2 left. On some of the figures in Pl. 11, the same point lies above horizontal 9.

27. Lepsius 1884, 100.

28. E.g., Blackman 1915a, Pls. 2, 10, 11.

29. E.g., Müller 1940, 84 Fig. b; Blackman 1915a, Pl. 10 right bottom. However, subsidiary figures often have narrower shoulders, e.g., ibid., Pls. 2, 10–11.

30. E.g., Müller 1940, 84 Fig. b.

31. E.g., Müller 1940, 86 Fig. a.

32. E.g., Müller 1940, 84 Fig. c, Pl. 36a, 86 Fig. b; Blackman 1915a, Pl. 2.

33. Blackman 1915a, Pl. 10.

34. EES archives Blackman photo B97 = Blackman 1953b, Pl. 11 left (grid not drawn) and Pl. 25, traces of grid just visible but clearer on B97.

35. Blackman 1915a, Pl. 3, Pl. 21 no. 2; 1953b, Pl. 19.

36. Robins 1984d.

37. Blackman 1915a, Pl. 10.

38. My thanks to Dr. Patricia Spencer for her help in providing me with copies of the photographs.

39. EES archives B85.

40. EES archives C73, Album p. 54.247.

41. EES archives B91, C76.

42. EES archives B95.

43. PM 1² i, 161(5), Wreszinski 1923, Pl. 265.

44. Mond photo 7002.

5. Proportions in the New Kingdom

1. E.g., TT 81, Mond photo 7116; TT 353, MMA photos M8C 189–191.

2. E.g., TT 92, Robins 1986, Fig. 15; observed by Bietak and Reiser–Haslauer 1982, 228.

3. E.g., Mackay 1917, Pls. 15.1–15.8; 16.1–16.2, 16.7; 17.1–17.3, 17.5–17.6.

4. E.g., Robins 1986, Fig. 26b; Iversen 1975, Pls. 13–14.

5. E.g., James and Davies 1983, Fig. 14 (reversed); TT 89, Mond photos 11006, 11013.

6. Contrary to Bietak and Reiser-Haslauer 1982, 228.

7. Scene in temple of Ramesses II at Abydos with surviving grid traces, PM 6, 36(31)–(32), Murray 1916, Fig. 10 (grid traces not visible); analysis on hypothetical grids shows that for some reason this elongated leg was rarely used in seated figures in the small temple at Abu Simbel (Figs. 8.9, 8.17, 8.18).

8. Robins 1983a, 21–23.

9. Hollander 1975, 98–99.

10. Iversen 1975, 35–36, 39, 41, 43.

11. E.g., Mackay 1917, Pls. 15.6–15.7.

12. E.g., ibid., Pls. 15.5–15.7.

13. E.g., Vandier 1964, 232–256, Pl. 7 Fig. 100, Pl. 8 Fig. 102.

14. E.g., TT 145, Baud 1935, 173 Fig. 80; TT 22, ibid., Pl. 4.

15. E.g., TT 75, ibid., Pl. 7b.

16. PM 1² i, 171(11), Mond photo 18030, MMA photo T2570.

17. PM 1² i, 304(5), MMA photo T3545 (given as 3145 in PM).

18. Dorman 1988, 66–109, has demonstrated that rather than Senenmut having two tombs, TT 71 was the tomb chapel and TT 353 the burial chamber, the two complementing each other architecturally, so that "only together do they function as a typical private tomb" (p. 109).

19. PM 1² i, 418(8), MMA photo M8C 183.

20. Lacau and Chevrier 1977, 1979.

21. Lacau and Chevrier 1979, Pl. 3 no. 233, Pl. 22 nos. 238, 191, 180, 253, 232, 206, 188.

22. Calverley 1958, Pls. 16, 19, 22, 25.

23. E.g., TT 154, Robins 1986, Fig. 24; Mackay 1917, Pl. 16.7.

24. The group comprises British Museum EA 43465–43467 (James 1985, Figs. 13, 21), University College London 28723 (Stewart 1979, no. 97, Pl. 23.1, called Middle Kingdom), Wellcome Museum, Swansea W 1377, Ägyptisches Museum Berlin (East) inv. nos. 18554, 18536, all acquired by Rustafjaell and sold at auction in 1906, together with Walters Art Gallery, Baltimore no. 32.2, bought by Walters from a dealer before 1930, and Brooklyn 05.390 (Fazzini et al. 1989, no. 32), bought by Petrie from an unknown dealer in Egypt. Similarities in style, and the presence of grid traces on all the pieces deriving from grids with approximately the same square size suggest that they may all come from the same tomb.

25. Fazzini et al. 1989, no. 32.

26. TT 353, MMA photos M8C 189, 191; temple of Ramesses II at Abydos, PM 6, 36 (31)–(32), Robins 1986, 21.

27. E.g., Baud 1935, Figs. 17, 19, 48–49, 74.

28. E.g., ibid., Figs. 25–26, 68, 80.

29. PM 1² i, 83(15), MMA photos T3441, 3445.

30. PM 1² i, 188(9), Mond photos 2060, 2067; Baud 1935, Pl. 20; Mackay 1917, Pl. 18.2.

31. PM I² i, 225(4), MMA photo T3003; Baud 1935, Fig. 68; Peck and Ross 1978, 32.

32. PM I² i, 182(10), Mond photos 11003–11004, 11011–11012.

33. Iversen 1975, 31–32.

34. What I call the elbow bone is anatomically the bony projection formed by the olecranon process of the ulna.

35. Brunner 1977; figures of deities in the temple of Luxor were not used because the originals from the reign of Amenhotep III were erased during the Amarna period and later restored.

36. Calverley 1933, 1935, 1938, 1958.

37. Epigraphic Survey 1930, 1932, 1934, 1957, 1963, 1964, 1970.

38. Epigraphic Survey 1936a, 1936b.

39. Epigraphic Survey 1979, 1981.

40. Blackman 1915a, Pl. 10 bottom right.

41. Ibid., Pl. 2.

42. British Museum EA 579, Bourriau 1988, no. 20.

6. Changes in the Amarna Period

1. Aldred 1988; Redford 1984.

2. Robins 1986, Chap. 6; Aldred 1973.

3. Wilson 1951, 208.

4. Cooney 1965, 4.

5. Hari 1985, 18.

6. Ibid. 18.

7. Lloyd 1961, 183.

8. Schäfer 1986; Robins 1986.

9. Smith 1981, 312; see also Aldred 1973, 55; 1988, 233.

10. E.g., Davies 1905a, Pl. 13.

11. Since the major private tombs at Amarna are unfinished and the innermost room or shrine is nearly always undecorated, it might have been intended to put more emphasis on the tomb owner here and to depict offering scenes and burial rites. A scene showing Panehesy, his wife, and his children (?) receiving offerings is shown on one wall of the shrine in his tomb, Davies 1905a, Pl. 23; for location, see Pl. 2. In the tomb of Any, two scenes show the owner receiving offerings. Both are only sketched in and are located in the shrine, Davies 1908a, Pls. 9, 10; for location, see Pl. 8. In the tomb of Huya, the shrine is almost completely decorated with scenes depicting the funerary rites before the mummy, the funeral procession, taking goods into the tomb, groups of mourners and the funerary equipment, Davies 1905b, Pls. 22–24; for location, see Pl. 1.

12. E.g., Lauffray 1979, Fig. 191.

13. E.g., Davies 1905a, Pl. 32.

14. E.g., Davies 1905a, Pl. 12; 1905b, Pl. 8.

15. E.g., Cooney 1965, nos.3, 3a, 19; Davies 1906, Pl. 31.

16. Russman 1980.

17. Ibid., 70–71.

18. E.g., Aldred 1973, Fig. 34.

19. Wilson 1951, 208.

20. E.g., Ghaliounghi 1947, 29–46; Aldred and Sandison 1962, 293–316; Aldred 1973, 54.

21. Aldred 1988, 231–236, rejected the attribution to Akhenaton of such a disorder.

22. Martin 1974, 91 no. 395, Pl. 54; Aldred 1973, Fig. 34.

23. Davies 1908b, Pl. 40.

24. Not recorded in Davies 1906, Pl. 15. Personal observation, spring 1984.

25. Personal communication from Christian Loeben.

26. Ashmolean Museum, Oxford inv. no. 1927-4087. My thanks to Dr. Helen Whitehouse for bringing this piece to my attention.

27. Davies 1941, Pl. 53. The traces are not marked on the drawing in Pl. 33 but can still be seen in situ.

28. Robins 1983b, 68–69.

29. Ibid., 67–68.

30. The traces show that the grid was in fact slightly uneven. Between horizontals 0 and 1, 5 and 6, and 6 and 7, the distance measures 4.5 cm, but between horizontals 1 and 2, it is only 3.5 cm. The highest horizontal, 7, lies at 30.5 cm, which falls short of the expected 31.5 cm by 1 cm, which is that lost between horizontals 1 and 2. The hairline measurement of 90 cm, however, shows that the lost centimeter must have been made up somewhere above horizontal 7.

31. E.g., Aldred 1973, 48–79, who recognized an early, middle and late phase of Amarna art. For my study of propor-

tions, I have amalgamated Aldred's middle and late periods as my later style.

32. Robins 1985c.

33. Davies 1908a, Pls. 26, 39.

34. Kestner Museum, Hanover, inv. no. 1570.22. My thanks to John Baines for making a photograph of the piece available.

35. Fitzwilliam Museum, Cambridge, inv. no. 2300.1943, Aldred 1973, 97 no. 11. My thanks to Janine Bourriau for providing a photograph of the piece.

36. Cooney and Simpson 1951, 1–12.

37. Cairo Museum 30/10/26/12, Westendorf 1968, 138.

38. Cairo JE 87300, Roeder 1969, Pls. 1–2.

39. Robins 1983b.

40. Davies 1906, Pl. 31.

41. Davies 1903, Pl. 22.

42. Davies 1908a, Pl. 3.

43. Davies 1905a, Pl. 12.

44. Davies 1908b, Pl. 16.

45. PM 1^2 ii, 560(5); Kamal el-Mallakh 1980, 67; Robins 1986, cover.

46. See n. 25.

47. Robins 1985d.

48. See n. 22.

49. See n. 34.

50. See n. 33.

51. See nn. 37, 38.

52. Davies 1906, Pl. 31.

53. Davies 1908a, Pl. 3.

54. Eaton–Krauss 1981, 260–262; Robins 1985d, 52.

55. Davies 1906, Pls. 15–16.

56. Ibid., 13.

57. Ibid., Pl. 15.

58. Ibid., Pl. 16.

59. Davies 1905b, Pl. 29.

60. Ibid., Pl. 28.

61. Davies 1905a, Pl. 22.

62. Davies 1906, Pls. 3–4.

63. Davies 1903, Pl. 36.

64. Ägyptisches Museum, Berlin (West) inv. no. 14145, Aldred 1973, 102 no. 16.

65. E.g., Davies 1905b, Pls. 4, 6; Edwards 1939, Pl. 23.

66. Davies 1905a, Pls. 32, 38; 1905b, Pls. 4, 6; 1908b, Pl. 17.

67. E.g., Martin 1987, Pls. 10, 11; Martin 1990, Pls. 27–31, 118–125.

68. PM 2^2, 77–86, Wreszinski 1935, Pls. 189–202.

69. PM 2^2, 76, Jéquier 1920, Pl. 78.2 (oblique).

70. Murray and Nuttall 1963, Carter nos.289b, 289a; Robins 1984a.

71. Murray and Nuttall 1963, Carter no. 266a; Carter 1933, Pls. 5, 7, 8.

72. Robins 1985d.

73. Eaton–Krauss 1977, 29–32.

74. Murray and Nuttall 1963, Carter no. 240; Robins 1984a, 21.

75. Murray and Nuttall 1963, Carter nos.237–239; Piankoff 1955, Pls. 18–33.

76. Murray and Nuttall 1963, Carter no. 108; Eaton–Krauss and Graefe 1985.

77. Murray and Nuttall 1963, Carter no. 255; Kamal el-Mallakh 1978, Pl. 13.

78. Robins 1984c; Kamal el-Mallakh 1978, Pls. 2–6.

79. KV 23, Piankoff 1958; Robins 1984c.

80. Hornung 1971; Robins 1983c.

81. Piankoff 1957; Robins 1983d. When I worked on this paper, I used the small-scale photographs published by Piankoff BIFAO 1957, Pls. 6A, 7B, 9A, 9B, since the tomb of Ramesses I was closed at that time. When I was subsequently able to visit the tomb, it became clear that my analysis of the seated figures in Pls. 7B and 9A was incorrect, as the two figures are in fact placed back to back on daises of the same height. Because of the position of the sarcophagus in the tomb, it was impossible to obtain a photograph of the complete scene, and I have been unable to reanalyze it. I was, however, able to ascertain that my analysis of standing figures was correct, thus demonstrating the presence of the short Amarna leg.

There is some evidence that the short Amarna leg persisted on some private monuments from Deir el–Medina, almost certainly drawn freehand, e.g., Cincinnati Art Museum 1947.55, Martin 1982, 83–84; British Museum EA 360, Bierbrier 1982, Pl. 7. Note also the large Amarna heads on these figures.

7. The Late Period and After

1. Mackay 1917, 83; Iversen 1975, 75 n. 4.

2. PM 2², 476(9)I; my thanks to Christian Loeben for drawing my attention to this grid. See also Bietak and Reiser–Haslauer 1982, 230.

3. Ibid., 230–231.

4. Mackay 1917, Pl. 18.3; Kuhlmann and Schenkel 1983, Pls. 31, 101.

5. Ibid., Pl. 31.

6. Ibid., Pl. 101, p. 89.

7. Mackay 1917, 83.

8. Robins 1985e, Fig. 1.

9. Baud 1935, Fig. 11.

10. PM 1² i, 324, *LD* 3, 282d = Prisse 1878, Pl. 2 no. 1.

11. CG 29314; Maspero and Gauthier 1939, Pl. 25; Edgar 1905, Fig. 5; Iversen 1975, Pl. 24.

12. Derchain 1961.

13. E.g., *LD* 4, 75d, 87d.

14. Mackay 1917, 83–84.

15. Prisse 1879, 126.

16. Iversen 1975, 16–17.

17. Petrie 1926, 38–41; Lepsius 1865.

18. Robins 1985e, 107–108.

19. Robins 1985a, Figs. 5a, 5b, 6.

20. E.g., Baud 1935, Fig. 11; Kuhlmann and Schenkel 1983, Pl. 31.

21. Robins 1985e, Figs. 4a, 4b.

22. E.g., Bietak and Reiser–Haslauer 1982, Fig. 109.

23. E.g., ibid., Fig. 109.

24. PM 3² ii, 401.

25. Firth and Quibell 1935, Pls. 15, 16.

26. Ibid., 5, 33–34.

27. Hodjash and Berlev 1982, 161; de Morgan et al. 1895, nos. 313, 318, 321; Edgar 1906, no. 33412.

28. E.g., *LD* 4, 75c, 87d.

29. *LD* 4, 32c, 75c, 87d. See also Iversen 1975, Pl. 29 (hypothetical grid).

30. Macadam 1955, Pl. 17e.

31. I would like to thank Dr. Helen Whitehouse for making this possible.

32. Kuhlmann and Schenkel 1983, Pl. 36 (17 squares).

33. Ibid., Pl. 37 (16 squares).

34. PM 4, 169(12)(14), 171(19)(20).

35. Clère 1961, passim.

36. Fazzini et al. 1989. My thanks to Drs. J. Romano and D. Spanel for providing me with photographs of the two pieces.

37. Kuhlmann 1988, color plate XII.

38. Ibid., color plate IV.

39. Edgar 1905; Steindorff 1946, 7–9; Young 1964.

40. Bothmer 1953.

41. E.g., Steindorff 1946, nos. 318–359; Hodjash and Berlev 1982, nos. 160–176; Edgar 1905, nos. 33402–33493.

42. Hodjash and Berlev 1982, 161, 171, 175; Edgar 1905, nos. 33404, 33405, 33409, 33414, 33430, 33434, 33448, 33453–33454, 33459.

44. E.g., Edgar 1905, no. 33434. The grid has been added to the finished surface.

44. Edgar 1905, nos. 33412, 33436, 33439, 33441, 33461, 33463.

45. See n. 41.

46. Edgar 1905, ix–x.

47. E.g., Steindorff 1946, 298–305; Edgar 1905, nos. 33327–33365.

48. Ibid., v–viii, 9–42.

49. Ägyptisches Museum Berlin inv. no. 3/70. I would like to thank Dr. Rolf Krauss for bringing the piece to my attention, and Dr. Settgast and the Ägyptisches Museum Berlin, Staatliche Museen Preussischer Kulturbesitz Berlin for permission to publish it.

50. E.g., Edgar 1905, nos. 33335–33337.

51. Ibid., vii.

52. E.g., ibid., nos. 33328–33330, 33332–33333, 33335–33343, 33348, 33350–33351.

53. E.g., ibid., nos. 33327, 33329–33330, 33335–33336, 33338–33339.

54. E.g., ibid., nos. 33340, 33343, 33348, 33350–33351.

55. E.g., ibid., nos. 33336–33338.

8. Composition and the Grid

1. E.g., Meir C1, Blackman 1953b, Pls. 29–30; Qaw el-Kebir, tomb of Wahka II, Petrie 1930, Pls. 25–27.

2. Blackman 1915a, Pls. 2, 10. For an example on a stela, see British Museum EA 579, Bourriau 1988, no. 20.

3. E.g., TT 22, 42, 81, 92, 96, 100, 154.

4. E.g., TT 89, PM 1² i, 182(10), Mond photo 11011; TT 108, PM 1² i, 225(4), Baud 1935, Fig. 68; TT 145, PM 1² i, 257(2), Baud 1935, Fig. 80; KV 57, Hornung 1971, Pls. 28–58 passim.

5. E.g., TT 75, PM 1² i, 147(4), MMA photo T2093; TT 77, PM 1² i, 152, 10, Baud 1935, Fig. 49; TT 78, PM 1² i, 154(9), Baud 1935, Figs. 50, 52; TT 143, PM 1² i, 255(4)(5)(6), Baud 1935, Figs. 75–78.

6. TT 378 contains a grid with the figure of a Ramesside king sketched on it. The tomb is otherwise undecorated, and there is no evidence that the royal figure is part of a scheme of decoration for the tomb chapel.

7. E.g., TT 22, PM1² i, 37(4), MMA photo T3408; TT 73, Säve–Söderbergh 1957, Pl. 17; TT 81, Mond photos 7020, 7037; Gebel es–Silsila shrine 5, Caminos and James 1963, Pls. 14–15.

8. E.g., TT 22, Mackay 1917, Pls. 17.5–17.6, MMA photo T3407; TT 42, MMA photo T3433; TT 82, Mond photo 15013; TT 92, Mackay 1917, Pls. 17.1–17.2.

9. E.g., TT 92, compare Mackay 1917, Pls. 17.1–17.2 with Pl. 18.1.

10. PM 5, 182(3), LD 3, 12a.

11. PM 5, 182(2), upper register.

12. PM 1² i, 82(5), MMA photo T3436.

13. Derchain 1961.

14. E.g., *chapelle rouge* of Hatshepsut, Lacau and Chevrier 1979, Pl. 14 nos. 153, 55; building of Amenhotep II, Van Siclen 1986, Pl. 41; lintel of Amenhotep III in the Open Air Museum at Karnak, Abdul–Qader Muhammed 1966, Pls. 1–2 (oblique).

15. E.40.1902. I would like to thank Janine Bourriau for permission to measure the figures.

16. Lacau and Chevrier 1979, Pls. 2, 3, 11.

17. Calverley 1933, 1935, 1938, 1958, passim.

18. De Mire 1982, Pls. 88, 127, 385.

19. Epigraphic Survey 1967, passim.

20. Epigraphic Survey 1930, 1932, 1934, 1940, 1957, 1963, 1964, 1970, passim.

21. Epigraphic Survey 1936a, 1936b, passim.

22. Epigraphic Survey 1979, 1981, passim.

23. Epigraphic Survey 1954, passim.

24. Desroches–Noblecourt and Kuentz 1968, passim.

25. One exception occurs in ibid., Pl. 114.

26. LD 4, 75c (Tiberius); PM 6, 254(1), LD 4, 87d = Prisse 1878, Pl. 2 no. 4.

27. PM 6, 206–207.

28. PM 4, 169(12) (14), 171(19) (21), Lefèbvre 1923, Pl. 6.

29. Blackman 1915a, Pl. 10.

30. Lacau and Chevrier 1979, Pl. 22, see also n. 48.

31. See Chap. 5 n. 21.

32. E.g., Calverley 1933, 1935, 1938, 1958, passim.

33. Personal observation.

34. PM 2², 225–227, Clère 1961.

35. Ibid., Pls. 44, 47, 64.

36. Lacau and Chevrier 1969, passim.

37. PM 2², 63–64.

38. Lacau and Chevrier 1979, passim.

39. Calverley 1935, Pls. 3–12, passim.

40. Epigraphic Survey 1979, 1981, passim.

41. E.g., in the temple of Amenhotep III at Luxor, Brunner 1977.

42. PM 6, 36(31)–(32), Murray 1916, 131 Pl. 10 (grid not visible, figure of Thoth omitted).

43. PM 6, 26(236)–(237).

44. E.g., Robins 1986, Fig. 21.

45. PM 6, 19(177)–(178) lower register, Calverley 1938, Pl. 16 lower middle.

46. PM 7, 113(17), Desroches–Noblecourt and Kuentz 1968, Pls. 41–42.

47. For scenes of purification, see Gardiner 1950; for a list of scenes of this type appearing in Theban temples, see PM 2², 543 (n). The majority of these scenes are unpublished or are published in a form unsuitable for analysis.

48. Epigraphic Survey 1940, Pl. 234; 1957, Pls. 296, 309.

49. Ibid., Pls. 296, 309.

50. PM 2², 220(19)–(20)2, Parker et al. 1979, Pl. 7.

51. Gauthier 1914, Pls. 62B, 65A.

52. LD4, 85a.

53. LD 4, 32c.

54. PM 2², 230(17)–(18)II 9, Epigraphic Survey 1979, Pl. 33.

55. PM 2², 476(9)I.

56. Clère 1961, Pls. 4, 14–15, 20, 26.

57. Ibid., Pls. 9–11, 22–23, 45, 47.
58. Kuhlmann 1988, color plate IV.

9. Nonhuman Elements and the Grid

1. E.g., British Museum EA 43465–43467, James 1985, 17 Fig. 13; Wellcome Museum, Swansea W 1377.

2. E.g., UCL 28723; TT 22, PM 1^2 i, 37(3), MMA photo T3416, (4)I, MMA photo T3408, 38(6), MMA photo T3418. The photo numbers for this tomb are cited as T3000 in PM. As this numbering had also been assigned to another series, those referring to TT 22 have been renumbered 3400.

3. E.g., TT 22, PM 1^2 i, 37(4)II, MMA photo T3408; TT 42, PM 1^2 i, 83(16)II, MMA photo T3444; TT 59, PM 1^2 i, 121(8), personal observation. In a similar scene in (7), neither the top nor bottom of the offering table appears to be on a horizontal.

4. E.g., TT 82, PM 1^2 i, 164(5), Mond photo 15013; TT89, PM 1^2 i, 181(3), Mond photo 11103.

5. E.g., TT 89, PM 1^2 i, 182(10), Mond photo 11006.

6. PM 1^2 i, 182(10), Mond photos 11006, 11013.

7. PM 1^2 i, 37(4)I,II, MMA photo T3408 (lower couple recorded by Mackay 1917, Pl. 16.6, but offering table not included).

8. Blackman 1915a, Pl. 10.

9. PM 1^2 i, 328(1), Baud 1935, Fig. 94.

10. British Museum EA 579, Bourriau 1988, no. 20.

11. TT 74, PM 1^2 i, 145(8), personal observation.

12. Blackman 1915a, Pl. 11.

13. Müller 1940, Pls. 32a, 36.

14. The third also originally held a lotus in the forward hand, but it is now almost totally destroyed.

15. E.g., Müller 1940, 84 left and middle.

16. Mackay 1917, Pls. 17.1–17.2; Mond photos 2072–2073.

17. Blackman 1915a, Pl. 2, the subsidiary figures but not the main figure of the tomb owner, Pl. 10 (but note this is not the case with the figures on Pl. 11); TT 55, Mackay 1917, Pl. 16.1.

18. Kayser 1971, front cover; Derchain 1961, Pls. 6–10.

19. Ibid., Pl. 4 and also Pl. 6.

20. Hildesheim 1973, 48 Fig. 10.

21. Edgar 1906, no. 33412.

22. Blackman 1915a, Pl. 7.

23. Hildesheim 1959, 38 = Derchain 1961, scene XII.

24. Hildesheim 1973, 48 Fig. 10 = Derchain 1961, scene X.

25. PM 2^2, 63, exterior, south side 1.

26. PM 2^2, 342(8) 2, Naville 1908, Pl. 161.

27. PM 2^2, 501, Epigraphic Survey 1957, Pl. 286.

28. PM 2^2, 476(9)I. Only a few traces remain, but these are clearly part of a 21-square grid.

29. PM 2^2, 226(3) (a) III, Clère 1961, Pl. 44; Blackman and Fairman 1949, Pl. 7. The scene is also drawn in LD 4, Pl. 12a, but this is not accurate, as the spacing between the calves is uneven, whereas Blackman's photograph shows that they are evenly spaced. Clère's drawing corresponds with Blackman's photograph.

30. PM 6, 60(128), Chassinat 1935, Pl. 104, grid traces omitted.

31. PM 6, 60(128)c, Chassinat 1935, Pl. 104 right, grid traces omitted.

32. Blackman 1915a, Pls. 10, 11, 15.

33. Ibid., Pls. 10, 11.

34. E.g., TT 92, PM 1^2 i, 188(9), Mond photo 2058, (10)–(12), Mond photos 2075–2077, (15), Mond photo 2000.

35. LD 3, 12a; photo kindly provided by W.V. Davies; personal observation.

36. See also Bietak and Reiser–Haslauer 1982, 225.

37. Derchain 1961.

38. Ibid., Pls. 4–10.

39. Ibid., Pl. 6.

40. Eggebrecht et al. 1979, 57; Hildesheim 1959, 338 Fig. 14.

41. Hildesheim 1973, 48 Fig. 10 right; Hildesheim 1959, 38 Fig. 14; Eggebrecht et al. 1979, 57.

42. Ibid., 57.

43. PM 5, 145; Bisson de la Roque 1930, Pl. 10 left.

44. Ibid., Pl. 10 right.

45. Lacau and Chevrier 1979.

46. Calverley 1933, 1935, 1938, 1958.

47. Calverley 1935, Pl. 18.

48. Desroches–Noblecourt and Kuentz 1968.

49. E.g., ibid. Pls. 33, 44, 52, 56, 70, 72, 76 left, 80 right, 99.

50. E.g., ibid., Pls. 25, 48, 50.

51. Ibid., Pl. 42.

52. Epigraphic Survey 1930, 1932, 1934, 1936a, 1936b, 1940, 1957, 1963, 1964, 1970.

53. Robins and Shute 1987, 47–48.

54. Robins 1982, 62 with n. 8.

55. Robins and Shute 1985, 113, 114 Fig. 1.

56. PM 2², 61–63, Lacau and Chevrier 1956, 1959; measurements made on author's photographs.

57. PM 2², 64–71, Lacau and Chevrier 1977, 1979; measurements made on author's photographs.

58. Robins 1985a.

59. Ibid., Figs. 6–8.

60. Calverley 1933, 1935, 1938, 1958.

61. Calverley 1935, Pl. 4, lower register right.

62. Robins 1985a, 54.

63. Epigraphic Survey 1936a, Pls. 15D, 15F, 45C.

64. Robins 1985b, 51–52.

65. Ibid., 55.

66. PM 5, 36(31)–(32), Murray 1916, Pl. 10 (grid not visible).

67. Müller 1940, Pl. 32b.

68. TT 92, PM 1² i, 188(9), Mond photo 2065.

69. PM 1² i, 189(11).

70. PM 2², 100(291).

71. Erman 1909, Fig. 125.

72. In order to compare slopes I have deliberately used a method that is analogous to the Egyptian procedure in architecture, substituting a drop of 6 units for a drop of 7 units. Like the architectural *seked,* it determines slope in terms of flatness rather than steepness, being comparable to the cotangent in trigonometry. It is applicable to very many, though not all oblique lines, since it appears that sometimes the drop is 5 or 7, not 6, units. A tempting alternative, which I rejected because it does not conform to known Egyptian usage, would be to employ the equivalent of the modern gradient, based on the tangent of the angle of inclination; this would give the drop for 1 unit of lateral displacement, the unit again being the grid square. With regard to actual ancient practice, in the absence of textual attestation it is unlikely that this can ever be recovered. It may well be that the draftsmen themselves did not think of the inclination of oblique lines in terms of a single unit of measurement, but simply learned combinations of drops and lateral displacements that would give them the desired effect. Reverting to the concept of gradient, although this may have been foreign to the ancient Egyptians, it has something to commend it in analysis when the object is to make comparisons. For instance, the relief of the pylon in the temple of Luxor has a gradient of 6, as compared with the actual pylon which has a steeper gradient of 7, corresponding to a *seked* of 1. The preferential gradients for the feathers of Isis in the temple of Sety I at Abydos are 6 for the front and 12 for the back, which is steeper than those of Amon–Re in this temple which have preferential gradients of 3 1/2 for the front and 6 for the back. The favoured gradient for the front of the royal apron in the temple of Sety I at Abydos is 1 1/3; this inclination can be compared with a result that I obtained from a preliminary survey of a single volume of the publication of the temple of Ramesses III at Medinet Habu, where the preferred gradient was 1 1/4 and therefore flatter. This stylistic difference is an indication of the extent to which the bottom of the apron juts forward.

10. Changing Proportions and Style

1. Saleh and Sourouzian 1987, no. 8.

2. Málek 1986, 29.

3. Donadoni-Roveri et al. 1988, 55.

4. Spencer 1980, Pl. 49 no. 460.

5. Firth and Quibell 1935, Pls. 15–17, 40–42.

6. Gardiner et al. 1955, Pl. 1 no. 1a (identified incorrectly as Smerkhet).

7. Ibid., Pl. 2 no. 5.

8. Smith 1981, 49 Fig. 32.

9. Quibell 1923, Pl. 27.

10. Kaplony 1963, Pl. 147 no. 853.

11. Ibid., Pl. 138 no. 833.

12. Ibid., Pl. 139 no. 838.

13. Quibell 1913; Borchardt 1937, nos. 1426–1430.

14. Simpson 1978, Figs. 33, 34.

15. Dunham and Simpson 1974.

16. Davies 1900, 1901.

17. Steindorff 1913; Epron and Daumas 1939; Wild 1953, 1966.

18. Duell 1938.

19. James 1953.

20. Simpson 1976, Fig. 31.

21. Ibid., Fig. 20.

22. E.g., Wild 1966, Pls. 149, 172.

23. Dunham 1937.

24. Bourriau 1988, 12–13; Robins 1990a.

25. Robins 1990a, 42.

26. Hanke 1959, 117–118 Fig. 2.

27. Bourriau 1988, 10; Barta 1970.

28. E.g., Bourriau 1988, nos. 36, 39–40, 48, 50; Bosticco 1959, nos. 31, 33–36, 38–39, 41–42, 47, 49, 50; Simpson 1974, Pls. 65–74, 76–79, 81–84.

29. E.g. Bosticco 1959, Pl. 31; Simpson 1974, Pls. 65 upper right, 71 left, 73 upper left, lower right.

30. E.g. Bosticco 1959, Pl. 31.

31. Hornung 1982, Pls. 76, 164–66; Piankoff 1954, Pls. 62–63, 138–141.

32. E.g., Davies 1927, passim; Martin 1987, passim.

33. E.g., Epigraphic Survey 1986.

34. Robins 1990b.

35. Brooklyn Museum 59.17. For identification with Iuput II, see Fazzini 1975, 98 cat. no. 89.

36. E.g., de Mire 1982, Pls. 161–162; Derchain 1961; LD 4, 49c, 75c, 87d.

37. Bianchi 1988, 55–80.

38. PM 6, 206–207.

39. PM 1^2 ii, 538–539, Room F, Capart and Werbrouck 1926, Figs. 176–178.

40. E.g., Peck and Ross 1978, nos. 29, 35, 38, 44, 48–50, 86.

Aldred, C. 1968. *Akhenaten Pharaoh of Egypt: a new study.* London.

————1973. *Akhenaten and Nefertiti.* New York.

————1988. *Akhenaten, King of Egypt.* London.

Aldred, C., and A.T. Sandison. 1962. "The Pharaoh Akhenaten: A Problem in Egyptology and Pathology." *Bulletin of the History of Medicine* 36. 293–316.

Aldred, C., et al. 1978. *Les Temps des pyramides.* Paris.

Barta, W. 1970. *Selbstzeugnis eines altägyptischen Künstlers.* Munich.

Baud, M. 1935. *Les Dessins ébauchés de la nécropole thébaine.* Cairo.

Bianchi, R.S. 1988. *Cleopatra's Egypt, Age of the Ptolemies.* Mainz.

Bierbrier, M.L. 1982. *Hieroglyphic Texts from Egyptian Stelae etc.* Part 10. London.

Bietak, M., and E. Reiser-Haslauer. 1982. *Das Grab des Anch-Hor Obersthofmeister der Gottesgemahlin Nitokris* 2. Vienna.

Bisson de la Roque, F. 1930. *Rapport sur les fouilles de Medamoud (1929).* Cairo.

Blackman, A.M. 1914. *The Rock Tombs of Meir* 1. London.

————1915a. *The Rock Tombs of Meir* 2. London.

————1915b. *The Rock Tombs of Meir* 3. London.

————1924. *The Rock Tombs of Meir* 4. London.

————1953a, *The Rock Tombs of Meir* 5. London.

————1953b, *The Rock Tombs of Meir* 6. London.

Blackman, A.M., and H.W. Fairman. 1949. "The Significance of the Ceremony ḥwt bḥsw in the temple of Horus at Edfu." *JEA* 35, 98–112.

Blanc, C. 1867. *Grammaire des arts du dessins.* Paris.

————1876. *Voyage dans la haute Egypte.* Paris.

Borchardt, L. 1937. *Denkmäler des alten Reiches (ausser den Statuen) im Museum von Kairo. Nr. 1295–1808.* Part 1. Berlin.

Bosticco, S. 1959. *Le Stele egiziane dall'antico al nuovo regno.* Rome.

————1965. *Le Stele egiziane del nuovo regno.* Rome.

Bothmer, B.V. 1953. "Ptolemaic Reliefs IV. A Votive Tablet." *Bulletin of the Museum of Fine Arts* 51, 80–84.

Bourriau, J. 1988. *Pharaohs and Mortals, Egyptian Art in the Middle Kingdom.* Cambridge.

Brewer, D.J., and R.F. Friedman. 1989. *Fish and Fishing in Ancient Egypt.* Warminster.

Brunner, H. 1965. *Hieroglyphische Chrestomathie.* Wiesbaden.

————1977. *Die südliche Raüme des Tempels von Luxor.* Mainz.

Calverley, A.M. 1933. *The Temple of King Sethos I at Abydos* 1. London and Chicago.

————1935. *The Temple of King Sethos I at Abydos* 2. London and Chicago.

————1938. *The Temple of King Sethos I at Abydos* 3. London and Chicago.

————1958. *The Temple of King Sethos I at Abydos* 4. London and Chicago.

Caminos, R.A. 1974. *The New-Kingdom Temples of Buhen* 1. London.

Caminos, R.A., and T.G.H. James 1963. *Gebel es-Silsilah* 1. London.

Capart, J., and M. Werbrouck. 1926. *Thebes: The Glory of a Great Past.* London.

Carter, H. 1933. *The Tomb of Tut.Ankh-Amun.* London.

Chassinat, E. 1935. *Le Temple de Dendara* 4. Cairo.

Clère, J.J., and J. Vandier 1948. *Textes de la Première Période Intermédiaire.* London.

Clère, P. 1961. *La Porte d'Evergète à Karnak.* Part 2. Cairo.

Cooney, J.D. 1965. *Amarna Reliefs from Hermopolis in American Collections.* Brooklyn.

Cooney, J.D., and W.K. Simpson 1951. "An Architectural Fragment from Amarna." *Brooklyn Museum Bulletin* 12, no. 4, 1–12.

Davies, N. de G. 1900. *The Mastaba of Ptahhetep and Akhethetep at Saqqareh. Part 1, The Chapel of Ptahhetep and the Hieroglyphs.* London.

————1901. *The Mastaba of Ptahhetep and Akhethetep at Saqqareh. Part 2, The Mastaba. The Sculptures of Akhethetep.* London.

————1902. *The Rock Tombs of Deir el Gebrawi* 2. London.

————1903. *The Rock Tombs of el-Amarna* 1. London.

————1905a. *The Rock Tombs of el-Amarna* 2. London.

————1905b. *The Rock Tombs of el-Amarna* 3. London.

————1906. *The Rock Tombs of el-Amarna* 4. London.

————1908a. *The Rock Tombs of el-Amarna* 5. London.

———1908b. *The Rock Tombs of el–Amarna 6.* London.

———1927. *Two Ramesside Tombs at Thebes.* New York.

———1941. *The Tomb of the Vizier Ramose.* London.

———1943. *The Tomb of Rekh–mi–re at Thebes.* New York.

Davison, M. 1979. *The Splendors of Egypt.* New York.

Dawson, W.R., and E. Uphill. 1972. *Who Was Who in Egyptology.* 2d ed. London.

de Morgan, O., et al. 1895. *Catalogue des monuments et inscriptions de l'Egypte antique.* Vol. 3, *Kom Ombos.* Vienna.

Derchain, P. 1961. *Zwei Kapellen des Ptolemäus I Soter in Hildesheim.* Hildesheim.

Desroches–Noblecourt, C., and C. Kuentz. 1968. *Le Petit Temple d'Abou Simbel 1–2.* Cairo.

Desroches–Noblecourt, C., R. Antelme, M. Kanawati, and D. Harlé. 1967. *Toutankhamon et son temps.* Paris.

Donadoni, S. 1969. *Egyptian Museum Cairo.* London.

Donadoni–Roveri, A.M. et al. 1988. *Il Museo Egizio di Torino: Guida alla lettura di una civiltà.* Novara.

Dorman, P.F. 1988. *The Monuments of Senenmut.* London and New York.

Dubery, F., and J. Willats 1972. *Drawing Systems.* New York.

Duell, P. 1938. *The Mastaba of Mereruka.* Part 1, *Chambers A1–10.* Part 2, *Chambers A11–13. Doorjambs and Inscriptions of Chambers A1–21. Tombchamber Exterior.* Chicago.

Dunham, D. 1937. *Naga–ed–Der Stelae of the First Intermediate Period.* London.

Dunham, D., and W.K. Simpson. 1974. *The Mastaba of Queen Mersyankh III G 7530–7540.* Giza Mastabas, vol. 1. Boston.

Eaton–Krauss, M. 1977. "The *Khat* Headdress to the End of the Amarna Period." *SAK* 5.

———1981. "Miscellanea Amarnensia." *CdE* 56, 245–264.

Eaton–Krauss, M., and E. Graefe. 1985. *The Small Golden Shrine from the Tomb of Tutankhamun.* Oxford.

Edgar, C.C. 1905. "Remarks on Egyptian 'Sculptors' Models'" *RT* 27, 137–150.

———1906. *Sculptors' Studies and Unfinished Works.* Cairo.

Edwards, I.E.S. 1939. *Hieroglyphic Texts from Egyptian Stelae etc.* 8. London.

———1976. *Treasures of Tutankhamun.* New York.

Eggebrecht, A., et al. 1979. *Pelizaeus–Museum Hildesheim.* Hildesheim.

Emery, W.B. 1958. *Great Tombs of the First Dynasty 3.* London.

Epigraphic Survey. 1930. *Earlier Historical Records of Ramses III.* Medinet Habu 1. Chicago.

———1932. *Later Historical Records of Ramses III.* Medinet Habu, vol. 2. Chicago.

———1934. *The Calendar, the "Slaughterhouse," and Minor Records of Ramses III.* Medinet Habu, vol. 3. Chicago.

———1936a. *Ramses III's Temple within the Great Inclosure of Amon,* part 1. Reliefs and Inscriptions at Karnak, vol. 1. Chicago.

———1936b. *Ramses III's Temple within the Great Inclosure of Amon,* part 2. *Ramses III's Temple in the Precinct of Mut.* Reliefs and Inscriptions at Karnak, vol. 2. Chicago.

———1940. *Festival Scenes of Ramses III.* Medinet Habu, vol. 4. Chicago.

———1954. *The Bubastite Portal.* Reliefs and Inscriptions at Karnak, vol. 3. Chicago.

———1957. *The Temple Proper,* part 1. Medinet Habu, vol. 5. Chicago.

———1963. *The Temple Proper,* part 2. Medinet Habu, vol. 6. Chicago.

———1964. *The Temple Proper,* part 3. Medinet Habu, vol. 7. Chicago.

———1967. *The Beit el–Wali Temple of Ramesses II.* Chicago.

———1970. *The Eastern High Gate with Translations of Texts.* Medinet Habu, vol. 8. Chicago.

———1979. *Scenes of King Herihor in the Court.* The Temple of Khonsu, vol. 1. Chicago.

———1981. *Scenes and Inscriptions in the Court and First Hypostyle Hall.* The Temple of Khonsu, vol. 2. Chicago.

———1986. *The Battle Reliefs of King Sety I,* Reliefs and Inscriptions at Karnak, vol. 4. Chicago.

Epron, L., and F. Daumas 1939. *Le tombeau de Ti.* Vol. 1, *Les Approches de la chapelle.* Cairo.

Erman, A. 1909. "Zeichnungen ägyptischer Kunstler griechischer Zeit." *Amtliche Berichte aus den königlichen Kunstsammlungen* 30, 197–203.

Fazzini, R. 1975. *Images for Eternity: Egyptian Art from Berkeley and Brooklyn.* New York.

Fazzini, R., et al. 1989. *Ancient Egyptian Art in the Brooklyn Museum.* London and New York.

Feucht, E. 1977. "Hilfslinien." *Lexikon der Ägyptologie.* Wiesbaden, 1201–1206.

Firth, C.M., and B. Gunn. 1926. Excavations at Saqqara. Teti Pyramid Cemeteries 1–2. Cairo.

Firth, C.M., and J.E. Quibell. 1935. *The Step Pyramid* 1–2. Cairo.

Fischer, H.G. 1963. "Varia Aegyptiaca." *JARCE* 2, 17–51.

———1973. "Redundant Determinatives in the Old Kingdom." *Metropolitan Museum Journal* 8, 7–25.

Fisher, C.S. 1924. *The Minor Cemetery at Giza.* Philadelphia.

Freed, R. 1981. "A Private Stela from Naga ed–Der and Relief Style of the Reign of Amenemhat I." In W.K. Simpson and W. Davis, eds., *Studies in Ancient Egypt, the Aegean, and the Sudan,* Boston.

———1984. "The Development of Middle Kingdom Egyptian Relief Sculptural Schools of Late Dynasty XI." Ph.D. diss., Institute of Fine Arts, New York University.

Gardiner, A. 1950. "The Baptism of Pharaoh." *JEA* 36, 3–12.

Gardiner, A., et al. 1952. *The Inscriptions of Sinai.* Part 1: Introduction and plates. London.

———1955. *The Inscriptions of Sinai.* Part 2: Translations and commentary. London.

Gauthier, H. 1914. *Le Temple de Kalabchah* 2. Cairo.

Ghalioungui, P. 1947. "A Medical Study of Akhenaten." *ASAE* 47, 29–46.

Hanke, R. 1959. "Beiträge zum Kanonproblem." *ZÄS* 84, 113–119.

Hari, R. 1985. *New Kingdom Amarna Period,* Iconography of Religions XVI, 6. Leiden.

Hildesheim. 1959. *Roemer-Pelizaeus-Museum Hildesheim.* Hildesheim.

———1973. *Führer durch die Sammlungen des Roemer-Pelizaeus-Museums.* Hildesheim.

Hodjash, S., and O. Berlev. 1982. *The Egyptian Reliefs and Stelae in the Pushkin Museum of Fine Arts, Moscow.* Leningrad.

Hollander, A. 1975. *Seeing through Clothes.* New York.

Hornung, E. 1971. *Das Grab des Haremhab im Tal der Könige,* Bern.

———1982. *Tal der Könige Die Ruhestätte der Pharaonen.* Zurich and Munich.

Iversen, E. 1955. *Canon and Proportions in Egyptian Art.* 1st ed. London.

———1971. "The Canonical Tradition." In J.R. Harris (ed.), *The Legacy of Egypt.* 2d ed. Oxford.

———1975. *Canon and Proportions in Egyptian Art.* 2d ed. Warminster.

James, T.G.H. 1953. *The Mastaba of Khentika Called Ikhekhi.* London.

———1961. *Hieroglyphic Texts from Egyptian Stelae etc.* Part 1. 2d ed. London.

———1970. *Hieroglyphic Texts from Egyptian Stelae etc.* Part 9. London.

———1985. *Egyptian Painting.* London.

James, T.G.H., and W.V. Davies. 1983. *Egyptian Sculpture.* London.

Jaroš–Deckert, B. 1984. *Das Grab des Jnj–jtj.f: die Wandmalereien der XI. Dynastie.* Mainz.

Jéquier, G. 1920. *Les Temples memphites et thébains des origines à la XVIIIe dynastie.* L'Architecture et la décoration dans l'ancienne Egypte 1. Paris.

Junker, H. 1943. *Giza* 6. Vienna and Leipzig.

Kaplony, P. 1963. *Die Inschriften der ägyptischen Frühzeit* 3. Wiesbaden.

Kayser, H. 1971. *Söhne des Sonnengotte.* Hildesheim.

Kuhlmann, K. 1988. *Das Ammoneion. Archäologie, Geschichte und Kultpraxis des orakels von Siwa.* Mainz.

Kuhlmann, K., and W. Schenkel. 1983. *Das Grab des Ibi, Obergutsverwalters des Gottesgemahlin des Amun (Thebanisches Grab Nr. 36).* Mainz.

Lacau, P., and H. Chevrier. 1956. *Une Chapelle de Sesostris Ier à Karnak.* Text. Cairo.

———1969. *Une Chapelle de Sesostris Ier à Karnak.* Plates. Cairo.

———1977. *Une Chapelle d'Hatshepsout à Karnak* 1. Cairo.

———1979. *Une Chapelle d'Hatshepsout à Karnak* 2. Cairo.

Lange, H.O., and H. Schäfer. 1902a, *Grab- und Denksteine des Mittleren Reichs im Museum von Kairo No. 20001–20780.* Part 1. *Text zu No. 20001–20399.* Berlin.

———1902b, *Grab- und Denksteine des Mittleren Reichs im Museum von Kairo No. 20001–20780.* Part 4. plates, Berlin.

———1908. *Grab- und Denksteine des Mittleren Reich im Museum von Kairo No. 20001–20780.* Part 2, *Text zu No. 20400–20780.* Berlin.

Lange, K. and M. Hirmer 1961. *Egypt: Architecture, Sculpture, Painting in Three Thousand Years.* 3d. ed. London.

Lauffray, J. 1979. *Karnak d'Egypte. Domaine du divin.* Paris.

Lefèbvre, G. 1923. *Le Tombeau de Petosiris.* Part 3. Cairo.

Lepsius, K.R. 1849–1859. *Denkmäler aus Aegypten und Aethiopien* 1–12. Plates. Berlin.

———1865. *Die Altägyptische Elle und ihre Eintheilung.* Berlin.

———1884. *Die Längenmasse der Alten.* Berlin.

———1897. *Denkmäler aus Aegypten und Aethiopien. Tekst* 1. ed. E. Naville. Text. Leipzig.

Lichtheim, M. 1976. *Ancient Egyptian Literature* 2. Berkeley.

Lloyd, S. 1961. *The Art of the Ancient Near East.* London.

Macadam, M.F.L. 1955. *The Temples of Kawa* Vol. 2, *History and Archaeology of the Site.* Plates. Oxford.

Mackay, E. 1917. "Proportion Squares on Tomb Walls in the Theban Necropolis." *JEA* 4, 74–85.

Málek, J. 1986. *In the Shadow of the Pyramids. Egypt during the Old Kingdom.* London.

el–Mallakh, Kamal 1978. *The Gold of Tutankhamen.* New York.

el–Mallakh, Kamal, with Robert Bianchi. 1980. *Treasures of the Nile.* New York.

Martin, G.T. 1974. *The Royal Tomb at El–Amarna* 1. London.

———1982. "Two Monuments of New Kingdom Date in North American Collections." *JEA* 68, 81–84.

———1987. *Corpus of Reliefs of the New Kingdom from the Memphite Necropolis and Lower Egypt.* London.

———1990. *The Memphite Tomb of Horemheb Commander-in-Chief of Tutankhamun.* Vol. 1, *The Reliefs, Inscriptions, and Commentary.* London.

Maspero, G. 1887. *L'archéologie égyptienne.* Paris.

Maspero, G., and H. Gauthier. 1939. *Sarcophages des époques persane et ptolemaique* 1. Cairo.

de Mire, G. and V. 1982. *Les Temples de Karnak contribution à l'étude de la pensée pharaonique* 1–2. Paris.

Monneret de Villard, U. 1927. *Il monastero di S. Simeone presso Aswan* 1. *Descrizione archeologica.* Milan.

Moussa, Ahmed M., and H. Altenmüller. 1971. *The Tomb of Nefer and Ka–Hay.* Mainz.

———1977. *Das Grab des Nianchchnum und Chnumhotep.* Mainz.

Muhammed, Abdul Qader. 1966. "Recent Finds." *ASAE* 59, 143–155.

Müller, H.W. 1940. *Die Felsengräber der Fürsten von Elephantine aus der Zeit des Mittleren Reiches,* Glückstadt.

———1973. "Die Kanon in der ägyptischen Kunst." In *Der "vermessene" Mensch—Anthropometrie in Kunst und Wissenschaft,* Munich, 9–31, 180–181.

Murray, H., and M. Nuttall, 1963. *A Handlist to Howard Carter's Catalogue of Objects in Tutankhamun's Tomb.* Oxford.

Murray, M.A. 1916. "'The Temple of Rameses II at Abydos." *Ancient Egypt* (London).

Myśliwiec, C. 1972. "Towards a Definition of the 'Sculptor's Model' in Egyptian Art." *Etudes et Travaux* 6. Warsaw.

Naville, E. 1908. *The Temple of Deir el Bahari.* Part 6, London.

Newberry, P.E. 1893a. *Beni Hasan* 1. London.

———1893b. *Beni Hasan* 2. London.

———1896. *Beni Hasan* 3. London.

———1900. *Beni Hasan* 4. London.

Osborne, H., ed. 1970. *The Oxford Companion to Art.* Oxford.

Parker, R., J. Leclant, and J.-C. Goyon. 1979. *The Edifice of Taharqa by the Sacred Lake of Karnak.* Providence and London.

Peck, W., and J. Ross. 1978. *Drawings from Ancient Egypt.* London.

Perrot, G., and C. Chipiez. 1882. *Histoire de l'art dans l'antiquité* 1. *L'Egypte.* Paris.

Petrie, W.M.F. 1900. *The Royal Tombs of the First Dynasty.* Part 1. London.

———1926. *Ancient Weights and Measures.* London.

———1930. *Antaeopolis. The Tombs of Qau.* London.

Piankoff, A. 1954. *The Tomb of Ramesses VI.* New York.

———1955. *The Shrines of Tut-Ankh-Amon.* New York.

———1957. "La Tombe de Ramses 1er." *BIFAO* 56, 189–200.

———1958. "Les peintures dans la tombe du roi Ai." *MDAIK,* 16, 247–251, Pls. 21–25.

Piankoff, A., and Hornung, E. 1961. "Das Grab Amenophis' III im Westtal der Könige." *MDAIK* 17, 111–127.

Porter, B., and R. Moss 1934. *Topographical Bibliography of Ancient Egyptian Hieroglyphic Texts, Reliefs, and Paintings.* Vol. 4, *Lower and Middle Egypt (Delta and Cairo to Asyut).* Oxford.

————1937. *Topographical Bibliography of Ancient Egyptian Hieroglyphic Texts, Reliefs, and Paintings.* Vol. 5, *Upper Egypt: Sites.* Oxford.

————1939. *Topographical Bibliography of Ancient Egyptian Hieroglyphic Texts, Reliefs, and Paintings* Vol. 6, *Upper Egypt: Chief Temples.* Oxford.

————1952. *Topographical Bibliography of Ancient Egyptian Hieroglyphic Texts, Reliefs, and Paintings* Vol. 7, *Nubia, the Deserts, and Outside Egypt.* Oxford.

————1960. *Topographical Bibliography of Ancient Egyptian Hieroglyphic Texts, Reliefs, and Paintings.* 2d ed. Vol. 1, *The Theban Necropolis.* Part 1, *Private Tombs.* Oxford.

————1964. *Topographical Bibliography of Ancient Egyptian Hieroglyphic Texts, Reliefs, and Paintings.* 2d ed. Vol. 1, *The Theban Necropolis.* Part 2, *Royal Tombs and Smaller Cemeteries.* Oxford.

————1972. *Topographical Bibliography of Ancient Egyptian Hieroglyphic Texts, Reliefs, and Paintings.* 2d ed. Vol. 2, *Theban Temples.* Oxford.

————1974. *Topographical Bibliography of Ancient Egyptian Hieroglyphic Texts, Reliefs, and Paintings.* 2d ed. J. Málek. Vol. 3, *Memphis.* Part 1, *Abu Rawash to Abusir.* Oxford.

————1981. *Topographical Bibliography of Ancient Egyptian Hieroglyphic Texts, Reliefs, and Paintings.* 2d ed., ed. J. Málek. Vol. 3, *Memphis.* Part 2, *Saqqara to Dahshur.* Oxford.

Prisse d'Avennes, A.C.T.E. 1847. *Monuments égyptiens, bas-reliefs, peintures, inscriptions etc., d'après les dessins executés sur les lieux.* Paris.

————1878. *L'Histoire de l'art égyptien, d'après les monuments, depuis les temps les plus reculés jusqu'à la domination romaine* 1–2. Paris.

————1879. *L'Histoire de l'art égyptien, d'après les monuments, depuis les temps les plus reculés jusqu'à la domination romaine. Texte par P. Marchand de la Faye d'après les notes de l'auteur.* Paris.

Quibell, J.E. 1909. *Excavations at Saqqara (1907–1908).* Cairo.

————1913. *The Tomb of Hesy. Excavations at Saqqara (1911–12).* Cairo.

————1923. *Archaic Mastabas.* Cairo.

Redford, D. 1984. *Akhenaten: The Heretic King.* Princeton.

Robins, G. 1982. "The Length of the Forearm in Canon and Metrology." *GM* 59, 61–75.

————1983a. "Natural and Canonical Proportions in Ancient Egyptians." *GM* 61, 17–25.

————1983b. "Amarna Grids: 1." *GM* 64, 67–72.

————1983c. "Anomalous Proportions in the Tomb of Haremhab (KV 57)." *GM* 65, 91–96.

————1983d. "The Canon of Proportion in the Tomb of Ramesses I (KV 16)." *GM* 68, 85–90.

————1984a. "Two Statues from the Tomb of Tutankhamun." *GM* 71, 47–50.

————1984b. "Isis, Nephthys, Selket and Neith Represented on the Sarcophagus of Tutankhamun and in Four Free-standing Statues Found in KV 62." *GM* 72, 21–25.

————1984c. "The Proportions of Figures in the Decoration of the Tombs of Tutankhamun (KV 62) and Ay (KV 23)." *GM* 72, 27–32.

————1984d. "Analysis of Facial Proportions in Egyptian Art." *GM* 79, 31–41.

————1985a. "Slopes of the Double Feathers of Amon-Re in the Temple of Ramesses III within the Great Enclosure of Amun at Karnak." *DE* 2, 51–58.

————1985b. "The Slope of the Front of the Royal Apron." *DE* 3, 49–56.

————1985c. "Amarna Grids: 3. Standing Figures of the King in the Early Style." *GM* 84, 51–64.

————1985d. "Amarna Grids 2: Treatment of Standing Figures of the Queen." *GM* 88, 47–54.

————1985e. "Standing Figures in the Late Grid System of the 26th Dynasty." *SAK* 12, 101–116.

————1986. *Egyptian Painting and Relief.* Aylesbury.

————1990a. "The Reign of Nebhepetre Montuhotep II and the Pre-unification Theban Style of Relief." In G. Robins, ed., *Beyond the Pyramids: Egyptian Regional Art from the Museo Egizio, Turin,* Atlanta, 39–45.

————1990b. "Proportions of Standing Figures in the North-west Palace of Ashurnasirpal II at Nimrud." *Iraq* 52, 107–119.

————1991. "Composition and the Artist's Squared Grid." *JARCE* 28, 41–54.

Robins, G., and C.C.D. Shute. 1985. "Mathematical Bases of

Ancient Egyptian Architecture and Graphic Art." *Historia Mathematica* 12, 107–122.

———1986. "Predynastic Egyptian Stature and Physical Proportions." *Human Evolution* 1, 313–324.

———1987. *The Rhind Mathematical Papyrus, an Ancient Egyptian Text*. London.

Roeder, G. 1969. *Amarna–Reliefs aus Hermopolis. Ausgrabungen der Deutschen Hermopolis Expedition in Hermopolis 1929–39* 2. Hildesheim.

Russman, E.R. 1980. "The Anatomy of an Artistic Convention: Representation of the Near Foot in Two Dimensions through the New Kingdom." *BES* 2, 57–81.

Saleh, Mohamed. 1977. *Three Old Kingdom Tombs at Thebes*. Mainz.

Saleh, Mohamed, and H. Sourouzian. 1987. *The Egyptian Museum Cairo, Official Catalogue*. Mainz.

Säve-Söderbergh, T. 1957. *Four Eighteenth Dynasty Tombs. Private Tombs at Thebes* vol. 1. Oxford.

Schäfer, H. 1986. *Principles of Egyptian Art*. 4th ed. trans. and ed. J. Baines. Oxford.

Schenkel, W. 1962. *Frühmittelägyptische Studien*. Bonn.

Shedid, Abdel Ghaffar. 1988. *Stil der Grabmalereien in der Zeit Amenophis II. Untersucht an den Thebanischen Gräbern Nr.104 und Nr. 80*. Mainz.

Simpson, W.K. 1974. *The Terrace of the Great God at Abydos: The Offering Chapels of Dynasties 12 and 13*. New Haven and Philadelphia.

———1976. *The Mastabas of Qar and Idu G7101 and 7102*. Boston.

———1978. *The Mastabas of Kawab, Khafkhufu I and II*. Boston.

Smith, W.S. 1946. *A History of Egyptian Sculpture and Painting in the Old Kingdom*. London.

———1981. *The Art and Architecture of Ancient Egypt*. 3d ed., revised with additions by W.K. Simpson. Harmondsworth.

Sotheby 1906. *Catalogue of the Collection of the Egyptian Antiquities Formed in Egypt, by R. de Rustafjaell, Esq.* London.

Spencer, A.J. 1980. *Catalogue of Egyptian Antiquities in the British Museum*. Vol. 5, *Early Dynastic Objects*. London.

Steindorff, G. 1913. *Das Grab des Ti*. Leipzig.

———1946. *Egyptian Sculpture in the Walters Art Gallery*. Baltimore.

Stewart, H.M. 1979. *Egyptian Stelae, Reliefs and Painting from the Petrie Collection. Part 2, Archaic Period to Second Intermediate Period*. Warminster.

Vandier, J. 1964. *Manuel d'archéologie égyptienne*. Vol. 4, *Bas-reliefs et peintures, scènes de la vie quotidienne*. Paris.

Van Siclen III, C. 1986. *The Alabaster Shrine of King Amenhotep II*. San Antonio.

Wenzel, G. 1990. "Struktur- und Hilfsliniensysteme in ägyptischen Wandbildern." Master's thesis, Munich.

Westendorf, W. 1968. *Painting, Sculpture and Architecture of Ancient Egypt*. New York.

Wild, H. 1953. *Le Tombeau de Ti*. Vol. 2, *La chapelle (première partie)*. Cairo.

———1966. *Le Tombeau de Ti*. Vol. 3, *La chapelle (deuxième partie)*. Cairo.

Wilkinson, J.G. 1880. In G. Rawlinson, trans. and ed., *The History of Herodotus* 2, 4th ed., London.

———1890. *A Popular Account of the Ancient Egyptians. Revised and abridged from his large work by Sir J. Gardner Wilkinson*. London.

Williams, C.R. 1932. *The Decoration of the Tomb of Per–neb: The Technique and the Color Conventions*. New York.

Wilson, J. 1951. *The Culture of Ancient Egypt*. Chicago.

Wreszinski, W. 1923. *Atlas zur Altaegyptischen Kulturgeschichte* 1. Leipzig.

———1935. *Atlas zur Altaegyptischen Kulturgeschichte* 2. Leipzig.

Young, E. 1964. "Sculptors' Models or Votives." *Bulletin of the Metropolitan Museum of Art* 22, 246–256.

Index

References to illustrations are printed in italics.

www.ingramcontent.com/pod-product-compliance
Lightning Source LLC
Chambersburg PA
CBHW081141180526
45170CB00006B/1885